Abracadabra!

Abracadabra!

SECRET METHODS
MAGICIANS & OTHERS
USE TO DECEIVE
THEIR AUDIENCE

Nathaniel Schiffman
Foreword by Henry Gordon

 Prometheus Books

59 John Glenn Drive
Amherst, New York 14228-2197

Published 2005 by Prometheus Books

Inquiries should be addressed to
Prometheus Books
59 John Glenn Drive
Amherst, New York 14228–2197
VOICE: 716–691–0133, ext. 207
FAX: 716–564–2711
WWW.PROMETHEUSBOOKS.COM

09 08 07 06 05   5 4 3 2 1

Library of Congress Cataloging-in-Publication Data

Schiffman, Nathaniel.
    Abracadabra! : secret methods magicians and others use to deceive their audience / by Nathaniel Schiffman.
        p. cm.
    Includes bibliographical references and index.
    ISBN 1–59102–248–7
    1. Conjuring. 2. Conjuring—Psychological aspects. 3. Magicians. I. Title.
GV1547.S2436 1997
793.8—dc21
                                                                                97–22288
                                                                                CIP

Printed in the United States of America on acid-free paper

Contents

Part Three: People, Places, and Things   211

Part Four: Off Stage and Out of the Theater   303

Foreword

Henry Gordon

In this age of information overload the inventory of magic books on the market is huge. When I started in this game, there were only a handful of books available for the neophyte. Today there are books on general conjuring, on specialty magic with cards, with coins, with sponges, with matchbooks, with cigarettes, with cigars, with napkins, with dice, with handkerchiefs, with newspapers—need I go on? This glut of books can be confusing for the beginner—where to start?

The problem is, most hobbyists begin by buying books filled with instructions on how to perform particular tricks. In that case they are leapfrogging the information they should first be acquiring: the knowledge of the basic principles of conjuring. This should include the subtleties of misdirection, the understanding of human perception, the basics of showmanship, and the understanding of visual and psychological illusion.

Books based on these principles are extremely rare. This book by Nathaniel Schiffman is one of them.

Having said this, I can anticipate the controversy this volume will raise among magicians now active in the field, particularly professionals. "The secrets of my illusions are being revealed—this is unethical—I'll be put out of business."

There are several ways of answering these complaints. First, I have never known of a professional magician who has had his or her career affected by revelations of this kind *when they appear in a book that has been purchased*. It is an entirely different matter when an opportunist uses public television to force-feed the viewers with these secrets. This is definitely unethical and uncalled-for—but even in that case it has been my experience, after years of observation, that most people who are more interested in the entertainment of magic than in the solving of the secrets will forget the revelations over time.

Another point: this is not the first book, and will not be the last, to reveal the methodology behind some popular illusions. Even the secret of David Copperfield's vanish and reappearance of the Statue of Liberty (if you could ever believe such a thing could happen) was revealed in a popular book. Evidently David still carries on.

Apart from some of the major illusions devised for TV presentation, there is very little that is new under the sun. Most illusions are based on the principles of effects presented many years ago. They are often updated with the use of modern technology, and to fit today's culture.

The secrets of conjuring will always be revealed. This serves two useful purposes. It promotes an interest that recruits newcomers to this wonderful hobby, and it challenges performers to devise new and improved methods of deception. And this challenge has always been accepted and acted upon.

Conjuring is an art and a craft. The hobby itself attracts people for various reasons. Some are curious about the modus operandi of the craft. Some wish to boost their egos by being able to deceive others and reap applause. Others just want to join a hobby group with similar interests. Many immerse themselves in the hobby by collecting magic books and paraphernalia and learning the history of the art—without ever performing a magic trick. Some attempt to turn professional—but I don't recommend leaving your day job too soon. The huge turnout at magic conventions reflects the interest in magic—the world's second-oldest profession.

When first leafing through the manuscript of this book the thought struck me, "This man has gone through a mountain of research to produce this opus." Nathaniel Schiffman has come as close as one can to touching all the bases on the subject of conjuring. The many examples and explanations of the art of misdirection are among the highlights of the book. They provide an excellent primer for the beginner and a memory jogger for the more experienced. The chapter on magic stagecraft is something any magician can benefit from.

In the last section, which deals with deception in our everyday activities, the author demonstrates how many of the principles of conjuring are used to hoodwink and mislead the gullible. A good example is how misdirection is sometimes used in advertising to create an illusion of excellence that really doesn't exist. And this principle is taken directly from the magician's arsenal of deception—the big difference being that the conjurer is using deception for the purposes of entertainment only.

If you are interested in conjuring, and want to develop your knowledge and skills in this craft, then this book is for you. If you're just reading this book out of curiosity and to delve into magical secrets, that's fine too. But then, when later you're watching a magician perform, there are two ways you can witness the performance. You can watch it with a knowing eye, as would other magicians, admiring or decrying the performer's technique—or you can just sit back, forget everything you've read here, suspend your disbelief, and be entertained.

Preface to Paperback Edition

There's nothing magical about magic.

It's fake.

We know that, but we are fooled anyway.

We are all experts on being fooled—after all, just about everyone knows how some magic trick is done, or has a few ideas on the subject, or has gotten tricked, or played a trick, or told a lie, or been lied to—at some time or another. We are so knowledgeable about tricks and deception, yet we are still fooled by the magician anyway. How can this be?

Let's start with a story. Not about magic specifically, but about the experience of being fooled.

We were sitting in a lecture hall, where a world-renowned architect was showing slides of his work.

"First let's look at the earliest conceptual drawings . . . and here's some balsa wood models of the same structure," he said. He advanced the slide again to show the finished product. "And here is what the building looks like on site," he said. We sat there a moment, gazing at the silver modern monstrosity.

"And finally," he concluded, "let's look at the finished building." As he advanced the slide, we wondered, what did *that* mean? Weren't we just looking at the finished building? Now there was another slide that also showed the finished building, which looked . . . a little different . . . from the previous slide. . . . Our confusion began to grow: *What did he mean? Isn't this the same as the last slide . . . ?* And then, throughout the auditorium, a "Communal Ah!" as we all realized we had been fooled—for the first photo had not been a photo at all. He drew back to the previous slide so we could take a second look at the "photo" of his building.

"Computer graphics are wonderful, aren't they?" he said.

We had been staring at a computer graphic, thinking it was a photo of his building, and we had been fooled. Give me a break! We use computers every day.

We are intelligent, well educated, cynical, savvy, we're inundated with computer graphics in movies and on television, yet *still we were tricked*. Not just me. Not just the guy sitting next to me. Not just some of us. All of us. The whole room full of people. Fooled. How could this be? How could a whole room full of people experience the "same thing" and then it turns out the thing we experienced was only a shared illusion?

Well, for one, the context of the experience. We trusted him. We didn't expect to be fooled. We were relaxed; we weren't sitting there in a skeptical frame of mind. Maybe he didn't even intend for us to be fooled. Maybe it just happened. But it makes one wonder: How else are we fooled? When else are we tricked, without ever being made aware of the fact? And how can we become smarter about the ways that we are deceived?

One way might be to learn about magic as practiced by magicians. If we see how magicians fool us in the controlled environment of the theater, perhaps we might learn lessons that can be taken to other areas of life.

After all, we live in times infused with illusion and artifice. Unlike our ancestors who lived in and among nature, today we live in an almost entirely artificially created environment. We have become separated from the natural world, our food supply, and the inner workings of the machines that we use every day. With light pollution many of us can barely see the night sky. We are more familiar with human-designed landscaping than the landscape of the natural wilderness. Air-conditioning and heating units separate us from the natural change of seasons while our supermarkets are stocked with fruit and veggies that know no seasons. The spontaneous sounds of our cafes and shops are drowned out by music piped in by corporate headquarters in hopes that it will influence us to buy. There is an all-around limiting of our sensory experiences. Many of us spend large portions of our day seeing the world through "screens"—television, computers—without the accompanying tactile and aromatic sensations that would surround us if we were really experiencing the real world in real life. We feel as though we have experienced the world, when in fact we have mostly only sat in a chair and seen a projected image of it.

We live in times infused with magic. Consider the past seven years since the hardback edition of this book came out: the recent successes of such magic-themed books as *Harry Potter*, television shows such as *Charmed*, and theater blockbusters such as the *Lord of the Rings* film trilogy. As we spend more time in the synthetic constructions of corporate environs than we do outdoors, movies such as *The Truman Show*, *The Matrix*, *eXistenZ*, *Vanilla Sky*, and so on coax into us the notions that perhaps the reality around us is less real than we think.

Religions with magical overtones such as Wicca and Witchcraft continue to grow in popularity,[1] as have various spiritual teachings infused with mysticism such as the Kabbalah. There is even exercise infused with mysticism, like Tai Chi and Yoga. All have grown in prominence over the past several years, demonstrating our society's continuing interest and need to imbue our lives with magic.

We can turn on the TV and find plenty of magic shows. But the magicians don't wear tuxedos and manipulate props, and they don't call themselves magicians or even mentalists. They call themselves psychics and claim to be predicting the future or speaking with the dead by utilizing "cold reading" techniques—educated guessing—to bring magic to a much wider audience than ever before. However, these magicians don't present their shows as stage magic, but as reality.

Unfortunately, a large portion of the general public is so unskilled in the dividing line between science and magic that it is possible for many viewers to plausibly believe that the psychics have supernatural powers. The consequence of this is that it induces some of those viewers to believe that they themselves may have magical powers. And sometimes, some of those people decide to act on their magical powers by volunteering their psychic predictions to law enforcement and so forth, which means that law enforcement agents have to run around in circles taking their prophecies seriously. These predictions are often unsolicited by the police, but the fact that someone makes a claim means that law enforcement has to respond to it. And of course the media has to take seriously what law enforcement is up to, so they produce balanced news stories about "psychic detectives" who are "helping to solve crimes," which reassures the public that there may be something to the psychics after all if the media is taking it seriously. Which leads to viewers who watch the news reports, and so the cycle continues. I think that a few more doses in the educational system teaching how even smart people can be fooled would be beneficial here (you'll get a few doses throughout this book).

An example of one such incident happened recently when an American Airlines flight was canceled after a "psychic" phoned in a premonition about a bomb onboard the plane.[2] The plane had to be searched by bomb-sniffing dogs, crew members were inconvenienced, and the passengers were delayed and rescheduled to later flights. How would you feel if you were trying to get someplace but your flight was canceled because of some nutjob who thinks he has magical powers? Do we prefer to have our law enforcement personnel fighting crime, or responding to the whims of cranks with delusions of magical powers? Should we be treating self-proclaimed "psychics" as trusted airline safety consultants, or should we be treating them the same way we would treat any other kook who calls in a bomb threat? "But in these times, we can't ignore anything," the director of the federal Transportation Security Administration explained. True, they can't ignore a bomb threat—so why don't they *call it that*. Call it a *bomb threat*, placed by a *troublemaker*. Instead, they say that a psychic made a prediction, followed by a rash of media stories glorifying this psychic who came *this close* to preventing a disaster!—thus legitimizing the claim, and teaching the public that the government takes "psychic powers" seriously.

Why do such cycles continue? Clearly it is a complicated issue, but one possible factor is hinted at by a recent article in the *Wall Street Journal*: "Psychic Cells."[3] For a fee, cell phone users can have horoscopes, tarot, aura forecasts, and coupons for psychics delivered to their cell phones. This short, unassuming article sounds so commonplace as to obscure the underlying message: that it is in the best interest of corporations to have as many consumers believe as many different crackpot ideologies as possible, for each ideology produces new ideas for revenue streams. Consider the ancient belief of Feng Shui, which has recently been commercialized. It's supposed to be about energy flow, but now it has become more about money flow—into the pockets of home redecorators. Similarly, in recent years we've seen other supernatural trends blossom, such as homeopathy and the use of magnets for curative purposes. Homeopathy involves diluting water until *no active ingredients* remain, and then prescribing a measure of this plain water to the patient. "The most common strengths have been diluted as often as 3, 6, 30, 200, 1000, 10,000, 50,000, or 100,000 times,"[4] reads one guidebook to homeopathy. I'm waiting to see the bottled water manufacturers come out with homeopathic line extensions. (It will still just be plain water in the bottle, but they can charge ten times the price.) Another example is magnets, which were being promoted a few years ago by marketers. You could walk into any supermarket and see displays for Dr. Scholls shoe inserts with magnets. What exactly are these magnets supposed to do anyway? They don't tell you that on the packaging, but leave it to your imagination (because of course they don't do anything). As we will see, this is the same thing magicians often do—leave things to your imagination.

So these trends wax and wane in popularity, and will wax again in the future as the merry-go-round of magical nonsense spins around. Soon some other trend based on mysticism will take its place.

As the world becomes a more complex place, these sorts of fantasies, conspiracies, and easy answers can be comforting. Unlike at the architect's lecture, there often is no one there to clue us in when we are being deceived or misled. The magician's trick comes and goes, and we never identify it as such, and we may be left with a false impression of how the world is. There are no easy answers, and only more complex investigations can inspire that "Communal Ah!" when we see how things really are.

More than ever before, it is crucial to be an informed citizen to understand societal mechanisms. Every year billions are spent to influence us,[5] as consumers and voters, to think and act in one way or another, and yet we go around believing it doesn't affect us. How many savvy, world-weary people do you know who would deny that they are influenced by advertising, marketing, or packaging—but when a celebrity sports a new hairstyle or fashion, those same people flock to buy the product, emulate the look. We think packaging doesn't affect us—but we have favorite brands of bottled *water.* It can be hard sometimes to know when an attempt is being made to influence us, and also when those attempts are succeeding. Nobody's going to teach us stuff like this when it's in their best interest to keep us in the dark and going along with it. That is the point of this book, to bring to the surface some of the methods that are used to attempt such manipulations of mind. Perhaps it can be advantageous for us to understand better the methods that magicians and others may use to deceive.

Understanding magic gives us another view onto our world. When we see how we can be deceived or influenced, we might notice when it is happening to us (or, as my lecture anecdote illustrates, we still may not). You might expect to be deceived when in the presence of high-tech, sophisticated gadgets and graphics, but as we will see throughout these pages, our senses can be fooled by a lot simpler things, ordinary things that we are familiar with from everyday life. (Like in the case of psychics—things as mundane as *words*.)

Stage magicians have assembled a bag of tricks that can be useful in life, the way knowing multiplication, or cooking, or other skills can be useful in life. However, unlike baking a cake, there aren't many classes available to teach you how magicians and others attempt to fool you.

For example, magicians have assembled an arsenal of techniques for manipulating our perceptions of space and time. Perhaps it can be useful to be aware of these techniques in this modern era, when we are always so short on time, so stressed from overwork, and when the slim difference between work time and leisure time is blurred, as we are crushed into diminishing personal space at the office and on the roads—perhaps under these circumstances it may be useful to understand how space and time can be exploited by magicians as a first step toward recognizing these same space and time manipulations in our own daily lives.

Understanding magic gives one the confidence and understanding that mysteries can be figured out. There are rational explanations for even the strangest events. It makes us aware of things from other people's points of view. There is the view of the magician who plans and tries to control the situation; and the view of the recipient who takes it in and is fooled.

But, some ask the question: Does deconstructing magic, learning how it works, take away from the surprise and wonder? Not if the magic is artfully conceived, practiced, and executed. After all, we go to movies knowing "it's all fake." Yet we are still drawn in and can be affected by the cinema, even while knowing how the special effects are done. (For that matter, you can learn how an optical illusion works yet still see the illusion.) Besides, most stage magicians don't inspire much wonder in the first place. They present flash, spectacle, and tricks, but not genuine emotion. Yet the more I've explored the art of deception, the more I've come to believe that the tricky part of it is the least interesting part of all. What is most important is not the secret "trick," but the vast preparation—the marshaling of resources, the planning of alternative paths, the layering of numerous details—in order to create a specific effect in the viewer's mind.

You can prove this to yourself with a simple test. Walk into a magic store with fifty thousand dollars. Buy yourself the largest, glitziest, most expensive, most complicated, most impressive magic trick in the shop—the kind professional magicians in Las Vegas use onstage. OK. Now you've plunked down your fifty thousand dollars (plus tax) for this thing. Go on; buy the "Make an Elephant Disappear Trick." Take it home. Unpack it. Put it together. And see what you'll find. I'll tell you what you'll find. Once you see how it works, you'll lose interest. You'll find that it is something as prosaic as a false wall or a trapdoor. The trick itself is not that interesting. What's interesting is how a prepared professional can make it look like something spectacular onstage.

Another question that gets asked is: Doesn't it hurt the magicians to reveal their tricks? Not as much as it hurts the audience to see a magician who relies only on a bunch of tricks, instead of presenting a transformative theater experience consisting of an engaging mix of patter, character, and emotionally charged narrative.

Besides, most people don't read too much. Most people don't seek out information like this but tend to use the information most readily available to them: that which is pushed at them by television, radio, and the first few sentences of some front-page headlines. Therefore magicians, including the TV psychics, use mostly the same tricks and techniques that magicians have been using for millennia, and audiences are still fooled.

"Osama bin Laden uses misdirection, look-alike decoys and fake caravans to foil pursuit," an October 2001 Associated Press article began.[6] Two years later we saw similar reports of Saddam Hussein during the buildup to the Iraq war, using doubles when he appeared in public to fool those who might try to pin him down.[7] But as we will see in chapter 6, magicians have used doubles throughout history to deceive an audience in the same way. The audience has no reason to believe the person they are looking at is not the real person, just as I had no reason to believe the photo I was looking at was not the real building. And so, if a technique is effective, it can be disclosed to the public and still remain effective and still be used year after year.

It is easier than ever now to locate almost any book that has ever been published on any topic, including many which reveal secrets of magic. Few people make the effort to do so. It is easier than ever now to visit the Internet site of the US Patent Office and look up online patents that the magicians themselves have placed on their own magical devices. But how many people bother? The dissemination of information is greater now than ever before, yet how many people take advantage of all the information out there, or even have the time to do so? Thus the information can be made available for readers like yourself, without harming the craft of magic.

Yet there are benefits to pursuing all those information sources available to us. Better-informed consumers mean a better product. Let's face it, most magic shows today are little more than the result of a magician going on some $X-thousand-dollar shopping spree and showing off the tricks he or she purchased. It's show and tell. Look at the toys I bought! This might produce spectacle, but I don't believe it engages the audience, and the audience feels this as a lack of involvement, whether or not they know how the tricks are done. But when the magic consumer learns more, it forces the magicians to get better, to be more innovative, to think through their presentation to add mystery and poignancy to the spectacle they are performing onstage.

Or, maybe it's just fun to learn how the trick is done. So let's get started!

Notes

1. Sample quote from one guide to Wicca: "Wiccan magic flows out of Wiccan religion. The energy raised during a ritual will, if left to itself, dissipate into the environment. Rather than allow the energy to go to waste, Wiccans use it for healing and empowerment. The point of spells is to change or adapt reality in line with the magician's will." Tony Grist and Aileen Grist, *The Illustrated Guide to Wicca* (New York: Sterling, 2000), p. 68.

2. "Feds Cancel Flight on 'Psychic' Bomb Tip," Associated Press, March 27, 2004.

3. Ann Grimes, "Psychic Cells," *Wall Street Journal*, February 26, 2004, p. B4.

4. You might not believe me that homeopathy prescribes plain water. Here is more of the quote from this typical book on the subject, Stehpen Cummings and Dana Ullamn, *Everybody's Guide to Homeopathic Medicines: Revised and Expanded* (New York: G. P. Putman's Sons, 1991):

> Potenization [of the medicine] consists of a process of successive dilution. If the medicine is soluble, 1 part is diluted in 99 parts of water or alcohol, and the mixture is mixed vigorously…. One part of the diluted medicine is then diluted again in the same manner, and the process is repeated as many times as necessary to achieve the desired final dilution strength. The most common strengths have been diluted as often as 3, 6, 30, 200, 1000, 10,000, 50,000, or 100,000 times…. By convention, a medicine that has been diluted fewer times than another is considered a lower potency. (p. 15)

(Reread that last sentence again if you didn't get it the first time. He's saying the medicine is more potent the more you dilute it in water.)

To translate all these numbers into something understandable, let's turn to Barrie R. Cassileth, *The Alternative Medicine Handbook: The Complete Reference Guide to Alternative and Complimentary Therapies* (New York: W. W. Norton, 1998), where it is explained that

> [i]n the end, [after the dilution process] the resulting solution can be more than a billion times more dilute than a solution of one molecule of salt placed in an ocean. Since a molecule is the smallest possible amount of any substance, most homeopathic remedies contain less than one molecule of the original plant or mineral extract. (p. 37)

(Imagine drinking an oceanful of water, and maybe only encountering one grain of salt, if that! That's homeopathy.)

5. Robert S. Lazich, ed., "Broadcast Ad Revenues (1999)," in *Market Share Reporter—2001* (Farmington Hills, MI: Gale Group, 2001), p. 297, shows broadcast ad revenues for the major television stations are in the billions of dollars.

6. John J. Lumpkin, "Bin Laden May Be Planning to Run," Associated Press, October 16, 2001.

7. Richard Price, "The Many Faces of Saddam: War on Saddam Dramatic Proof of Why You Shouldn't Necessarily Believe Everything You See on Television," *Daily Mail* (London), March 21, 2003; "German Scientist: Saddam Has Doubles," Associated Press, September 27,

2002; and "War in the Gulf: Double in TV Walkabout," *Scottish Daily Record & Sunday Mail*, April 8, 2003, are three of many press reports on the subject.

PART ONE

WHAT IS MAGIC . . . REALLY?

In this first section we try to answer the above question. What is magic . . . really? Even if you're not a magician you probably have some ideas about how magic tricks are done . . . but you probably have a lot of misconceptions as well. This section attempts to set your thinking on the right track so you'll better understand what magic is and how it is performed.

1

The Foundations of Deception

How does a magician stand up there on stage and fool an entire audience? How can *one person* deceive a whole room full of people?

Theories

There are a few theories that come up every now and again, theories that have been with us for many decades and attempt to explain the phenomenon of magic:

"THE HAND IS QUICKER THAN THE EYE"

This theory states that the hand can move quicker than the eye can see. The magician is trained to move fast (or by extension, to talk fast) so the audience cannot follow what he or she is doing. As magician Horace Goldin of the early 1900s was wont to say: "Don't blink or you'll miss a trick."

This theory was debunked by psychologist Joseph Jastrow at the turn of the twentieth century, when he tested two great magicians of the time, Harry Kellar and Alexander Herrmann. Surprisingly, Kellar tested about average for motor skills, sensory acuity, and memory; while Herrmann actually fell below the average population in such factors. Clearly something other than speed is at work.

As anyone who has ever witnessed hands moving across a piano keyboard knows, the hands can be quick, no doubt, producing music that comes fast and elegant, and yet every motion of the hands and fingers are there to see. We *can* see those fast hands! So this theory must be invalid. The hand is definitely *not* quicker than the eye. There is a small element of truth to this theory, but it's not that the hand is quicker than the eye. The hand is not invisible because it's *quicker* than the eye—it's invisible because the eye is distracted away from the hand at crucial moments. More on this later.

THE "SUPERNATURAL" THEORY

Another theory of how-it's-done is the supernatural theory. We're a lot more sophisticated now than we were a hundred years ago, but sadly the supernatural theory is still pretty prevalent. *Every* magician I interviewed and almost every magician I read about or researched had stories to tell of audience members who believed they used psychic powers or metaphysical powers to produce their illusions. The skillful escape artist Harry Houdini had to contend with those who charged him with slipping out of jail cells by "dematerializing" his body. Magicians who perform mentalism and séances are frequently accused of harnessing real supernatural powers. One magician said he has gotten phone calls from desperate people wanting to purchase magic potions and inquiring whether he has the power to cast spells on people. Needless to say, magic is not done by supernatural means. If it were, there would be no point to the show. The point of a magic show is that you *don't* know how it's done. You know it's done by some natural means, but you have no idea how to explain it. That leads us into . . .

THE "HYPNOSIS" THEORY

Another theory that gained a level of popularity in years past is that the magician is performing some kind of hypnosis on the crowd. One of Britain's master magicians of the early 1900s, David Devant, explained magic this way. He said that magic "is an art by means of which a man can exercise . . . a spell over others, and persuade them into believing that they have seen some natural law disobeyed."[1]

Regardless of his opinion, the hypnosis idea is also more or less nonsense. It's true that some magic does involve making suggestions and offering subtleties much as a hypnotist does. However, at no time is the audience pulled into a trancelike state. Someone wide awake and scrutinizing the action closely can often be fooled even more than a less observant person—because the observant one will notice those subtleties and become misdirected from the true source of the magic. As we will see, the magician merely sets up the necessary prerequisites for an illusion to occur. Your mind does the rest in actually creating the illusion. If anything, the audience members hypnotize themselves, but even that is pushing the idea a tad too far.

The "Brainwashing" Theory

Similar to the hypnosis theory, the brainwashing theory states that the magician brainwashes the audience into believing miracles are occurring. Once again we have a theory that is not wholly accurate by itself, but we can take some smidgens of the theory and work with them. While the magician does not technically brainwash the audience in the traditional sense of the word, many of the techniques of brainwashing are extremely similar to those a magician uses to lead and direct an observer's mind. Both brainwashers and magicians attempt to fill one's mind with nonsense. They use a fast pace that doesn't give one a chance to logically think through the situation. Both use techniques to control the victim/spectator's behavior while making it seem the victim or spectator is acting under their own direction. A fuller comparison will be made in chapter 15, where we discuss applications of magic outside the theater. There are some overlaps in technique because both have to do with audience manipulation and influencing ideas. But there are some divergences as well, because brainwashing and magic have different ends to their means. Brainwashing is for ideology; magic is for entertainment.

None of these theories—brainwashing, hypnosis, the supernatural, or hand quickness—is completely able to explain how stage magic is accomplished. None can completely explain how one person stands up and fools a whole roomful of people. What then? How? What is the theory that does explain it all?

Theories Today

Today we are as sophisticated as ever, and yet more often than not we are still fooled by the magic. Our theories today will vary depending on what kind of trick is presented. If the trick is very simple, with no fancy apparatus, then we are likely to believe it was done with a special skill the magician possesses, perhaps palming, or maybe it "went up his sleeve."

If the trick does involve apparatus, then our tendency is to suspect the apparatus. Maybe it's done with mirrors or strings, or a trap door in the stage. But as we'll see as we delve into it, just because you don't see any apparatus, doesn't mean none was used. And just because a fancy box or gizmo is employed, doesn't mean the trick was self-working. Later on we'll go into mirrors, sleeves, string and stage in greater depth. And we will delve into all the different areas of magic to see what's going on backstage and behind the curtain.

What we will see most of all is that a successful magic trick is a lot more brilliant and complicated to pull off well than most audience members would suspect. And while this may be an arguable point, I believe that out of everything, the most important technique for deceiving an audience is—*misdirection*.

Misdirection of Actions, Objects, and Illusions

All magic tricks rely on misdirection to some degree. The question is, what part of you is being misled? Your eyes? Your ears? Your brain? A little of all three? It's a lot more complicated than you may think.

Let's start by discussing misdirection in space and time and thought and mind. When you emerge from this section of the book, you will know the signs that a misdirection is occurring. And even if you're not exactly sure how the trick was done, you will have a better understanding of when it was definitely *not* done.

SPACE MISDIRECTION

You know about misdirection. The magician waves his left hand in the air. Meanwhile his right hand is covertly sneaking into his pocket and pulling out the rubber balls. That's *spatial* misdirection, because while your attention is focused on one point in space, the action is happening at another point.

Sound can also be used to misdirect. As I write this, I'm sitting on an outdoor patio adjoining a restaurant. Lots of white metal chairs, and tables with umbrellas. People are sitting around chatting and eating. A few moments ago, a new mother came out through the sliding doors of the restaurant, her screaming baby in her arms. How many of us sitting here looked up and turned our heads around on our necks to see what was making the noise? All of us. It's part of the animal survival mechanism to seek out the source of potential trouble. The baby doesn't know it, but she has misdirected us from our tasks, our eating, our writing, as skillfully as any master illusionist. With sound.

FREE THE FLEA!

Now you're going to perform an illusion. It's going to involve spatial misdirection. The audience will be misdirected by your use of physical gestures and sound. (Are you in a public place? If so, people will look at you like you're crazy if you try this experiment! Maybe you'd better skip this until you're safe at home in your bedroom. The trick is meaningless if you read it silently.)

We will perform the illusion in stages, each time building on a new level of misdirection. We will also refine the illusion in other ways. This will give you an idea of the kind of practice and preening that goes into any magical performance.

Okay, here's the illusion. Make a fist.

Hold the fist in front of you.

Now read these two sentences:

This is my pet flea.

Hey, let me out of here!

Not a very effective illusion. No one would believe you really have a flea in your fist, let alone that the flea was pleading to get out! But that's okay, we can improve upon the effect. Let's start with the wording.

This is my pet flea.

Right away we see there's a problem with the way this is worded. This says your *fist* is the flea. That's wrong. The flea is inside your fist. So let's change the first sentence to illustrate that idea.

My pet flea is in my fist.

By changing the wording we have changed the image the audience will see in their minds. I have an image of that fist opening up to reveal tiny circus tents with little fleas hopping around, and a ferris wheel spinning in the background. You might have a different flea image in mind!

We're not done yet. Let's put in some misdirection—or rather, some direction. When you read those two sentences, the audience had two points to focus on: your face and your fist. Which should they look at? They don't know! This is important because you are trying to implant an illusion in their brains. To do that you must have complete control over what sensory input the audience takes in. You begin by showing them where to look.

You want to direct the audience to look at your flea-filled fist. When you start talking you should look at the people you are talking to, but when you mention your fist, look at it. Truly believe in your mind that a flea is in your fist!

As you're looking at your fist, you might want to gesture with your other hand. Hold your fist up. With the other hand open, palm up, fingers pointed toward your fist, eyes looking at your fist, say:

My pet flea is in my fist.

Hey, let me out of here!

Good, good! You gestured so that audience knew to look at your fist. But we're not there yet. Three more steps to go. The voice is all wrong. Fleas don't speak in your voice. Next time you do this, use a squeaky flea voice when you read the second sentence, as if you were a flea trapped inside a fist. The second thing is, we want to project the image of the flea calling out from inside that closed, dark fist. To do that, curl your tongue up and back inside your mouth, so that the underside of your tongue touches the roof of your mouth. This makes your squeaky flea voice sound muffled, as if it were coming from inside a fist. Finally, as the flea is talking, wiggle your fist ever so slightly, to give the impression that the flea is frantically trying to escape.

(fist, gesture)

My pet flea is in my fist.

(squeaky, muffled, look, wiggle fist)

Hey, let me out of here!

What was once mere words is now an illusion. Look at all the steps needed to convey physically and mentally the idea that a flea is trapped in your fist. . . . That's the magic of misdirection!

"Bah, humbug!" somebody sneers. "That's not magic, that's ventriloquism." Yes, you're right. But ventriloquism is a kind of illusion, which is what this book is about. When you watch a ventriloquist don't you really feel, at least for a little while, that the dummy is the one talking? You *do*. And notice how your eyes travel back and forth between the dummy and the performer as they engage in conversation. That's absurd! Why should you look at the dummy when it's "talking"? When the dummy is talking it means the ventriloquist is doing the performing ("throwing" his voice). It makes more sense to look at the ventriloquist when the dummy is talking, so you can admire his ability to speak through a closed mouth! And yet we don't, because the ventriloquist misdirects us. He looks at the dummy and makes the dummy look at him when he talks. He acts as if the dummy is alive. That's the key to creating effective magic: acting.

The magician must believe his illusion is real, and must use acting to convey that belief to the audience. Like the ventriloquist throwing his voice, the magician throws his belief. If the audience catches it, an illusion is created in their minds.

TIME MISDIRECTION

One of the biggest secrets of magic is another kind of misdirection that no one talks about or thinks about. Not spatial, but *temporal* misdirection. Misdirection in time.

NOT NOW

The vanished assistant is about to reappear inside the locked-up crate. You want to know how the trick is done so you concentrate on the crate. You stare at every aspect of the stage, looking for some clue. That's fine by the magician, because what you don't know is that the assistant was back inside the crate five minutes ago when they were locking it up and throwing drop cloths over it. That's misdirection in time because what you think is happening now, already happened. Sometimes it works the other way—what you think is happening now isn't going to happen until later. Either way your attention is misfocused onto irrelevant events.

One of the greatest achievements of the legacy of illusion is the almost complete coverup of time misdirection. People know about space misdirection, but temporal misdirection has been in a sense misdirected from the public's eye. The magicians don't want you to know about it, obviously, because to have such a great secret allows them to be lazy when performing illusions that require temporal misdirection. Furthermore, as you watch magicians performing, you will often see the more experienced ones using one kind of misdirection as a coverup for the other kind. They make it look like they are hiding something spatially when in fact they are hiding it temporally. Sometimes they "accidentally" mess up the trick along one misdirection to fool the audience into believing that is the method of secrecy they are using for that trick. For example, imagine a trick where the magician transforms a red scarf into a green scarf. Towards the end of the trick, the magician has the red scarf in his closed fist, and he places it into the "magic box." Now, the audience is watching carefully for signs of trickery. They know the red scarf is in there, so they're looking to see how he will try to switch it for the green scarf. But they won't see the switch take place, because they're wrong—he *didn't* just put the red scarf in the box. He actually put the green scarf in. The switch had been accomplished five minutes previously (time misdirection) when no one was thinking about switched scarves. Five minutes before, as he was secretly switching the scarves, he "accidentally" revealed an extra green scarf sticking out of his pocket. The kids in the audience jump up and start pointing at the green scarf in his pocket, thinking that he was going to try switching the red scarf for the green scarf in his pocket. Of course, the magician acts bewildered and throws the green scarf away. The audience now has the idea that the magician was going to make the transformation by exchanging the red silk for the greenie in his pocket (a spatial maneuver that would require spatial misdirection). In reality, the "accident" has become spatial misdirection to cover up the fact that the scarf has already been exchanged. Now that they know what to look for they won't be able to find it, because they've been temporally misdirected. If this all seems too complicated for you, imagine what it's like to be the magician having to focus on all this *and* put on an entertaining show at the same time!

One of the best uses of time misdirection can be found in the Metamorphosis illusion. Metamorphosis is a feat of magic popularized by Houdini and his wife Bess. Now it is performed regularly by many magicians, the husband/wife team The Pendragons being the most prominent.

In Metamorphosis, the magician is placed into a large bag, which is tied at the top with thick cord. The bag is placed into a trunk, which is buckled, locked, sometimes tied shut with ropes. As Mark Wilson performed this illusion, the trunk was covered with a canvas which was extensively laced up to make certain the magician could not escape. The assistant then stands on top of the trunk, holding a large silk curtain. Now comes the magic, and it happens in a split second: the assistant lifts the curtain over her head, and just as quickly lowers it again. She's not there! The magician now stands in her place atop the trunk. Thunderous applause. The magician throws aside the curtain and proceeds to unlock the trunk, tear open the bag, and there is the assistant astoundingly inside.

What is amazing about Metamorphosis is the sheer rapidity in which the transposition takes place. In a mere *moment* the magician and assistant change places. In a blink of the eye!

What is not so apparent is the time misdirection at work here. Think about it. The magician is placed into the bag, which is then placed into the trunk. As soon as the trunk is closed you can expect that the magician has gotten out of the bag, and is waiting in the trunk (or perhaps has exited the back of the trunk via a trap door, depending on the make of the trick). The buckles, locks, ropes, and canvas that cover the trunk make the illusion appear more difficult to accomplish, but in reality they are making it somewhat easier. It takes quite a while to apply all the buckles, locks, and coverings to the trunk. During that time the magician is actually escaping from inside. Rather than making it more difficult, the magician actually has all that extra time in which to effect his escape!

A similar process of time misdirection works after the body exchange takes place. The assistant stands on the trunk, lifts the curtain above her face, then drops it down again to reveal she has become the magician. The audience feels that the assistant is now magically transported through the locks, into the trunk, into the sealed bag. However, there's no need for such an instantaneous exchange! First we must wait through the audience applause. Then we must let the assistant unlock those locks and buckles and ropes, all of which gives the assistant lots of extra time in which to wrestle her way into the sealed bag. It should also be mentioned that in some versions of this effect, handcuffs are also used. The magician or assistant uses the time gain to effectively slip in or out of the handcuffs, depending on which part of the trick is being done.

Now you'll notice I didn't mention exactly how the effect is accomplished. Just how does the magician escape from a tied bag, or locked handcuffs, or a locked trunk (or how does one get into such containers?). These are questions that will be answered throughout this book. The important thing to realize for now is the basic understanding of time misdirection at work. In Metamorphosis, as in many other tricks, we are under the impression that the trick takes place in a *snap*, in a fraction of a second. In reality our impression is merely an illusion.

*   *   *   *   *

Another kind of time misdirection involves the *passage* of time. In this kind of misdirection, the magician will hope that the passage of time helps you to forget an action that was taken earlier. Time misdirection is often used in "card forces."

Magicians have ways of forcing a card on you. When they say, "Pick a card, any card," you may be surprised to learn that the card you "randomly" selected may actually have been controlled into your hand by the magician. Card forces often follow a procedure such as this:

1. The magician secretly places the card he wishes to force on the top of the deck.
2. The deck is shuffled (actually, false-shuffled, to keep the top card on top where it belongs).
3. The deck is cut.
4. The magician coercively switches the top half of the deck with the bottom half.
5. Time misdirection comes into play now. The magician makes a joke, or tells the spectator what's coming up next. The magician will look into the person's eyes.
6. At this point the audience should have forgotten which half of the cut deck came from the top, and which came from the bottom. The magician offers the "center" of the deck to the spectator, "All right, now take this card from the center of the deck, exactly where you cut it." The spectator is really taking the top card.

A few moments of distraction is all it takes to make spectators lose their concentration. It is important to realize that if you want to figure out how the tricks are done, it's not enough to observe each individual action carefully. You must also observe how actions lead into each other, and what the relationships between actions are. The magician often will intentionally mislead the audience into thinking that an action (or option or object) is something very different than what it actually is.

BRACKETING AND FRAMES

Time misdirection involves "the bracketing of a trick," explains Peter M. Nardi, a magician and sociologist at Pitzer College who performs magic for his students.

> The beginning and end of a trick often is never clear. Often what the audience sees as the beginning of a trick may already be the middle of it. Something may have started already, loading the deck, forcing it, shuffling it in certain ways, and all of that. So the trick actually begins at a certain point and your job as a magician is to indicate *false* beginning of when it starts. Or conversely, the same thing at the ending. If you did a coin disappearing from the hand (you did a French drop [sleight of hand maneuver] or something) and you open up the hand real slowly and it's gone, well

what looks like the ending has already disappeared moments before. So the trick for you ended before, but for the audience it's just ending now.

This is another of those important concepts that consistently fool audiences: the fact that a trick may have started long before we had any idea that trick was going to be done. That means there's no way to prepare, no way to say, "I'm going to be extra vigilant and find out how it works!" You can certainly try, but it makes it very difficult to detect.

DECEITFUL CAMOUFLAGES

We have been discussing misdirections of *actions* (i.e., misdirecting the action of switching scarves by talking to the audience about a duplicate green scarf that then gets discarded). Other illusions require the misdirection of *objects*, which basically means the object must appear on stage, remain functional to the magician, and yet stay invisible to the viewing audience. One of the best examples are the strings needed to perform levitation effects. The strings have to be on stage, and yet they must remain invisible. Other effects require other things to be invisible, and various camouflaging techniques are used for this purpose. For instance, many stage shows have made large animals "disappear" from boxes suspended high above the stage by hiding the animal behind a sheet of material that matches the background curtain.

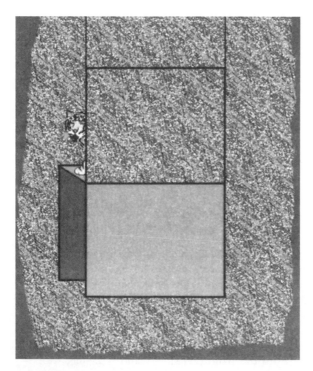

Fig. 1. The sides drop down and the tiger has vanished! Actually it's concealed behind a swatch of cloth that matches the backdrop. The next step will be to divert attention elsewhere—quick!

Another way items are camouflaged on stage is through the use of black art. Black art is the use of blackness to hide objects. At the back of the stage is a black curtain. The stage itself is kept dark except for black lights. The magician is visible in a white outfit. There might be objects hidden all over the stage—half the object is painted black, the other half painted with pigments which glow in response to the black lighting. To make objects appear, the magician need only spin them around so the colored side shows. Invisible assistants dressed all in black glide out from the wings, unseen by the audience. Those invisible assistants can cause objects or people to fly around, or appear and disappear. Black art tends not to be used as much in magic shows any more, due to its being widely known. More often it can be found in puppet shows and stage shows like Mummenschanz, where colorful characters seem to fly and float above a darkened stage—held aloft by invisible, black-clad puppeteers.

A different kind of camouflage occurs when the natural traits of an object are disguised. For example, a metallic steel ball might be covered with cloth knitting to give the impression it is a soft, fluffy thing. On the other hand, if the ball is to float through space, it will probably be a light, hollow ball disguised to look like a heavy, solid iron orb. Such disguises can help conceal the working of the trick (no one suspects the cloth ball could stick to a magnet, yet a magnet is used to draw it out of sight); or disguises can be used to enhance the illusion (it's amazing that such a heavy metal object can float like that).

Breaking Trusts

I remember seeing a show in high school where the "psychic" concentrated real hard and then managed to read the thoughts of the audience.

"I'm receiving a number . . ." he intoned. (Clasps hand to head.) "It's a . . . it's a long number. Nine digits. 3-2-7 . . ." (face contorts in concentration). "6 . . . 4 . . ." and in one final burst: "1279." He looks up smiling. "Does this number mean anything to anybody?" The words are barely out of his mouth when there is a squeal from the crowd. "That's my Social Security number! How did you know!"

"Wait, wait." The psychic-magician puts up his hand in protest. "You're Michelle, right?"

"Yes." She looks at her date with a surprised smile.

"Your birthdate is August—no!—*December* eighteenth."

"Yes!" she grins. The psychic is right!

This went on for a while, until the psychic had managed to psychically read the names, birth dates, names of pets and significant others of half a dozen people in attendance. Quite impossible, and yet this is what he did. My friends left the show feeling amazed and awestruck at this display. I left feeling empowered because it was so "obvious" how it was done. Later I talked to a student who had helped set up and usher the show, and I found my initial hunch to be correct. . . .

When we read a mystery book, we expect the author to play fair with the reader. The clues should all be laid out before us, no matter how tortuous they are. It is the extraneous details that misdirect from the clues. Fair play means you can't suddenly introduce a new character on the last page who turns out to be the murderer—that doesn't jibe with our notions of fairness in mystery-reading. Similarly, audiences come to a magic show with certain assumptions about how the magician will behave. Like the mystery writer, they expect the magician to perform his magic in front of them, in full view, while misdirecting away from those certain actions that constitute the trick-to-the-trick. The audience probably doesn't realize they are making those assumptions, because they have no reason to believe their assumptions are being broken. But very often a magic trick works because the magician has broken the unwritten rules of theatrical performing.

There is a sense of trust established between magician and audience. The magician agrees he will use "magic" to perform illusions—not unfair practices like camera tricks. The audience believes the magician is honest. But magicians very often breech that trust. For instance, we all know the rule about audience volunteers. "Have we ever met before?" the magician asks. "No, never." Technically this is true, but when you're a professional magician doing a nationwide television broadcast and your reputation is on the line—not to mention that you have to put on a good show for people—you want to make sure beforehand that the "random" audience volunteers you choose are:

- Sane
- Lively, bubbly, and happy
- Photogenic
- Happy to be on camera
- Sitting in an aisle seat or otherwise easily approachable
- Complacent (not going to heckle or mess up the trick), and
- Preferably, beautiful women.

David Copperfield has members of his staff scout out the audience before a show. They locate enough volunteers that meet this description, and cue Dave in on who he should choose during the show. Are these "random" volunteers in on the act? No, almost certainly not. But the volunteers are certainly not complete unknowns to the magician. One magician tells the story of his friend, a young woman, who was the daughter of the man responsible for booking Copperfield at a particular show. The previous night she had gone out to dinner with Copperfield (as well as her father, and others). The next day she was selected by Copperfield as a "random" audience volunteer for one of his tricks. They had met before the show, but she swears they did not discuss the trick. The magician who tells this story concludes, "Maybe [Copperfield] just likes to meet his volunteers for some of his tricks so he doesn't get some heckler for an 'assistant.' " As always, the magician does whatever is necessary to put uncontrollable aspects of the show under his thumb.

"Psychics" such as Kreskin, and the high school performer who was mentioned at the beginning of this section, also defy assumptions about their intentions.

When a "psychic" tells a person personal information, he has no way of knowing there is only one solution to "How'd he do that?" The magician *had to have contact with the person* and found out those items of information through that contact by meeting with audience members before the show. This is called "working the crowd," and is shown humorously and honestly in the movie *Leap of Faith*.

In the movie, Steve Martin plays a conniving evangelist who, deep down, has a heart of gold (*awwww!*). Martin uses his confident personality along with some stage tricks to milk audiences for whatever they can afford. Martin and his company expect to take in $4,000 a night. During his evangelistic performance, Martin uses the power of God to mysteriously perceive items of interest about the local townsfolk. This young girl is pregnant, that man has a back problem, one woman has a dispute with her neighbors. The audience gasps in religious awe as they sit spellbound by Martin's otherworldly knowledge (and incidentally, stuff money into the buckets being passed through the crowd). Their need to believe coupled with Martin's sneakiness creates a convincing illusion of divine word handed down.

When you think about it, there really are a lot of assumptions people make without realizing it when they go to a magic show. Look how many assumptions Martin's audience made about the tent show:

1. The unthought-of assumption that the man on stage alone is performing the magic (here, Martin had a team of helpers to listen in on audience conversation, and deliver these secret messages to Martin through a miniature earpiece).
2. The unthought-of assumption that all the magic is done in "real time" as the performance is happening (here, the gossipy tidbits are actually collected *before the show begins*—time misdirection!).
3. The unthought-of assumption that the magic is done on stage. After all, that's where the show is! (Of course, here, Martin's sneaky assistants were not on stage at all, but meandering through the crowd.)

James Randi explains how the Israeli magician Uri Geller has used the same techniques to fool many people, often quite intelligent people, into believing he has psychic powers. Randi relates how at one performance, Geller instructed a trusted assistant to "stand by the door of the theater as people came in and report to him backstage who had what in their purses or pockets as they paid for their tickets. [The assistant] watched Geller take down the license numbers of various cars in the parking lot outside and note details about the people who got out of them—all for later use onstage."[2]

This is basically what I found out by talking to the usher at my high school show: that the psychic had talked to people as they came in, and had his assistants do the same. That is as much as my friend saw. It's possible that the psychic went so far as to gather information on students by pick-pocketing, rifling through student records, talking to teachers, or looking up last year's yearbook in the school library. Mentalists have been known to use all of these sorts of detective methods to work their mind miracles.

Notice the sneakiness of this: in a standard magic show, we see the assistants on stage. Here we just saw that one man performing solo. Our minds make the unthought-of assumption that what we see is what we get. No, what we *don't see* produces what we get.

It is no wonder that a person can stand up there on stage and deceive a roomful of people when, unknown to them, their minds are secretly harboring such betraying ideas about the nature of the show. What it all boils down to is *illusions*. The magician sets up an optical, audio, in fact total-sensory illusion that involves even the very familiar mechanics of your mind. The fact that familiar concepts are being silently broken only makes the illusion that much more mystifying.

The point of all this is that, contrary to what magicians would have us believe, what unfolds on stage does not include enough evidence to explain how a trick is done. Conversely, just because you cannot find a solution to the puzzle does *not* mean real psychic powers or otherworldly explanations must be the answer.

There is one magicians' rule that is important, but not as strictly adhered to as the "never tell how a trick is done" rule. It is a rule that has much to do with this idea of trust and fair play, and it is a fourth unthought-of assumption that was defied in Martin's evangelic tent show.

The magician should never cross the line, presenting himself as a magician and psychic, or perhaps not even a psychic at all, as that would be dishonest. The magician creates a role for himself and sticks with it. That role defines how he deals with the audience, and if he breaks from that role he is being dishonest. Many magicians break that bond, presenting themselves as a hypnotist but doing psychic stuff as well. They often conduct hypnotism in a scientific way, and stress the truthfulness of it, and the reality of hypnotism. But then they go ahead and simply *lie* by performing "psychic" acts. This whole thing is an issue of lying. The magician should not lie to the audience. The audience expects magicians to be truthful in their dealings. When they are not, the result can be anger, outrage, and even tragedy.

In *Leap of Faith*, good magic performed for the wrong reasons results in destitute people delivering the last of their money to a greedy bunch of fakes. Later we'll talk about how magic is used by all sorts of people to extract money, manipulate minds, and otherwise reconstruct the reality of its victims. For now, let's continue examining how magicians consistently break the trust we place in their honesty.

BREAKING THE LIMITS OF THE SHOW

When spatial misdirection occurs, the magician is doing something in a place where the audience does not think to look. Misdirection in time can go one step beyond this. The magician works his trick at a time when the audience *cannot even think* to look because the show has not started yet. The magician breaks the trust of real-time performing. We have already seen examples of how pseudopsychics start performing a trick before the show even begins. Some tricks are accomplished because crucial moves are made earlier in the show. For example, magician John Bannon has a transposition illusion he performs in which a selected playing card turns up inside a box of lozenges—and the lozenges end up inside the box of cards. It is a mysterious effect, but Bannon explains that a duplicate card box, containing lozenges, is in his jacket pocket before the show. Bannon probably starts off his show with a fresh deck of cards, sealed and fully wrapped in cellophane. Throughout the performance, the audience sees that box as *the* card box that the cards came in. He therefore needs to switch the legitimate box with the prepared one sometime before the lozenges trick is performed. "Since virtually no heat is on the box, making the switch is fairly easy. Keep it simple," he advises. "Since I use this routine as a closer, I remove the box from my pocket *at the end of the previous trick*."[3] In other words, he is breaking the limits of the trick, starting the trick before it even starts—or anyway, starting the trick before the audience sees the trick begin. In a sense this is a form of time misdirection. The audience is easily fooled because things are happening before they know to look for things to happen![4]

There is a reverse way of breaking the limits of the show—to *pretend* to perform some action before the show, but actually save the performance for some time during the show. For instance, some mentalists make predictions weeks in advance of the show about what the headlines of the day will be. They make their predictions, then mail them in a sealed envelope to the host of the show for safekeeping. The mailing is opened for the first time on stage the day of the event. One mentalist at a show I attended mailed an envelope to the theater owner prior to the show. During the show, he had the owner stand up with the envelope in hand. "You have not opened that, and I have not opened that, and no one has seen the contents of that envelope since I sealed it weeks ago, correct?" the magician asked.

"Yes."

"Open the envelope," commanded the magician. As the envelope is being torn into, the apparently psychic magician reminded us that he had not touched this envelope for weeks. The theater owner is startled to find a poster-sized sheet of paper inside. He unfolds it, and there, in bold print big enough for the entire room to read, are today's tidbits from Washington, current sports scores, and an accurate reporting of the weather. Applause!

Question: How did he predict these things weeks in advance?

Answer: He didn't.

Devices are commercially available to magicians that will shoot a message packet into a sealed envelope to achieve this effect. But in this particular case the large sheet of paper was clearly too big to have been subterfuged into a sealed envelope, and besides, the magician never touched it! Or did he?

A talk with some of the janitorial staff revealed that one of the magician's assistants had been poking around in the theater's offices well before the show began. With only speculation to go on, it is fair to assume that this assistant replaced the original envelope with one done up that day by the magician. How did the magician forge postmarks on the mailed envelope? The same day as he mailed the original envelope (containing blank paper) he also mailed *himself* an unsealed, twin envelope, with his own address printed on a removable label. The letter was received by the magician; he removed his own address, replaced it with the theater owner's and then waited for performance day.

What if the original packet wasn't available for the switch on the day of the show? Then the magician would have had to ask the theater owner to pass the envelope up to him on stage. There, he could use the device to shoot in his prediction of the day. Or he could use some standard magician switcharoo to covertly switch the mailed blank paper for one done that day with predictions on it. Good magicians are always prepared for such contingencies, as James "The Amazing" Randi has explained. At least one book has been written on the subject: *"Outs," Precautions, and Challenges*, by Charles H. Hopkins. He wrote the book with the card magician in mind, describing methods for getting out of difficult situations with spectators. "Ever run out of endings?" I asked Randi. "No, no," he answered. "There's always a way." The trick is to be prepared for it.

Concessions in Control

I have a feeling that most magicians do not like breaking trusts and would rather use a more honest method if one was available to them. But if they want to deliver a particular effect, sometimes it is impossible to do so honestly. A concession in their values as a magician is one thing, but sometimes magicians will go so far as to trade off their one prized possession to deliver an illusion—control. Control means everything to the magician, for without it, he can not control your mind.

SACRIFICING AUDIENCE MEMBERS

Sometimes it is more useful to give away some control in favor of making a trick work. I call this "sacrificing." The magician sacrifices a secret by revealing it, in order to accomplish the effect.

One of the magicians I spoke with (I'll call him Wizard X to protect his anonymity), explained his amazing card prediction trick, which involves sacrificing an audience member. Wizard X is an experienced magician who has been in the business for many years. This is what he said:

> Sometimes there will be a confederate in the audience, or a plant. There's a trick I used to do (I haven't done it in a long time now), I would say to the guy, "Have we met before?" "No, no." "Here's a deck of cards in the case. Take out a card and put it in your top pocket. Put the cards back in the case again." The guy does that. I say, "Now you have a card in your pocket. Does the audience know what card you have?" He says, "No." "Do I know what card you have?" He says no. (You'll be on opposite sides of the stage.) "Concentrate on your card." He concentrates. I tell him, "The card you have in your pocket . . . take it out with the back towards the audience. It's the four of spades." And the guy turns it over—there it is—the four of spades. Knocks the devil out of the audience. Knocks 'em out. Knocks 'em out.
>
> The guy never met me before. I never met him before. Now what happens? The deck of cards. . . . Maybe I shouldn't tell you this . . .

There was a long pause at this point as he considered whether or not to reveal the trick. After awhile, he continued speaking . . .

> As he opens the deck of cards, on the flap, on the inside of the deck it says, "Please take the four of spades." Now when you give the guy the cards you wink at him, you know, like something's going to happen. So when he opens up the deck he looks back at you and you wink at him. And the guy knows that he's going to be in cahoots with you. So most of the time, *most* of the time, the guy will take the four of spades out. He'll go along with the gag.

A beautiful, amazing magical trick, to everyone in the audience—almost everyone that is—except for that one audience volunteer, because that one volunteer has been sacrificed so that the rest of the audience can have a baffling magical mystery. Magicians have a name for this technique. It's called *impressionment*, because they are impressing or drafting the volunteer into their service.

Wizard X said that on the way out the door, the volunteer's companions will ask "How'd he do it?" And the volunteer will sometimes tell them. However, the volunteer's story sounds so obvious and so simple that they refuse to believe him. "You're full of baloney, come on!" they taunt. Even if one table of people walks out of the nightclub knowing how the trick is done, there's still a roomful of audience that goes away mystified. In this case Wizard X is sacrificing one spectator for the good of the entire audience. One spectator loses the magic of the trick, but in return dozens or hundreds of spectators gain a very special magical effect.[5]

If one reads through the literature exposing faith healers, there are many examples of sacrificial lambs being used to generate money to line the faith healer's pockets. An old crone who can barely walk is scouted out before the show and offered a chair by a nice young man. He's so nice, he rolls her in the chair to the very front of the tent. At some point during the show, the nice young man rolls the woman on stage where the faith healer is blabbering a yarn about how this woman will walk again (praise Jesus!) once his mighty hands have touched her skin. He presses flesh to flesh, and orders her to rise from her chair. Of course, the woman was never really immobile in the first place; the stiffness in her joints is just enough to make is seem that she hasn't walked in years. "She can walk! She can walk! Praise Jesus!" and the nice young man collects her into the chair and rolls her the hell out of there, or maybe he just escorts her off the stage. Everyone in the audience assumes that she came to the show in a wheelchair, immobilized by old age or paralysis, and the touch of God has given her the strength again to walk. You can almost hear the coffers filling up with dough, and yet very often the one who has just been healed hardly questions why she was placed in a chair to begin with. If she does happen to question it, it doesn't matter. She's been sacrificed for the good of the audience. She knows the trick—but the "healer" gets everybody's money.

Penn & Teller performed an effect where they sacrificed an entire studio audience for the much larger TV audience. Or, to put it another way, they sacrificed the *trick* in order to produce an *illusion*. What they did was teach the audience how to vanish a small silk handkerchief. After teaching the studio audience the method, P & T led the group through the illusion as it was filmed for the folks at home. The end result was that the studio audience was given a piece of secret magic information. The tradeoff was, they became P & T's accomplices in fooling the larger, home-viewing audience.

Magician Theodore Annemann, best known for his contributions to mentalism and for creating *The Jinx*, a magazine for magicians, was known for saying that in a roomful of seven people, he would have no compunction about making six of them his confederates in order to fool the seventh.

Penn & Teller play havoc with the idea of sacrificing volunteers and sometimes the entire audience. They will sometimes pretend to be sacrificing the audience, while in reality they are *fooling* the audience. For instance, on one of their television specials, Penn had someone on the street pick a card from a new deck. He then quickly fanned the remaining fifty-one cards towards the camera and announced that he would use magic to divine the selected card, which of course he did.

Previous to the trick, Penn & Teller, being Penn & Teller, had graciously invited us (the home viewing audience) into their inner sanctum and explained how the trick was to be accomplished: A computerized optical recognition system was hooked up to the camera. When Penn fanned the 51 cards before the camera, the computer was busy scanning the rapidly moving card images and processing the data to determine which card of the deck was not presented to the camera, and hence the chosen card. Of course, Penn had to make sure his fanning was even and complete, so that the computer would have complete and good data to work with. His partner Teller was sitting in a control room somewhere, and when his computer spit out the name of the missing card, Teller typed that card into another computer that was connected to an electronic sign that displayed in the street where Penn and the audience volunteer was standing. The sign was behind the volunteer, so that Penn could see the card displayed upon it, but the volunteer could not. Thus, to the volunteer, the divining of the card was nothing short of miraculous. To the home audience, it was not an illusion, not a mystery, but merely a clever prank played against the volunteer, because the audience had been let in on the gag.

Ah, but remember, you can't always trust magicians. In fact, you can hardly ever trust them, especially when they're Penn & Teller. There was no computerized optical recognition device to read a quick riffling of cards before the camera. Such a notion is preposterous (where would they get such a thing?) Indeed, the selected card had been forced. (A magician can secretly force a volunteer to select a particular card, even when the volunteer believes they have a free choice of any in the deck.) So in essence, the trick appeared to be the volunteer being fooled by Penn & Teller and the audience when in reality it was Penn & Teller fooling the audience. Many people, including some very bright people, went away from that magic show thinking they had gotten a real "behind the scenes" look at how a magic trick is performed. What they really got was hoodwinked. I don't want to give the impression that such techniques (letting the volunteer in on the trick, or conversely, pretending to let them in) are typical of what magicians use, because those are very atypical maneuvers. Just realize that such techniques can be used. In fact, any technique that gets the job done will be used by some magicians sometimes, so you should never rule out a technique just because it seems unlikely, or too "unethical."

Finally, I would like to point out that very often a magician must bend the rules and reveal secrets when he is trying to pull off a super-big stunt. I'm sure that when Copperfield made the Statue of Liberty disappear,[6] or more recently when Franz Harary made a space shuttle vanish, they had to reveal full details of their plans to the governmental agencies involved. The French magician Majax once surprised a television news host by removing a golf club from the host's personal golf bag and then using "psychic powers" to effortlessly bend the club as if it were a thread wilting in his fingers. Of course, the host was astounded to see one of his golf clubs melt away like that. What he didn't know was that Majax had previously had one of the show's secretaries insert a gimmicked club into the bag. The bending club was designed by an electronics expert a week prior to the show.

In these cases, and perhaps many more that we will never know about, the magic occurs in part because the magician must reveal some secrets to outside parties, and in so doing must give up some of his control. In these cases magicians are forced to sacrifice their secrets to the people who have control over the magician in order for the trick to take place at all.

Opportunistic Events

Sometimes a magician yields to the currents of chance that flow around all of us, relying less on control and planning and structure, and turning his attention to some opportunistic event that comes his way. For instance, there have been a few times when I was performing for a friend or family member when my audience of one was distracted for a moment by a ringing telephone or a dog bark . . . and at that moment I snuck a peek at the picked card, or hid a few more quarters on my person, or whatever the current trick required. When attention was resumed, the trick proceeded *even better* than planned, because of the opportunistic event. One magician told me that when he's performing, "I also watch for other things . . . telltale signs of employment or hobbies or something to work into the act. The more personal you get with your audience the more they remember you." Critics have often offered exposés on Uri Geller, remarking on the many opportunistic devices Geller will make use of and then add to his résumé of alleged psychic ability.[7] Other magicians have reported using similar tricks, such as happening to notice an identification card or nametag of a complete stranger at a party, and then proceeding to "read the person's mind" for that data. The great Houdini stunned the staff of one European police station when he escaped from their jail cell in a matter of minutes—the officers had forgotten to lock it before they left.

For most stage shows, you can safely assume that the majority of the performance is well-rehearsed and not based on the currents of chance. However, in an impromptu situation, a party, a gathering of friends . . . you never know to what extent someone will go to fool you.

Mirrors, Sleeves, and String

There is a short story by Stephen Leacock in which a wonderful magician is beleaguered by a heckler throughout his performance. For every astonishing illusion, the Quick Man has the same criticizing comment to make: "He hid it up his sleeve!" Everything from a loaf of bread to a rocking chair was adroitly concealed up this magician's sleeves according to this blunt fellow. Worst of all, the heckler begins to have the makings of a cult following in the auditorium. There are rumblings of agreement as the rest of the crowd becomes disenchanted with the illusions. Even if they realize the Quick Man is wrong, the heckler's comments remind them that it is, after all, only a trick. The fragile thread of illusion is broken like a spiderweb blown apart by a breeze.

The magician in the story is frustrated. *He* knows his methods are far cleverer than the old sleeve trick. And yet, if that's what the audience believes, he will have a hard time perpetuating the illusion that his illusions are magical.

So how common are these standbys of magic of which we are all aware? We all know that magicians use mirrors—somehow!—to perform illusions; that strings lift assistants to unbelievable heights above the stage; and that sleeves are used to conceal an amazing variety of produced and vanished objects. That is the common perception—but is it a misperception? That's what this section is about.

MIRRORS

Do magicians really use mirrors in the working of their tricks? The "Wizard of Fun," Leigh Hotz from Cleveland, Ohio, had this to say on the subject:

> Mirror based illusions are not used much these days because of more "modern" methods needed to go with today's performance conditions. In the "old days" stage magicians only did their acts on stages with limited viewing angles ... and the audience always viewed the act from the front with little or no side viewing due to the layout of the theater ... but these days magicians find themselves under conditions where they are sometimes surrounded, or unusual performance conditions (example: shopping malls, gym floors, theatre in the round, etc.) where certain methods can not be used properly. ... This restricts certain types of illusions we can perform but any good professional has enough variety of routines and props, that he can work it out. ... YES [mirrors] exist but not nearly as much as 20 years ago.[8]

One of the most well-known uses of mirrors is the Owens table, and variants thereof. It is a table whose legs form a triangular shape underneath, and has mirrors placed deceptively between them. The mirrors reflect the opposite legs, giving the appearance of four visible legs and a clear view underneath the table. In reality the mirrors create a small wall, behind which the magician can hide an assistant. These mirror constructions were used in many different effects, usually to cause bodies to appear or vanish; or in "torture" tricks where someone (stupidly) steps into a box that is thrust through with swords and the like. There are also versions where a volunteer places his or her arm through a long rectangular tube. Doors open to reveal the central portion of their arm missing! The magician promptly pokes his own arm straight through. All these are done with diagonally slanted mirrors reflecting a curtain or side of a box, creating a place to hide from the audience.

Mirrors can also be used on a small scale. There is a gimmick that is popular in magic books that I've never actually see anyone use in real life, called a "mirror glass." The mirror glass looks like an ordinary drinking glass, but it is split into two compartments by a mirror. Actually it's a double-sided mirror. Standard magical apparatus, you can buy it at any magic store. The magician fills one half of the glass with candy, leaves the other half empty, and shows the empty half to the audience. The audience sees the outside of the glass reflected in the mirror, and so it appears to be an ordinary empty glass. The magician covers the glass with a silk, utters magic words, boom boom boom (secretly giving the glass a half-twist), and lifts off the silk to show the other compartment, the one filled with candy. Once again the mirror reflects its own half-side of the glass, and so the audience sees not a half glass, but a full glass of candy. The magician ends the trick by graciously handing out candy to the audience.

Obviously any trick that relies on mirrors relies on the reflecting property of mirrors, which leads anyone with half a brain to wonder: "Gosh, why doesn't the *audience* get reflected in the mirror along with the empty glass?"

Ah, good question. Time for an experiment.

CREATE MAGIC!—EXPERIMENT WITH MIRRORS

Find a small mirror. For this I use a 1½" by 2" travel mirror, but you may have one of different dimensions. Try to get a plain mirror, one that is not attached to a case or compact, or inside a frame.

After you've found a mirror, go into the kitchen and find a drinking glass, any glass that the mirror will fit into is fine. If the mirror is too big for a glass, try a glass jar, or even a glass vase if it's in a glass-like shape. Whatever glass you use, it should be round. The mirror is not going to exactly fit and fill the glass the way a store-bought magic prop would, but that's okay. We're not making a store-bought magic prop here. We're simply doing an unscientific bit of fooling around.

Now look at your empty glass. You can see your hand through it. You can see the other side of the room through it. Now drop the mirror in and take another look. The first thing you'll notice is that the mirror is not as noticeable as you might have thought it would be. In my case I'm using a mirror that is two inches high in a glass that's six inches, and while the mirror is very visible, it doesn't exactly jump out and grab my eyeballs and force me to look at it. In fact, I can easily imagine that if the mirror was cut to fit the glass exactly, it would be pretty difficult to see the mirror in the glass. Your reaction might be somewhat different depending on the shape of your glass, the size, how sloping the sides are, the thickness of the glass, and how well the mirror fits into the glass. Commercially available mirror glasses tend to have decorative fluting to further obfuscate the mirror. If you were a manufacturer, you would have taken all these things into consideration when designing your mirror glass before putting it on the market.

One of the reasons the mirror is somewhat inconspicuous is because some weird rules of light-bending and refraction are at play. Look at your face in the mirror in the glass. Your face will be smaller than actual size, and there may be some distortion as well. No need to call the plastic surgeon, just remove the mirror from the glass for a moment, and compare your face out-of-the-glass to the face in-the-glass. There is a striking difference between the two reflections.

Also, I'm noticing that today this experiment is not working as well as it did yesterday, because today I'm wearing a bright yellow and red shirt that reflects quite visibly in the mirror. In a real-life magic situation, the mirror glass would be facing an audience that is probably sitting a few yards away. Thus there would be lots of small images, distorted, made even smaller by the curvature of the glass, all of which makes those images hard to recognize, hard to distinguish from the normal shininess and silveriness of the glass itself. You can begin to see how this mirror principle works.

Are we still in the kitchen? Turn on the cold water faucet, and fill up the glass with water. Don't get the pages wet! Not all mirror glass tricks employ water, of course, but the water is sort of a "bonus scrambler," further making the reflection less obvious to an outside observer. And throw in these additional facts to further clinch the deal:

1. The audience is expecting to see an ordinary, ungimmicked drinking glass. It's harder to notice the mirror when you don't know it exists.
2. The audience is not exactly at eye level with the drinking glass. For instance, at a children's show where this sort of trick is likely to be done, the kids are sitting cross-legged on the floor. If the magician is on stage, the audience is even further below the level of the glass.
3. Stage lights, or even normal everyday lighting, create misdirecting reflections in the glass.

The result is a glass that looks full, even when the audience is just seeing half of it.

TRAP DOORS

The magician holds up a curtain, and with a swish of his hands, a tiger appears behind it. Another swish, and the tiger changes places with a lovely lady in leopardskin leotards. Even Leacock's Quick Man would realize there is not enough room up a sleeve for a lady or a tiger. But that would not faze him, because he could conveniently point out, "They came up through a trap door in the stage!"

And perhaps the audience would buy it.

But trap doors are uncommon in magic, for several reasons. First of all, most of a magician's large stage illusions are purchased. Let's say I'm in the business of creating illusions and selling the blueprints to magicians through mail order. For the most part those blueprints have to be self-contained. I can't expect there to be a trap door in the stage, and I certainly can't expect a trap door to be at a certain spot on the stage, or a certain size, or even that the illusion will be performed on a stage at all. In short, if I'm going to create a trick, I'd better make sure it's something that I *can* sell you. I can't sell you a trap door in a stage.

Secondly, there is the problem of touring shows. Trap doors are not so commonly found on smaller stages, and much of magic is not performed in a full-scale theatrical setting anyway. Magicians have to be prepared for senior citizens' centers and junior high schools and the like.

Trap doors exist—but they're not in the stage, they're in the props. In other words, the magician uses traveling trap doors, such as the one on top of the Metamorphosis trunk, or in the packing crate from which an escape artist breaks free. The trap doors are well constructed in the crates. One collector of magical apparatus bought a trick steamer trunk and even with unlimited hands-on access to the thing was unable to figure out how it worked. "There's got to be a secret panel. Or a trapdoor. Something" he said. But he couldn't find it.[9]

SLEEVES

In Stephen Leacock's short story, the Quick Man thought everything from a loaf of bread to a rocking chair got hidden up the magician's sleeves. Surprisingly, magicians rarely use their sleeves for any effect. Sleeves have gotten such a bad rap that many magicians roll up their sleeves at the beginning of the show as a way to establish trust with the audience. Many magicians will wear a sleeveless T-shirt or tank top for the same reason. As a result, the sleeve is not readily in the magician's bag of tricks, and so if a magician were to use the sleeves it might be the one way in which he could fool other magicians, who are looking for other solutions to the sleights. There has been at least one book devoted to the art of sleeving, *The Encyclopedia of Sleeving* by Jack Chanin, a monograph self-published by the author in Philadelphia in 1948, and more recently a video on the subject.

A more common use of sleeves is with "pulls" and "takeup reels." These are devices the magician hides inside the back of his sports jacket. A *pull* is used to make items vanish. A length of elastic runs through the sleeve and into the hand. A cup or clip is fastened to the end of the elastic. The magician will show an object to the audience, place it in his hand (really placing it into the cup or clip), and then secretly let the elastic pull the object deep within his sports coat. The magician opens his hand and shows the object gone . . . it went up his sleeve!

There are some variations on the pull. It doesn't have to go up the sleeve. Some merely go into the body of the jacket. It all depends on the trick, but the magician will be careful to incorporate the necessary body postures and movements into the act. For example, when Blackstone did his famous birdcage vanish (a cage with a live bird vanished from his bare hands) he would hold his arms outright in front of him, seemingly presenting the cage to the audience for their inspection. Actually it was very helpful to hold his hands out, because that tightens up the elastic. The cage was specially designed to collapse on command. At the appropriate time, Blackstone would toss it forward, and the collapsed cage would be pulled up his sleeve—bird and all. Savvy adults watching the show might shake their heads and say, "Nah, it couldn't go up his sleeve because he wouldn't want to injure the bird." But truth be told, the cage was constructed so as not to injure the animal. After all, if you're going to design a prop, aren't you going to design it so it doesn't hurt your animal?!

Actually, in many cases the bird was injured or killed. So with a sad nod towards realism, magicians abandoned their real birds in favor of realistic-looking dummies.

STRING

If the magician made his assistant float into the air, the Quick Man would shout out, "It's strings! He's doing it with strings!" And he may be right— or he may be wrong. Strings are in fact used for some levitations and many animation effects when objects seem to move around and float through space on their own accord, but it's not as simple as the Quick Man would like us to believe. First of all, there's the problem of how to hide the strings. Go on, Quick Man, answer that one! If the magician is standing there in broad daylight making a rose float in the air, why don't you see the string? Or for that matter, if he's making his assistant float in the air with string, how can he pass a hoop around her body? These are the core mysteries of these kinds of illusions, and they will be explored at great length in the next chapter.

Foundation's Edge

This chapter attempted to give a basic introduction to some of the foundations of magic, including misdirection, the use of gimmicks and fakes, lying, and concealment on stage. Even though a lot has been explained already, we have only just begun to skirt the edge of how a professional magician creates fantastic illusions. The next chapter takes a methodical approach to explaining the different kinds of magic tricks. After that we will begin to explore further the complexities inherent in even the simplest of magical illusions.

2

A Magician's Dozen

A magic show is a showing of impossible feats. Magician Peter Warlock divides these impossible feats into eleven magical forms:

1. The production of an object.
2. The evanishment of an object.
3. The transposition of objects.
4. The change in form, size, color, weight, or temperature of objects.
5. The penetration of one solid object by another.
6. Defiance of the laws of gravity.
7. Proof of invulnerability.
8. Making the inanimate animate.
9. Making whole something that has been mutilated or destroyed.
10. Accelerating a natural process such as inducing the rapid germination of a seed into a bush.
11. Producing pseudopsychic phenomena, such as telepathy, precognition, or thought-transference.

Others have used other categories, some more, some less. But let's use these eleven as our "magician's dozen."

So if you're a magician, and if you're doing magic tricks, any magic trick you do is going to have one of these eleven effects. Something will appear or disappear, or two items will switch places; objects may move or float in the air, their properties may be impossibly altered, restored from destruction, or grow unnaturally fast. Or you the magician may appear to have knowledge that is impossible for you to have obtained.

Illusion of Illusions

Now let us make a very important distinction between illusion and reality. The illusion of a trick may look like one of these forms of magic, while the reality underlying it is based on a completely different form of magic. Understanding this distinction frees your mind to better imagine how the illusions are performed. You knew that the magician was deceiving you to a certain extent. This distinction says that the magician may deceive you to *every* extent, going so far as to deceive you into believing one form of deception is going on when in reality another form is being used.

For instance, look at solid penetrations. I'm going to push the salt shaker through the solid wooden table. That's illusion number five—solid penetration. The "reality" is not penetration—that's impossible! The reality is a disappearance (number two) and then a reappearance (number one). The salt shaker disappears from the top of the table, and reappears underneath it.

Another example. We would all say that to transpose objects is quite a magical event. The transposition is the illusion. The reality is two "productions" and two "evanishments," which ends up looking like a transposition. An escape artist may appear to escape from bonds and shackles. Perhaps the reality is not an escape, but a solid penetration or even a disappearance.

My point is that sometimes it is difficult to determine the "trick to the trick" because the audience is looking for an answer of one form when really the answer is of another form entirely. You might say that this is a fourth kind of misdirection—misdirection of the process by which the illusion is created. Then again, it is an illusion created by necessity, not artifice.

Most importantly, when attempting to analyze magic tricks, you must first remember that after all, they are *illusions*, and illusions of any form may underlie the surface appearance.

Now we will look specifically at the eleven magical forms, and see how these various misdirections interact to create those illusions.

Magic Form #1—Productions

Oh, don't you wish that you had $1 million dollars . . . or a Bengal tiger . . . or a bunny rabbit? Productions are the magician's way of creating something out of nothing, a dream everyone has.

Probably the two most famous productions (most famous magic tricks?), at least in America, are (1) pulling a rabbit out of a hat and (2) pulling a coin out of someone's ear. These are uncomplicated illusions, very easy to understand, and startling. Look at the words used to describe the illusions: "Pulling ____ out of ____." The act of "pulling" is a tangible physical gesture, easily visualized in your mind, an easy motion to make with your own hand. One of the things we'll notice about the most magical magic is that when you look at it being performed it is obviously impossible and yet so realistic you believe that you could do it too if only you tried hard enough. Other illusions rely on the magician making lots of quick, complicated gestures, which don't give a magical impression. The rapid, hard-to-follow motions make it look like the magician is doing something tricky to make the magic work, rather than the magic flowing naturally from nature. Thus it is my contention that the best magic is simple, done slowly, and proceeds logically from one portion of the trick to the next, building up like steps in a geometric proof. At the end, when the "proof" is reached, it is obvious that no trickery was involved (all the steps were plainly visible), and yet it is also obvious that something magical has transpired. The effect is real magic.[1]

A magic trick consists of a series of proofs showing that no physical mechanism is used to produce the effect, and yet the effect occurs anyway (thus making it magical). So how does the magician "prove" something that, if we stop to think about it, is impossible? A question as broad as the universe, and just as meaningless. For there is not just one way to create a production. There are always many solutions used by different magicians for different tricks, sometimes even by the same magician for the same trick. For a production the basic question to consider is, "Where was the item hiding before it was pulled out?" The ear did not contain the coin, but perhaps the magician's hand did. The bunny was most likely hiding on a shelf or in a pouch hanging behind the table.

But just knowing these simple answers is not enough. The magician's hand? A bunny in a bag? Do these solutions sound too simple? Look at a more large-scale production, like a car appearing suddenly in an empty box. Could the same simplicity lie behind something as mysterious as that? Well, the answer is yes and no. Yes, the answer to almost all questions in magic is quite simple. And because of the simplicity, the answer is often disappointing.

However, there's more to a trick than just "the trick." The bunny was hiding on a shelf? Well, how did the magician get the bunny in the hat, in full view of the audience, without being seen? (Answer: the magician scooped it up into the hat.) Why did no one see this bold, sweeping gesture? (Answer: because the move was made at a psychologically noncritical time during the performance, and was further played down by the magician's eye contact with the audience, and perhaps misdirection with the other hand.) So you see, as it turns out, simplicity is not so simple when you really look at it closely. Behind every simple act in magic there are dozens or hundreds or thousands of hours of practice, study, failure, trying, memorizing, and learning. These are all topics that will be expressed throughout this book.

Magic Form #2—Evanishments

Where there's bread, there's butter. Evanishments—also called disappearances—are the butter of magic. You see, you very rarely have *just* an evanishment. There's always something else with it, usually a production (appearance). If something vanishes, the magician must make it appear again. An evanishment might also have a solid penetration or transposition go along with it. But you can't have an evanishment by itself: that would be like selling a mystery book with the last chapter purposely ripped out. The plot would never be resolved, the tension would never relax. Evanishments might be the only magical form of this kind—a form that, for aesthetic reasons, does not stand by itself on its own merit.

Certainly there is great power in evanishments. The person who can vanish another person, or an army of enemies, is one to reckon with. There are so many different kinds of evanishments, so many different things that can be made to vanish, that it's hard to give a general explanation for how vanishes are accomplished. But it is safe to say there are three main techniques: (1) The item is somehow removed from the stage; (2) the item is kept on stage, but is hidden; or (3) the item remains where it was originally.

- *The item is somehow removed from the stage.* This is usually accomplished with time misdirection. The item is removed at the earliest opportunity (usually, the first time the item is covered over with a scarf, hand, or box). The magician may lead you into thinking that the item is still hidden in his hand or under the cloth, when in reality it has been passed off to an assistant and shunted into the wings. A person can be "removed off stage" by various means such as trap doors or by hiding behind a screen or piece of equipment that's being moved around by other assistants. Another way this is done is via the "Curtain Switcheroo" to be explained later.
- *The item is kept on stage, but is hidden.* The item may be hidden in a secret compartment in a piece of equipment. Or perhaps it was slipped into the magician's pocket or sleeve or elsewhere out of sight.
- *The item remains where it was originally.* The last case is the simplest, and is usually done only in the most complicated illusions. Suppose some well-heeled magician brings out a Bengal tiger, puts a funny hat on its head, and leads it into a box. He closes the box, there's a puff of smoke, and suddenly the tiger is being led onto the stage *from the back of the theater.* All eyes swivel to see the sight, as the box is quickly rolled off stage. In this case the tiger remains where it was originally. No one refers to the box again after the tiger has reappeared from off stage. No one questions whether there were two tigers with funny hats, one of which has stayed in the box. This may sound like an obvious ploy when I spell it out to you here, but you have to remember, when you're watching a spectacular magic show with lights, smoke, wild animals, and dozens of dancers in

feathery costumes, you don't notice things like this. You're already watching the next two miracles, the original box long forgotten.

Magic Form #3—Property Changes

Property changes create the illusion that an intrinsic property of an object has been altered.

- A silver ring is held in the hand and turns to gold.
- A glass of water changes into a glass of ice cubes.
- A scarf of one color passes through a tube and emerges another color entirely.
- A selected card shrinks to half its size; or for large stage shows—enlarges to jumbo size.

All sorts of properties and characteristics can be changed to produce a startling trick. Later we'll see how in World War II, Hitler used a property change trick on one of his aircraft of war, giving the illusion it was much faster than it really was and thus bolstering the opinion that his Luftwaffe was invincible.

The color of an object, the size of an object, water to wine, silver to gold. These are all examples of property changes that, if they were to happen to us in our everyday lives, we would think we were going insane. Things have certain characteristics that don't alter willy nilly. That we know. That's why property change effects are hard to pull off effectively. After all, if the magician makes a red scarf turn blue, the whole audience knows that it hasn't really changed colors—the scarf has been switched. Therefore it's up to the magician to do a good job of creating a convincing ambience that encourages the audience to believe that a property change has taken place.

Of course there's nothing wrong with a magician turning one silk into another silk. But if that's not the desired effect, then the magic hasn't been done effectively. As a naive audience member you may previously have thought that a magical event is pretty self-evident, but now you can see that a lot of thought must go into achieving each effect exactly as desired. In some cases the magician might want the audience to believe the glass of water has disappeared and has been replaced by a new glass, this one containing ice cubes. Perhaps the storyline of the trick calls for that sort of effect—a transposition—rather than a property change. If you've ever witnessed "unrealistic" magic, it's a good bet that the reason it was unconvincing was that the effect you saw was not the effect the magician believed he presented.

Magic Form #4—Transpositions

A transposition occurs when two objects exchange positions. The classic example is the Metamorphosis illusion, in which the assistant is locked inside a trunk, and the magician stands on top of the trunk. In an instant, they transpose positions. Transpositions are another example of a magic trick that must be clearly defined for the audience to "get it." After all, a transposition is a composite trick, composed of two productions and two evanishments. Once again good direction is needed so that the audience understands exactly what is occurring, or rather, what the magician wishes them to believe is occurring on stage.

Magic Form #5—Solid Penetrations

When I started my first job after college, I didn't have much to do the first few weeks except sit around and learn about how the company worked. This turned out to be pretty boring, so I would walk over to the Chicken Holiday next door and buy food and bring it back to my desk to eat. For some reason unknown to mankind (and chickenkind), when you get food at Chicken Holiday, they put the food in cardboard cups that they then either staple or rubber band together. Anyway, after a few weeks I had accumulated a heaping mound of tan rubber bands on my desk, and I would play with them as I stared out the window at the sunny days outside. I didn't want my days at work to be a total waste, so I decided I would learn how to make two rubber bands pass through each other. I had seen a magician do a trick where she visually snapped one rubber band through the other. They seemed to penetrate each other like mist passing through clouds. I figured I had the time and I had the bands, and I had the ability to figure out how the illusion was performed.

After a few days of playing, I came up with the basic principle that allowed the two bands to pull through one another. A few more days of playing, and I had become quite good at it. After a few weeks I had altered the method slightly and mastered the technique. Now I could also pass the bands through each other in full view of the audience, had there been an audience. It was about that time when my boss started giving me work to do, so I had to put down my rubber bands and make myself useful.

Penetrations as a magical form can be surprisingly convincing and quite forceful when done properly, perhaps because they seem to defy a physical principle that is so common to our everyday lives. Matter cannot pass through matter. We know that. And yet, when we look at a magician sliding two Linking Rings together, their fluid motion seems so very natural. The way they slip through each other looks so real you think you could do it too. But of course, when the rings are passed out to the crowd to try, they are found to be solid and hard metal frames. It's like waking up from a dream: the abilities that seemed so logical a moment before are now as logically impossible. Of course the next time you dream, or when the magician takes the rings back into his hands, the abilities once again appear fantastically possible.

The trick of the linking rings is possible because some of the rings have a tiny gap in them. If the magician hands out some rings for inspection, he makes sure to hand out the normal, unbroken rings. The rings he keeps holding onto (with thumb and forefinger covering the gap) are separate, while some of the other rings are permanently linked together. Telling you this reveals all but reveals nothing. A well-planned routine is so seamless and fast that you wouldn't know where to look for the hole in the ring even if you did know about it.

Penetrations are not limited to inanimate objects. Houdini made famous his "Walk Through a Wall." Many of the sicko torture tricks are also penetration-based. Often these have an assistant or audience volunteer putting their body parts into a box or basket or guillotine, and having it plunged through with swords, sliced off, or cut in half. The worst part about these tricks are the lousy jokes about half-price sales at second-hand shops.

In some ways, escapes can be thought of as penetrations. Most contemporary escapes are done in full view of the audience, which implies the escapologist is using a special skill to escape, rather than the magic of matter-through-matter. However, there are hidden "escapes" such as Metamorphosis which are accomplished by "magic" rather than "escape skill," due to the manner in which they are presented. Because of the ropes, chains, blankets, and whatnot that go into them, this sort of trick would also be counted as a solid penetration of sorts. But you don't need ropes, blankets, and an assistant to do amazing penetrations—you can use simple rubber bands. This is how my "Band Through Band" illusion works:

Create Magic!—Band Through Band

A rubber band is linked across the thumb and index finger of the left hand. Hang another rubber band off the end of your right index finger. Dangle the second rubber band in the hole between your left hand and the rubber band that you are holding in the left hand. Now insert your right thumb inside the bottom loop of the right-hand rubber band. The two rubber bands are now solidly locked (figure 2).

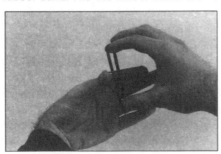

Fig. 2. The two rubber bands are solidly locked . . . for now.

Show the rubber bands to your close-up audience. Show them how the rubber bands are linked together. It is impossible for them to be separated.

Gently rub the right band up and down against the left with a sawing motion. Show how you are trying to slide one magically through the other. It doesn't work.

Stretch the bands apart so they are elongated and tightened. This is a more tense kind of pulling apart than the sawing was. Your audience (and you) will really feel the problem at hand. It feels so easy to be able to just pull one rubber band through the other. And it looks possible to do just that. They are so thin you think the god who regulates physical wonders of the world should allow these two slender bands to slip apart. . . . Perhaps a little more force will do the trick.

Let the rubber bands slacken a little, but still keep them taut. Slip your left middle finger into the left band. Put it next to your left index finger. *Simultaneous* to this action, insert your right middle finger in the right rubber band, next to your thumb (figure 3).

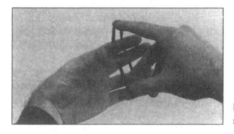

Fig. 3. Left and right middle fingers are inserted.

Then pull the bands apart tightly while twisting your right hand away from you to create a very twisted, complicated-looking intertwining of the bands (figure 4).

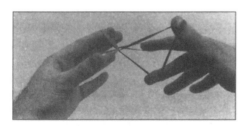

Fig. 4. The right hand is twisted away from the body to produce this complex intermeshing of the rubber bands. Let the band slide off the right index finger to separate the bands.

Once again pull the rubber bands tightly, and as you do so, quickly let the rubber band slip off the end of your right index finger. Your hands will fly apart and the rubber bands seem to penetrate each other. As your right hand is flying back, slide your right index finger back into the rubber band loop. The rubber bands seem to have penetrated, to the amazement of your audience!

The trick lies in the fact that the left hand pretty much stays where it is, while the right hand moves away. In this case the hand is quicker than the eye! People have a hard time moving their line of vision fast enough to track your moving right hand.

After your right hand slips back, you should immediately bring it close to the left hand again, to show the two rubber bands still linked squarely on your fingertips.

It takes some practice before you can easily slip your right finger back into the rubber band, but once you get used to the proper way of holding your fingers, you can slip the finger in as the right hand is being snapped backwards. One helpful hint is to make sure, at the beginning of the routine, that the rubber band is slipped around the very tip of your right index finger. As you improve you'll be able to slip it further back somewhat, but it's good to have it as high up as possible in the beginning, to allow it to easily slip off at the end.

An alternate method of performing the illusion allows the rubber bands to penetrate in a slow and graceful manner, not the fast snap just described. Begin the illusion as described above. Place the rubber band on your left hand, then link the other one through it with your right hand. Show your audience that the two bands are materially inseparable. Use a light sawing movement to impart the sense of disappointment in the physical world, that it forgot to allow such a simple want to be fulfilled.

For this effect we won't be stretching the rubber bands. This version is gentle and relaxed. After sawing to no avail, pull taut the rubber bands, and insert your second fingers as before. After inserting the fingers, twist your left hand towards you and your right hand away from you. You will end up with your right thumb on top of the left-hand rubber band. Touch your right thumb to the rubber band; as you do, slip your right index finger out of the loop that it's in, and slip the right index finger into the same loop as your right middle finger. This action is fast and subtle, and hidden from the audience by your left hand.

Now you have two choices: (1) You can untwist your two hands (keeping your right thumb touching the left rubber band) then pull your hands apart. The rubber bands will give a gentle little tug as you separate your hands, making the penetration visible and real; or (2) With your hands twisted, stretch apart your fingers to tighten the rubber bands, and make a soft sawing motion. After a while, allow your hands to separate, and the rubber bands (which aren't really joined at all at this point) will seem to pass through each other.

You can see there are many options to this illusion, as there are to many magical effects. The situation can be enhanced by an accompanying story, multiple rubber bands, or other devices that you come up with. Of course, as with any sleight of hand, practice is the key component.

Finally, I should mention that after a few weeks of Chicken Holiday I decided to try out the Bagel Express, also next door to the office. The food was healthier and the women working there were a lot friendlier than the greasy guys at the chicken store. Bagel Express wrapped their food in paper. "I guess if my boss lessens my workload again," I said to myself, "I'll be ready to try and learn a paper-tearing trick!"

Magic Form #6—Proving Invulnerability

Proving invulnerability is about cheating death, cheating injury, or escaping the destructive consequences of mutilations. These tricks are sometimes accomplished by the usual means of trickery and misdirection. Other times they are done quite easily because the magician is fibbing—he's doing something that everybody could do, if only they got up the nerve to try it. Many of these illusions are "geek tricks," the kind of effects done in circus sideshows to gross out the crowd. One example is the performer who pounds a long metal spike up his nose. Other variations use a spoon or nail. The trick to the trick? There is none—you just shove it up there—very carefully! The nasal cavity can take a lot if you tilt your head back and shove just right.[2]

Most sword swallowing is legitimate, although the performer might carefully choose a sword that fits exactly to the bottom of the stomach, and no further. Some even learn to partially swallow a metal tube which stays in their throat during the performance to protect their insides. Of course many hours of practice went into learning how to overcome the gag reflex and lining up the mouth with the esophagus, but the effect itself is genuine. As you might suspect, some people fake it. For every legitimate sword swallower there are plenty more who wear a fake beard and actually slide the sword into the beard and down the front of their costume. Some may even use a sword with a retracting blade.[3]

These illusions also have a long history of performance by East Indian fakirs. These performers would show their ability to withstand self-inflicted tortures, like sitting calmly under the heat of a roaring flame, lifting heavy weights with their eyelids, and walking across red-hot coals. A publication of the early 1970s, *Swami* magazine, often featured fakir-like effects such as eating light bulbs, razor blades, and fire, drinking scorching acid, or cutting off a person's tongue.

Now, all these effects are pretty much believable to one extent or another. You can believe that someone is stupid enough to actually snack on a razor salad, washing it down with a beaker of hydrochloric acid. But other, similar effects start involving what is obvious "magic." One effect calls for the yogi to place needles in one eye and remove them from the other eye, or swallow a length of thread, then slice open the stomach with a razor and pull out the thread through the incision. This sounds like the magical performances given by faith healers, who purport to remove tumors and other yuck from the bodies of the infirm. Actually they use standard magicians' tricks, as we shall see later on.

Magic Form #7—Animations

An animation is the bringing to life of an inanimate object. If the magician's handkerchief suddenly pokes out of his pocket and goes dancing across the stage, that's an animation. It would seem that animations would be one of the most realistic and breathtaking of all magical illusions, especially if the magician takes great care to imbue the inanimate object with a lively personality and festive dance. It's true these illusions can be most stunning, but only if done properly. The sad fact is, everyone knows how animations are done: with wires, ropes, strings and things. The illusion comes from both hiding the wires and making the floating so realistic that the audience forgets to think about the cables.

Okay, now wait a minute. We've just thrown away a thousand years of magical history down the drain, without so much as a second thought about what we were saying. Animations are done with wires and threads. The illusion comes from hiding the threads. It's easy to dismiss this whole category of conjuring, but look at what we're saying here!—how in god's name does someone *hide* wires? The wires are strung up right in front of the audience, so how could they not be seen? It's easy to dismiss animations and levitations as "obvious" but when you put your mind to it you begin to see that even if you know how it's done, you really don't know how it's done. Let's examine some of the theories about how people and objects are levitated and animated in a magic show.

THE BLACK THREAD THEORY

The black thread theory is that a black thread is used to animate objects. The thread is dark, so you can't see it from far away in a darkened theater. The black thread theory is pretty darn good. Most magic books for kiddies have one trick or another that makes use of black thread. The prototypical example is the Ghost Pencil trick, otherwise known as the Pencil in the Bottle. A corked bottle is shown with a pencil inside. On command, the pencil dances and jumps mysteriously. There is no visible means of support, and the cork makes the puzzle even more baffling.

The method given for this trick is always black thread. The thread is attached to the eraser of the pencil, and the pencil is dropped in the bottle with the eraser side down. The thread runs up the length of the pencil and out of the bottle. Small tugs on the thread produce a jiggling effect. The cork poses no problem, because a slit is cut into the side of the cork that the thread fits into nicely and gives it room to move around. The magician will have two corks ready—one with the slit, the other perfectly normal. The normal cork may be passed around for inspection, and then casually switched for the slit cork. The ungimmicked bottle can of course also be passed around freely, and the magician will probably also have a duplicate pencil ready to show around as well.

This is just one of many illusions that rely on a black thread. As one magician told me, "What most magicians use is simply black or dark blue [thread]. A standard sewing thread is unraveled to its component threads, and that's what we use." If you don't feel like doing the unraveling yourself, there are different sizes of threads, and it's in the magician's best interest to take the thinnest thread possible. Sources list various sizes (A or 0 or 000) black silk thread as thin enough for this purpose. It is said that if the thread is thin enough, it will be invisible under most lighting conditions, except perhaps direct illumination. The magician might position himself so his shadow falls on the thread. The spotlight might be focused exclusively on the magician or the floating object, keeping the thread in the dark. One important point to remember is that the magician will only be using black thread if the background is equally dark, or a mixed pattern in which a dark thread will melt away. Also, animations and levitations are often done in a dark séance environment. Horns and bells and other objects might move about as if ghosts were present in the room. Certainly the darkness of the room helps to cloud the black thread from view.

This brings us to a theory-within-a-theory. It's been suggested that if the magician doesn't want to perform in darkness, he can create a devilish or hellish appearance on stage by shining red lights. Instead of revealing the thread as you first might suspect, red lights supposedly serve to make the thread more invisible. I decided to put this claim to the test. I bought a red light and a blue light at Home Depot, and tried looking at black threads under both conditions (they also had yellow and green, but I figured blue is at the opposite end of the spectrum from red so it would make the most significant comparison). The red-lit thread *did* seem harder to see than the blue-lit one. But the red light was also darker overall than the blue, so I was left unsure if it worked or not. I took the matter to Mohan S. Kalelkar, a professor of physics at Rutgers University, whose reputation precedes him as one of the department's most well-loved members. He made it clear that he was no magician, but could explain the physics stuff. Is there any reason why red light might make the threads hard to see? "Yes," he explained, "In fact, anything (whether black or not) is harder to see in red light than in ordinary light of all colors.

> The reason is that red is the color with the largest wavelength: about 650 nanometers or so. Ordinary white light is a mixture of all colors, averaging to about 520 nanometers. The smaller the wavelength, the greater our ability to see things and distinguish objects. If you'd like to read more about this, look up "Rayleigh's criterion" in the index of any introductory physics textbook.
>
> Although it is true that it is harder to see things in red light, I would not expect it to be a major effect; after all, the difference between 650 and 520 nanometers isn't huge. I don't think the use of red light is the decisive factor; it is probably one of several factors that all help to disguise the thread.

In this case I suppose the theory is partially verified. This, along with all the evidence for the black thread theory seems pretty convincing. Magicians and magic books recommend black thread, and black thread certainly is invisible against a dark background. But there are still some problems. What about magic done in broad daylight? Or when the magician is not wearing black? Or for that matter, when a human assistant is levitated? Certainly thin black thread isn't used to lift a full-grown woman! This takes us to . . .

THE ARMY MENTALITY THEORY

The army mentality theory states: "Camouflage, camouflage, camouflage!" The theory is that you can't see the thread because the magician has camouflaged it to match the background. This is similar to the black-on-black approach, but it is more versatile, because it allows the thread to be any color—so long as the background matches it. Smoke may also be used to offer some concealment. While you probably won't be seeing magicians use khaki green thread, sometimes they use a zebra-stripe thread. The pattern breaks up the line and blends into a mottled background.

There are other tricks used to camouflage threads. According to one magician, "the backdrop usually provides linear camouflage and soft focus, or a contrived shift in the apparent depth of field is used to complete the illusion of no support." That means the background doesn't necessarily have to be a solid color matching the thread; in fact it's much better if the background is *not* a solid color. It should have some sort of a pattern to it. If the pattern has a line in it, the line will help conceal the line of the thread. If the pattern is vertical, that will help guide the audience's eyes upward, away from the thread, which may actually be strung along a slanted angle. David Copperfield uses a shiny, silvery, glittery backdrop for his flying illusion, and you can bet its purpose is to diffuse his method of support.

THE MISDIRECTION THEORY

The misdirection theory was stated best by one physicist who was trying to explain to me why the thread is invisible. I was hoping that by talking to physicists I could come to a physical understanding involving optics and the reflection of light that would explain how thread can be invisible. But this physicist replied that the thread's "invisible nature has much less to do with physics than with perception; if you look for it, you'll see it. The trick is that the magician prevents you from even considering it as a possibility."

Now this seems a hopeful theory. We know that misdirection can be a powerful force. But somehow it doesn't seem to jibe with levitations and animation effects where the whole stage is visible all the time. I myself always look for the strings, but I never see them. If the trick really only relies on misdirection, shouldn't we see the strings, at least some of the time? After all, misdirection is usually only good for a second or two. If the magician was doing the Ghost Pencil trick described above, and he wanted to switch one cork for another, it would require a misdirection of only a moment to perform the switch. But a levitation effect can go on for several minutes. Can a magician misdirect our eyes and minds for that long? Our intuition says "No way!"

Yeah, but our intuition is what messes us up in the first place! The reason most illusions work is because our intuition tells us to look where the action is, where the climax is. Of course that's the very moment something sneaky is going on someplace else. If our intuition can lead us astray, how might it be betraying us in levitation effects?

Well, for one thing we might assume the threads run straight up to the ceiling. Actually, most often the threads don't run straight up at all. They run diagonally from the top corner of the stage, down to the object, and up to the other top corner. Often the magician isn't even the one controlling the floating object—an off-stage assistant pulls the thread. You never thought of that, did you?

With some effects the thread is strung diagonally, from the magician's shirt button (for example) to an "anchor" object on a nearby table. Or consider for a moment if the thread ran from the back of the stage, over the audience's heads, to the back of the theater. The audience would receive a foreshortened view of the thread (if they could see it at all) and they probably wouldn't see it, never suspecting that it was strung that way.

You might also say that there's misdirection in the cork. An intelligent observer might think, "Hmm, it couldn't be done with threads because the bottle is corked. There must be another solution." The spectator's own reasoning misdirects.

So, even a theory that at first seemed so unrealistic as misdirection turns out to have some good practical merit. Still, there are plenty of questions left unanswered.

PHUN WITH PHYSICS THEORIES

One budding physicist/magician speculated on why invisible thread might be invisible. What if, he asks, "the thickness of the string is comparable to the wavelength of the visible light"? Or what if we "make the string non-reflective and small enough in diameter so, at the distance it is being observed, it falls below the resolution of the human eye?" Both of these arguments he dismisses as implausible, because the thread would have to be too thin for them to work. Indeed, the wavelength theory is certainly wrong. "The wavelength of visible light is in the range of about 400 to 700 nanometers," explained Kalelkar. "It is quite impossible for the thread to be so thin. Even a single strand of human hair is about 100 times thicker than the wavelength of light! The thread is undoubtably thin, but not that thin." However, he agrees there is some merit to the nonreflective theory. "We see things on the stage because light reflects off them and into our eyes. What is needed is to minimize reflection from the thread."

THE FISHING LINE THEORY

The final theory is that the thread is invisible because it is clear, like fishing line. It must also be very pure and clean, so that everyone sees right through it. This is an interesting theory because, first of all, it directly contradicts the black thread theory (how can the invisible thread be both black and clear?) and secondly, because we *can* see fishing line, so why can't we see the magician's thread? The theory rests in the physics of refraction.

When light passes through a transparent material it does not go straight through. Some of the light tends to bend (refract) slightly off course. It is this refraction that makes things underwater look funny (like when you look at a straw in a glass of water, it looks bent). Physicists use the term *refractive index* to describe how much bending the light exhibits as it passes through an object. Normal air is said to have refractive index of 1, because light passes through air without bending at all. If some particles of steam were suspended in the air, the refractive index might be higher than 1, meaning that light was being bent due to the particles (and perhaps creating a mirage in the process).

All this is what caused one magician to speculate that if "the refractive index of the material the string is made of is close to 1" that "in combination with proper lights" such a string would be invisible to the audience. That way there would be no light bending, and no light bouncing back towards the audience. The string would have to be as thin as possible so it would refract as little light as possible. The problem with this theory, he argued, is that, "Such a thin string couldn't hold anything." Professor Kalelkar also doubts this explanation, "although I could certainly be wrong. I would not have thought that refraction is particularly relevant." He goes on to stress that nonreflectance is probably the crucial point.

THEORIES UNITED

At this point we have a mishmash of contradicting theories. Is the thread black or clear? Or camouflaged? What's going on? As you've probably guessed by now, all the theories are partially correct. It depends on the situation, where the illusion is being performed and under what circumstances. Some levitations/animations rely on black thread, others on white thread, striped thread, or silver wire. All will rely on misdirection and camouflage of some variety to further conceal the thread.

One physicist/magician explained, "The usual materials are 'kevlar' mono-fibre; with round or trilobular cross-section, and even the silk from the Golden Orb spider has been used in close up TV shots in advertisements." Trilobular is a textile term meaning the cross-section of the thread has three lobes, like a clover leaf. Mono-fiber means it's thin (that is, one fiber) so as to make it that much harder to see. Still, it seems odd that people don't see the thread. After all, we *do* see thread under normal circumstances. Well, he says, to prove his point, "I have on occasion used invisible thread with up to three feet of thread exposed, in broad daylight, on a sidewalk (in front of the Hollywood Magic shop) to perform 'miracles.'" He explains: "A fine nylon thread can be invisible in full sunlight to a person of normal vision." The key words here are "sidewalk" and "sunlight" and perhaps also "Hollywood." In such a setting, shadows are minimized. Bright sunlight is shining down from above, and more sunlight is reflected off the sidewalk. Sunlight is hitting the thread from all directions, meaning there are no dark places where a shadow can exist. And glare from a bright sidewalk certainly impedes one's ability to see clearly. But the trick will work even in not-so-bright places. I've seen magicians float dollar bills in their dimly lit magic shops. Part of the concealment is due to the fact that the thread is rigged up in an unusual, unexpected way (i.e., from the animated object to the pinkie of one hand, to the magician's left ear). In some cases the magician actually turned away from me, apparently putting the thread on the other side of his body. Also, if the magician is doing a good job, he is occupying the audience by calling their attention to the floating object, rather than the space around the object. (This ploy is at work from the very start. He might ask you if you have a dollar to lend him. You reach for your wallet, and while your eyes are thus misdirected, he uses the time to get his thread ready.) While the object is floating, he is perhaps making sure to foreshorten the thread, and is filling your mind with an engaging patter which cues you in on where to look. Not only that, but the thread itself is *extremely* thin. Magicians often use a special Invisible Thread they buy at magic shops. "Invisible" is hardly an exaggeration. Against a suitable background the thread is impossible to see from mere inches away. Wanna know how thin it is? Pluck a hair from your head—invisible thread is even thinner than that! (I know, I've done the comparison.) This thread is so thin that one time I was holding a strand of it in my hand (and could barely see it), when suddenly I realized I was actually holding two strands wound around each other. I separated the two strands and now the thread became even thinner! If you handled some of this thread yourself you'd have a new respect for thread tricks. The thread really is nearly invisible, even from just a few inches away. It slips between your fingers so you hardly know whether you're holding it at all. It rolls up, it floats away. It's unbelievably strong yet seems to break at inopportune times. It's ignorant to say "done with strings" when you find out how hard it is to use the thread. In short, it's not "just strings" but all of these many things—physical, mental, and emotional, practice and talent—combining to make the thread invisible.

CREATE MAGIC!—EXPERIMENTING WITH LEVITATIONS

It can be an enlightening experience to try out some of these techniques just as a magician would. First let's work with black thread. Pull off a few feet of black thread. Hold it at arm's length against various backdrops, and in different lighting conditions. I find that when I hold the thread in front of a dark carpet, I can't see it—even though I'm staring straight at it! If you can still see the thread, make sure the thread is not being directly illuminated. Allow your shadow to fall across it. In one case I put a yellow blanket over a navy blue couch, and held the thread so half was in front of the couch, and half in front of the blanket. It was a startling contrast! I could see the yellow-backed thread just fine, but as soon as it went in front of the dark blue couch, it disappeared!

Try thinning the thread by separating its fibers into individual strands. I had to experiment a while before finding a method that works. I took a length of thread and taped one end to the desktop. Then I twirled it through my fingertips, so the strands started to unravel. Then I slid a pin between the strands, separating them. Often the thread spirals up when you do this, but be persistent! You will be rewarded with extremely thin thread that should be even harder to see.

Now let's work with some clear fishing line. For this experiment, put on a lightly colored shirt. Any pastel, light blue, or light tan shirt should do fine. You'll also need a dollar bill and about a foot of fishing line. Crinkle up the dollar into a ball around the center of the line. Hold the ends of the fishing line loosely in your hands, with the crinkled dollar floating in the center. Hold it up in front of you. You will probably be able to see the fishing line. Now look at yourself in the mirror. It is very difficult to see the fishing line against the backdrop of your light-colored shirt. I first tried this with a light blue shirt with a pattern on it, and was amazed at the results! What's truly amazing is that you can see the fishing line clearly from your perspective, but when you look at your mirror's image, it is invisible. You begin to appreciate how it is that magicians fool us with this stuff. (You can try this same experiment wearing a dark shirt and black thread.)

You might have to play with the lighting and positioning of the line to get it absolutely invisible. Another helpful hint is to avoid pulling the line taut. If you let it hang loosely, the line will be at an unusual 45-degree angle that makes it harder to locate against the shirt.

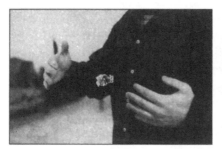   

Fig. 5. Invisible thread is used here to float the dollar bill. You can't see the line because it blends in with the dark hue of my shirt. The careful observer will notice a piece of transparent tape in my left hand, which holds the invisible thread. The other end of the thread is tucked in my pocket.

Fig. 6. Here's the dollar bill from my perspective. I can see the thread perfectly from my angle even though the audience is mystified!

Well, well, well, we're so smug, aren't we! We know how the magician makes the thread invisible right before our eyes. We're pretty smart, aren't we! Then answer me this one—how do a few mere threads levitate a person high above the stage? Threads may be thin enough to levitate a rose or a dollar bill—but a person?

Okay, let's turn to the eighth magical form for that answer.

Magic Form #8—Defying the Laws of Gravity

When I was a boy I wanted to be Peter Pan so I could fly above rooftops. I would daydream about this, and I suspect that many other people had the same daydreams at one time or another. To be able to defy the laws of gravity is to ignore one of the most basic physical laws that we face every day. Magicians allow us a vicarious glimpse into this world of unlimited flight when they cause themselves or their assistants to lift above the stage and fly around before our eyes. Let's run through some of the methods that have been used through the years to bring those daydreams of flight to life:

THE POLE LEVITATION

The simplest levitations keep the performer close to the ground. The sorcerer hypnotizes his nubile female assistant into a deep trance. She sways backwards and he guides her body to lean against a chair. He lifts one of her legs off the ground. Then he lifts her other leg off the ground. Then he lets go. Amazingly, she remains suspended there in mid-air. This sort of illusion uses an iron pole hidden inside the assistant's clothing. Basically the woman is lying on this iron pole or rod, which is connected to the chair with a strong hinge. She must have physical strength and the ability to act hypnotized while actually receiving one hell of a noogie in her side by the damn pole under her clothes! This form of levitation has many variations. Old East Indian fakirs would sit cross-legged and show their ability to levitate above the ground with only a feather for support. The feather had a solid iron rod embedded inside it for vertical lift, and two rods sticking out horizontally which the fakir would sit on, the rods being hidden under his robes.

THE "BOUNCY-BOUNCY" LEVITATION

Some gurus trying to push transcendental meditation as a way of life have claimed that those who master TM can reach new planes of consciousness not only mentally, but physically as well. To prove it, the gurus circulate promotional photos that show themselves sitting in lotus position and levitating in the air wearing nothing but a toga and a tranquil expression. How do they do it? The photos are faked. They sit on a trampoline and start to spring up and down. A friend snaps a photo when they're at the top of the bounce. They make sure to crop out the trampoline from the photo. Other swamis have mastered their darkroom techniques. They take a photo of themselves standing on a ladder, and then bring it into the darkroom and have all traces of support airbrushed out!

THE "STICK OUT YOUR LEGS" LEVITATION

This levitation is commonly found in magic books for children and can occasionally be seen at séances and haunted houses. A person lies down on a bench and is covered with a white sheet. Just her head and feet stick out the ends of the sheet. Then slowly the person begins to levitate off the bench, until she is about five feet in the air. She will hover there, and then eventually come back down to earth. This one is done with a pair of fake legs and feet. These can be broomsticks or long pieces of wood, with shoes and socks attached to one end, and covered in padding to look leg-like. The fake legs are hidden behind the bench. When the woman lies down, she actually keeps her legs on the floor. She picks up the fake legs and places them under the sheet. She then stands up under the sheet, keeping her back arched as if she were playing Limbo, and holding the fake legs straight out in front of her. The audience sees her head sticking out one end of the sheet, and the fake feet sticking out the other end. She slowly stands up higher and higher, lying backwards in the air, to give the appearance of levitation.

THE SPURTING FOUNTAIN LEVITATION

In this artful illusion, a person levitates on streams of water rising from the stage. The water isn't the only thing coming out of the stage, for the person is supported by transparent Lucite cylinders that are invisible in the water.

THE HOLLOW SHELL LEVITATION (WITH BONUS VANISHING!)

This levitation also uses a sheet covering the floating person from head to toe. But in this illusion the floating person can rise higher and higher and higher above the stage. Finally the magician whisks away the sheet to reveal—nothing. The person has vanished. The effect is often known as the Asrah illusion, and is accomplished with a lightweight hollow frame resembling a human form that fits under the sheet. It turns out that the person never gets under the sheet in the first place. Instead of lying down on the platform, she slips through a trap door in the stage just as the sheet is placed over her. No one realizes she's gone because the wire framework takes the shape and form of her body laying there. It's so lightweight that almost any kind of thin wire can be used to lift the sheet and hollow shell up into the air. Finally, the magician pulls off the sheet (the shell remains hidden underneath it), and the audience sees that the lady has vanished.

THE GOOSENECK LEVITATION

The traditional levitations—the "real" levitations—involve no sheet, no photos, just a person lying down on a raised platform. All supports are removed and the person remains floating in the air. Then hoops are passed around to prove there are "no strings attached." Indeed, there aren't any strings attached. The levitation works because a sturdy metal support beam juts out from behind the curtain. The beam is supported backstage by metal supports and strong assistants. The woman is supported in air by this raised beam. It's almost as if she is being lifted off the ground by the raised prong of a hidden forklift. The audience can't see this beam for several reasons: The assistants and supports are hidden behind a curtain. All that sticks out from the curtain is the one "forklift prong." But even that isn't visible because it's foreshortened, and positioned almost completely behind the woman being levitated. It might also be black against the black curtain of the stage. Furthermore, the woman may be wearing a loose-fitting dress which hangs down and blocks the audience's view of the beam.

There is still one sticking point. The magician passes a ring around the floating assistant to prove there are no means of support. How does a solid ring pass through the solid beam? It doesn't. If the ring is wide enough it can pass around the support beam as figures 7 and 8 show.

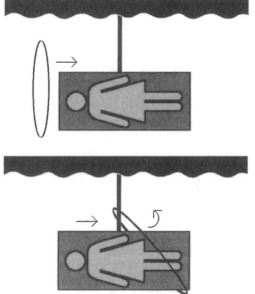

Fig. 7. The floating person is supported by a secret support beam extending from back stage behind the curtain.

Fig. 8. The hoop must be larger than half the assistant's body, so that it can pass across the body while one end is stuck at the support beam.

At that point the ring is threaded on the beam, as in figure 9. The magician need only pass it around the assistant again to free it (figure 10). The whole double motion is done so gracefully, it seems like a double proof. Not only is the magician passing it around the assistant one time, but *twice*. It truly seems she is floating there with no means of support.

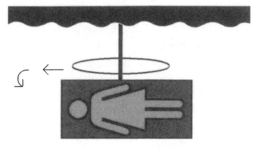

Fig. 9. The magician can see the support beam clearly, so he must bring all his acting ability into play. At this point the ring has passed around the person, but it is stuck on the support pole. The magician must bring the hoop back to the other end of the person without arousing audience suspicions.

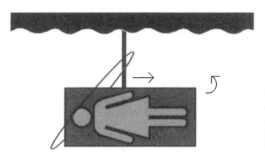

Fig. 10. The second pass begins. To the audience it seems like a second proof of no support, but to the magician it is a necessary step to remove the ring from the support bar.

As always in magic, there are multiple methods to performing the trick. Some magicians won't want to use a humongous ring. The straight support beam also hinders the magician's movement. He has to stay where he is or walk all the way around the front of the assistant to get to the other side. The audience might notice that he never crosses fully in back of her. To solve these problems, the support beam is often shaped like a flattened S. This is called a gooseneck support.

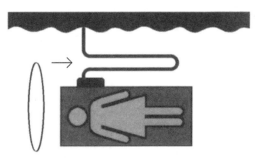

Fig. 11. The gooseneck support can be used with smaller rings. The ring can pass all the way up the length of the assistant, but a second pass in the other direction is required to unthread it from the support bar.

As the hoop is passed around the assistant, it gets threaded onto the gooseneck support. The magician can pass the hoop clear across the woman in one fell swoop. (He must then bring it back the opposite direction to remove it from the support beam.) Watch carefully when magicians do the hoops. You will probably never see a magician pull the hoop straight across the body only once. He always has to bring it one way, then back again, to remove it from the gooseneck support beam.

PROOFS IN FLYING

One thing you may have noticed about these different forms of levitation, is that they are all very limited. Most require the floater be covered with a sheet. Other versions are restricted to flat, unconvincing motion close to the stage. Compare these limited levitations to the more realistic flights in theater. There's *Peter Pan*, where Peter and three children fly around Neverland like migrating doves. In Wagner's *Das Rheingold* characters are seen flying above the stage. Other plays and operas also include characters who fly. And in all these plays the characters *really fly*. They don't just lift straight up off the stage. They don't just lean against a chair or move up a little. These actors are literally flying through the air! It brings an interesting question to mind. Question: If actors can have such realistic flying scenes, why are magicians' levitations so limited? Answer: The actor's flying may look more realistic—*but it's not a magic trick!* A magic trick requires proofs. The audience has to be *shown* that the illusion is not accomplished through ordinary means.

In theater, a flying actor is connected to wires hanging from above the stage. It's hard to have proofs with such a setup. Besides, there are no proofs in theater. Peter Pan flies around, but he doesn't fly through a hoop to prove he really can fly. In theater everyone knows it's a trick, and no one complains. But at a magic show, it's expected that the magician uses *magic* to do the tricks, and he's supposed to use proofs to prove that it's magic. It's hard to pass a hoop around a person when she's attached to wires hanging from the ceiling!

Actually, this isn't entirely true. There are several ways a proof could be accomplished. There could be a hole in the hoop. This method has been used in the past, and it is the way the Linking Rings illusion is performed. Another proof can be found in the Ghost Pencil trick mentioned earlier. In that trick, the pencil moved inside a corked bottle, because the cork had a concealed hole through which the thread passed. A similar technique can be used in large stage shows with the magician's wires. (The most amazing large-scale illusions often rely on the same principles as dopey little tricks you find in kiddy magic books!)

Perhaps the most convincing reason why more magicians don't do *real flying* is for the same reason they don't use trap doors: magicians have to be in control. They have to be prepared for any situation. They can't set up wire riggings every place they perform. Almost any small stage can accommodate pole levitations and gooseneck supports. But most stages are simply too small, too close, for flying. Most important of all, most performance spaces don't come equipped with a loft system with pulleys and counterweights and beams, hidden behind curtains above the stage. Most magicians are performing at comedy clubs, civic centers, club rooms, shopping malls, kids' birthday parties, and other places that are not equipped for realistic flying. It's just not financially sound for them to invest in such a system when they won't be able to use it most of the time. However, there are theaters that do have flying actors, proofs or no proofs, and there are some magicians who do real flying routines, cost and all. Let's take a look at how this is accomplished.

How to Fly

Theaters are built with a complicated system of rigging above the stage, with ropes, pulleys, and fly bars, horizontal rods from which scenery can be hung. Crew members off stage (called flymen) pull on ropes to raise or lower scenery as needed. Sometimes electric winches are used when a heavy piece needs to be dropped into place. In all these cases the setup is quite straightforward for normal theatrical usages. In most theater shows, the scenery is a flat backdrop or scrim that extends from the floor to above the stage: therefore the audience need never see the cables since the backdrop is as high or higher than the top of the stage. Furthermore, stage backdrops need only be raised straight up and straight down.

Flying an actor, on the other hand, is a bit different. When Peter Pan flies, he doesn't just go straight up and down. He flies *across* the stage. Furthermore, he has to fly with wires exposed. So here are two problems: how do we get horizontal movement? And how do we make the wires disappear?

First of all, the actor wears a harness under his or her clothing, to which the wire is attached. The harness is made of heavy-duty canvas, reinforced with leather and webbing material. It has shoulder and thigh straps. The harness covers the entire torso, stomach, and back of the actor, hidden under the costume. Generally the actor is hanging by a single wire. The harness is designed to provide support and balance, and one important consideration is where exactly to attach the wire to the actor, because that influences what the flying will look like. If the wire is attached to the top of the actor's back, the actor will be almost completely vertical (like someone treading water). If the wire is attached lower down, the actor will tilt forward a la Superman.

There are several methods for rigging the wires above the stage. The most popular uses two wires: one vertical, and one horizontal. The vertical wire drops down from the top of the theater and attaches to the actor's back. The second wire is called a "breast" line because—well, gosh, I guess stagehands just like having an excuse to talk about breasts. The breast line runs horizontally and attaches to the *middle* of the vertical wire, between the top of the stage and the actor. To get the actor up into the air, the flymen pull up on the vertical wire. To fly the actor across the stage, they pull on the horizontal line.

Okay, now that we've got down the basic gist of what's happening, let's throw some monkey wrenches in our mental model. First of all, it should be noted that flying is more than just pulling on ropes. The takeoffs and landings have to look convincing, otherwise people will notice that the person is just being pulled around by wires. The actor and stage crew must practice working together thoroughly to present a realistic image of flight. The stage manager or show director must think about what kinds of flying are most needed for the show. In *Peter Pan* there might be a number of "takeoff" scenes where Peter Pan is shown leaping into the air and flying across the stage. For this reason, the vertical wire would be placed to one side of the stage rather then directly in the middle. Consider what happens if the actor is standing on the *right* side of the stage, but her vertical line is hanging down from the *left* side. As she leaps into the air, the stagehand pulls her up on the vertical wire. But since the wire is on the opposite end of the stage, she is pulled laterally across the stage as well, thus lending some nice horizontal flying to the scene. On the other hand, the *Das Rheingold* Rhine Maidens are seen flying around in a more unstructured lateral dance of flight. Some stage management textbooks describe vertical wires running directly up, to produce a graceful pendulum arc to their flying. But the majority of the textbooks recommend a system where the actors are rigged with two lines, running diagonally to the upper opposite corners of the stage.

Some plays involve levitations of objects, not people, and therefore they can get away with techniques that don't require such heavy wires and support systems. In *Dracula*, a vampire bat flies from the back of the audience onto the stage during a climactic scene. A thin thread is all that's needed to support the fake bat. A play with Olympic themes might sport a javelin throw, which can be rigged to run along an invisible line. Same with a bird that flies across the stage. Some shows might have an underwater scene with fish swimming about. These will be accomplished by off-stage flymen carrying "fishing poles" with fish dangling down on invisible threads.[4]

Other kinds of riggings are possible. One method uses a trolley that runs along a horizontal cable high above the stage. The actor hangs by wires that run through pulleys in the trolley, down to the actor's harness. The pulleys allow the actor to be pulled up or down; and the horizontal trolley allows the actor to be pulled left or right. It is the flymen's job to expertly combine the horizontal and vertical motions to produce realistic flight. This version of rigging will include a swivel at the point where the actor is attached to the trolley wires, to allow the actor to rotate.[5]

Another method, called "differential drums," is used to levitate things like ghosts and skulls diagonally up across the stage. This method involves a large pulley, a small pulley, a horizontal cable, and a trolley that rides along the cable. The trolley is pulled left or right along the cable, which allows the flying object to move left or right across the stage. The size differential between the two pulleys causes the object to fly in a diagonal path, as more and more wire is released.[6]

Now let's tackle our second concern: how does the wire remain invisible? It would seem that any wire that is strong enough to carry an actor's weight must be so thick and heavy that everyone will be able to spot it from their seats. Apparently this is not so. The guidebooks for stage managers mention two kinds of wire that are both strong and invisible: piano wire, and airplane wire. Piano wire is strong and thin, but it doesn't bend well. All of the rigging techniques require pulleys that the wire runs through. But once piano wire starts bending around a pulley, it begins to become brittle and weaken. Therefore piano wire is not used.

What *is* used is called airplane wire, or wire rope. It's a strong cable but without the problems that piano wire has. Aircraft wire can bend without weakening, which is necessary for stage work, since the wires have to be curled around pulleys to lift the heavy load of the actor. Furthermore, airplane wire is almost invisible on stage; thus it is used for all these flying effects. The wires disappear for the same reason that threads disappear in a dollar-floating trick. It's a combination of several factors: misdirection (if the wire is hooked up off-center, it creates a diagonal effect that might be missed by an audience looking for wires directly above the flying figure); a patterned and shifting background (shiny mylar curtains, for instance, which may be ruffled into moving waves by a breeze from backstage fans); and perhaps a clever combination of lights lighting the actors and not lighting the wires.

It should be said that the flying illusion is *not always so great*. At a high school production of *Peter Pan*, the teacher promised us she was using a professional flying system, just like they use on Broadway. They must've done something drastically different on Broadway because the moment the curtains opened, the audience collapsed into peals of laughter: Wendy, Michael and John all had thick white cables snaking out from their backs and up to the top of the ceiling. The flying itself was smooth and realistic: but the wires were there for all to see.

It's notable that out of all the textbooks I looked at dealing with on-stage lighting, set design, and theatercraft, *none* of them gave any indication about how the lighting should be set up to make the wires invisible. You would think they would have all sorts of techniques and hints and lighting lore passed down from one production of *Peter Pan* to the next. But they don't. This, I think, is the strongest indication of all how easily we are fooled.

Magic Form #9—Restoring the Destroyed

Restoring the destroyed can be the most mystifying of illusions. Consider a twenty-dollar bill borrowed from an audience member. The bill is signed across the front, then torn to shreds. The pieces are rubbed together and in a few moments, they are unfolded to show the restored bill whole again. The act is astonishing, and prays on every person's desire to get back what we've lost through our own negligence or misuse.

One of the most preeminent illusions of this kind is "Sawing a Woman in Half." The trick created a sensation when first performed by British magician P. T. Selbit in London in 1920. His early version of the trick would be not at all convincing to a modern audience. Unlike the sawing illusions of today, Selbit's female assistant was completely enclosed in a wooden crate the size and shape of a regulation Army coffin. He sawed through it with either a two-man crosscut saw or a rotary power saw. The crate was padlocked and placed on a wooden bench. Her head did not stick out the top, and her feet did not stick out the bottom. Her legs did not show through a window in the side. A modern audience would suspect the truth: that once the box was closed, the woman bunched up her legs into the top half of the coffin, giving the saw a clean path to slice through the middle.

It didn't take long for other magicians to bootleg the idea and improve upon it. For the 1921–22 theater season, Horace Goldin allowed the New York vaudeville audiences to see the woman's head, hands, and feet extending through holes in the ends and sides of the crate. Goldin played up the danger aspect by keeping an ambulance nearby the theater, and stationing a uniformed nurse and a stretcher in the theater lobby during performances. One wonders how a single nurse could carry a stretcher, but this is just showmanship after all! Goldin was also known to hire a group of men, dress them like undertakers in dour black coats and top hats, and carry the handsaw in a procession through the city streets and right up to the theater where the performance was being held.

Since that time there have been many variations on the illusion relying on several different principles of deception:

- *Hollow recess in the platform.* The "coffin" sits atop a platform. The platform is designed to look too thin to house a human, but that is an optical illusion. An extra woman or two can actually hide inside the thin platform. In one version, two women are used. One woman lays down in the cabinet so her head and maybe her arms extend out visibly for the audience. However, her legs don't stretch out straight in front of her—they slip down into the hollow recess of the platform. Another woman is hiding underneath the other half of the platform, and her legs extend out through the cabinet for the audience to see. This allows the boxes to be separated, all the while showing very convincingly realistic body parts extending from the boxes. No one suspects the body parts belong to two different women.
- *Fake body parts.* The second version uses just one woman, who scrunches up in one half of the box. Her head and arms are visible to the audience, but her legs descend into the hollow area in the platform, or are scrunched up in the box with her. The box is deeper than it appears, allowing more room for her to scrunch. Fake legs are used in the other box to give the illusion she is lying flat across. Sometimes the legs are me-

chanically animated to give the impression they're real. A low-cost version uses a thread that runs to the leg box—the woman in the head box pulls the thread to wiggle the fake legs. The movement is seldom convincing if you know to look for it. Some versions use robot feet, which are undoubtedly wearing socks because it's so difficult to make plastic look like human flesh!

- *Dummy middle.* The third method also uses one woman, but in this one the center of her body descends down into the platform. What the audience sees as her stomach (or back, depending how she's lying) is really a faked dummy which the metal panes or buzzsaw can safely pass through. In this version of the illusion, you'll notice, the two halves of the body can't be separated since it's really only one person stretched across the table!

We will come back to each of these variations further along in this book.

Those are the explanations for the sawing illusion, but what about all those other tricks where something is destroyed and then restored? We've all seen a playing card burned to a crisp and then made whole again. Or a rope that's cut up and then the two segments magically joined together. How do those kinds of restorations work? Well, in general there are only three ways to restore something that has been destroyed: Either a whole duplicate item is substituted for the destroyed thing, or the thing was never really destroyed in the first place, or, in rare instances, the thing destroyed really is somehow made whole again. Let's take a look at each of these methods and how they are applied.

RESTORATION METHOD #1: SUBSTITUTION

There is an old magic trick called Fresh Fish that follows this format. The trick, which has innumerable variations, goes something like this. The magician shows a large paper banner that reads FRESH FISH SOLD HERE TODAY! The magician explains that the owner of a fish store hung up this banner to advertise his fresh fish. Then some prankster came by and pointed out and said, "Hey, why does it say TODAY? Of course you're selling it *today*—you can't sell it *yesterday!*" So the store owner (and the magician) rips off the word TODAY from the sign. The prankster says, "HERE?! Why does it say the fish is sold HERE? Isn't that obvious? After all, you wouldn't be advertising for the fish store across town, would ya?" The store owner takes his advice and rips off the word HERE. This goes on with all the remaining words of the sign, until the sign has been torn into five pieces. The store owner yells at the prankster to get out of his shop, as he eyes the destroyed sign wistfully. The store owner needs his sign back, and happily the magician is present to do that for him. With a wave of the hand, the magician pulls apart the paper in his hand to reveal all five pieces have restored themselves into a whole-again banner.

The trick is accomplished with a duplicate banner. The magician starts the trick with two lookalike banners in his hand. One is stretched out to show the full wording, while the other is folded up and attached behind it to the other side of the banner. As the magician rips words off the sign, he stacks up the ripped pieces one by one behind each other. He does it in such a way that at the end of the ripping he can turn over the stack and unfurl the duplicate banner. It takes some preplanning to figure out exactly how to stack the pieces so the folded duplicate banner ends up underneath the stack at the end. The magician then has to subtly turn over the stack of papers, unfold the whole "restored" banner, and conceal the ripped pieces behind the sign. A good magician will sneak the pieces into his pocket so he can let the audience inspect the restored banner fully.

Restoration Method #2: Never Really Destroyed

It is not always possible to have a duplicate item on hand. For instance, consider a trick where a spectator donates a dollar bill, signs it, and the magician rips it up, burns it, then pulls the fully restored dollar out of the ashes. That would be a pretty amazing trick! The problem is, a duplicate bill cannot be used because there would be no way to forge the signature ahead of time, and besides, the serial number of the bill wouldn't match. Instead, what happens is that the money is never really ripped up or burned up in the first place. You'll probably see the magician do something like this:

- The spectator signs the bill and hands it to the magician. The magician places it in an envelope, rips it, burns it, etc. (Reality check: There was really a thin slit in the bottom of the envelope. When she pushed the dollar inside, she was actually pushing it out the slit and into her hand. She hides the bill in her hand while ripping up the envelope. You'll probably notice she didn't use a standard letter-sized envelope. Instead, she used the tiniest envelope she could find. That's so she would have an excuse to fold up the dollar bill real small. That way you wouldn't notice it when it was folded small and hidden in her hand. Now the magician goes into her pocket to get the matchbook to burn the torn envelope with; while her hand is in her pocket, she drops off the concealed dollar and takes out the matches. Now she can relax with the dollar safely tucked away until it comes time to reveal the "restored" dollar at the end of the trick.)
- A more skilled magician doesn't need to use the envelope trick. She will have a duplicate folded bill hidden in her hand; after taking the spectator's bill, she folds it up and substitutes one for the other. There's no need to use an envelope because this magician is an expert at sleight of

hand. As she shows off the folded bill to the crowd, she's doing the drop-off in the pocket as she removes the matches for the burning part of the trick. Is the duplicate bill real? Is she really ripping and burning a real dollar bill? Maybe, maybe not. The important thing is that she has managed to switch the spectator's marked, signed bill with something that superficially *looks* like it.

I would estimate that the vast majority of destroy-and-restore tricks rely on the thing never really being destroyed to begin with. Most rope tricks work this way. For instance, when the magician cuts a rope in half and then restores it whole again, usually some ruse is pulled so that you only *think* he cut the ropes in half, while in fact the rope remained almost entirely whole.

RESTORATION #3: RIGGED UP TO DESTROY AND RESTORE ITSELF

This last method of restoring the destroyed is rare, and usually only occurs in very specific circumstances. For example, there are special magic wands that can be purchased called "breakaway wands." The wand looks solid and whole, and can be tapped against a table to prove its solidity, but as soon as it's handed to a spectator, the wand droops over like a dead fish. Similarly there are breakaway Oriental fans, twirly guns, and similar items. In these cases you can say that the thing is rigged up to destroy and restore itself on the magician's command (in the case of the wand, the magician secretly removes a small segment of the wand before handing it over to the spectator; the wand loses tension with the piece missing, and so it droops over). It's not really a magic trick, more of a novelty gag, and so this method has only limited use.

Magic Form #10—Accelerations of Natural Processes

One of my favorite illusions I performed as a young, budding magician involved the tenth form of magic: acceleration of natural processes. I passed around three items for inspection: a bath towel, a clay planting pot, and a cardboard box filled with dirt. I would then invite the audience to dig through the dirt with their hands to be sure it was dirt and nothing more. Once they were satisfied that the pot was empty, the dirt was dirty, and the towel was just a towel, the trick would commence!

I explained to the assembled group that I would plant a seed in the pot, and would use magic to make the plant grow and flower within a few minutes. I held up three packets of seeds and had a volunteer select one of the packets. (They weren't real packets, just envelopes with glued-on photos cut from a gardening catalog, with the names of the flowers printed neatly underneath: roses, forsythias, and pansies.) The volunteer selected one of the packets and I escorted her back to her seat and had another volunteer fill the pot with dirt. I then planted the seed in the pot. Sometimes I "watered" the seed with magic water, or sprinkled it with sparkling fairy dust to help the magic kick in. Then I folded my arms before me, with the towel draped over them, covering the pot. I stared at the audience as I spoke to them about the power of magic to cause the impossible to occur. After a moment, I would lift up the towel to reveal some small forsythia branches now growing in the pot.

This was greeted with some gasps, but the plant was not done blooming. I placed the towel in front again, and after a short time, it was removed to reveal the branch had grown, and delicate yellow flowers had bloomed up and down its length. Applause! Bows!

Magicians through the centuries have performed similar illusions. In the year 1615, Sir Thomas Roe, on expedition for the British East India Company, reported seeing an Indian magician grow a mulberry tree from seed to fruit. Over a hundred years later, a London clockmaker and trickster named Christopher Pinchbeck would team up with magician Isaac Fawkes to create a mechanical tree that accomplished the same effect. "The Pinchbeck tree was carried in a box. The limbs and trunk were hollow and the leaves pressed tightly against the limbs. Compressed air pumped through the hollow limbs and trunk caused the tree to expand and 'grow' before the audience's eyes."[7] Pinchbeck used this method to create an apple tree and later an orange tree for the magician. Another century would pass before the trick was improved again, this time by Robert-Houdin, a "David Copperfield" of the mid-nineteenth century in that he was a popular magician who liked to use technology to make his tricks work. (He was also skilled at sleight-of-hand conjuring.) Robert-Houdin improved the tree trick by including a separate hydraulic line so that after the tree grew to full size, air could be pumped through this second line to uncluster the leaves and reveal fruit hidden underneath.[8] Later the Americas would get into the act, with grand style and flair. Harry Kellar, known for his mysterious and solemn displays of intriguing illusions, would grow stunning bouquets of live rosebushes before an astonished audience. Other cultures have magically grown corn, mangoes, and cucumbers.

My own version of the tree-growing illusion was much simpler than these (I was just a kid after all). How did I do my trick? How did I accelerate the natural process of plant growth? *Shhh*, I'll tell you. There are two parts to the trick: (1) choosing the seeds and (2) growing the plant.

The first part involves leading the spectator to choose the "correct" packet of seeds so they will match the plant that emerges. I'll describe how that's done later on. For now let's concentrate on how the plant is grown. I used a technique similar to the one most likely used by the Indian magician witnessed by Sir Thomas Roe back in the seventeenth century. The Indian magician probably used dwarf trees in various stages of growth. By misdirection and sleight of hand, subsequent trees were substituted for each other to give the impression the tree was growing.[9] This is how I did it. Before the show I went into my backyard and clipped two branches off the forsythia bush. One was small and runty, and I swiped off most of its leaves. The other was chosen specifically for its thickness and bright, flashy flowers. I dress up for the show and wear a sports jacket. The branches are hidden under my jacket with paper clips.

The trick is done early in the show, because it's hard to move around nonchalantly with the branches hidden under there. The jacket is kept buttoned.

The trick is straightforward to start. The audience is allowed to examine all the props. I plant the seed, then drape the towel over my folded arms. I make sure the towel is draped well over my shoulders. With the towel in position, I support the towel with my left arm. That leaves my right arm free to do as it pleases under cover of the towel! I unfold my right arm, sneak it into the jacket, remove the first branch and plant it in the pot, and rebutton the jacket. All the while I'm talking to the audience to focus their attention on my face. It's important to do this part carefully, because the arm movements should remain invisible underneath the towel. Furthermore, I have to give the impression that two arms are holding up the towel, when really it is only one.

To make the branch bloom, I once again cover the plant with the towel, draping it over my shoulders. This time I make sure my left arm is free to move around, because I have to reach under the opposite side of my jacket to get the flowery branch stored there. Before doing that, however, I pull out the first branch, and raise it to my right hand. My right hand holds it above the pot, under the cloak of the towel. I can then pull out the flowery branch from my jacket and plant it in the pot. This time when I pull away the towel, the first branch is concealed underneath it. I might toss the towel into the box with the dirt, so no one will suspect a thing.

I enjoyed performing this trick as a child, and I got to perform it twice to two different audiences. At the time I reasoned that if I ever had to repeat it to the same people, I would make sure to prepare beforehand by securing some rose branches and flowers—that way no one would get suspicious about it being forsythias all the time.

Acceleration of natural processes doesn't only have to refer to magically growing trees, of course, but that is probably the most popular illusion of this form that magicians tend to do. A neat trick in this vein might be if a magician held aloft an ice cube, and said she was going to cause it to melt *extremely quickly* using magic. She closes her fist around it, gives the fist one good shake, and opens up to reveal nothing but dripping water. The effect could be accomplished by a combination of sleight of hand—perhaps the ice cube is switched at the last moment for a plastic replica filled with water that's made to burst when squeezed. With all these effects the magician must be sure to do proper "magic management" on two levels: On the lowest level, he has to make sure he's performing the underlying moves correctly. On a more general thematic level, the magician has to structure the effect so it *looks like* the natural process is being accelerated. Otherwise everyone will just assume that the forsythia got there by "magically appearing." Or that the ice cube merely vanished, rather than melted away. For this reason, it's important the magician think carefully through every utterance, every movement, and make sure that it all works together to promote the theme that the natural processes of the universe are being magically accelerated.

The Final Magic Form . . . Magic Form #11—Mentalism

One might be tempted to think that feats of mentalism are merely the abstract equivalent of productions (producing objects from thin air). After all, in a mind-reading trick a piece of knowledge appears out of nowhere, into the magician's brain. In fact very often the abstraction turns out to be very true. As we've seen already, the mentalist may open a sealed envelope to reveal the prediction that was apparently sealed within many days earlier. However, the reality is that the envelope was empty all along. Suppose the psychic wants to predict newspaper headlines for the day of the show. The prediction is made on the day of the performance. The mentalist writes up the prediction that morning on a piece of paper, and now the trick becomes how to get that paper inside the sealed empty envelope. You see, it looks like a feat of mentalism—predicting the future—but really it's a penetration effect (or an appearance). Of course, the audience never realizes that. This is a prime example of the illusion of illusion.

So that's one kind of mentalism trick, the newspaper prediction. But what about reading of minds? Mind-reading tricks are incredibly spooky, as the performer seems to somehow know intimate thoughts and has no qualms about revealing them before an audience! How does mind reading work?

The Amazing Kreskin, known mostly for his television appearances in the 1970s and 1980s, poo-pooed many of the theories critics had of his mind-reading ability. He starts by talking about the thick glasses he wears:

> The glasses are not transistorized bugging devices. I have no second set of hidden eyes, no mirror built into my ring, no periscope in my belt buckle, no assistant concealed in the ceiling and transmitting to me through a miniature radio—all of which have been advanced as "how-to" techniques.
>
> After a Johnny Carson "Tonight" show, one critic, quite seriously, said he suspected I planted tiny mikes in numerous audience seats and then listened backstage to pick up key information as the audience chatted pre-

show. What strikes me so funny about this is the picture of myself crawling around the floor at Studio B in Burbank prior to show time, stringing wires and cutting holes in upholstery. Such an NBC "Watergate" would be more hilarious than the show itself, and Carson would be better off photographing that rigging than what I do later.[10]

Please keep in mind that it's the magician's job to misdirect you, and here Kreskin is doing just that! No, I'm sure Kreskin doesn't crawl around or hide a periscope in his belt buckle (but what good would a periscope in a belt buckle do anyway?). But he, and other mentalists like him, use similar tricks to gather information about the audience prior to show-time (we've already examined some of those tricks). By laughing about these suggested methods, Kreskin is saying, "Oh, my act is so awe-inspiring and mystical and magical that how in the world could that amazing magic be due to such lowly subterfuges as microphones and assistants transmitting information?" He wants you to believe that he wouldn't stoop to such low-brow hijinx as that. But the truth is, there's nothing low brow about them at all. It gets the job done. That's what magicians do. They do what needs to be done, using whatever methods are available to them at the time. The tale is told of the Amazing Randi astounding a roomful of incredibly observant magicians with his feats of mentalism. Then he revealed to them his glorious secret: he used a trick deck of cards. The same deck anyone could buy at a toy store in the mall. We don't expect the magician to break the rules, and here Kreskin is trying to convince you that he doesn't break the rules, but you've got to remember—there are no rules! The game is Trick the Audience. You're the audience. They're going to do whatever they can to win the game! There's nothing wrong with planting mikes if it creates a fantastic illusion. If it elicits awe and the audience has its breath taken away, then the magician has done a swell job and should be congratulated. Many, many, *many* magic tricks are done with what might be considered "low brow" tactics. An unbent paper clip holds an extra playing card under the jacket. Or a slip of tape affixes an extra coin under the table. The methods of the magician are sometimes very crude, but that's why they hide them from you. And besides, who are we to argue that a method is no good, if that method has been used for years to confound us into a sense of magical reverie?

Another thing you should look for when watching a mentalist perform is when exactly he reveals information. For instance, does the audience volunteer first say her mother's maiden name and only then the psychic rips opens the sealed envelope? Or is the envelope ripped open without anyone mentioning confidential information about themselves? If the first—if the audience member reveals information and only then the psychic reveals his prediction—then you must suspect a "nail writer" or similar gadget. A nail writer is a small ring that fits on the finger. Fitted to the ring is a tiny pen or piece of graphite. Once the information is revealed, the psychic nonchalantly scribbles with his fingertip nail writer onto an index card, and when the envelope is ripped open, the appearance is given that the card is pulled out of the envelope. (Actually the card is behind the envelope.) Techniques of spatial and time misdirection are used so that the audience does not possibly believe that anything unusual is going on. As far as time goes, the audience believes he wrote his prediction long before, so they have no reason to suspect he's writing now. And as far as spatial misdirection goes, while the performer is scribbling on the card, he may be looking at the audience and making funny banter with them. Why should they suspect that he's also, covertly, scribbling with his thumb on an index card?!

There are many other variations on the psychic game. Some tricks use a hidden slip of carbon paper to make a secret copy of the message a volunteer writes down. The volunteer folds up her message and seals it in an envelope, but the magician is able to steal a peek at the carbon copy.

CREATE MAGIC!—PSYCHIC PREDICTION

This is a fun trick because it gives you a good excuse to throw a party.

The Effect

Hold a Super Bowl party and announce at the beginning that you will make a psychic prediction as to who will win the game. Write your answer on a paper in full view of the audience (don't let them see what you're writing though) and seal it in an envelope. Let the envelope be in full view for the entire game. At the end of the game, dramatically tear open the envelope, pull out the card and hand it to your friends, who read it and wonder how you knew the outcome. This trick is most effective when there is some great upset and the longshot ends up winning. It becomes more effective if you repeat the illusion year after year, every year making a correct "psychic choice."

Backstage

This is the trick to the trick. When you scribble your prediction, you are writing something like this:

> # THE JETS ARE
> # THE WINNER
> # IS THE GIANTS

The trick is accomplished when you rip open the envelope. You have to remember which end of the card is facing up. If the Jets won the game, you would turn the envelope upside down and, as you ripped it open, also rip off the words "is The Giants." Then the card would read "The Jets are the winner."

Similarly, if the Giants won, you would rip open the envelope by tearing off the top of the card—"the winner is The Giants." You might want to subtly indicate on the outside of the envelope with light pencil marks where the cutoff points to tear at are. Naturally the card should fit snugly in the envelope, with no extra room to move around.

An alternate way of doing the trick is to simply write the name of one team at the top of the card, and the other team at the bottom, upside down. (One of these names could be secretly on the card before you make your public proclamation.) The tearing would proceed in the same way as described above.

Finally, you should consider the magician's rule to never repeat a trick. Now, if you're going to be doing this over and over again every year, you should: (1) Bet money on it: you'll clean up! (2) More importantly, vary your wording somewhat. For instance, sometimes you can write the card to say:

THE JETS ARE
THE LOSER
IS THE GIANTS

Then you have to remember to always tear off the end that *won* the game, not lost it.

One thing to be wary of is hecklers. And grabbers. If you leave the envelope lying around, someone's going to think it's theirs to peek at. Don't let that happen or the jig is up!

MENTAL TELEPATHY CODES

Codes were used extensively in the mid-nineteenth century to provide the appearance of psychic powers. The mentalist would be blindfolded and possibly covered with a blanket, to shield him or her from sight. An assistant would walk around the room collecting objects from audience members. As each item was held up, the blindfolded mentalist would say exactly what the item was.

If these acts were done in modern times, we might suspect the mentalist of wearing a secret radio earpiece and listening to a description of the item as described by an accomplice watching from the back of the theater. Or we might even suspect a miniature television set underneath the blanket. But such technology was not available then.

We might also suspect the blindfolds and blankets are rigged, or are not exactly obstructing the mentalist's view. Indeed, such methods are used in some effects, such as when a psychic takes a blindfolded drive down the road in an automobile. The psychic carefully controls how the blindfolds are applied to his eyes, furrowing down his eyebrows, as if in deep concentration. After the blindfolds are in place, he raises his eyebrows. This gives enough lift to provide sneak peeks out the bottom or sides. Consider what the mentalist Dunninger has to say on the subject. After devoting six and a half pages to explaining the reality of "eyeless sight," he admits that if you're really in a bind you should start "leaning slightly over the table and opening your eyes beneath the blindfold. You'll find that if you look straight down, you can see past the sides of your nose and get a good look at the setup on the table. No matter how tightly they blindfolded you, there's no way of preventing you from getting that needed glimpse. In fact the tighter, the better, because you can keep scowling while they tie it, as though it really hurts."[11] And this is revealed after trying to convince the reader that eyeless sight is really possible!

But neither of these techniques were used by the mind readers of the past. They used a complicated code system. Every item that a spectator could possibly have was represented by a code word. Further code words conveyed descriptive adjectives, colors and numbers. As the assistant went around the room, he would hold up items and make comments:

"Here's a fine object you'll never guess."

"A watch? A gold watch!"

"Yes! Oh, and look, can you see what nice thing we have here?"

(He thinks for a moment.) "A silk scarf. Beautiful."

"Now form a vision of this item . . ."

All the code words are embedded in the assistant's speech: "fine" is the code for "gold." The word "guess" means "watch." Perhaps the word "Oh" means "silk," and "nice thing" means "scarf." If an audience member brought a scarf embroidered with golden thread, the assistant might say: "Here's a fine nice thing for you to concentrate on." The assistant and mentalist had to have their code completely memorized. Some of these codes were enormous! Often there would be dozens of words and phrases used, covering the entire range of objects and descriptions of objects. The assistant had to be quick in coming up with a sentence or two that incorporated the code words, making it probably a tougher job than that of the mentalist, who of course was allowed to pause, consider, focus his thoughts, and think a bit before responding.

While it may have been difficult to memorize and perform such mental telepathy acts, there were certainly a number of stage teams who put in the practice and made a show out of it. It's even said that by age four, the young Harry Blackstone Jr., "was performing feats of 'mental telepathy' for visitors to the Blackstones' Michigan home. When he first performed it, he even astonished his mother and father: he'd learned their complicated code while eavesdropping on rehearsals!"[12]

COLD READINGS

A cold reading is a conversation between the mentalist and a subject. The mentalist tells the subject things about himself or herself that the mentalist could not possibly know. The mentalist might also make predictions about the future. There are many tricks mentalists use to do this. They might use some of the data-gathering techniques we talked about before in conjunction with the movie *Leap of Faith*. Some psychics who work from their homes will rig up a monitoring device in their waiting room, to listen in and collect data on their gullible customers before they venture into the psychic's mystically festooned reading room. A common baby monitor is sufficient for this purpose. The psychic might listen in on idle chatter (carefully making sure to schedule some appointments with overlapping times, so there are always several people in the waiting room); or her spouse or assistant may chat with clients, eliciting valuable personal information in well-heard whispers. Houdini himself had his home rigged up, and would surprise friends by knowing what they had on their mind.[13]

Sometimes the psychic doesn't intentionally go out and sneak around and collect data; she collects the data merely from being around the person whose thoughts she is attempting to read. On an episode of the "Oprah Winfrey Show," the psychic Rosemary Altea was shown reading the thoughts of a random woman in the studio, and she made the astonishing declaration that the woman's mother had died of cancer a few years back. The woman began screaming and crying hysterically. It was a big, dramatic moment on the show. What home viewers didn't see was Dr. Michael Shermer, another guest on the show, explaining that he had shared a limo with the woman, and that she had had a reading with the psychic the day before. The woman was not as random as she appeared. Shermer's information was edited out of the televised show, as such information often is.

Data-gathering and preknowledge are sometimes used, but more often the mentalist relies on good guesses and careful word choice. For instance, the mentalist may approach a young woman in the audience and ask her, "I sense a problem . . . ?"

"Yes."

"You're concerned about something. But I also see good fortune. You will overcome challenges, but in the end all will work out."

The subject goes away feeling refreshed and satisfied.

A skeptical onlooker might point out what hogwash this is. First of all, everyone has problems and concerns of some kind or another. To predict good fortune is meaningless, and besides, it isn't a real demonstration of psychic abilities unless the predictions are shown to have come true! Likewise with "overcoming challenges." And the final bit is nonsense: it will "all work out" in the end. Of course it will! Life always continues forward, regardless of what occurs. These are words known as "nominalizations," words that sound specific but don't actually refer to anything in the real world. "It's not what you say," advises Kenton Knepper, who performs mental acts of this kind, "so much as what they hear. And when you use the proper nominalizations, words that cut both ways, it will *have* to fit their experience, because they—the person listening—*make it fit* their experience simply to understand what you're saying."[14]

Now, all that is what skeptical onlookers might say (if they had a chance to really think it through), but let me show you why all that is not important. In a certain sense it doesn't matter what other people think, as long as the subject herself is satisfied with the exchange. The mentalist didn't just pick anyone at random from the crowd: she specifically chose someone with wide eyes, sitting rapt at the edge of her seat. Someone who appeared intrigued and interested to find out about her future. In other words, the mentalist chose someone who would make a good subject. To satisfy the skeptics, the mentalist will also perform more traditional mental magic tricks where a definite outcome is achieved. In the case of performers who bill themselves as genuine psychics and all they do is cold reading, well, they have very few skeptics in the audience whom they must please.

THE AURA OF THE MENTALIST

Mentalists, more than any other kinds of magicians, love to play up the public's uncertainty about all things spiritual and psychic. One time I took a business card from a psychic. The card showed an eerie drawing of the astral planes on it (or some such nonsense). I wasn't sure what it was a drawing of, but it looked like a weird diagram of the human psyche or something. The psychic wanted laypeople to look at it and be in awe of his mystical knowledge of the cosmos. Years later I took another look at the card, but this time I understood the drawing: It was a diagram of a computer hard drive!

You see, these professed psychics are always trying to fool you, however they can. They do whatever they can do to promote an aura of supernaturality. Such magicians as Kreskin, Dunninger, and many others offer themselves as people who genuinely have mental powers in excess of normal people. I wonder if they believe it themselves. It certainly keeps most of the audience in awe.

A Dozen Explanations

A dozen explanations to the "magician's dozen" doesn't even begin to do justice to all the creative ways magicians have come up with to deceive audiences throughout the centuries. This chapter has been a brief summary of all that is available in the illusionist's repertoire, as far as tricks go. But we have yet to answer the basic question "What is magic . . . really?" We know magic is fake. We know it relies on all sorts of deceptions, but why is it that some deceptions work while others do not? Why are some fakes plausible while others stand out like a sore thumb? For instance, a cartoon is fake—mere drawings on paper, that's pretty obvious. A sculpture is a fake made of rock. But when we observe the fakeness of magic, we don't interpret it as fake. We see it as very real. Even when we know in our hearts that a person cannot fly, that a silver sword cannot penetrate a body and come out bloodless, even when our eyes betray our common sense, we see magical illusions as *real*. Why is that? What is this stuff that magic is made of that is fake and yet real at the same time? That question is the one we will begin to uncover in the next chapter and in part 2 of this book.

3

What Is Magic Made Of?

We've gone through this whole catalog of magic, begun to see some of the complexities underlying the illusions and presentations of the illusions. But what is this magic made of? Some magicians have tried to categorize deceptions in various ways. Arthur Buckley, a skilled prestidigitator of the 1930s and 1940s, defined all magic as the product of these components:

Manipulation	False Partition
Substitution	Concealed Mechanism
Duplication	Falsification
Camouflage	Arrangement
Imitation	Preparation

Some tricks use combinations of these components. Other magicians have used different classifications. Penn & Teller do a routine called "The Seven Principles of Magic" where Penn explains to the audience the principles of sleight of hand. (Their seven principles are: palm, ditch, steal, load, simulation, misdirection, and switch.) While Penn describes the sleights, Teller stands there and performs the very sleights that Penn is describing. The audience is enthralled and baffled. The point, well taken, is that even if you know how a trick is done, you can still be utterly baffled if the presentation is flawless.

Naturally, most magicians aren't going to be as talented as a Teller, but many are. On a recent trip to the Walt Disney World resort, I had the pleasure of watching a strolling magician at work. He produced sponge balls from the air, caused them to multiply miraculously at his fingertips, and even produced them within the closed fists of his close-up audience. I was pestered by my traveling companions to divulge how he accomplished the tricks. "Uhm . . . well . . ." I began, wondering how to boil down that magician's many years of steadfast study and practice into a fifteen-second explanation. "Well, it's misdirection. Whenever he shows you the balls in his hand, he's secretly removing an extra ball from his pocket, or dropping something in there." A minute later the magician came over to us and surprised my group. "I'll never figure that out!" was the joyous proclamation. I had just *told* them how it's done!

So what is it about a trick that causes us to perceive it as magical? The essence of magic is easily felt but not so easily created. I've seen plenty of magicians that are as uninspiring as the practical joker who puts a whoopee cushion on your chair. A whoopee cushion isn't magic, it's a . . . trick. A *magic* trick should be more than that. For a trick to be magical, it has to be more than just a trick. There has to be an illusion behind it.

The illusion supports the trick, enriches the trick. The illusion is prepared by the magician, but ultimately the illusion is created by you, the audience, in your own mind. The illusion that is created is what lends believability to the trick. In essence, the magician is a persuader, like the advertiser who persuades you that his product will solve all your problems, or the politician whose rhetoric tries to persuade you that voting for her will save you money. When done properly, magic may be the most effective persuader of all, since the ones being persuaded—the audience—are actually persuading themselves.

A giraffe is covered with a huge dropcloth. The shape of the animal is visible beneath the cloth. Therefore the giraffe must still be under there. Now the magician whisks away the drop cloth. The giraffe is gone! I know a three-thousand-pound giraffe cannot vanish into thin air. I didn't see it go anyplace. Therefore, magic has occurred.

But the audience never really sees the giraffe vanish. They merely think they see its outline under the dropcloth. It's the persuasive evidence that builds up in the audience's minds that causes them to believe that the giraffe has been vanished.

Author James VanFleet applies this principle to business, saying that the key to persuading others in the workplace is to let them think that your proposal is their own.[1] If your proposal is intelligent and the right choice, they can't help but be impressed by their own ingenuity.

When a magician performs an illusion, he has to simultaneously do three things: (1) tell the story of the effect, (2) manipulate the secret mechanisms that provide the "magic," and (3) create "proofs" or "clues" that show no secret mechanisms are occurring.

These all have to be done as simply and elegantly as possible, while keeping the audience entertained. A tall order! One that many so-called magicians are not fully capable of carrying out. They'll do number two (perform the magic), usually do number one (create an overt and engaging pretext for performing the illusion), and sometimes complete number three effectively (enrich the illusion with subtle actions and misdirections).

Number three is increasingly more important, especially when magicians turn to the old standby tricks. I asked magicians why they thought that audiences today can still be befuddled by illusions that are centuries old (or that work by principles that are that old). Teller had this to say:

> Many of the tricks which fooled people centuries ago do *not* work any more. People know a lot more nowadays. It's basic training for adulthood in Western society to go through a phase where you learn magic. It happens when people are around between eight and twelve, and usually entails a magic set or a magic book, and six months of hell for the parents and siblings. Those tricks that persist, like the Cups and Balls, are usually complex in choreography (and so, hard to follow even if you know just what's going on) and flexible enough to admit of many variations, so that even if you know the trick, the performer can catch you with some new wrinkle.

Take something like the Linking Rings. To look at the magician performing the illusion, you would first say he is "doing the trick." But it is more than that. He can't be *just* doing the trick. He also has to be hiding the trick of the trick from you. Thus, he has to simultaneously pass rings through the gaps in the rings, while at the same time hiding the gaps from the audience. Furthermore, he has to do these things entertainingly, telling a story, or at least allowing the separate components of the trick to flow together effortlessly. So, where once we might have said the magician is doing a magic trick, now we have to say he is doing three things—tricking, hiding the trick, and choreographing the trick.

But wait—there's more! You can't just say he's "doing the trick." Doing the trick is actually a whole sequence of moves, each of which is a smaller trick. Similarly, choreographing some stupid metal hoops into a delightful and mystifying tale involves good storytelling ability, acting, memorizing patter, and good timing.

We can go on and on, taking each of these details in turn and expanding them out to what they really mean. The best magicians will do so, analyzing these components of the illusion, finding out the best ways to work them together to create an effect that is truly magical. Just like we refined our flea-in-the-fist illusion, the best magicians will refine their illusions over and over again. The less-than-best magicians may stop as soon as they have the moves memorized, if they get that far at all. Many stop at the "doing the trick" part.

Throughout this book, whenever I'm talking about the subtle techniques of a magician, I will always be referring to a good magician, a practiced one, a magician whose act rests on a solid base of skill and devotion and not on trips to the magic store to buy plastic tricks. Keep that in mind. This book is not about bad magicians. It's not about clowns or comics who happen to use a magic trick in their act. Herein we will be discussing only the suavest, most magical of magicians—the ones who can present an illusion in a startling and mystifying way such that you really believe, as you watch it, that there was no logical, realistic way for the feat to have been accomplished. Those are the magicians I speak about here. The rest are not worth mentioning.

Optical Illusions

Illusions, illusions! We keep talking about illusions here! But none of the illusions mentioned are like anything you're used to reading about when you read about illusions. Usually when you hear about an illusion, it's an optical illusion, a visual design that confuses the eye and mind. How do optical illusions fit in with the mind-benders that magicians use to distort reality?

The connection is simple to see. Let's start with one of the most famous optical illusions of all, invented by German psychologist Franz Carl Müller-Lyer. In the figure below, which line is longer? The line from A to B, or from X to Y?

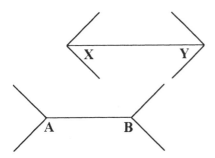

Fig. 12. The Müller-Lyer arrows is a well-known optical illusion.

Ha! I tricked you! If you guessed "they're both the same size" you're wrong! Actually, the X–Y line is longer than A–B. However, the placement of the arrowheads, and our preconceived notions about optical illusions, cause us to incorrectly believe that the lines are the same size. An illusion of this sort can be directly translated into a magical effect. We can imagine a magician using these lines as the basis for a three-dimensional stage prop. Perhaps these could be two halves of a box to hold an assistant who vanishes. Because the sides of the box look the same length, the audience assumes that the two halves fit neatly together. However, since one half is larger than the other, the assistant can slip out the gap. Later the box is opened to show that the assistant has vanished. With a little ingenuity, most optical illusions can be recreated on a grand scale for stage in some manner or another.

Many of the large-scale magic tricks use optical illusions to get you to believe a wall or platform is thinner than it really is. For example, consider a box that an assistant climbs into and then disappears from. One way to do the trick would be to have the assistant hide inside the wall of the box. The wall is designed to look thin, much too thin to contain a person. However, the assistant can hide inside it because it's not as thin as it looks. Optical illusion is at play here! The edge of the box can be painted matte black with a reflective strip down the middle. This divides up the wall into three thin stripes. The black bands visually recede while the narrow, reflective band stands out, looking like a thin ray of light. The eye is deceived because we don't see the three separate bands as one large piece (which it is). It looks like three *thin* bands, none of which are wide enough to contain a person. It's reminiscent of the heavy person who wears vertical stripes to look thinner. In this case it's the magician's apparatus that wears stripes for the same reason.

Why are there optical illusions? Perceptual illusions? Most of us take our eyesight for granted. We see things all the time; they are what they are. This thing here is a book. You know what a book looks like, and this thing you're holding happens to look exactly like a book. Ergo, this is a book. Why then do our eyes deceive us at times? This issue comes up again and again in this book, and will come up in any discussion of magic. You know this is a book because it is "obvious" that it is a book. However, there are plenty of situations that are not so obvious. In those cases your eyes and mind don't have enough clues to determine with certainty the true nature of the object, so your brain takes its best guess. When you look at the arrow illusion above, you made an initial best guess automatically, just by eyeballing the arrows. Being a skeptical person, you may have then looked at the arrows more carefully to revise your answer, maybe even going so far as to make rough measurements of the arrows with your fingers. At that point you would have come up with a different, more correct answer. But it remains true that to get the correct answer required supplying more information to your brain.

Let's do a neat "arts and crafts" project that will demonstrate one way in which magicians use our minds' "best guesses" to trick us.

CREATE MAGIC!—MAGIC TUBE ILLUSION

For this project you will need two rectangular sheets of paper (8½″ x 11″) and clear tape. The paper can be construction paper or notebook paper or copier paper, but just make sure it is bendable and has four straight sides. Now follow these instructions:

1. Take one piece of paper and hold it so that the long ends are at the top and bottom.
2. We are going to make a tube. Gently curve up the bottom of the paper so that it meets the top edge. Do not fold or crease the paper; simply edge the corners to-

gether. Use two or three pieces of clear tape to fasten the two long sides of the page together.

3. Fluff out the paper so that it is a long, round tube.

At this point we are going to repeat the process with a second piece of paper, but we are going to tape together only one end of the tube.

4. Pick up a second sheet of paper, and curve it along its vertical axis as you did the first piece.
5. Apply a piece of clear tape on the right-hand side, where the edges meet.
6. Hold this semi-tube vertically, with the open end at the top. The tape should be facing you. Take the top two corners of the paper and overlap them by about an inch or an inch and a half. Use a piece of clear tape to fasten the overlapped corners.

You now have a tapered, cone-shaped tube whose top and bottom are taped together, and whose top has a smaller diameter than its bottom.

7. Carefully slide the second, cone tube inside the straight tube. Make sure you insert the cone tube all the way inside the straight tube.

Congratulations, you now have a magic tube! Look through the "large end," where the inside tube is the same size as the outside tube. You can see through to the other side, and it looks perfectly normal. Now look at the "small end," the tip of the inside cone. Here you can see empty space between the inside cone tube and the outside straight tube (figure 13).

Fig. 13. The magic tube from the magician's point of view. The magician sees the cone-shaped inner tube, but the audience sees straight through what looks like a completely normal, empty tube.

This tube-within-a-tube is something that magicians will often use. Imagine the possibilities! You can hide scarves, ribbons, or ropes in that empty space. Make sure to show only the large end to the audience, and they won't see any of it. You can then mutter some magic words, rip the tube in half, and pull out a colorful assortment of items from inside what was obviously empty just a few moments before.

You might have to experiment with different sizes for the small end of the cone. You don't want to make it too small, because then its small size becomes apparent. But you don't want to make it too big, because then there is no room to hide items.

Try pointing the large end of the tube at a mirror, as if you were a magician showing your audience that the tube is empty. You will be amazed at how real and natural the tube looks. Even though you know the gimmick and you know the secret, the perceptual illusion persists. That's what this is, after all: a perceptual/optical illusion. Our minds are used to seeing the road in front of us stretching out to the horizon—we know very well that faraway points of the road are smaller than the near-to-us parts. Just like in this tube. We expect the further-away end to look smaller, and so the mind is not surprised to see exactly that effect. Furthermore, the tube is so flimsily constructed and looks so homemade, it is doubtful that there is any trickery involved, especially when the magician takes the reassuring steps of showing the tube's emptiness to the audience, and to poke his magic wand through its center, reaffirming the hollowness that the eyes have already seen.

Optical illusions can help to psychologically direct the audience's thoughts. Consider figure 14. Which doughnut has the bigger hole?

Fig. 14. Which doughnut has the larger hole?

It looks like the hole on the left is bigger. Both holes are actually the same size.

The principle behind this very convincing illusion is that our brains like to compare things with their surroundings. It is very difficult to just compare the two holes. We find ourselves comparing the holes in relation to their "doughnuts" first, and then comparing the results of that comparison with the comparison that was made about the other hole and its surrounding doughnut. The hole on the left takes up more of the doughnut's surface area than the hole on the right, thus when the two ratios are compared, the one on the left appears to be bigger.

Magicians can use this principle in their magic. For example, linking rings are always thin (like the left doughnut). In the linking rings illusion, the big hole is emphasized as the rings are seen to effortlessly pass through each other. But in other illusions, like when a thick rubber washer or thick wood blocks are made to magically appear threaded or unthreaded on a string, the thickness promotes an illusion that the hole is smaller so it would be very difficult for the ring or block to pass through the string. In those cases the solidness of the ring is emphasized. I'm also reminded of a stage illusion, sometimes called Permeability, that is currently popular. This illusion has an A-frame in which a woman is standing. There is a triangular hole through the frame. The magician pushes his body through the hole in the frame, and therefore through the woman's body as well. In this illusion, the thickness and wideness of the frame serves to make the inside hole appear smaller than it actually is, just like in the right-hand doughnut above. Also, black rubber covers the hole in the A-frame to further obscure the fact that it is a big, gaping hole.

I once saw a startling and effective illusion at a mall. I was riding down the escalator trying to find the electronics floor but discovering only women's underwear and Mexican crockery. Hanging from the ceiling of the lower level I was descending to were ornamental glass slabs bordered with gold trim. Looking through one I could see the sales floor of the lower level, and standing there was a woman purchasing the very stereo I wanted to buy. Something caught my eye in the other direction, and when I turned back toward the woman she was gone. Literally vanished in a single moment, along with the heavy stereo carton. My eyes searched the sales floor and then I saw her again, standing exactly where she had been before—behind me!

I knew what had happened. I thought I was seeing her through the glass, but really I was seeing a reflection of her in the glass. When I was on the escalator, her reflection was very real and visible in the hanging glass plate. I turned away, but when I looked forward again I was now looking at the actual sales floor, not the floor behind me that was reflected in the glass. Poof! A disappearance in an instant.

You often see a variation on this illusion while riding buses or trains. Looking out a window on the opposite side of the bus, traffic is clearly visible passing the bus. However, looking closer, one sees that the traffic is coming *at* the bus from the opposite direction. The traffic is not directly through the window, but rather, reflected in it. What you see is not what you get.

Sometimes similar effects can be seen at night looking through a window. A restaurant has sliding glass doors. Looking outside at the patio at night it is impossible to tell if someone is approaching the restaurant from outside, or is coming up behind you. With preparation and proper misdirection, a magician could make an audience think he is approaching from the outside. Then the doors open to reveal he has vanished! While all eyes are on the empty space outside, the magician could sneak into a "locked" trunk to add an extra element of surprise to the disappearance. This would work particularly well as a Metamorphosis-style illusion—the assistant who had been in the trunk reappears when the doors open. She then goes over and opens the trunk to show the magician unexplainably inside.

That is about all I want to say of optical illusions at this point, except perhaps to say you should always be suspicious of frames and glass panes in magic shows. It is important to remember that there are illusions of all kinds. Optical illusions deceive your eyes. Audio illusions mislead your ears.

Tactile illusions dupe your fingers. Taste illusions confuse your tongue. The brain is an imperfect organ—any kind of sensory input into it can be played with, messed around, and can fool you to some degree.

But illusion by itself is not enough to make a good magic show. That is a point I want to stress and repeat and stress again. By itself an illusion may be clever and deceitful and intellectually interesting, but it's not an entertaining magic show. Too many would-be amateur magicians buy a plastic little "magic trick" from the toy store, and then go off in a few minutes and show it around to all their friends and family. You know what I'm talking about; that's not a good display of magic. That's just someone who knows the gimmick underlying the illusion. Showing off the illusion to everybody does not make for *magic*. MAGIC! A magical atmosphere. A mystical, wondrous, awe-inspiring air of miracles. No, the illusion alone doesn't do that. The magician must have certain knowledge and skills. The magician must know how to enhance the illusion, drawing out its mysticism the way salt brings out flavor in foods. The magician is more than just a presenter of tricks. The magician must be specially trained in the fine art of creating and sharing a magical atmosphere. These are the kinds of skills we will talk about in part two.

Magic Is Non Sequitur

The students walk into their Logic 101 class, sit down, and the professor stands up and says, "Good day, class, my name is Dr. Roberto. Today's lecture is going to begin with a brain problem. I'm going to prove to you that every person on earth is the same height.

"There are lots of people in the world, and many of them are the same height. I can make this assumption because I'm six feet tall, and my friend is six feet tall. And I'm sure that for other people, there will always be someone else who is the same height as them. Let's assume that I choose to compare people of the same height. I start by comparing myself to my friend. Good, so far the theory is working, for we are both the same height. Now I compare myself to Person A, and again we are all six feet tall (because I can choose to compare people of the same height). Next I compare my friend to Person B, also the same height.

"Incidentally, even though I'm the same height as Person A, and my friend is the same height as Person B, that doesn't mean that Person A and B are the same height as each other. So I compare them together, and they too are the same height, as logic dictates they must be. Now I continue pulling out people in groups of two, comparing them, then pulling out representatives of each group who have matching heights to make further comparisons. In this fashion I can continue on to prove that every person on the planet is the same height!" The professor smiles.

Clearly something has gone terribly wrong here. Either the professor's proof is bad, or there are six-foot babies walking around. I sincerely hope that it's the professor's logic at fault, because I'm not thrilled with the prospect of having to change diapers on six-foot babies.

The professor's error lies in the initial assumption. The professor assumes that any two people that are compared must be the same height. The professor ends up assuming the conclusion from the premise, a logical no-no. It's like the tail chasing the dog.

Stage magic is like the professor's puzzle in the sense that magic is based on invalid initial assumptions. The magician presents a logical "proof," but obscures the fact that the original assumption (that no trickery will be used) is actually the conclusion that we are meant to draw from the act. In any case, it is an invalid assumption because the magician certainly does use trickery of one form or another.

A magician's proof consists of visual clues. For instance, if the magician is levitating a tiger, he will pass hoops around the tiger to "prove" there are no strings holding it up.

The magician will use other kinds of proofs as well, to prove the assumption that he is not using trickery. For instance, he will use various ruses to hide the trickery from us (for example, misdirection, camouflage), and will not let us see the gimmicks that make the tricks work. The illusion is real only if the magician proves to us that it is real. And his proof is based on our assuming that the proofs he shows us are themselves real. But obviously they are not real. Obviously there is something fishy about the proofs. We make an incorrect assumption when we believe that the hoops mean anything if they are passed around the levitating tiger. Our impression of the event—that the tiger is levitating—is a non sequitur. A non sequitur, translated literally from the Latin, is a conclusion drawn incorrectly from the premises. Magic is a non sequitur because the proofs that the audience is given are never truthful enough to draw a magical conclusion from. However, lacking certain consequential evidence to the contrary, the audience is forced into believing the non sequitur as true. If I show you the hat is empty and then proceed to pull a bunny rabbit from it, I have obviously left out an important part of the proof. I've left out the part where I prove that I will *not* scoop up a rabbit from a bag behind the table when I tip my hat. Clearly I cannot prove that I won't scoop up a rabbit into the hat from a ledge, because to do so would give away the trick. Instead, I as a magician have to pretend that I've covered all the bases. Hopefully with my confidence and acting I manage to convey to you that I have sufficiently proven that what you are about to see will be magic.

Let's get back to Professor Roberto for a moment. Let's say the professor wraps up class for the day, heads out the door, and walks quickly to the faculty bathrooms, mindful of a full bladder (and late for a faculty football game). Right before getting to the men's room, the professor suddenly stops walking. Professor Roberto refuses to go into the men's room, regardless of the aforementioned full bladder. The question for all you detectives out there is, "Why does the professor refuse to go into the bathroom?"

Magic is mystifying because it breaks our logical assumptions about how we believe the world works. Logic is so ingrained in us that even animals and senile people have been shown to be surprised by and appreciate magic, even when others might have deemed their minds not capable of distinguishing the impossibility of magic. But they can distinguish it. Both senile people and animals have been shown to understand spatial relationships between objects, the barriers between them, and what are possible and impossible operations on those objects.

It seems quite illogical for the professor to refuse to step into the bathroom. There must be a dead body in there, or at least the stench of one, to cause the professor to stay away. A lack of logical proofs often leads us to "make up stories" like this, to explain what is unexplainable. We simply don't have enough clues to figure out why Dr. Roberto won't walk into the bathroom. The magician always hides or obscures some clues from you. If you're reading this book, you want to try and find ways to unhide and unobscure those clues. That may not always be possible, but by using these techniques you can usually come up with a good guess. In this case, I'd guess Professor Roberto won't step into the men's room because she's a woman.

Of course, I'll never know if this guess is right or not. Magic is an eternal suspense. Like I've said, the working of an illusion is often compared to the building tension in a mystery story, with the magician as the devious murderer who plots a crime that looks as though it could not have been committed by him. In both cases, clues are left behind (the magician's proofs) that reveal a certain story to the audience or reader. The difference between magic and mystery is that there comes a point in a mystery story where the suspense is over and the murderer's method is revealed. That never happens in magic. Even if you figure out how it's done, the suspense isn't over, because in magic, the murderer never reveals the method of the crime.

I'd like to end this talk of logic with a magic trick that uses, or, rather, misuses logic in such a way that the conclusion of the trick—the magical illusion—stems very clearly from an illogical premise that is presented as valid truth.

CREATE MAGIC!—THAT'S KNOT POSSIBLE!

This can be presented as a magical effect or as a puzzler. Either way it is startling. You show a rope to your audience of one. I use a short length of clothesline for this. Hand over the rope, telling the person to hold both ends and tie a knot in the rope without letting go of them. After some unsuccessful trying they soon realize it is impossible to tie a knot in a rope without letting go of one end of the rope.

It is very important that *they* realize it is impossible to tie the knot in the rope. It may be that they think it's merely *difficult* to do so. If they think that, then when you do it they will see it as a trick rather than a magical illusion. So, as they are trying out different approaches, you should offer them helpful advice such as, "Try making two loops and pushing your hands through both simultaneously." Say anything that sounds reasonable, and show a genuine concern for their figuring it out. After a while, they will realize for sure that it is topologically impossible. Take the rope back from them, and agree that it is impossible to do through ordinary means. Thank goodness you're not an ordinary person!

You hold both ends of the rope and, without letting go, begin to form the knot in it. As the knot takes shape you say, "This is the point in the trick where people most often think I'm cheating. So why don't you, without letting go, hold the ends of the rope and pull it tight." Your loyal subject then takes the rope ends off your hands, and pulls. A nice knot is formed and the person is left holding the rope, evidence of your supernatural abilities flaunted in his face, because it is indisputable that a pair of hands was holding the rope the whole time and never let go, thus there was no opportunity for that knot to form in the rope.

The trick is actually simple to do, and the method I describe below is not the easiest way to do it. The reason I describe a more complicated version is because if it looks too simple, the spectator will be more inclined to realize it is just a dumb trick. But if you make it look like you're working hard at it, the spectator will be more inclined to believe some skill or magic is involved.

Take the ends of the rope between your index and middle fingers of each hand. "Notice how the knot forms without ever letting go of the rope." Start off by making some false moves with the string, to confuse the person watching. Pass your right hand above and around your left. There will be a loop of string under your left hand. Push your right hand around the left and down through the loop. "See how I scoop it up?" you ask. Now pull your left hand out from the loop of string. At this point you can do some more moves to hide those crucial moves. You might want to wrap the string around your left hand a few times then pull the string through the loops. When you're done misdirecting, tell the spectator: "This is the point in the trick where people most often think I'm cheating. So why don't you take the ends of the rope and pull it tight." Pass it over to the sucker and let him pull the knot tight for you.

The Magical Life and Mindset

"When my father was in vaudeville," said actor Alan Alda in an interview,

> I would stand in the wings and watch the magician. I could see how he made the audience think there was nothing in the box. I was seeing him from the side; I'd see how he'd reach under the table and put the pigeons in the box. Standing on the side—watching and hearing the reaction of the

audience and seeing the performers five feet away, reading their thoughts, watching them time their performance—is an education that you can't get from the other side of the footlights. You can watch actors create their illusions, but if you don't see where they get the pigeons from, you don't really know how they're doing it.[2]

Alda suggests watching from the sidelines to see how actors find the secret pigeons that motivate and enrich their acting. That of course is a fruitful way to learn how magic is performed as well. Watching from backstage, being able to see things from the assistant's side, would certainly reveal a lot more than the magician would care to make public.

However, if you do learn magic that way you're still missing some very important things. With magic, seeing things from backstage can only teach you mechanical gimmicks. But with magic, the most important stuff is not the particular gimmick used for particular effects. What is important is the stuff available on stage—in sight of the audience every night—that never leaves your line of vision. And that is the magician himself or herself, the way the magician presents the magic, the psychology of the magic: the things that are so obvious and so visible that they are invisible. As a watcher and analyzer of magic shows, it is up to you to separate the invisible from the nonexistent. If you see a subtle movement that looks like it is hiding a palmed coin, it will be up to you to decide whether the movement really was hiding a coin, or if the movement was there as a subterfuge, or if it was intended at all.

ACTING AND REACTING

"A magician is an artist, that's all. He's just another artist. He's an actor." This said by magician James Randi, and that's all there is to it. Magicians are actors who know how to make us believe the character they play, which is a magician, and that the magician can perform acts of magic. Or they make us believe that acts of magic are happening around them.

Matthew Dwinells, an illusion artist from Talkerton, New Jersey, explained, "Magicians have to make themselves believe what is obviously not real, and the audience has to believe that from the expression on their face, from their gestures."

Therefore, it is not surprising to find that a number of actors and entertainers started out as magicians: Harry Anderson, Johnny Carson ("The Great Carsoni"), Dick Cavett, Arsenio Hall, Carl Ballantine ("McHale's Navy"). Jimmy Stewart was once an assistant to his magician friend Bill Neff. Woody Allen has always had a fascination with magic, which shows up occasionally in his writings and films. Steve Martin was a "kid magician," said Sandorse, a local conjurer. "He worked in Disneyland for years and years behind the magic counter." He also did magic tricks at birthday parties and would later incorporate magic into his writing, such as his play *Floating Lady*; of course, he also later appeared in *Leap of Faith*. Milton Berle also was a magician ("You wanna see a card trick, kid?"). Orson Welles was also at one time a professional magician. Some other magicians have made repeat acting performances, including Penn Jillete in the movie *Hackers*, and both Penn & Teller in "Sabrina the Teenage Witch." The nineteenth century's "Wizard of the North" acted in theater in *Rob Roy*. And in modern times, conjurer Christopher Hart played the role of Thing's hand in the movie *The Addams Family*!

Look how many of these notable names are talk show hosts. Dwinells explains this succinctly: hosts are "good with reactions." They have to rehearse their comedy and bits just as any magician needs to rehearse his magic.

However, what he and other magicians point out is that while a magician is an actor, an actor cannot be a magician. (Unless the actor actually is a magician.) "Magic is a mindset. It's not something you can pick up in six months . . . even the jargon, facial expressions, how you handle your hands." Dwinells talked about how actors playing magicians on TV don't look right—they don't move and act the way magicians do—because they don't know how to be magicians. "A real magician, magic is in his brain. He knows the way to look to make the audience believe. But when actors play magicians, there's something missing." There's actually a lot of things missing. That jargon, the facial expressions, and the like, all of which sound so insignificant when compared to the ultimate magical effect being achieved, actually are very meaningful. It is because of those slight, understated mannerisms used by magicians that the magic performed becomes believable. When actors play magicians, they look like they are doing tricks. When a good magician does magic—he's really doing magic.

You should keep all of these things in mind as you read this book. The ways that a talented magician will try to create an impression in your mind are many and varied and often so slight as to seem insignificant. But it is because of their insignificance that they are so effective. And all of these small impressions are planted in your mind by acting.

PART TWO

WHAT ARE ILLUSIONS MADE OF?

With that background behind us, the next section continues to examine magic from an on-stage perspective. If you were a magician, what would be going through your mind on stage? As it turns out, there's a lot more to think about than just the current trick. The magician tries to control as many aspects of the theater experience as possible, and in so doing, creates his illusions. After exploring the art of chicanery, we will start to really analyze the action. This section ends with an encyclopedia of "Things to Look For" when watching a magic show in order to decode the mysteries and figure out how the trick is done. As a final step there is a chapter on "Crashing the Clan" so that you can further break through the shroud of secrecy that surrounds magic and perhaps even become a magician yourself.

4

The Art of Chicanery

This section looks at the skills of the magician and the things he is thinking about while on stage. You may not realize that the magician has a lot more on his mind than just making the current trick work. Every motion and every utterance is carefully devised and controlled. The entire layout of the performance space is arranged in a certain way, and the way the audience interacts with the show is cleverly orchestrated by the magician and his crew to achieve a desired effect. As one magician told me, "There are ways to control the audience. [We] give a suggestion, like a hypnotist." These "suggestions" are things you would never think about if you didn't know to look for them, but once you know about them you will see them in every show by a skilled performer. This section focuses on these hidden aspects of the art of chicanery, aspects that are used to control the performance . . . and you in the audience.

Movement

Magicians move their bodies with fluidity, grace, and poise. Look at the way David Copperfield dances through his routines. All magicians put a certain fancy flair into every gesture, every wave of the hand. Even the way they hold a deck of cards is so beautiful you could take a picture of it and frame it. This all looks like showmanship, and in fact there is an element of show to it. But there is a more important reason for all the posturing. As usual, there is hidden meaning behind the showy gestures.

Have you ever tried palming a coin? Palming is the act of hiding a small object in the palm of the hand. Most people can do it to some extent. Try it with a large coin, like a half dollar. There are many different kinds of palms.

All have one thing in common: they force your hand into an unnatural contortion. Nobody walks around with their hand like that! True, the best magicians can palm coins and make it look very natural. But even the best have difficulty palming a playing card and making it look natural. Palming a card (or in some cases, an entire deck of cards) requires keeping the fingers straight, and the whole hand slightly arched. There are many such moves, most particular to a single trick, that require the magician to move in a certain way, or act in a certain way.

That is why magicians *constantly* move with that dramatic gracefulness. They want you to believe that the elegant suaveness is part of themselves, not part of the trick at hand. When they always move like that it brings down your defenses, it imparts a sort of mysticism over the whole event, *and it hides the few times when the motions are being done to actually conceal something.* Movement plays such fundamental roles in magic that magician Charles Pecor, a professor of speech and drama, has advised the student magician to read a book on body language in order to better understand the ways that gestures and body motion communicate through nonverbal means. Only then, he suggests, will the magician have the fullest sense of how those motions can be exploited to misdirect the audience's eyes and thoughts. As a painter or sculptor must study anatomy, the magician must study natural motions and holdings of the body in order to know what "looks" correct and what does not.

Some magicians have resorted to cheap gimmicks to help them attain a natural look. Early in this century, a magician named Berthold Reese was going around doing a mentalism act that had many of his viewers fooled into believing he really had supernatural powers. He had the showmanship down pat, though perhaps not the technique—he smoked a fat cigar throughout his performance because the cigar gave him an excuse to curve his hand, thus making it easier to conceal a folded slip of paper that contained the prediction he was supposedly using his psychic powers to unveil.[1] Every time he lifted the cigar to his mouth it would afford him an opportunity to peek at the hidden paper.

Some lissome dancing can set the mood while also helping out the trick. Dancing may be necessary to get the magician (or assistant) to a certain spot on stage, so they are standing over a trap door, or standing near the back wall or a curtain through which they will slip out. Without the choreographed dancing, there would've been no logical reason for them to *be* at that part of the stage in the first place! Remember, the magician is in control of every action on stage, and any action may be a clue to the mystery.

A final reason that magicians must pay attention to how they move is so that their message is conveyed with the least distractions. This is true for any public speaker, whether it be the president of the United States, a stand-up comedian, an actor, or a magician. There are certain distracting movements oft-performed by ill-at-ease lecturers such as rocking back and forth, holding the arms stiffly at the sides, and keeping the hands clenched over the crotch or held rigid. These will be distracting to the audience and take away from the words being spoken. They are even more damaging to the magician whose voice and body must combine into one flawless performance. Unwanted gestures may take away from any intentional misdirections the magician is trying to set up. These movements are *dis*tracting, but a magician's movements must be *at*tracting—they must attract the eye in a certain way, at a certain time, to achieve a certain effect. Magician Gary Kurtz wrote a set of lecture notes called "Leading with the Head" in which he describes how he exploits constantly shifting weight to misdirect the audience by creating alternate bands of tension and relaxation.[2] Thus the magician, more than the stand-up comic or lounge singer, must be aware of how his body is moving or not moving at all times.

PANTOMIME

Pantomime, also called mime, is the art of creating illusion through gesture, movement, and motion. The voice is not used, although some mimes will use music, sounds or noises to enrich the illusion. Pantomime is an important part of stage magic, but magicians can use pantomime in a surprising way—sometimes they accompany it with their voice. Magicians are allowed to do so: after all, they're magicians, not mimes.

Let's look at pantomime as a pantomimist does it. A mime tries to create a *full-body* illusion. Emotions like sadness or fear can be easily expressed via exaggerated facial expressions. But a mime will not use just facial features to communicate the emotion, but his or her entire body. To show fear, the arms may be outstretched, posture crouched, the body fearfully retracted away from some horrid thing, stance low to show lower status—it all adds up to a poise that communicates fear. The face may be entirely emotionless and yet the illusion is achieved because the contortions and movement of the entire body indicates the emotion. "If any part of your body is not working with you, it detracts from that image" says master mime Mark Stolzenberg.[3] Of course, magicians will try to do the same thing—using every available option to form and enhance the illusion.

Not only emotion, but motion too, can be illusionistically created by the mime. For instance, one of the fundamental miming techniques, "countermotion," occurs when part of the mime's body moves in one direction, indicating motion in that direction, while simultaneously another part of the mime's body moves in the opposite direction.[4] For instance, the mime is pulling on an imaginary rope hanging from the ceiling. He grasps the pretend rope and lifts up on his toes as if he were pulling himself up. Simultaneously, the mime will bring down his hands in countermotion. The countermotion helps create the impression that the mime is pulling himself. It also leaves him some "growing room." Now he can stretch up his arms again as he pulls up on the imaginary rope. Countermotion may also be used to help simulate walking or running a great distance. The audience focuses on the direction the mime is facing as he "walks" or "runs," and therefore pays attention to the arm and leg motions that seem to propel the mime in that same direction. However, they are not attuned to the countermotion in the opposite direction by those same arms and legs, which keeps the mime standing on the same plot of floor.

To summarize, mimes can create the illusion that they are moving their bodies (when the motion is actually ineffective), but they can also create the illusion that they are *not* moving their bodies (but motion occurs anyway). For example, one technique is called the conveyor belt side glide, where it looks as though the performer is being pulled sideways on a conveyer belt.[5]

The upshot of all this is that mimes have the ability to create familiar images, actions, motions, and movements, almost literally out of thin air. In the hands of a skilled performer these techniques can be convincingly played out in such a way that the audience believes the movements are real, to a certain degree. On one level, the audience knows there is no conveyor belt pulling the mime across the floor; but on another level the audience has become absorbed and interested in the performance, and so they don't think those heretical thoughts. On this accepting level, the audience's collective mind looks at the gestures and the movements and they use the physical clues to recognize what the movements mean. On this level, wanting to be entertained and to enjoy the show, they pay attention to the meaning they have inferred from the motion, and less to the reality of the situation. On some basic level, the audience really does see the mime "sitting in a chair," then "pulling on a rope," then "running a marathon." These mechanisms of shifting attention can be quite useful to the magician. We'll get to that a little later.

As you know, the typical mime wears whiteface. The functional reason for whiteface is to make facial expressions stand out; the psychological reason is that "it identifies you as a mime. You are able to draw attention to yourself more easily."[6] Later we will look at the dress code of the magician. The highly stylized look of both kinds of entertainer is important in the sense that if you can look at a man and know that he is a mime, then you know what to expect from him. And you don't try to turn up the sound on the television.

When the audience knows that someone is a mime (or a magician, or a comedian, etc.) it puts them in a certain state of mind. They will become more accepting of the performance. The audience feels the walls of the box that enclose the mime, they can see the bicycle he rides, feel the tug on the rope that he pulls. In short, the audience identifies with the mime's actions and reactions to common physical situations. They know exactly what it's like to knock on a door or put their hand up against a wall. If the pantomime is good enough, we can almost feel the imaginary wall pressing against our hands.

Now take that illusion, that physical feeling that has been transferred off the stage and into our nerve endings, and put the illusion into the repertoire of the magician. Mime offers the magician yet another subtle way of creating deception. With mime, the magician can seem to perform simple acts—such as moving a sponge ball from one hand to another—that never really happen. The sponge ball stays in the first hand *in reality*, but in the physical feelings of our minds, the ball has switched. We know it has switched because we have *felt* it. We know what it feels like to transfer an object from one hand to another. Magicians don't call it pantomime. They call it sleight of hand.

Magician Jeff McBride incorporates silent mime effectively into his act. In the show I attended, a candlelit nightclub venue in the Mardi Gras Showroom at the Showboat Hotel in Atlantic City, McBride performed an almost voiceless act. His gestures, dance, and the musical accompaniment told the magical story.

In one illusion he ripped up a plastic streamer into tiny shreds, and put the pieces in his mouth. He swallowed the pieces, let them churn in his stomach, regurgitated the now fully restored streamer, and let yards and yards of streamer unfurl out of his mouth whole again, new. The trick is a variation on the "threaded needles" that Houdini made popular in his 1925 full-length magic show. Houdini would put loose needles and thread into his mouth, make chewing motions, then pull out the thread with the needles threaded at intervals along the length. The trick has also been done with razor blades, and is always pretty much accomplished the same way, by having two sets of needles (or razors, or streamers), one of which is hidden in the mouth in a safety packet, before the trick begins. A substitution is made inside the mouth for the pre-threaded needles or razors (or restored streamers). Doing a pantomime act, McBride has the advantage of not having to talk. He won't accidentally spit out a piece of streamer while pronouncing a diphthong. He was also able to make use of mime to convey the swallowing, churning in the stomach, and upheaval of the streamers. His hands, half dancing and half physically representing the ongoing mending in his stomach, whirled circles around each other, visually demonstrating the action in what the audience could not see—the inside of his stomach. Then his hands (and suitably rising, stuttering music) traced upwards the path of the streamer up from his stomach, through his throat and into and out of his mouth. We could "see" the streamers as they were pushed up from his stomach by his throat muscles, because his gestures and movements indicated its happening. His movements were not iconographic. That is, he did not simply point to his stomach, his chest, or his throat as the streamers supposedly worked their way up his body. No, his movements were emotional, they were reflections of what he was feeling. We could see and feel the movement of the streamers because he painted this gesture picture of *how he felt* as the streamers rose through his system. We could feel the sensations McBride conveyed in his miming.

If he hadn't mimed, the streamers would never have left his mouth, so to speak. If he hadn't mimed, then we wouldn't have known that they did leave his mouth and got restored in his stomach. On the other hand, ever since I saw the performance, whenever I think about this illusion, I think about how he swallowed and regurgitated the streamers. I know logically that he didn't swallow them, but emotionally I can't get it out of my head that that's what he did. Yes, the magic has worked. The illusion has been created in my mind. Even knowing how the "trick" is done, the illusion has still been effectively created.

The whole act was accompanied by musical accompaniment and also by a side-of-the-stage drummer obscured behind a black gauze curtain. The sounds and the mime were effectively integrated into a routine that made use of the Lota Trick. Lota is a common prop, a gimmicked bowl that can be purchased from magic dealers. It is often used for comedic effect. The magician keeps emptying water from it, and every time he thinks he's dumped out the last of the water, some more appears inside it. The gimmick is an ancient one that has appeared in East Indian magic, and perhaps in Peruvian pre-Columbian cultures centuries ago. The bowls come in different shapes, with different names. One version is shaped more like a spittoon or a squat vase, thus giving it a flared-out part on the bottom. The walls are hollow, and extra liquid is stored inside. The flared-out design offers more liquid capacity than straight sides would allow. The magician keeps his finger on a secret airhole while pouring the water. When he lets go of the hole, water flows from the flared portion into the mid-section. With a finger on the hole, he can empty out all the water from the vase, thus giving the impression it is empty. As soon as he puts it down, however, the airhole becomes uncovered, and water rushes in from the flared outer portion to fill the mid-section. By carefully controlling how much water has been poured, the magician can come back to the vase several times during the course of the performance and make it seem as if the vase is continuously replenishing itself.

Here's how McBride used the Lota. He held out the empty brass bowl, and an invisible water droplet fell from the sky into his bowl. Then another drop fell, and another. Now the bowl was magically filled with quite visible water, which he thirstily drank down. Of course, nobody believed that invisible water fell from the sky, but a good illusion was created. Every time a droplet fell, a musical *plink* would sound as the drop hit the bowl, and McBride would lower the bowl a few inches, as if the water had hit hard and heavied the bowl in his hands.

Now I come to the crux of the issue. I've just been talking about water droplets falling from the sky. It was a very convincing, realistic display. But of course, in reality no droplets fell at all. The sound and the downward movement of the bowl combined to *become* the falling water droplet. As an audience, we know exactly what is happening, even when absolutely nothing is happening. That's amazing. That's illusion.

Sound and Music

I mentioned before Jeff McBride's mixing of dance, music, and mime to create illusion. The whole show creates an alien atmosphere, with his use of weird masks, exotic Asian costuming, strange lighting, thundering drums, and smoke. The other component was the sound and music that accompanied almost the whole presentation. Sometimes the music *was* sound—the sound of beating drums. At one point McBride rolled out a giant drum (from which a woman would later magically emerge), and "proved" that it was solid by banging on it to produce a thunderous boom. By that time the on-stage drumming by his assistants and the off-stage music had culminated together into a loud, booming, pulsating rhythm, blended together so well that it was impossible to say whether McBride was really banging on the drum to produce the noise, or if it was part of the music accompaniment. Of course, these were not thoughts that the audience was supposed to have. The audience sat back and watched and enjoyed McBride banging on the drum, producing the marvelous sound. One little girl screeched, "He bang so *loud!*" and covered her ears. But of course, he wasn't banging at all.

Sound is used by the magician in such tricks as Miser's Fortune, where a great quantity of coins is pulled from thin air, little boys' ears, and, in raunchier shows, cleavage. The sad fact is, coins can*not* be pulled from the air (you can verify this for yourself right now), and so the magician must rely on a trick to accomplish the miracle. Primarily, most of the coins produced are actually the same coin. The magician somehow hides it in his hand, produces it, then pretends to drop it in a metal bucket where it produces a hearty metallic *clang* upon hitting bottom. Sound is used as proof. The metal bucket may also have a spring-mounted lever secretly implanted in its handle. The magician can press the lever with his thumb to create the sound of a coin falling into the bucket. Of course, since the magician has in reality retained the coin in his hand, he can go on to produce it again and again, assuming there are plenty of little boys' ears and grown women's cleavages on hand.

Instructions that accompany such rigged buckets tell the magician to shake the bucket vigorously so the audience can hear the coins rattling around inside. What the audience doesn't know is that there are coins hidden under the false bottom of the pail. The magician can pretend to drop a coin, the bucket is empty but we hear the coin drop due to the secret lever, and then we hear all the many coins rattling around due to hidden coins inside the pail bottom. There doesn't have to be many coins to make a large sound. We've all heard the ferocious bark of a watchdog and later found out that the monster we imagined was really a poodle.

We human beings rely so much on visual cues that we often don't realize how much we really do rely on sound cues, and to what extent our mind takes those sounds seriously. We shut a latch or a door and unconsciously expect to hear a click or thud as the door slams into place. We may shut the door a hundred times and never really notice the click, but the one time it doesn't happen, we will give the door an extra shove until we're sure it's closed right, until we hear the door clicking into place.

I've noticed that the elevators in the *Rolling Stone* building on Sixth Avenue in New York make use of sound misdirection, or direction. When the elevator door opens, the elevator may be on an upward path or a downward path. A sound cue is used to indicate which one. If the elevator is going down, a low tone is sung. If it is going up, a high note is emitted.

Certain jobs that rely on computers, like food checkout at a supermarket, use sounds as a cue. A supermarket cashier need not even have a brain, some futurists have lamented, since all cashiers need to do is listen for the beep from the laser scanner announcing that the food package has passed through the scanner properly, indicating that the cashier can move on to the next item, and the next item . . . the next customer, and the next customer.[7] It's a way of "dumbing down" the workforce, by having them rely solely on audio tones, and not needing to think for themselves. Does the name Pavlov ring a bell?

Video games are a good example of effective use of sounds. A buzzer sound may indicate that your on-screen character has been shot at. A triumphant musical call indicates that you've shot down a villain. When the sound is turned off or if the television is on too loud to hear the sound effects, it's more difficult to follow the game, because you get used to the subconscious processing of sounds. Donald A. Norman, a cognitive scientist at the University of California, points out that sound is an essential and effective way that the world reflects the complicated interaction of objects. Parts rub together and make a noise; other sounds are generated when objects are breaking, tearing, crumbling or bouncing, or hitting each other.[8] So much information can be transmitted and received and understood, even in a brief amount of time, that it only makes sense that the magician would try to make use of such cues, either by shaking some imaginary coins and conjuring up the image of a full pail, or the way McBride "shows" water dropping from the ceiling with only some tiny plinks of sound.

Music is used to evoke a certain mood. Envision a movie that shows a woman strolling through a wooded area, picking berries and smelling flowers. Now imagine the same scene accompanied by pulsating heartbeats, tempestuous pounding music, and a heavy, lecherous breathing. The choice of music and overlaid sounds gives an entirely different meaning to the scene. What was once a peaceful display of nature and beauty is now a monstrous, suspenseful trek through a dangerous forest. Veteran movie composer David Raskin has said about the music he makes for movies: "We're manipulators. It's about affecting the audience subliminally. The manipulation involves the music that helps tell the story."[9]

I've seen magicians use this technique to create suspense in their acts. Magicians can buy specially made music on tape or compact disc. The music has "an intense driving force" as one catalog describes it, for use in their acts. One magician I saw played this pounding, suspenseful music at a particular time, and the whole audience was on the edge of their seats waiting to see what would happen. As I was watching the show I suddenly thought, "Hey, almost nothing's going on on stage." All of the excitement and suspense we felt was artificial, built up solely from our knowledge that a certain kind of music equates to suspense. An illusion of suspense was created in our minds when in reality the magician was just walking around on stage tapping a box with his wand or whatever he was doing.[10] This just goes to show how really powerful music is in creating a mood. After all, I remember the music, the suspense, the edge-of-the-seat feeling. But I don't remember at all what was happening on stage or the context of that suspense. In other words, I remember emotions but not specific physical things. This is an issue that will become even more important when we look at how fake psychics, advertisers, politicians, and the like try to deceive us. Often they do so by evoking a mood. If we "believe in them" we can get trapped into doing things for them—even when there is nothing happening on stage. Even when there is no substance to the mood that we are feeling, we act as paramours forever scribing poetry to an unrequited love.

The trick in description is merely a puzzle which requires the necessary dressing to turn it into entertainment. Such dressing is called presentation.—Peter Warlock

Patter and Padding

We've been talking about the importance of sound to the show. The most noticeable sound is that which comes out of the magician's mouth. Words alone have the ability to sway our opinions, to cause us to rise to actions against our will, or to make us empathize with another human being. Mary Matalin, who led President George Bush's re-election campaign against Bill Clinton, tells an anecdote that shows how critical even one word can be. Bush was addressing an audience, and at one point in his speech he deviated slightly from the prepared text. He was saying: "I went along with one Democratic tax increase, and I'm not going to do it again. Ever. *Ever.*" And, as Matalin recounts, "The second 'Ever' was ad libbed." A single word . . . *ad libbed?* Does a single word have such power? Matalin seems to think so:

"Even in my sweat and fatigue, it registered . . . On the way back to the motorcade [Marlin Fitzwater] and I bumped into each other and said, at the same time, 'Ever. *Ever*,' acknowledging that we'd noted it, hoping that nobody else did.

"Well, they did. One extra word made the promise more definitive than the President had been on the subject this campaign."[11] Matalin writes that the media noticed the word, took it as a promise, questioned them relentlessly on the point, and made Bush look as though he were setting himself up for another round of "break the pledge" (for he had broken a similar promise not to raise taxes just a few years before). Bush had given this speech many times before, but he had never gotten himself into trouble with it before. But he had never deviated from the speech as written before. And now, by deviating by just one four-letter word, he was digging a hole for himself.

Magicians, of course, have their own script to follow. *Patter* is the script the magician follows, the words that are said, and the way in which those words are coordinated with the physical movements of the performer and his props. Patter "locates a trick; it gives that trick a meaningful place in the magician's show and in the spectator's daily lives," wrote Robert Stebbins, a social psychologist who has studied the work and lifestyles of magicians. "The trick may actually be impossible to do without the patter, in that the patter justifies the bodily movements and positions shielding the magician's deceptive manoeuvres."[12]

In earlier times, a magician's patter was strange words and incantations. Magic was more easily believed then, as were the magic words. Thus, in the early part of the seventeenth century, there was a magician who called himself Hocus Pocus. While performing every trick he would repeat the words, "*Hocus pocus tontus talontus, vade celerite jubeo.*" Looking through the historical tracts of magic, one can find lots of pseudo-Latin mumbo-jumbo, weirdo words and magic phrases that magicians have bandied about in an effort to confuse the minds and busy the ears of the crowd. Whether it worked is anybody's guess. If the audience believed even a little bit that the magician had some sort of elite knowledge or ability, then perhaps the words served as further proof that the magician was living in a higher plane than they.

Magic words, hocus pocus, abracadabra, and other nonsense sounds are still used, mostly for comedic effect nowadays, and sometimes to dramatize a particular moment in the course of an illusion. However, modern patter is more likely to be very straightforward and subsequently much more deceptively effective. Words are used to introduce an illusion, often by setting a scene of nostalgic childhood or faraway lands or by creating some other emotion in the listener. Words are used throughout a performance to enhance it with a fanciful story. And of course, words are used to misdirect and direct. For example, if I say, "Look at this cookie on a plate." You'll get a totally different picture in your mind than if I say, "Look at this planet in the solar system."

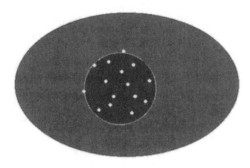

Fig. 15. Cookie or planet?

In ambiguous situations, the magician's words can be the extra shove that pushes people's minds to accept one reality over another. In selecting his words carefully, the magician "elicits certain perspectives and inhibits others."[13]

For instance, as the magician is being lifted high above the stage in a suspended crate he might call out: "I have a fear of heights!" He might describe a trick by saying, "I'll attempt to . . ." Such comments give the impression that the magician has never done this before, that there was no preplanning or rehearsals. It furthers the illusion that the trick is impromptu and that it could be done at any time by the magician.

The stereotypical idea of the con man and used car salesman is of the fast talker who speaks eloquently, smoothly, and quickly so that what comes out of his mouth sounds correct and you can't really argue with it. This is somewhat true of magicians too, although more frequently it is their movements that come out fast and smooth, making it difficult to recall the exact sequence in which the moves were executed. However, there is something to be said for the smooth-talking magician. Certainly the skill comes in handy as an accessory to illusion. It is important that when the magician talks, he is intelligible and believable. That's where the acting comes in, and also where good diction comes into play. When Houdini was starting out, he was known to have been poor at speaking clearly while performing. He would rush through his tricks, trying to quickly get on to the next one, in order to show as many tricks as possible. Few people stuck around to watch his whole performance because they couldn't follow the fast movements and couldn't understand what he was saying. One day a short, red-faced stranger approached the young Houdini and told him to do fewer tricks, do them well, and do them so the audience could follow the action. (The man also pushed Houdini toward concentrating on what he loved most—escaping from chains and locks.) Houdini took the advice to heart and soon was building a reputation for himself as a competent magician. And the crowds started staying.

Another magician, the great Kellar, sacrificed his look for comprehensibility. Kellar always wore a thick, furry mustache until someone criticized that it "muffled his words and prevented those in the rear of his theaters from hearing him."[14] Out came the razor; away went the mustache. Words are too important to a magician to risk having them muffled by a mustache!

PATTER QUIZ

Now we're going to have a pop quiz about patter. But beware, for the quiz consists entirely of trick questions. Here's how the quiz works. First you will read a transcript of a magic trick. Then I'm going to select two quotes that the magician said during the course of the magic trick, and ask you questions about those quotes. Here's the transcript:

A magician standing on stage with a deck of cards has just called up a member of the audience to help him.
Magician: "Take a card. Look at it, show it to the audience. Don't let me see it. Then put it back in the deck."
The volunteer does this.
Volunteer: "All right."
Magician (shuffling the deck): "What'd you say your name was, again?"
Volunteer: "Lucy."
The magician cuts the deck into two halves and places them on the table.
Magician: "Great, now point to a half, Lucy."
Lucy does so.
Magician: "Very good, Lucy, you chose the left half, please turn that deck over. You will see that the bottom card—the card from the very center of the shuffled deck—is the one you randomly selected earlier."
Lucy does this, and is surprised to find her chosen card.

Okay, now here's the pop quiz. Look at the following two quotes excerpted from the transcript, then answer the questions that follow:

(1) "What'd you say your name was, again?"
(2) "Very good, Lucy, you chose the left half, please turn that deck over."

1. Which of these quotes was planned and which was simply tossed out impromptu?
2. Which quote is "patter" and which is simply "padding"?
3. The magician, you'll recall, prepares and pre-plans every aspect of the performance. Why then would the magician include such a spontaneous throwaway line?
4. Which of these question(s) were really trick questions?

The first quote is obviously just a spur-of-the-moment line he threw out because he forgot the girl's name. The second quote is very important to the trick, and it is a line that was thought out beforehand. Right?

No, absolutely not! That's all wrong! In fact, the total opposite is true.

The first question seems very innocuous and nothing that you would attend to. Look what happens when the magician says "What'd you say your name was, again?" All eyes in the audience, and on stage, go up to the magician's face. The volunteer looks at the magician's face, and as the volunteer answers the question, the audience's eyes travel to her face. Nobody's looking at the deck of cards! Here's the behind-the-scenes explanation: When Lucy inserted her card back into the deck, the magician used his little finger as a bookmark, to save the place where the card was. As he was nonchalantly shuffling the deck, he asked the question that further misled everyone's eyes away from the fact that he was cutting the deck so that the selected card ended up at the top of the deck. (Funny how in magic, "behind the scenes" is often right in front of your face!) The question is so innocent, so trifling, that no one at all would even bother to think about it. It just sounds like meaningless chitchat, and yet the question was one of the most planned-out lines of the entire routine. Consider all that is going on at the moment when the question is asked:

- The fact that he speaks at that moment misdirects our eyes, so we are physically misdirected from the secret action.
- We are not only physically, but emotionally misdirected from the action, because we would never suspect that he's doing anything funny with the cards at that moment, because he has turned the moment into just a guy standing there casually shuffling the deck.
- The magician must use good acting technique to make the question seem meaningless, while at the same time his hands must be performing a crucial move that will make the trick work.
- The question was premeditated by the magician, perhaps written and rewritten until he came up with something that was perfectly forgettable.
- The magician's voice, hand movement, and head and face movement must all be coordinated to achieve the desired effect of plainness.

You can see how a lot of thought must go into every utterance. And remember, this was the utterance we thought was issued on the spur of the moment. Imagine how much prethought must go into something that is obviously an unchangeable piece of patter from the show. Such as quote number 2: "Very good, Lucy, you chose the left half, please turn that deck over."

This quote, "obviously an important immovable line from the show," actually might not have been spoken at all, depending on circumstances! The magician used what is known as "magician's choice" to force Lucy to pick the left-hand pile. Magician's choice is a way of seeming to allow the volunteer to make a choice when really the choice is totally under the control of the magician. Here the magician said, "Point to a half." By chance, Lucy happened to point to the correct half, the half that contained her card. If she had pointed to the other half, the magician would have said, "All right we will discard that pile and look at the other pile..." and continued from there. In other words, the trick could have progressed totally differently from that point forward. But as an audience we get to see the trick performed only once, under one timeline, and so we never know "what coulda been."

MAGICIAN'S CHOICE

Magician's choice can be done with many cards or piles of cards as well as the two illustrated in the quiz. In my Growing Forsythias illusion, I used it to force the packet of forsythia seeds from three choices. I fanned out the three packets and said, "We have to take out some of these, which one should we take?" Notice how vague that is. First I'm saying we have to take out "some," but then I say to choose "one." If they choose the forsythias, then I just go with that and continue the trick. But suppose the roses are chosen: "As you wish, we'll take out the roses." I put it aside. "Okay let's finish this up—Now which one do you want to take?" If they choose forsythias, I say, "Okay, you've finished it up, and you chose the forsythia." But if they chose pansies I can put the pansy packet aside and be left with the forsythias, which I want. Magician's choice is versatile in this way. As long as magicians are quick on their feet, they'll be able to use such double-talk to make our decisions for us. Can you think of some ways to do magician's choice with four options? Five? Ten?

In any case, I find it interesting to look at quotes like these. The one that looks impromptu is actually a well-established part of the show. And the quote that looks like a well-established, needed part of the show could, under the right circumstances, never be spoken at all. The audience attends to one and disattends to the other, and yet both are planned out beforehand and both are misleading in one way or another.

The answers to the quiz are: (1) Both quotes were planned. (2) Both quotes are patter. Neither is padding. (3) The above discussion answers question 3. (4) Questions 1 and 2 are definitely trick questions. Maybe question 3 is too, I'm not sure.

Notice the magician said, "Point to a half." Not "pick a pile" or "choose a half," but simply, "Point to a half." The magician is being smart here, being very explicit about what he wants the volunteer to do. After all, if the magician told the volunteer to "pick" or "choose" a half, then the volunteer might pick it up and hold onto it. If the volunteer picked up the wrong half, the trick would be ruined. Incidentally, notice that at the start of the trick, the magician said, "Take a card." The magician here is following the advice of the nineteenth-century magician Robert Houdin, who advised magicians to say, "Take a card," not "pick a card" or "choose a card," because by saying "take," the magician is subtly implying that the volunteer should just take a card without thinking about it. Just take any damn card! In any case, I just wanted to point out these two other phrases used by the magician to further drive home the point that *any utterance, no matter how banal* can be developed by the magician in a certain way to elicit the maximum benefit, to get the audience to think or act in a certain way, or to create a certain illusion in your mind. The magician always has control over everything, but more importantly, the magician really does exercise this control over everything.

MAGIC WORDS

"A la, peanut butter sandwiches!"

That's a sentence you probably haven't thought of in a while (unless you have young children at home). "A la, peanut butter sandwiches" is the magic word (or phrase rather) intoned by "Sesame Street"'s resident magician before each of his magic tricks. As mentioned earlier, nowadays the magic word tends to be used comedically if at all. Hocus pocus! Shazam! Alacazoo! Abracadabra! Siegfried and Roy shout out a dramatic "SAR-MOTI!" at crucial moments—their code for "Siegfried and Roy, Masters of the Impossible."[15]

But there is a little bit more going on behind the scenes than just humor. A magic word focuses the audience on itself, on that point in time. The magic word is a good way to solidify a trick based on time misdirection. Suppose the trick to the trick happened ten minutes ago: scream out "SAR-MOTI!" now and you concentrate the viewer's attention on the present, rather than thinking about the past, when the magic really took place.

A magic word is also a "known quantity." We will see more and more as this book progresses how important clichés are to magic, because when a cliché is presented the audience knows how to react to it. When the magician raises his hands in the air and shouts out the magic word, people instinctively know to concentrate on the magician because "he's making the magic happen" at that moment. Children's magicians will often start the show by teaching the kids a magic word, and then throughout the show whenever some magic is needed, they elicit the kids' help in screaming out the word. The children are participating in their own misdirection.

STORYTELLING WITH MAGIC

As a final note on patter in a magical performance, let us look at the role of storytelling in magic. A story helps motivate a trick. Instead of just having a trick for the sake of a trick, a storyline offers meaning to the audience, a reason for the trick's existence. One cannot underestimate the importance of motivation. After all, it's the magician's job to convince the audience that what they're seeing is *real*. Motivating the trick with a storyline can only help the illusion gain reality. Motivation can also provide a cover-up of certain sleights. Earlier I mentioned how dance can be used to subtly bring the magician to a certain place on stage in order to effect a trick. Similarly, a storyline may offer a logical reason for the magician to casually do something that would otherwise seem suspicious. Perhaps the magician has just slipped an object into his sleeve and he doesn't want it to fall out. Incorporate the trick into a story about bedtime, and the magician has an excuse to raise his arms as he yawns an exaggerated sleepy yawn. With arms raised, the object will slip further down into the sleeve and won't problematically fall out down the road. The story is used to conceal the true series of events that creates the illusional series of events the magician seems to perform.[16] It gives a concrete foundation for those events, more noticeable and easier to pick up than the subtle cues of misdirection that make up the bulk of illusion.

Magicians value storylines so much that it's possible to purchase routines from magic dealers. A routine is like a screenplay for a magic act. It explains how the magician should act, talk, what should be said at each point along the way, and how the props should be manipulated. Usually the routines aren't giving away any secrets. The magician already supposedly owns the equipment and has practiced the sleights. The routine is purchased in the same way a movie director would purchase a screenplay—so that it can be acted out, transformed, and realized into a piece of entertainment to display before an audience. That should tell you how much magicians value a good narrative (rather than just presenting tricks randomly), that they would go to the trouble of studying the routines of other accomplished magicians to learn from them. Routines can sell for anywhere from twenty-five cents on a photocopied sheet of paper to five or seven dollars or more. Routines are often printed in book form so that fledgling magicians can study the routines used by masters of the craft.

Pacing

The pace of a show is another factor the magician must think about while on stage. Pace is one of those slippery factors not much talked about, hard to get a hold of, and not much thought about by amateurs. It's a finesse often lacking when an amateur performs, so that even when the tricks work out okay, the audience may still walk away not feeling entirely satisfied, but not quite sure what exactly to put the blame on. The smart magician will arrange tricks in a certain order so as not to bore the audience. A dozen fabulous tricks—even if they are all mystifying by themselves—can still be boring to a lay audience if they are all derived from the same form of magic (all disappearances or all escapes, for instance). And it hardly needs to be mentioned that the liveliness of the show depends on the magician presenting the tricks slowly enough so that the audience can follow the action, but quick enough so as not to be boring. As you may know, magicians of olde used to be adept at other skills such as juggling, and sometimes even the modern-day magician thinks of magic as little more than juggling props around to dazzle the audience. One way to alienate the audience is when the magician tries to impress them with his agility or deftness. Magician Ken Barham asked the question of himself:

> Am I quick? I find that being smooth is far more important. I have seen many magicians who perform at hyper speed. This has two effects: First it wows the audience with their speed rather than fools them (you often hear "gee he's fast" as opposed to "How in God's name did that happen!?") Second, it robs the magician of appreciation. He is halfway through the next trick before the audience has time to grasp that something impossible just happened. They miss the next one because they are still on the last one and he deprives himself of a few seconds of applause. Both sides lose.

While it's important not to go too fast, sometimes a fast speed is in fact desired. In these cases it's not so fast that the audience gets confused, but just fast enough so that the audience doesn't get a chance to think about what's transpiring. In this manner, a quick pace can aid in the creation of illusion, and if you'll indulge me a moment of extended metaphor, I'd like to hearken back to our earlier comparison of magic to psychological brainwashing. Brainwashing too involves movements of sorts. Robert Jay Lifton studied Westerners and nonconformist Chinese who were being re-minded by the Chinese Communist government so they would understand and believe the Communist ideology. A good portion of the time spent in "re-education schooling" (that is, prison) was spent with the prisoners working on their "confession document." Each prisoner was made to confess everything. What is everything? Everything is . . . *everything*. The prisoners were not told specifically what it was they'd done wrong, and in most cases they believed they were doing good for the community. Many of them were religious missionaries or doctors who gave medical attention, food, or other help to the sick and poor of their communities. Certainly they had nothing evil to confess. And yet, their captors would torment them into confessing everything, and so these innocent bystanders who had been dragged into a topsy-turvy world where kindness is evil would begin to confess. Of course, since they had nothing evil to confess, they would confess lies. For instance, a doctor might confess that while visiting sick patients in their homes, he used the opportunity to engage in espionage, gathering information that he would funnel back to the United States embassy. The lies of confession would grow and grow (for if they did not confess to anything, they would be punished further); the victims would say anything to appease their captors. They would be grilled endlessly on minor details of their confessions, as their captors tried to ferret out the truth from the falsehoods. These oral inquisitions were the precursor to a written confession document in which the victim would spell out in writing the evil which he had committed.

Now, the people who ran these prisons were not stupid. They didn't fall for the lies, the "wild confessions" their prisoners would tell them. They knew they were being handed false confessions. Why then were such falsehoods allowed? They were allowed because the false confession was merely the first step in the total brainwashing experience.

For many weeks or months the prisoner would be thinking that he's making progress, that the captors are buying his falsehoods and perhaps would release him based on these confessions. But after weeks of hoping, all that hope would be lost. You see, there would come a point where the captors would yell "Hogwash!" They would call their prisoner's bluff, admonish him for lying, punish the captive in some way, and make it clearly known that false confessions would not be tolerated.

The captors would then offer some clue as to what they're *really* after. They're not after falsehoods. They're after legitimate evils. But what evil has a Christian missionary or a medical doctor perpetrated? The Communists would explain that it is evil for them to be there in the first place. When the Chinese people see Westerners coming in with Western medicine, Western religion, and Western ideas, it makes them lose faith in the Communist doctrine. The Communists had recently taken over the country. They were imposing their rule in order to improve conditions within the country. The last thing they needed was meddling outsiders thrusting their own, differing viewpoints onto an already resisting populace. That was the evil in their good deeds, and their evil acts of good were what needed to be confessed, orally, and in the written confession document. Now, with this newfound knowledge that they had in fact done wrong, the captives could confess their sins. They might not completely believe that assisting the poor and infirm was evil worthy of confession, but they at least would now understand and even sympathize with the reasons they had been captured by the Communist government.

> Although fantasy and falsehood are by no means eliminated, this shift does give the prisoner the sense that he is moving in the direction of truth. His confession changes from an uncontrolled dream-like (or nightmarish) vision to a more responsible reinterpretation of his own life. Thus he becomes more "engaged" in the confession process, more closely bound to his own words. At the same time, the effect of his wild confession has not been entirely lost upon him; he is apt to retain feelings of guilt over it, as if he had really done the things he described.[17]

What's most important to realize is that as the prisoners move to a more realistic sense of what they have done wrong, they believe they are making that movement upon their own volition. They believe they've made a personal discovery of what is expected of them, and also a personal discovery of the wrong within themselves. But only later, when they are far removed from the prison and their controlling captors, might they realize that "the official's manipulations had made this reaction inevitable."[18] The brainwashers are magicians controlling the minds of their prisoners. The prisoners believe they are making discoveries, gaining understanding, forming new beliefs about their predicament, when in fact those new beliefs and ideas are merely sprouts from the seeds the brainwashers had begun to plant from the moment they were thrust into the prison environment.

In a magic trick on a stage, the magician offers proofs to belie the wild imaginings of how the audience thinks the trick is done. The audience travels closer and closer to the "truth" as the magician provides more and more proofs as to the illusion's impossibility. The audience starts out with several explanations for how a trick might be done, but one by one the magician knocks down those ideas by passing a hoop around the levitating figure, or by rolling up his sleeves, or by showing his hands to be empty. The audience moves closer to the truth—that the trick is inexplicable, impossible, and therefore done by means unfathomable.

Another sort of movement also facilitates the layering of proofs upon the truth, and that is the movement of the show itself, the pace of the show. The magician spins the box around, showing every side of it, then proceeds to pull rabbits and streamers from it—but the showing of the box was done so fast you can really only assume that you were shown every side of the box. Perhaps one side was not shown at all. In card magic there's something called the Elmsley Count (which we'll discuss later) that allows the magician to deal out a number of cards while hiding one or more from the audience's view. The parallels to brainwashing (not to mention cult indoctrination) are astounding. In the Chinese Communist brainwashing, when a victim began his move from fantasy to "reality," it was accompanied by constant movement in the form of round-the-clock interrogations, being forced to promenade around in chains "to increase his physical discomfort, and to give him a sense of movement."[19] By day he was given tasks aimed towards exerting the confession from him; when not that, other activities were designed for him. After eight days of unrelenting movement, motion, struggle, confession, dictation, torment, he was finally allowed no sleep at all. One victim said afterward, "You are annihilated . . . exhausted . . . you can't control yourself, or remember what you said two minutes before. You feel that all is lost. . . . From that moment, the judge is the real master of you. You accept anything he says."[20] This is not unlike the magician who quickly presents image upon image, sound upon sound, without giving the audience a chance to digest or think about the individual components, let alone synthesize them together into a meaningful conclusion. Part of brainwashing consists of learning to spontaneously express all reactions and thoughts as soon as they occur;[21] in other words, no thought should be allowed to simmer and ricochet in the head. If it's a thought it must come out immediately; if it is a thought beneficial to the ideological cause, then it will be agreed with; if it goes against Communist ideology, then it is treated as a problem to be solved. The brainwashers actually used the terms "problem" needing to be "solved," usually by a "schoolmate" who "helps" one obtain the "proper standpoint." "They have to explain the facts until I am convinced," said one former inmate in the brainwashing prison. "If I am not convinced I must say I don't understand, and they bring new facts. . . . You are all day under the compulsion of denouncing your thoughts and solving your problems . . . You understand the truth of the people—day by day, moment by moment—and you cannot escape."[22]

The purpose of the brainwashing was "thought reform." In other words, the Communists wanted to permanently alter the thought processes and beliefs of their victims. Magic is more of a temporary brainwashing. The magician need only confuse and befuddle the audience for a few minutes while the trick is underway. Afterwards, once the trick is done with, a new trick starts up, and the process begins anew—new "wild imaginings" to be undone with new proofs to prove one's assumptions wrong. Within each trick the audience is not given a chance to think about what is transpiring, and also *across* tricks they are not given the chance to think. By "think" I mean "analyze closely" the proceedings. Like Dr. Roberto, the logic professor, who offered her students a series of logical statements that led to a puzzling and impossible conclusion, in magic as in brainwashing, the puzzle pieces don't necessarily fit together entirely, but the audience gets the sense that they do. Clearly this is not true for all tricks; however, for many stage illusions, it is the misleading proofs coupled with the magician taking over the thoughts of the audience, plus a quick pace that leaves no room for second thoughts, that begets an audience who ends up believing the absurd might be possible.

Another way that audience members participate in their own "brainwashing" is when they discount certain methods as being too far-fetched. This is especially true of adults, says Eddie Gardner, the owner of Diamond's Magic, Inc., a mail order magic supply business. "The more educated they are, they look at it in a complicated way." He tells of baffling a roomful of engineers: "You could see their heads churning, lots of head scratching. They couldn't figure it out" because they overlook simple solutions in favor of complex rigmarole. Many tricks are so unbelievable—or so simple—you would never think that's how it could be done. For example, magicians used to do a large stage illusion where the assistant would disappear from a box suspended high above the stage. At the crucial moment, the front of the box would fall open to reveal emptiness inside. The trick was unthinkably simple, yet it was that simplicity that made it so astounding. The secret was a trap door in the bottom of the box—and a trap door in the stage underneath the box. When the front of the box fell down, it temporarily blocked the audience's view. The assistant would actually fall straight down through the trap door in the box, right through the stage, and onto a cushion underneath below. The timing had to be perfect for this to work! An idea like this is so preposterous the audience discounts it as a possibility. This illusion eventually turned out of fashion because there were too many injuries, and too many problems with it. But while it lasted, the effect had audiences participating in their own brainwashing—as they hoodwinked themselves into the mystical, magical, *unknowable* aura of the secrets of the magician.

You should look the part. . . . It is a simple and easy, yet extremely valuable, method you can use to increase your unlimited power with people by inspiring them to have complete confidence in you.—James VanFleet, *21 Days to Unlimited Power with People*

Character

People see magicians as . . . magical. They know that it's all "a trick" but at the same time, the illusions are created with a specific learned skill on the part of the magician. People understand there is a talent behind it, the same way talent underlies the ability to juggle balls, shoot free throws, or bake a pie from scratch. Therefore, once learned, the magic is something inherent to the magician. There is something *about* the magician that allows him to do magic, where an ordinary person could not.

Many magicians are asked, "Hey, show me a trick." People know that magic requires preparation, and yet they also believe the magician can perform miracles on a moment's notice—as if the magic really is done with mysticism. Many magicians carry around an impromptu trick or two for just such occasions.

You would never walk up to a famous actor and say, "Hey Brando—*act.*" So much of our theatrical entertainment is planned out in advance—movies, musicals, theater, concerts, lectures and seminars, and comedy pieces. We expect these to be prepared beforehand. A person might go up to a comedian on the street and ask for a joke, because the person believes comedy is in the nature of the comedian. So too, mysticism is viewed as in the nature of the magician. Even though we realize illusions are prepared before the show, the show itself is easily viewed as flowing naturally from the performer. For instance, Suzanne the Magician tells how when she performed on a cruise ship she was constantly pestered by passengers for impromptu performances. "I couldn't even eat in the lounge without people wanting to see magic. I would be dressed in shorts, not even looking like a magician, and people would want to see magic." The *tricks* are staged; the magician's magical presence is impromptu.

Or so it seems. Magicians would like to appear as though what they say is unplanned, but you can be sure there is hidden meaning behind everything they say and do. As the Amazing Randi instructs beginner magicians, "The most important rule is: make sure you are in charge of what's happening. It's *your* show, so stay in control."[23] Later on we will see why and how even the simplest instructions to participating audience volunteers are carefully planned out before the show.

The role that the magician plays will determine how the audience perceives his magic. Does he play a bumbling clown? An ancient wizard figure? A classical magician in top hat and tails? In the early twentieth century, several Caucasian magicians went so far as to don Oriental garments and makeup to achieve a character that was mystical to Western eyes. The chosen character is the first step toward defining the character of the show, whether it be comic, mystical, uplifting, or, in the case of such magicians as faith healers and psychic charlatans, money grubbing.

WOULD MAGIC BY ANY OTHER NAME SMELL AS SWEET?

One of the ways a conjurer establishes character is by choosing a stage name. Here are some of the stage names that have been used throughout the history of magic.

Real Name	Stage Name
Jacob Meyer	Philadelphia
Ehrich Weiss	Harry Houdini
William Ellsworth Campbell Robinson	Chung Ling Soo[1]
Chee Ling Qua	Ching Ling Foo
Siegmund Neuburger	Lafayette[2]
Theodore Bamberg	Okito[3]
Percy Thomas Tibbles	P. T. Selbit[4]
Delbert Hill	Donna Delbert[5]
Harry Bouton	Harry Blackstone
James Randall Zwinge	The Amazing Randi
David Kotkin	David Copperfield[6]

1. Robinson, a native New Yorker, dressed in Oriental garb and makeup to present his mystical feats. He thus fooled audiences in more ways than one. His deception went to such extremes that he even insisted on using translators when interviewed by the press.

2. This German Siegmund, born in 1872, was using a lion in his act a century before this century's Siegfried and Roy, used one.

3. Another American who guised himself in Japanese makeup and garb, and was even able to fool his Asian audiences. He became Chinese during the war years.

4. This magician derived his stage name from his real name—spelled backwards.

5. How did Mr. Delbert Hill become Donna? After going AWOL from the United States Air Force, Delbert lived four years in drag as a female magician named Donna Delbert. His stage name and persona was less a matter of establishing a character than keeping himself out of jail.

6. He named himself after the Dickens book of that title. Earlier in his career he was Davino.

James Randi is a conjurer well known for his magic and escapes, but also for his fervent efforts to educate people about the truth behind phony supernaturalists. Randi is one magician who has cultivated a magical look, with a flowing white beard and dark eyes often ominously glaring in publicity photos. "I think it probably helps [to have a magic look]. Because it makes people think of magicians when they see you," Randi said. He went on to explain, "If a man looks like a tailor or looks like a bum on the street and everything, no matter how skilled he is, it still hasn't produced the *atmosphere*. What do you think a magician should look like? A tailor? Or a doctor? A haberdasher? What? He should look like a magician. Wouldn't you think?"

Apparently people do think that, because when I survey laypeople about what they thought of magicians, the words most often used to describe them were simply "magic," "mystical," and "magical." Some commented on a magician's "magic eyes," which harkens back to the hypnosis theory of magic.

A psychologist might think of Stanley Milgrim's classic 1974 study, *Obedience to Authority*, in which he showed how authority figures tend to bend us. We will follow authority figures, listen to them, be influenced by them, often unthinkingly. Magicians clearly are authority figures of some stature. In fact, magicians of an earlier age often used the title "Doctor" or "Professor" before their name. An air of authority connotes access to privileged information and special powers. Thus it makes sense that people either consciously or unconsciously comply with those in authority, which can only do a great service to the presentation and production of a magical illusion.[24]

DR. COPPERFIELD, I PRESUME?

Magicians have a long tradition of trying to lend authenticity to their performances by proclaiming themselves doctors or professors of science. There was Professor De Vere, whose act included slicing off and restoring his assistant's head. Professor Cummings promised his audience "Dancing Babies" and "Piece-Work Magic." Professor John Henry Pepper of the Royal Polytechnic Institution performed his ghost illusion at the Egyptian Hall in London. Others included Professor Krosso ("The Modern Samson & the Strongest Man in the World"), Professor Anderson ("The Wizard of the North"), Professor Carl, who, among other marvels, performed "Feats of Natural Philosophy," Dr. Walford Bodie, M.D., who put on a show that included magic, bloodless surgery, escapology, hypnosis, and electrical experiments, Dr. Valentine ("In Eccentric Delineations of Character"), and Professor Harrington ("whose name is as familiar as 'Household Words,' " proclaimed one of his billboards).

Perhaps the best use of alleged titles and degrees was made by the eighteenth-century magician Pinetti, whose bountiful qualifications read: "Pinetti, Knight of the German Order of Merit of St. Philip, Professor of Mathematics and Natural Philosophy, Pensioneer of the Court of Prussia, Aggregate of the Royal Academy of Sciences and Belles Lettres of Bordeaux and financial counselor to H. R. H. the Prince of Limburg-Holstein." One wonders, after spouting all that out, whether there was any time left for the magic show!

(Information garnered from posters and billboards depicted in Milbourne Christopher's *Magic: A Picture History*.)

Magicians have, over the ages, created these auras of authority, power, and mysticism for themselves. Still, it's easy to point out magicians who don't follow the mold, who don't present an image of magic, power, and special knowledge—Penn & Teller, for instance. Randi dismisses this with a verbal punch: "They're comedic magicians, so they try to look like comedians." And what of all those other magicians out there? The ones who dress in jeans, go clean-shaven, act whimsical when they should appear mystical, and generally don't play the role of magician? What about them? Well, they're not famous, *are* they?

Clothing

Clothing is part of one's character, but to a magician it is much more as well. It serves as the magician's pocketbook, chest of drawers, and file cabinet. Magicians of a bygone era wore formal coats with tails, and a vest underneath. They would literally have about a dozen secret pockets and sliding tubes hidden throughout their clothing. Pockets hidden under the jacket lapels. Pockets in the tail of the coat. A tube of silk embedded in the jacket that led from the breast pocket to the tail pockets, so items could be imperceptibly transferred from here to there. Another large pocket inside the jacket was big enough to hold a fold-up bouquet of flowers. Huge pants pockets would extend down past the knee, making an ideal hiding spot for a multicolored parasol or bushel of bright feathers. Magicians can't wear such formal wear today without arousing suspicion.

The Orientally garbed magicians wore long, flowing robes with beautiful, colorful patterns. The robes and layers of fabric offered many hiding places on their person, to hide all sorts of objects that would be produced as if from thin air. The best costumes are functional as well as providing appropriate character. Even such immense items as a goldfish bowl (with live goldfish happily a-swimming) could be produced from under the robes. The bowl was covered with a specially fitted rubber lid, and hung vertically by a strap underneath the magician's garments. Another version uses an oddly shaped bowl, shaped like a letter C, which fit snugly against the magician's body underneath the clothes. From the audience's perspective the bowl looked normal.

The modern magician's jacket may be outfitted with a *topit*, a large secret pocket that the magician throws stuff into when he wants to get rid of it, or can pull items out of as needed. Now, how does someone get a topit in their jacket, you might be wondering? For starters you can look in the L & L Publishing Catalog of magic, and you'll find a topit sewing pattern that "comes with step-by-step instructions for your tailor or seamstress." One walk-around magician wrote that he had his "most recent dinner suit (tuxedo!) specially made with extra pockets and a built-in Ammar-style topit. . . . When not in use, the built-in topit provides useful extra storage double valuable because it is accessible from my left outer pocket."[25] In other words, there's a secret passage from his outside pocket into the topit. A typical use of a topit was presented by a comedic magician who had made a bird appear at his finger tips. He made a joke about the bird pooping on his hands, so he brought out some toilet paper to wipe up. But the toilet paper stuck to his hand. He shook his hand to get it off. He kept trying to shake off the sticky toilet paper while the audience laughed at his predicament. When he finally shook it off, he realized to his surprise that the bird had vanished. The violent shaking, and the broad gestures that went with it, was perfect cover for his tossing the fake bird into his topit.

Control of the Theater

In 1987, Siegfried and Roy were preparing a dazzling stage show for the Mirage casino hotel in Las Vegas. The Mirage had offered to build a theater to the magicians' specifications, as well as to set the stage and let them put on the show however they wanted. Total control to the magicians. They designed their theater with one thought in mind, that the magical quality must "begin from the minute the audience entered the theater: the lasers, the lighting, the music, the miracle workers. The environment would prepare them for the experience."[26] The resulting show is a multimillion-dollar extravaganza featuring seventy-five tons of scenery, a mechanical dragon, and a zoo of jungle animals. Not too many magicians have the capacity to realize full control over the theater the way S & R have done, but magicians do exert some kinds of controls, which, though they may be small, do their part to control the audience.

"When I do shows for children," explained Suzanne the Magician,

> I put down a line, either with tape or a rope. When I introduce myself at the beginning of the show, I say I have three rules:
> The first rule *is*: You have to have a lot of fun!! Can you do that?
> "Yes!!!" the children yell.
> The second rule *is*: You can be as loud as you want, as long as you stay in your seats!! *CAN YOU DO THAT?*
> "YES!!!" They love to yell.
> And the third and most important rule *is*: You see this line? Everything on this side of the line is the stage, I'm the entertainer so I'll stay on the stage. Everything on that side of the line is the *audience*, and that's you guys. So you stay in the audience until I ask you to come up to help me. Okay?

All three rules are significant and revealing. This last rule especially. The line dividing stage and seating is made to seem so distinct, and yet in reality it is so vague. Skillful magicians know that the first step in controlling the audience's mind is to control the stage. In fact, they have to know at every moment what is going on not only on stage, but with the audience as well, because the audience is so much a part of a magic show. In this section we will look at how the magician plays with that dividing line, shifting it, crossing it, making it disappear when the need arises, and pointing it out when it serves his purpose. And we will see that this line is not only drawn across a physical boundary, but across a psychological one as well.

SEATING

Magicians will often control how the seating is arranged. Certain illusions won't work if audience members can peek around the side of a platform, or behind a strategically placed curtain. Earlier, when we discussed the use of mirrors, it was mentioned that in bygone days the sightlines of the audience were restricted by performing in a theater, perhaps restricted to the extent of not allowing certain seats to be filled if they were too revealing. Nowadays magicians perform under all sorts of conditions, including walk-around shows, and on television, both of which can devastate a magical performance.

If the show is being performed in a nightclub setting, you might see the tables by the sides of the stage pushed away, depending on what the act entails. Come back next week when the entertainment is a rock band, and you'll see that the tables have been pushed into their original position close up to the stage.

Many of the magicians I spoke with downplayed the importance of seating. For instance, Dwinells explained, "I do arrange the chairs so the people are all in front of me. Not always for the angle . . . just so that they're in front. It's for their benefit." (So the audience can see what's going on.) However, he admitted, "Definitely there are angles to all sorts of tricks," and he mentioned the fact that tricks are often advertised as "angle proof" in the magic catalogs, thus belying the existence of a whole class of manufactured tricks, which are not angle proof.

There clearly are many tricks that can be detected if the seats are improperly arranged. In the words of one magician: "I know that no competent magician can have his trickery detected, given his choice of viewing angles and distance. Wouldn't be much of a magic show otherwise." That's the thing: To create magic—to create an imaginary illusion of control over the environment—the magician has to have a real and visible control over it. One conjurer commented; "Though I've never had occasion to use this, I've heard where a magician chooses certain people from the audience to help him out on stage, because those people happened to be sitting at a bad angle where they could see something they shouldn't. Maybe this is more true in walk-arounds than in stage shows."

A magician could also give audience members a task to perform if they are sitting in bad seats. For instance, they could give out some props and have the audience members inspect them while the magician performs another effect. Hopefully they are too preoccupied with the props to take advantage of their angle. Magician Leigh Hotz admitted,

> Sometimes I find myself in a location which may not be ideal for certain effects and I have to manually restrict certain viewing angles. This can be done by "reserving" a block of "bad" seats for my sound/lighting crew to work from, or simply blocking out a bad angle with a piece of scenery or large prop. Lighting also can be used to do the job in some cases. Luckily, many modern illusions CAN be surrounded but we still like to be viewed from the front for artistic reasons.

Magicians with even more money to spend might fill in those bad seats with living, breathing people. One magician reported that there are bad angles to the David Copperfield flying illusion. In the illusion, Copperfield pushes against the air to float, soar, and do loop-de-loops in the air, even inside a closed Plexiglas box. The flying effect is very realistic, except, as my source reported, from some of the front side seats. A different contact explained that an actor friend of his was hired by Copperfield to play an "audience member" at show performances. He explained that the first few rows of the audience were plants, but he stressed that no one was in on the tricks. When the flying illusion was televised, at the end of the show Copperfield was shown walking outside the theater with the audience as they left the theater. Then he magically takes flight into the night sky. My source informs me that the audience members whom he was walking out with were also plants. Of course, they would have to be. A slightly different story was offered by a Virginia magician who said, "I have a friend who was in the audience and he had a friend who they recruited to [be a stooge]. They had them come to a soundstage before the show and 'watch' him fly, then they went to the real show and went backstage while they showed the tape to the rest of the audience." I don't believe his story is particularly accurate, in fact it sounds bogus (the old Friend of a Friend fallacy). And in other news, I've heard from at least one nonstooge who sat in front row seats at a show with two friends. Perhaps only some of the seats are filled with stooges. Copperfield himself denies using stooges. But it does point out that some people might be paid to sit in as stooges to some extent at the performances (can those pro-stooge reports be completely bogus?).

You might ask yourself, why would Copperfield go through the bother of paying people to pay audience members to sit in bad seats where the illusion may be revealed?—that still reveals the trick to the same number of people! Ah, but Copperfield has an ace up his sleeve. (Actually he has a cable up his sleeve—the ace is for a different trick!) All participants in his show are required to sign a legal document to the effect that they will not reveal any secrets. This may not be the most effective way to bind and gag someone, but it's the most legal, and it's what Copperfield relies on to keep many of his stooge-dependent tricks hush hush.

Finally, there are traditionalist magicians who, unlike that whipper-snapper Copperfield, are going to rely on their magic skill to produce their effects. Copperfield sees a way to control the audience by planting an audience. Purists maintain the best way to control is to be in control of themselves.

> *The Amazing Randi:* The audience comes into the theater and sits down. It's my job to entertain them no matter where they're sitting. Or how they're sitting or how they're distributed. That's not under my control.
> *Me:* Your tricks are usable under any conditions.
> *The Amazing Randi:* Generally speaking, yes. Under some conditions you can't use certain things. You have to adapt them or not use them. Depends on the theater.

And it depends on the magician.

Sometimes you, as an audience member, have a unique opportunity to catch the magician in a situation that is less than ideal. As one magician told me, "All magicians eventually do a show outside or with less than ideal stage area or accommodations." When you see a trick out of the proper location, it shows. And it can help you in determining how the tricks are done. For instance, one time I had the opportunity to see a magic show in a local theater with a small stage, close to the audience. The magician was using this local theater as "practice" to get the kinks out of his stage act before heading out to Atlantic City, where he would perform his act on a larger stage with flashy lights and effects. It seemed like a good deal: we would get a big stage show at an inexpensive price. Some people might point out that it's not such a good deal because I wouldn't be getting the full show with the glitzy special effects, and besides, there might still be some bugs they hadn't worked out. But that was exactly the reason I wanted to see the show! It was a great opportunity to catch a magician in a situation that he wouldn't have complete control over! The reason magicians can fool us so often is because they have that control over the theater, the seating, and the way the stage is set. But here the magician would be performing tricks close-up that should be done on a larger, faraway stage. And he would be performing tricks that were not as well-rehearsed as he would've liked. This was an ideal opportunity, and I was glad I took advantage of it! As it turned out, some of the tricks didn't come off correctly because we were too close. He did a lot of "box tricks" where an assistant is pushed into a box, and is then cut up, rearranged, made to disappear, or changed into a different assistant. A few of the tricks were revealed to my attentive eye because I was closer than I should've been. In one case I could see clearly that a pair of legs visible through a window in a box were fakes. On the farther away Atlantic City stage, that robotic ruse would not have been so apparent. In another instance, my particular angle allowed me to just barely detect that the assistant was not standing straight in a vertical box that was meant to hold her rigidly vertical. Her body was curved to the side, thus allowing metal stakes to pass through the box and seemingly pass through her body as well. Again, at the larger stage show I would not have had the opportunity to witness such a slip-up!

It should be mentioned that the audience applauded wildly for each illusion, and the crowd walked away with big smiles on their faces. I didn't hear anyone chattering about the secrets they spied on stage, or commenting on how they thought the tricks were done. The fact is, mistakes were made right before their eyes, and probably not one of them had noticed it! They didn't think to notice, or they didn't realize that what had drawn them to the show (a cheap price, a big-stage magician on a small stage) was in fact *clues* they could use to their advantage in figuring out the methods to the magic. Those factors seemed insignificant to them, and yet they made all the difference in the world to the performance. The moral of this story is that it can be a real eye-opener when a magician loses any kind of control over the theater, stage, or show.

It's even better when it's a bad magician.

PLANTS, BUSHES, STOOGES

The theater has a long history of using audience plants and stooges. Comedian Groucho Marx related in the March 1933 issue of *Redbook* that his father (whom the Marx brothers called Frenchie) gave their early performances a boost by sitting in the audience and providing his "prop laugh" as Groucho put it, in order to satisfy the theater manager that the boys were funny and should be allowed to continue performing their act. Long after he had heard their jokes, Frenchie would provide his raucous guffaw "which nearly always proved infectious," leading the rest of the audience to laughter. He spent much of his spare time laughing at his sons' jokes, until the manager "became as familiar with Frenchie's mechanical merriment as we were." Groucho's mother (who herself had come from a theatrical family—her parents were strolling magicians and musicians in Germany), implored Frenchie to hire paid "boosters." Frenchie would pay for the boosters' tickets and give them an extra dime for their time. For an important show at Chicago's Majestic Theater, Frenchie brought in fifty boosters to cheer the boys on. Groucho also relates how one "sad afternoon" six boosters mistakenly "yelled and stamped their feet to express approval" of the wrong act. They remained blissfully quiet while the Marx Brothers appeared. The brothers' act was canceled after the opening matinee, thus attesting to the power of the planted stooge.[27]

Nowadays we have canned laughter on TV sitcoms to provide the function of boosters, to convince *us* that what we're watching is funny. In a TV studio the whole audience become boosters as they react amiably to the applause signs and off-camera prompting of the director to whoop, laugh, or emote impassioned sighs. In a related twist, local theaters will often give away unsold seats before showtime as a way to fill the theater. This is not so much for the audience's benefit as for the performers who would be disheartened to play before an empty house.

Television infomericals also use a whole studio of paid-off seat-fillers to applaud the products and be "amazed" as the product is demonstrated. Legendary TV pitchman Ron Popeil readily admits he hires boosters: "We pay them $35 for being there all day and give them a lunch," but shudders at the suggestion that such an audience likes the product only because they're being paid to do so: "I don't hire shills, my audience has always truly been amazed at my products. . . . Many want to trade their $35 for whatever product we might be marketing."[28] Sure, when some of the products sell for $35 in "three easy installments" I'd trade my $35 bucks for the thing too!

Magicians who appear on television will occasionally use a similar ploy to increase suspense and audience involvement. During a dramatic escape or stunt, the camera will close in on some wide-eyed women pleading with their hands that the magician be delivered unharmed from his situation. Sometimes I've noticed the front rows seem to be stocked with only beautiful women. Coincidence?

Plants and stooges exist in magic, though not as much as the layperson might believe. But it does happen. When my father was recently selected as an audience volunteer to appear in a pickpocket act, it was no surprise to him—the pickpocket had come around before the show, gave him a phony tie to wear that could be slipped off easily, and slipped another guy an extra pair of underwear. Stooges are also used sometimes when a particular trick might embarrass or offend an audience member, or shower them in seltzer water. In those cases it isn't necessary to have a stooge, it's just the gentlemanly thing to do. Magician Theodore Annemann, best known for his contributions to mentalism and for creating *The Jinx*, a magazine for magicians, was known for saying that in a roomful of seven people, he would have no compunction about making six of them his confederates in order to fool the seventh. Mentalism is one of the areas where it's common to use stooges or plants to some degree or another.

Most magicians don't use stooges because (1) Who wants to pay them? (2) Most tricks can be done without stooges anyway, and (3) In a closed environment (say, a cruise ship) the stooge will then have the rest of the journey to "blab all" to every retiree on board. The magician might not mind sacrificing one stooge for the good of the show, but being stuck on a boat in the middle of the water enlarges the sacrifice to everyone the guy comes in contact with. In other words, he ruins the trick for everyone.

On the other hand, consider the words of one bar worker, who writes, "The use of a stooge . . . unethical? No way! A stooge to me is just like a thumb tip or a short card. It (he or she) is just a hidden "gimmick" to be used at the right time to create the magic. I don't care about ethics of performance here, simply effect."[29]

The wisdom to plan and order is one of the essential characteristics you will need if you are to lead, control, manage, and gain unlimited power with people.—James VanFleet

Audience Participation

Audience participation is where the magician really has to be sure of himself, because to allow a stranger from the audience to come up on stage is to allow room for randomness into an otherwise perfectly coordinated act. That's why you'll notice that a skilled performer gives very precise directions to audience volunteers. I remember watching David Copperfield instructing a volunteer after she had drawn a magic triangle or some such thing with a black marking pen. When she was done, he said, "Now put the cap back on the pen. Now hand me the pen." Even something as simple as handing off a pen has been carefully thought out and requested as a sequence of two specific moves. I asked some magicians what they thought of this. Sandorse the Magician recognized the need for such meticulous planning, commenting that as a magician, Copperfield always knows where he's going with a trick. "It may be well planned out. It may be when the [volunteer] put the cap back on the pen, David may take the pen and put it in his pocket now or something." A gesture as simple as that may be innocent, or it may conceal the secret removal of something from his pocket. You can see it would be necessary then to put the pen in his pocket, even if the act appears to be extraneous. And what if the pen were uncapped? That would delay the action, throw off the flow of the trick, and waste time on nationwide television. What if there was some gimmick to the pen that required it to be capped for it to work? Again, the same problems arise. The thing is, we never know which actions are important to a trick in a magical performance, and which actions are there to prod the story of the trick along. Each kind of action is important in its own way, and so each must be considered beforehand. "David does very, very good magic," Sandorse concludes. "It's well thought out."[30]

Even if you realize that a show was planned down to the very last detail, it can still be surprising how minuscule some of these details are. For instance, magicians are as choosy wordsmiths as the Bard when composing the scripts for their tricks. Consider the simple act of allowing an audience volunteer to select a card from the deck. We've already mentioned the virtue of saying "take a card" instead of "pick a card." Another magician might prefer to say, "Point to a card," because he knows if he says, "pick a card" the volunteer will grab the card, which is inappropriate for his particular trick. Another magician says, "Take a card," because he knows if he says, "Select a card," the volunteer will spend the next ten minutes trying to decide which card to select. To "take" a card forces a rapid action. Right here we have four different ways of saying the same thing—but meaning very different things indeed.

Other tricks may require the volunteer to provide complex moves, perhaps intricate workings of a deck of cards, that may be confusing to both volunteer and audience alike. When a magician gives precise instructions, it is for "clarity, so the audience knows what's going on every step of the way," said Dwinells. "It's a subconscious thing—the magician hasn't done this—I have." Especially with an illusion that involves suspicious or tricky moves, this will be important—that the volunteer (and the viewing audience who lives vicariously through the volunteer) hear exactly, step by step, what the volunteer is doing. Anything that could give away the trick was done not by the magician, but by the volunteer. The magician has had no part in it. Or so the appearance is given.

When instructions are misunderstood, the trick can go awry in big or small ways. Some tricks based on mathematical principles will be fouled up if the participant adds or subtracts incorrectly. The mentalist grandly announces, "Your number is 32!" but the volunteer shakes her head "no." Now the mentalist knows that the volunteer has screwed up the math, but at that point he's stuck. That's why it's important for the patter to be well-planned out, to help guide the volunteer and to avoid such a catastrophe. One solution is for mentalists to engage a committee of audience members to do a calculator check on the volunteer's math.

The special words a magician uses are accessories that help create a more realistic illusion. The trick may still work without it, but perhaps the illusion will have failed. For instance, a magician was working a synagogue to an audience of mostly children. At one point he was going to do something with an egg. He called up a little girl, and as he handed her the egg to inspect, he whispered in her ear, "*Pretend it's real.*" Unfortunately for the magician, she misunderstood what he had whispered. She thought he was telling her to *throw the egg across the room*, which, obediently, she did. To the audience's surprise, the egg did not break (it was wooden). That made for a moment that was both awkward and a drag to the show. The trick could still proceed, but now everyone knew the magician wasn't being honest with them. He could've lightened the moment by telling a joke. One magician in the same bind quipped, "That's a special egg. Comes from a chicken called a Plymouth Rock."

WHO TO CHOOSE?

Whenever a magician starts trolling for volunteers, invariably he will get finger-pointers, people who volunteer the person sitting next to them. The so named finger-pointee then sits cowering with their head down and hands concealing their face, so as not to be chosen and hopelessly embarrassed by the magician. The smart magician is not going to pick Mr. Shy Guy, because shy people do not make for a good show. They may be easy to bully around, but the awkward tension will translate to the rest of the audience, who will see the magician as a tormentor rather than a person they can admire and whose mysticism enthralls them.

The smart magician may choose the finger-pointer, or he may not. The pointer has shown himself to be a jokester, a prankster, a person coming very close to being a heckler. This the magician wants to stay away from. The finger-pointer may not be an ideal choice for a volunteer, but the magician might end up choosing him for the simple reason that the pointing he does points back to himself. The magician wants to choose an outgoing person, because such a person will make a good temporary assistant.

Psychologically this can be explained in part by the Reciprocity Rule, one of many principles of social psychology that manipulative people use to influence us. Certainly magicians count as manipulative. The Reciprocity Rule states that a person will give to you if you give to them. How does the rule apply to audience volunteers in magic?

Think of a trick like Wizard X's card in the box, where the volunteer gets to be in on the gag. There the magician is *giving* to the volunteer and the volunteer complies due to reciprocity effects. What does the magician give the volunteer?: (1) a good story ("Hey I got to be part of the show!"), (2) a part in a conspiracy (he lets the subject in on the secret), and (3) exposure and attention. Remember, if he's a volunteer—he *volunteered!* He likes being the center of attention. It gives him a chance to ham it up in front of the crowd. "Oh my lord! How did you know my card!?"

That's the theory underlying the selection. In practice, magicians are often as unaware of what they're doing as we are. It boils down to a hunch. Randi says he picks "someone with a good sense of humor, someone who'll cooperate. You can't tell, but you try to make an educated guess at it." One magician said she would pick a big, burly male for "box pounding"— pounding on a magic box to prove to the audience it is solid; but a female for psychological stuff and mentalism. She also mentioned choosing someone who looked strong for certain psychic effects that involve the volunteer secretly writing on carbon paper to make a hidden copy of a message. "I've had one too many experiences where I chose a young girl whose writing did not show through four layers of pages!" Other magicians said they prefer to stick with female volunteers from the audience. Magician and professor of sociology Peter Nardi explains,

> If I do a card trick, the man will say, "No." They try to undermine it. Women tend to go along with it much more easily. Or when you finish doing it, a man will say, "Oh I can do one too—watch!" Or a man will say, "How did you do it?" They want to know. The women will say, "That was great! Do another one?" The slight differences. That's why I think magicians often pick women

... because they're more likely to collude than men are. Men are more likely to challenge and undermine, refute, guess, all those kinds of things.

Readers of Deborah Tannen's bestselling books on "manspeak" and "femalespeak" are nodding their heads now, because these kinds of reactions from men and women are not only very accurate, but ingrained within us. It's interesting that Nardi points out how encouraging women are. "Do another one?" Sure the magician is choosing a volunteer who will make the show entertaining, but perhaps the magician is also choosing someone who will give him positive feedback. Someone who will make the magician feel good about what he's doing up there on stage.

CONTROL OF INSPECTIONS

One of the common reasons for introducing audience members into the show is when they are called up to inspect a prop to ensure that it's genuine. Often the prop is in fact genuine, and so the magician has no qualms about showing it off. Other times the prop is gimmicked or rigged in some way, and so the magician must exert his control to see to it that the volunteer is convinced it's real, even when it's a fake.

One way to do that is to have the audience inspect a genuine article. Then the magician substitutes the gimmicked item with some sleight of hand. That's possible for small items (like the rigged cork in the Ghost Bottle trick), but not in cases like the trunk with a trap door in it. Or at least it is much more difficult. The magician must rely on some form of controlling the spectator. They might do this in any number of ways:

- *Control the examination.* Instead of telling the spectator, "Examine this trunk thoroughly," the magician says, "Make sure this trunk is solid— give it some good hard thumps, like this." And then he proceeds to rap each side. The spectator obligingly does the same, thinking that he or she is doing a good job of inspecting it for trap doors. Of course the trap door is sturdy enough to withstand such a thump without flopping over, but the audience is convinced that the trunk has been proven okay by one of their own.
- *Speed.* The magician can set a fast pace that the volunteer instinctively knows to follow. Besides, few volunteers want to look like they're anal-retentive dorks, compulsively examining every prop under a microscope. It's a weird irony that the people who are called up to judge the magician's honesty, usually give him the benefit of the doubt.
- If the volunteer is lagging behind (and the magician fears he's about to latch on to some secret) the magician is ready to *jump in and move the show* along with a snappy one liner ("Don't bang it *that* hard, ha ha! Moving right along . . ."), or merely by asking if everything looks okay. The ma-

gician is joking of course. Or is he? It doesn't matter. He gets the same result, whether or not the inspection would have revealed something—the spectator feels socially obligated to move on, and they do.

- *Misdirection.* Magician Milbourne Christopher offers a splendid example along these lines, one that relies on a basic facet of psychology. If a spectator is asked to examine a die to ensure it's "legit," have the volunteer count the spots on each side. By getting their mind into a counting mode, they won't notice other irregularities, such as slight variations of color on each side of the gimmicked die.[31]

- *Use a stooge.* In rare cases the magician could let a stooge inspect a gimmicked item because a "regular" audience member would be tipped off to the gaff. This is almost never done. However, stooges are used occasionally to *switch* a real item for a gimmicked duplicate. Here's how it works: the magician passes around a genuine prop (a cork, let's say). The last person he gives it to is the stooge. The stooge is sitting there with the gimmicked cork in his hand, so he can make the secret switch and hand the gimmicked prop back to the magician. This trick is also used sometimes in mentalism tricks—the stooge secretly substitutes an empty envelope with a duplicate envelope that has an accurate prediction inside it.

One of the best ways to control inspections is to use ungimmicked props. That way there's nothing at all that needs to be hidden from the volunteers or the rest of the audience. Magician John Bannon points out that at the end of a certain mystifying card trick he liked to nonchalantly offer the cards for inspection. "Don't wait for him to ask, just hand them to him. . . . The examination actually enhances the trick by eliminating all of the spectator's easy outs."[32]

What conclusion can we draw from all this? Primarily, that magicians are fooling you—*always fooling you*—even when they seem to be acting genuinely forthright you simply never know if that genuineness itself is bogus.

Lighting

The colored lights, spotlight, strobe, and other flashy illuminations that are present in a theater are very common to us. We see these lights at every rock concert, play, and TV awards show. Their commonness leads to our taking them for granted, something a magician cannot do. Matthew Dwinells the Illusion Artist, said, "Lighting is important. Back lighting could expose certain tricks." Lights must therefore be chosen carefully to achieve the desired effect. Lights are also great for hiding things from the audience. I'm not just talking about shutting off the lights to hide in the cloak of darkness. Much can be hidden by shining lights brightly too.

One way that lights are used to hide things on stage is the strategic placement of lights to shine in the audience's face. This can usually only be done at large stage shows in a big theater, and even then is not used that much. However it is used at times to keep the audience from getting a good look at what's going on at a crucial moment of the trick. Stage lights are allowed to spill toward the audience during black art effects: the stage is kept black, but confounding the audience's ability to see the black-on-black on stage.

Once I saw a magician walk through a mirror that had been wrapped in paper. At the end of the effect, after going through the mirror and ripping through the paper to emerge on the other side, he stood in front and basked in the applause. I tried in vain to get a good look at the hole in the paper, but could not because the magician's body covered the hole, fog was rising up from the stage, and a bevy of spotlights moved and circled about, highlighting the amazement that we were to feel at that point. The magician stood so confidently there while the audience cheered—none of them realized that while they were cheering he was covering up the secret to the trick. If only he stepped aside, if only those spotlights had been turned off, or the fog dissipated, would we have been able to see a hole straight through a gimmicked mirror?

Lights used in combination with fog is cunningly employed. Both impart a mystical atmosphere to the show, but both used together also combine to obscure the proceedings. Movie director Peter Weir: "I think all filmmakers like fog. There is less information that comes through on the screen. It's closer to black and white. You have more control. Part of the appeal of fog is that it isolates and obscures and it's full of secrets."[33] This is just as true for magic as for films. You will notice this effect if you have the unfortunate opportunity to be driving through a dense fog, as I had recently. I was driving down a two-lane road. There was a lot of space between my car and the car ahead of me, which was pretty visible even though the fog was bad. I noticed that when a car was approaching from the opposite direction it was almost completely invisible at the same distance as the visible car ahead of me. Why should two cars, equally distant, have differing levels of visibility? Because the car coming towards me also had its headlights shining in my direction. The headlights funneled out into the fog, creating a wall of light behind which the car itself was invisible. Even when the car was a bright red or dark black, it was visible only as a light gray, whitish blob in the fog. If a chance encounter of cars in the fog can produce such a strong illusion, imagine how effective it would be if it were planned out by the magician, who specially selected colors and materials and specifically directed the lights to achieve the invisibility effect.

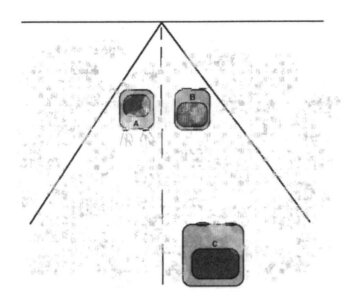

Fig. 16. Three cars on a foggy road. Even though cars A and B are the same distance from C, it is much more difficult to see car A. One might think car A's headlights would make it easier to spot, but they actually hinder the car's visibility. Such techniques of light and fog are used in stage shows to hide certain things and bring out other things.

The human eye's reaction to lights and darkness can be exploited in large stage shows. The build-up of the trick can take place on a well-lighted stage. If the lights are dimmed suddenly, our eyes won't be able to adjust quickly enough: the tricky part is accomplished before our eyes make the adjustment. No one suspects a thing because time misdirection is at work—the dimming of the light occurs well before the climax of the trick. But as you know by now, the tricky part of many tricks occurs well before the climax.

Some gimmicked props may also rely on lighting. There is a kind of fake playing card called a *transparent card* that changes from one suit to another when held to the light. It may look like a three of clubs at first, but after the magician gets through with some incantations, he holds it proudly aloft to show it has been promoted to king of clubs. Spectators don't realize that the king is painted on a secret layer inside the card—holding it up to the light exposes the inside, and the three clubs dotting the card's surface gets subsumed into the larger portrait of the king. Another variation on the card makes extra pips appear when it is held to the light. Keep in mind that this sort of thing is used rarely (for there are ways of achieving the same effects without bought cards) but it is something to keep in mind if you notice the magician holding the card one way one time and then a completely different way a little later.

Even though lighting can be used in this tricky way, the illusionist Dwinells insisted his main interest in lighting is visibility for the audience: "Usually spotlights directly on the magician are good." He explained that backlighting is bad because the audience cannot see the magician, and anything he does with his hands in front of him lies in shadows. Lighting is also important when the magician is performing "small" tricks on a large stage. For instance, the magician who swallows needles or razor blades makes sure to use shiny steel blades that will nicely catch the glint of the spotlight.

For most tricks, for most magicians, visibility will be the primary issue where lighting is concerned. But for the million-dollar magicians whose effects require gimmicks and stage presence above skill, lights can be used to both bring out what the magician wishes the audience to see, and conceal what he wishes to remain hidden.

OTHER THEATER CONTROLS

Besides lighting, seating, and the stage, there are other ways the magician might reinvent the theater for his own purposes. Magicians sometimes *salt* the room before starting. Salting means to hide small items here and there throughout the room well before show time. It can make for a lively surprise if the coin that is vanished turns up stuck to the bottom of your very chair! Another common salting is to stick a card to the ceiling. Nobody notices it (usually) and it makes for waves of applause when the magician later has someone select a card, return it to the deck, and then he throws the deck at the ceiling. What a shock when the selected card is found stuck up there! Little does the audience know it got there by salting long before they arrived.

One of the most drastic overhauls of a theater belongs to Pepper's Ghost. A man named Henry Dircks invented an illusion that was produced by Dr. Henry Pepper in 1862, in which the audience was treated to live actors cavorting on stage with semi-transparent ghosts and skeletons. The otherworldly creatures would fade away from view or appear again from thin air, just as ghosts and undead skeletons are wont to do. The illusion relied on Dr. Pepper having complete control of the theater. The ghosts and skeletons were actors dressed in costumes (*duh!*). They resided in a black orchestra pit in front of the audience, but concealed from the audience by a low wall. Up on the stage above, the real live actors performed behind a tilted sheet of glass. We've mentioned previously the fact that glass can sometimes be invisible to the eye given proper cleanliness and lighting. This glass was no exception. The audience would look directly through this fourth wall, never realizing it was there. The glass was angled so as to catch the reflection of the ghosts and skeletons down below. By adjusting the lighting in the orchestra pit, the ghosts would become more or less visible, more or less corporeal, or they could disappear altogether if the light was entirely extinguished. The actors on stage and under stage would have to choreograph their moves beforehand so it would appear they were reacting to each other's presence.

This is the kind of trick you wouldn't see at a sidewalk performance because it requires the magician to have complete control of the theater.

Stage Managers and Stage Presence

Lighting, music, dance, sound, patter, audience interaction, and don't forget to smile. The magician sure has a lot to think about while on stage. All of it contributes to perpetrating illusion, controlling the audience to get the desired reactions, and making the performance a more enjoyable one. Magicians with big bucks also have a paid crew of people looking out for the magician's best interest, trying literally to put the magician in the best possible light. Sandorse the Magician explained about such big-name magicians as Copperfield:

> Unbeknownst to you, David has around fifty people that work for him backstage that you never see . . . Behind the scenes there's a tremendous amount of things you never see or never even know about. There's a guy on the microphone saying, "Hit David with the little spotlight now. Hit him with this. Take him towards the left. Take him towards the right. Bring the music up. Bring the music down." *You* never hear this. *You* never see this. And then, neither does the audience, but it's that particular gentleman's job not to be seen, not to be heard. But his job is in the audience to make David look good. And he does. And this is why David comes across so well, because the light will hit him at that right angle and the right time. All the things just don't happen by accident. It's all planned out.

Copperfield himself has said his show involves a staff of fifty, and he has twenty experts to dream up new illusions.[34] Some of those assistants wait in the wings for signs of trouble. Someone who had a side view of the stage at one Copperfield show noticed that a side panel on his "elevator" illusion failed to drop into place. Like a wink, a prop man was pulling a rope to drop an emergency black cloth.[35]

Sometimes you can also spot assistants sitting in the audiences of magic shows (and regular theater shows). Look for someone with a clipboard taking notes. Like the boosters of yesteryear, these assistants are probably the ones laughing loudest at the jokes, clapping and hooting the most boisterously whenever the magician does anything as miraculous as blowing his nose. It's been said that Copperfield has a notetaker at the ready for each of his illusions. At the end of a trick, his microphone is cut from the speakers and goes directly to the notetaker. Copperfield dictates his thoughts on how the illusion went, and the notetaker writes it all down. This all goes on as the show progresses from one illusion to the next. He then goes over the notebook later at his convenience.[36]

Even if the magician doesn't have a pantheon of assistants, there are things he or she can do on stage to exert an invisible control. One helpful product is the "John Cornelius Toe Switch." This is a secret switch the magician can hide in his shoe to activate almost any electronic device by pressing down with a toe. Certain magic tricks depend on electronics for their wizardry, and so the magician can use the toe switch to invisibly switch on and off electronic devices—right in front of you—without you or anyone else being the wiser. The Quick Man was wrong—nothing up his sleeve—but did you check the socks?

When Is Control Not Such a Good Thing?

Part of being an expert magician means knowing when to throw control out the door. Magicians won't get rid of their control haphazardly. No, they'll do it in a very controlled way. Especially when a magician must work in close settings like a nightclub or a small room, the audience can (and sometimes must) be used as a guideline for how the show proceeds. Firstly, the professional magician will know enough to alter his patter to fit the room. At one lousy show I attended, the performer made an off-color joke as part of a routine and a man instantly jumped up in the audience and yelled, "Watch your mouth, there're kids here!" The magician sheepishly put away his props and went on to the next trick. He simply could not continue with his routine in any form other than blue. Harley Newman, an escape artist and practitioner of various stunts and sometimes magic in Allentown, Pennsylvania, explains that many budding bad magicians have an idea that "professionalism is memorizing a routine from a book." He says that while his show is preplanned, part of that preparation involves being able to react to the changing moods and actions of the audience. "In my head, I've built up a show, a generalized way of doing it. . . . [But] I leave room open, I'd rather have fun with the audience."

The Many-Faceted Magician

Look at all that we have discussed in this section—gestures, movement, lighting, sound, music, control of the stage and of the theater, audience manipulation, and on and on. Most important is the magician's ability to combine all these elements into a smooth performance that controls the audience's attention and mood. "By making instantaneous adjustments to audience mood and attention level, by imaginative handling of hecklers (we will touch on this later), by attractively presenting one's personality, by establishing eye contact to create in each spectator the feeling of being given special attention, performers keep their audiences tuned to their acts and, thereby, succeed in entertaining them.[37] Stebbins points out that this combination of talents can only be accomplished through extensive experience on the stage. If any one thing is missing, the magic is not magical. It's just a trick. If all are present, then you've produced an engaging, exciting, mystical performance. And that's what magic really is. All that stuff is what illusions are made of.

5

Analyzing the Action

The Contemplative Mind

One of the things you're not supposed to do at a magic show is try to figure it out. You're supposed to sit back and enjoy yourself. Let the magic wash through your soul and smooth your mind into a mass of awestruck jelly. That's the intention. That's what most magicians would tell you: For best results you should just sit back and enjoy it and not think about it too much. Of course, that's what cult leaders and religious figures will tell you too. So I asked some magicians if *they* try to figure out the tricks when *they* go to a magic show. Teller, from Penn & Teller, said—

> Magic persists because its principal theme ("Where does reality leave off and make believe begin?") is one of the most fundamental concerns of civilized mankind. Even a bad magician is interesting to watch, because there's something you can DO while watching him; you can catch him trying to fool you, which is a good feeling. You can't say the same of bad actors.

—which I suppose is a wordy way of answering "yes." On the other hand, the great magician and escape artist James "The Amazing" Randi said that he does not try to figure out how the tricks are done.

> No, I essentially don't. I figure that I should try to get the kind of impact that the audience does. If I see it a second time I might try to look for the solution then. It's usually transparent to me anyway, but sometimes it's not.

Randi has been doing magic for quite some time. He has a respect for his peers, and he understands all the persistence, thought, study, and intel-

135

ligence that goes into making a piece of magic into an artform. And he holds these talented conjurers in high esteem, wishing to enjoy their craft as a botanist enjoys the delicate scent of a flower.

Luckily we're laypeople, so we can be as barbaric as we wanna be!

Let's get into some no-holds-barred, let's-figure-out-how-the-trick-is-done *snooping*.

We know better . . . we know that there is more to the trick than just the "trick." You can't explain away an illusion by just discovering the tricky part of it. There is still the whole underlying question of how the magician made you believe, how did that stupid little self-evident-in-hindsight trick seem so realistic on stage? We know there are subtle and complicated issues involved. But that doesn't lessen our curiosity! This chapter will give you the knowledge you need to figure out how the tricks are done. Let's sit down and analyze the action.

The Liars' Club

The magician stands up there doing everything in his power to trick you, deceive you, make you think that something *else* is happening than actually is. Basically the magician is a liar. It seems appropriate then to turn to the psychology of lying to help us investigate that tricky magician on stage.

Psychologists have studied almost every physical gesture, facial movement and vocal utterance to see how it betrays the liar. For instance, the voice is one clue that gives away the liar. When a lie is spoken, the voice tends to rise higher in pitch. Other factors such as trembling, unusual stuttering or stumbling for words, and speech errors are also common.[1] Another common indicator of lying are unnatural "illustrators." Illustrators are those hand gestures we make almost involuntarily while talking. Ask almost anyone to describe what a spiral staircase looks like and you'll see some illustrators at work. (Or ask them to define "zig zag.") When a person is lying, illustrators may be nonexistent, because the liar is trying to restrain himself as much as possible. Or the illustrators are there but they don't match up properly to the words being spoken.

The human face, with all its tiny muscles crammed together to control everything from the wiggle of a nose to the flutter of lips, is another goldmine of movements that can betray a lie. "The face . . . can lie and tell the truth and often does both at the same time. The face often contains two messages—what the liar wants to show and what the liar wants to conceal."[2] For instance there is something called a "micro expression," which is a split-second showing of the liar's true feelings in the midst of a longer-lasting false expression. The liar may be putting on a false front of happiness, in the midst of which comes a quick burst of sad-face. The sadness is quickly squelched—it's often so fleeting as to be undetectable to anyone but a trained observer.[3] Another common facial clue to deceit is asymmetry. Fake smiles tend to be crooked, for instance, and other facial components won't line up exactly across the face. Yet another clue that many people know about is pupil dilation—the pupils of the eye get larger when someone is lying, excited, or otherwise mentally engaged.

There are tons of such clues that we can look at to judge whether a person is lying, but, as it turns out, research has shown that most people *get away with lying because onlookers believe that the falsified facial expression is genuine.* Not only that, but people tend to pay attention to the false face while ignoring these subtle clues that reveal true emotions.[4] That could easily explain why we're so easily fooled. We just happen to be untrained in all these many physical and vocal clues to deceit. Lie researcher Paul Ekman notes that he and others "have trained people in how to look and listen more carefully and accurately, and most people do benefit. Even without such formal training, people can on their own practice spotting clues to deceit."[5] Surely if we sit down to one of Ekman's lectures we'll come out all set to face those liars in a head-on confrontation! It seems we're on the trail to catching those magicians in the midst of their deceit!

So we should be able to catch those magicians pretty easily, right? It's just a matter of training ourselves in the fine art of lie detection . . . right? I mean, suppose the magician is talking to us about his pet bunny rabbit he had when he was a kid. Suddenly in the middle of this touching story, you notice his voice starts to stumble a little, and perhaps raises in pitch a mite. Most of the audience believes this is just a touch of sentiment on his part as he thinks back nostalgically to his long-lost pet. Ah! But you know the truth! *Those are clues,* you mutter to yourself, and you know that at that moment his mind must be elsewhere. He may be acting nonchalant on the outside, but you know that he's really secretly doing . . . something . . . that will cause a baby bunny rabbit to appear in mid-air.

Sounds good, huh? But how realistic is that goal?

Unfortunately, probably not too realistic at all. You see, even though magicians are liars, the lying they do is very different from your everyday "the dog ate my homework" kind of lie. First of all, magicians are always very practiced in their lies. While "many [casual] liars are betrayed by their words because of carelessness,"[6] the stage magician has carefully planned out what he or she is going to say and do. Besides, the whole act is a big lie, so it's hard to judge that one moment when the trick occurs from the rest of the magician's actions and persona. That would be a nice thing to do, after all, to use those facial clues and vocal clues to determine when the gimmick is being employed, but you have to remember that the magician has all of the act memorized, including his voice and movements, and the coordination of the two together, so to single out one moment out of many moments would be nearly impossible by facial clues or voice falterings. The entire act is a lie! Besides, remember what we said before about constancy of gestures? The magician has planned ahead. He knows that later on he needs to hold his hand in a certain way to conceal a coin, so he goes through the entire show using that weird way of holding his hand. That way you can't separate the one true "lie moment" from the rest of the act. He gets so used to that unusual gesture that he doesn't distinguish it from the rest. If *he* doesn't distinguish it, how can you hope to? As far as facial expressions go, the magician will have a fake smile plastered on his face through the whole act, so what difference does it make if you can tell if it's asymmetrical or not?

Illustrators may offer clues to deceit in real life, but, as with facial expressions, they are not too helpful in uncovering a magician's lies. First of all, magicians are always doing weird things with their hands anyway, so it's hard to distinguish what was prearranged from what wasn't. Furthermore, it's very likely that any gestures the magician does make has been learned as part of the act, and because they're learned rather than natural, they look phony anyway. On the other hand, a bad magician may have solely concentrated on learning patter and so any gestures that accompany that patter will have a forced and unnatural appearance for the simple reason that they're putting on an act, like an actor. In that case you might be able to detect the lie.

I'm reminded of a friend I had in high school who used to perform acts of vandalism on school property. When he was approached by his parents or school officials about the damage he would tell the same lie over and over again until, as he put it, "I told them the story so many times even *I'm* starting to believe it!" That's exactly what magicians do. They practice their illusions so much and so well that they start believing the magic is reality. Any top-notch magician will tell you that they have to believe in the magic in order for the audience to believe in it. And if the magician believes it's real, certainly that will cut down on facial clues and verbal slips.

No, I don't think the usual methods of catching liars apply to magicians, although they are useful to know. If you're being entertained by a close-up magician (especially if it's an amateur or hobbyist magician) then you will want to look for such things as pupil dilation and faltering of speech, because an amateur very likely hasn't practiced as much as they need to get it right. And any small twitch or slip is so much magnified in close-up magic that such things are probably worthwhile to look for.

But if you're watching an illusionist far away on a darkened stage, you're not entirely out of luck. Stage magicians have their own sorts of slips they are sometimes prone to doing. While they probably won't falter for words, you may catch a magician doing a sudden, fast movement, an awkward pause or stalling for time, or any of the usual misdirection tactics such as having only one obvious action occurring so as to obscure another more subtle action elsewhere on stage. I will talk about these in greater length later on. For now let us continue with other means of analyzing the magic show to try and discover the methods to the magic!

The TV Magician

Magicians have two problems when they allow their acts to be recorded and then viewed later. First of all, television is notorious in magicians' circles for revealing certain kinds of tricks. The threads used in levitations and animations are often visible on the small screen; close-ups can reveal that a leg or head in a box is just a mannequin, not a live person; and black art magic can be subtly revealed on television as well.

Magicians have another problem with television—illusion is a thing to behold live, immediately, on stage before you, where you can see it and know it is real. TV magic has a ring of fraudulence to it. We know that magicians are out to deceive us, so who's to say they aren't simply using video effects to make the trick work?

Happily, we can say truthfully that most television magicians do not use special editing or video effects to create their magic. To do so would turn the magician into a charlatan in his own mind. However it has always been a big concern to the magicians, and you will notice the great lengths they go through to stress to the viewing audience the "authenticity" of the magic being performed.

Now, this doesn't mean they don't use the medium to their advantage! When a magician has control of camera arrangements, he will invariably do just what he pretends not to be doing. The magician will try to inform the producer or director of photography that certain camera angles are bad and should not be used, otherwise they'll give away the trick. The camera operators still have lots of other camera angles and camera tricks they can use (zooms for instance), so the audience doesn't notice their viewing is being restricted in this way.

Let's look at David Copperfield, because he is, after all, TV's number one Magic Man. Listen to what Copperfield says very carefully. On one TV special he says, "Our camera—this shot—will never cut away. No camera edits, no video effects. You'll see it at home just like you'd see it if you were here with me." He emphasizes the "you'll see it as if you were here with me" part, mentioning it more strongly and more often than the "no camera tricks" part. His conscience does not allow him to tell an outright lie. Over and over again, Copperfield blatantly choreographs camera angles as extensions of the movement and dance so characteristic of his work.

A prototypical example of this is Copperfield's train car evanishment. The illusion is set up with our seeing Copperfield stride confidently through the corridor of the train car, and emerge from its solid hull to prove the car's solid fortitude. Next Copperfield surrounds the train with spectators, covers it with a huge white hanky, levitates the thing, swishes it around in the air like it's a balloon on a string, and finally, whisks away the silk blanket that covers the car to reveal—nothing! Empty air! Surely this is a miracle!

A miracle that anyone with a few million bucks can buy.

The first time I watched this illusion, I was baffled. I had it on tape, so I watched it again in slow motion. Then again. And again. One thing is very clear from seeing this on tape: The train never leaves the ground. Oh it *looks* like it is suspended above the floor with cables, but it's not. This is the luxury that TV and VCRs allow you, to see something again and again. The train car is covered by a large dropcloth, then supposedly raised in the air. From watching it, it's not apparent how he snuck the train out from under the dropcloth, but it is very clear that once it's in the air, it's gone. In it's place is a hollow frame or shell.

After the train is lifted up, the cables start moving it horizontally for some reason. As the train moves, the resulting breeze pushes in the cloth slightly. Obviously if the train were still in there, the breeze would blow the cloth *against the hard side of the train.* The next suspicious event is when the cloth is whisked away. When it's time to reveal the train has vanished, Copperfield pulls a rope, and the cloth falls down to the floor. But it doesn't fall uniformly. By watching the tape you can see that the two ends fall faster than the middle. Not only that, but two curved supports are visible underneath the cloth, as the cloth is dropping to the floor. The curved supports are apparently what gave the empty cloth its train-like appearance. When the cloth falls to the ground, those two hard, heavy endpieces bring down the ends of the cloth faster than the middle, which stays afloat a mite longer, like a parachute.

The power of the taped image seems to have triumphed once again! By careful viewing and re-viewing, one can piece together much of the process used to vanish the train car.

Oh, but there is that one sticking point. We haven't yet explained exactly how it is the train car vanishes from under the dropcloth! Since I knew the train doesn't get pulled up into the air, that meant it must vanish while it's still on the ground. At first I thought it must fall through a trap door in the floor. But then a report by *Spy* magazine came to light. The report alleges that Copperfield's

> audiences are actually paid extras who are required—as are crew members—to sign oaths that they will not reveal how he does his tricks. This "audience" will be paid to hold hands around, say, the Orient Express. Then, during a sneak camera cut, they drop their hands and stand aside while the train is moved out of sight—reclasping hands for the "disappearance" denouement.[7]

I think the author of the above quote is being somewhat unfair to Copperfield. Not all of his audiences are paid extras, as the *Spy* article seems to imply. Copperfield might look at it as hiring a group of short-term assistants, no different than hiring assistants for the other parts of his act. Still, it's very clear that one must be aware of TV tricks at play.

Using VCRs

Videocassette recorders are great for analyzing magicians doing their thing. When you're done with this book, you'll know how most of the illusions are done the first time you view a show, as you're watching it. But there will always be some things you missed. Some things you want to go back and check, or some illusions that have you completely baffled.

VCRs are particularly useful when looking at close up magic. Magicians who do close up magic have to be very good at what they do, since the audience is focused in on a tight area, with not much room for hiding, and not much room for slip-ups. These magicians may be so well-versed at their slight of hand, that you may *think* you know what's going on, but require a second going-over to prove it.

You'll be making good use of the freeze frame, rewind, and slow advance buttons on your VCR.

The first time I utilized my freeze frame and slow advance was for a magician that appeared on the short-lived ABC show "Incredible Sunday." The magician sat down at a table with the big-toothed, big-haired host, and proceeded to do two magic routines. The first, which involved coins appearing and disappearing from under a small cup, had me stumped. It obviously relied on some fancy fingerwork, but the actual methodology was so well practiced as to be invisible. The second routine, a variation on the cups and balls, was absolutely stupendous. Throughout the routine a multitude of sponge balls, fruit, and other items were produced and vanished from under the magician's hands and hat. At the end, the magician placed his empty hat on the table and asked the host to feel it. "There's something in the hat that wasn't there before," the host said, laughing at the impossibility of it. He lifted the hat to reveal a ten-inch, solid metal lug nut, which he then picked up and dropped on the table with a thud. There was simply no way for any of that stuff to have gotten inside the empty hat. And yet it did.

I watched the routines several times, but the performance was so well done that the more I watched, the more seamless it became. Some slowing down with the remote control was in order.

Using the pause and slow advance buttons revealed certain things. For instance, the magician would have his empty fist on the table, and open the fist to reveal some items that had magically appeared inside. As this flourish was going on, the other hand was bringing the hat into his lap. At one point a bit of orange was visible as the hat came up from his lap. Of course, the orange was the next thing produced.

At the end of the routine, a gigantic flourish on the table drew attention away from the hat, which again dipped down to scoop up the nut. After the invisible scoop, he handled the hat lightly, gently, and carelessly, suggesting it was empty, when in fact, if you saw the action in slow motion, he was very plainly gripping the heavy nut inside the apparently empty hat.

The entire routine crumbled under the omniscient gaze of my VCR eyes. I could see what twenty-four frames a second could not see. True, I had lost the magic of the routine, but I had gained an understanding: yes, those old tricks do work. You really can misdirect an audience by poofing your hand here while secretly loading up your other hand over there. But this was not merely a technician, but a magician. His skill lay in his ability to create *magic*. I didn't feel that he was doing a trick. I felt, and the host who sat knee-to-knee with him at the table felt, that something extra special was going on before our eyes.

Still, the magician's first routine left me stumped even when I viewed it in slow motion. Coins were mysteriously appearing and disappearing under an innocuous metal cup. The moves looked like standard magician's moves in real time, but in slow motion a different story was revealed.

Watching the action slowly, you would see something like this: a coin would be placed on the table. The cup is placed over the coin. The cup is lifted, and the coin is gone. In slow motion, it was obvious that the magician had no chance to steal away the coin. I still didn't know how the trick was done, but I was led to the unshakable conclusion that it was only a trick, accomplished by a gimmicked cup.

Years later I shared the story with a number of professional magicians and they agreed that this close-up artist was most likely using a *chop cup* for the trick. A chop cup is a standard magician's prop that works by having a magnet concealed inside its bottom. Fake coins (that will stick to a magnet) or steel balls can be made to appear and disappear by allowing them to be drawn up inside the cup by the magnet, or letting the magnet release its hold on the objects.

VCRs are an invaluable way to get to the heart of the mystery, if that's what you're after. In some cases you'll see how it's done. In others (like with the chop cup) you will see how it's not done (in this case by a gimmick, not by sleight of hand). This magician made effective use of his gimmicks, because his use of it was skillfully accompanied by patter, gestures and movement that added up to a magical effect. That is to say, if a magician does a trick that essentially boils down to one store-bought gimmick, that trick will not necessarily be successful, even if the gimmick always works on time, as expected, and without a hitch.

A VCR can also be helpful in your pursuit of the truth because if a magician appears on a show where he doesn't have directorial control, he's giving up some of his control over the situation. "Many performers who establish excellent stage routines are done in by television. For example, I have on tape a performance from a major television show in which a Las Vegas card-worker—well known to all magi—did some close-up one-on-one work for the show host, who was flabbergasted as expected. The performer failed to instruct the director, who used the wrong camera angles, revealing almost everything to the viewing audience. It was a disaster."[8]

FINDING MAGIC ACTS ON VIDEOCASSETTE

It is difficult to find magic acts on video, to study them as described above. Video rental stores don't stock them. Hardly anyone makes them. Every once in a while one of the television networks will host a magic special, but these end up sitting on the dusty shelves of the network closets, never to be played again, and certainly not to be made available on videocassette. I searched relentlessly to try and get a copy of that "Incredible Sunday" show to view. The trail ended coldly in a bitter maze of voice mail and phone tag. (So please excuse me if my recollection of the show doesn't match your knowledge of the performer.) It's hard to find magic acts on video.

Luckily there are lots of magicians in the world. Many magicians keep a library of magic on TV. If you want to get videotapes of magical performances, your best bet would be to ask around. Talk to the folks behind the counter at the magic store. Talk to people at magic clubs and organizations. Talk to people on computer bulletin board systems and on-line services. Often it is enough to simply mail a fellow magician a videotape and some money for return postage, and they will be glad to copy over some show or shows they've collected through the years. The Society of American Magicians is one of the best sources of magical performances on video, but one must be a society member to borrow from their extensive library.

Complete listings of magic seen on television shows and in the movies is maintained on the Internet, and is posted monthly to the alt.magic newsgroup. It may not be possible to obtain videos of every show in these lists, but they are certainly good pointers to magical appearances in mainstream entertainment.

If you own a video camera you may (or may not) be able to tape a live show. Most theaters prohibit the taping of performances (and the darkness of the theater makes for a grainy tape anyway). But in a Disneyland or Cypress Gardens or other touristy environment you can generally get away with capturing a live show for posterity on tape. Also, theme park shows tend to be outside, and video cameras operate best under natural sunlight.

It should be said that there are plenty of instructional videos available to teach magic. Most video stores do not carry these. You are most apt to find them in magic shops or magic catalogs. These are usually not magic performances. These are professional magicians demonstrating their sleight-of-hand techniques. Many of these tapes are so technical they are worthless to anyone except an expert. Again, you should ask around in magic circles to see which tapes real magicians recommend for someone of your skill level.

Photographs

Stage magic is like the visual equivalent of the fast-talking con artist. As such, the magician moves quickly across the stage, allowing little more than a fast glimpse of props. That's why still photographs can be so revealing, for they allow you to analyze the action at your leisure. Not only that, but often photographs are taken head-on, without considering the fact that the illusion may have been designed to be optimally viewed at an angle. For instance, in the Siegfried and Roy biography *Mastering the Impossible* there is a promotional shot that shows an assistant being squooshed in a box that is much too small to contain her body. Her smiling face pokes out of one end, and her wiggling tootsies out the other; the head and feet are separated by a mere eighteen inches of space—she's been squooshed. Ordinarily this would be an amazing illusion, given the sparking lights and pulsating music, fast spins of the table and box, and the angle from which the stage is viewed. However this photograph shows the box head-on, and it is painfully obvious that the table on which the box rests is thick enough to secretly hold the woman's body. Seeing the show live it would be harder to recognize this fact, since the box would be spun around, moved around, and viewed from an angle, diverting one's attention elsewhere.[9]

Another example of photographs allowing a revealing glimpse into the doing of a trick presents itself in the November 16, 1995 issue of *Rolling Stone*. On page 52, James Iha from the band Smashing Pumpkins has his body pulled apart by the Zig Zag Illusion. Unfortunately, the careful observer can plainly see that his wrist bends up at an odd angle, and his foot is also bent peculiarly, offering clues as to how the illusion is accomplished. As with the Siegfried and Roy squoosh box, the still photograph allows for leisurely viewing of the photograph, and the optical illusion that causes the Zig Zag Illusion to work is ripped away like the Wizard of Oz getting his plug pulled. On the next page of the magazine, lead singer Billy Corgan's disembodied head rests on a sword that is thrust through an elegant velvet chair. Did some *Rolling Stone* reviewer dislike the band's latest effort so much that he'd slice off the guy's head to get the photo? Once again the photograph provides the detective in all of us with the answer. Directly under the sword there is a panel of red velvet that matches the back of the chair. Corgan's body is hiding behind this panel, and extends out through a hole in the back of the chair. The fact that a patch of velvet is concealing his body is apparent to the sharp-eyed observer because the way the photograph has been taken, the patch of red extends farther to the left than the actual back of the chair extends, causing a slight but observable visual inconsistency.

We've all seen paparazzi snapshots of a beautiful actress or model who looks horrible without her makeup and designer gowns. Looking at photographs of magicians caught at a moment in time can be similarly revealing—showing off the real face behind the glossy exterior.

Movies and Television Shows

Hollywood is illusion. Consider the on-screen lovers who take jabs at each other's bad breath off screen. Consider the special effects, makeup and lighting, sound effects crews and all the rest of it that go into the making of a TV show or movie. Yes, Hollywood *is* illusion, and because of that, Hollywood has a higher-than-usual interest in illusion. Because they need to put out intriguing movies, deception comes up again and again in films. If you're interested enough you can use TV and movies to ferret out some explanations as to how some tricks are done.

Your guide can be the "List of Magic in Movies" and the "List of Magic in Television Shows." These listings are posted monthly to the alt.magic newsgroup on the Internet by Jeff Isozaki. Magicians send in magic sightings to Jeff, who maintains the lists. The current lists contain about 130 movies and even more television shows and videos in which magic has appeared.

A typical example is the movie *Colossus: The Forbin Project*. This 1970 sci-fi movie featured Dr. Charles Forbin as a martini-drinking computer scientist who builds a massive computer capable of independently regulating the national defense of the United States. But the Russians have built an equally sophisticated computer and once the two computers find each other, they decide to link up and together control all mankind. (In 1970 there was no humankind.) The computers have control of the nations' weapons, including nuclear weapons, and whenever the humans try to interfere with the computers' plan, the computers unfeelingly bomb the hell out of some poor village somewhere. The humans won't stand for such disregard for human life (although the computers rationalize that it serves the world population to kill a few people here and there).

Dr. Forbin, who walks through the movie like a cross between James Bond and a store mannequin, is aghast that his creation is running amok. It's up to him to regain control of his Machiavellian machine, and he sets about on a complicated plan to fool the computer. But as one scientist in the movie remarks, that's like "trying to fool a superior brain that's programmed to get smarter every day." They realize that when the missiles come up for reservicing they can replace the warheads with dummies. The dummy missiles can be fired but won't detonate, and therefore won't be destructive.

In order to carry out the deception, the scientists make use of a standard magician's prop—a box with a hidden compartment. The dummy module is inside the false top in a small silver box. The real module is removed from the missile and placed in the box for safe-keeping while they "retarget" the missile to its new computer-specified setting. Before replacing the module they subtly flip the box over, which causes the false panel to fall on top of the real module, exposing the dummy module, which they then remove and place inside the missile. A twist of the wrist is all it takes to enact the deception, and they manage to replace many of the deadly missiles with impostor dummies. They also get to reveal this standard magician's trick to the movie-going audience.

Revelations abound in the movies and on TV. Some are accidental. In an interesting twist, recently an Indian swami who supposedly has psychic powers was being filmed for a propaganda film that would prove to the world the validity of his claims. Unfortunately, during his amazing production of a gold chain from thin air, the camera accidentally revealed his magic method on film. The government tried to suppress the film, but it was distributed underground throughout India, and the BBC used it in one of their documentaries.[10] Gosh, I guess the guy wasn't psychic after all.

Watching Live Shows

Videotape may afford the magic investigator such luxuries as rewind and pause, but only a live stage performance can convince us for certain that what we're seeing really is magic, as opposed to some fantasy inside a wooden box. Although we've talked at great length about all the controls a magician imposes, there are plenty of mistakes made in live shows. Loopholes are left that allow the knowledgeable spectator to take a sneak peek at some secrets the magician inadvertently reveals.

How can you sneak a peek? First of all, select seating that is front and off-center. Seats way up front and off to one side seem to be a good bet for watching large-scale stage shows, assuming you have a view of the stage at all from that vantage point. Oftentimes side front seats allow views into the wings, which may reveal assistants scurrying back and forth, or someone slipping on or off stage, or a prop being handled "out of view" of the audience. Side seats also give you advantageous angles at times. For instance, in box tricks (where a woman is put into a box) sometimes having a side seat gives you a good view of exactly how she is slipping into or out of the box. From the front she may appear to be casually entering the contraption; from the revealing side seat you may see that her legs are curled up under her abnormally as in a sawing illusion, or that otherwise her actions are not as innocent as on first glance from the front.

The balcony is another trouble spot for magicians. Under utopian performing circumstances, the magicians would be able to have an audience of fellow magicians sitting in every seat during rehearsals, to make sure there are no bad angles, but such a thing is of course impossible. Especially when a magician is touring from one stage to the next every few nights. One magician reported that he saw a performance of the Metamorphosis illusion at a magic conference, and apparently the performers did not consider the balcony when staging their effect. At the climax of the effect, when the magician and assistant change places in an instant, everyone in the balcony could see behind the curtain, straight down into the top loader (trap door) of the trunk. So if you're into analyzing the action, don't be too upset about the balcony, just bring your binoculars and enjoy.

Certain kinds of shows will reward those who come early or stay late. If you come early and the venue is not large you may get to see the performers set up the stage and maybe even get to talk to them. Sometimes at the end of a performance audience members can walk close to the side of the stage and take a look at props or stage settings from a behind-the-scenes view. If you get to talk to the magician or assistants, naturally your first thought will be to blurt out, "How did you . . . ?" but be assured they are too well trained to answer that sort of query. A better approach would be to compliment the magician on the show, throwing out some magician jargon as you do so (see the Glossary to bone up on the cant). The magician is liable to make some comment that assumes you know more about magic than you really do, using some technical term that explains how the trick was accomplished. You may not understand the terminology they mention, but you can piece it together later after having had some time to think it through, and with some good magic reference books in front of you. One time I bullshitted my way through a conversation so beautifully that the clerk in the magic store finally backed up, said, "Whoa, I see you're a lot more skilled than me," and started asking *me* questions. I made a hasty getaway at that point.

Another time I happened to come early to a magic performance and saw a group of people in black chain-smoking outside the back of the theater. I approached and talked with them, and found that they were the magician's assistants. No real secrets were exchanged, but it was fun to learn the latest gossip on the show and the personalities behind it.

It was mentioned earlier that coming early to a psychic's performance can give you insights that late-comers don't get. For instance, you may spot the psychic or assistant(s) scouting the crowd, gathering personal information from them. Assistants or the magician might also come out to salt the room, or hand out props to confederates or volunteers in the audience. One trick to keep in mind as you're looking for these roving assistants is to be aware that the assistants may not be the same age as the magician, and probably don't look at all show-bizzy.

If the psychic performer has a large enough show you can come prepared with a shortwave radio receiver. That's what James Randi does when he attends evangelistic faith healers' services. As the faith healer struts around on stage divining confidential information about his flock, assistants backstage are feeding that info to him via radio. With the proper equipment you can tune in to all the back and forth chatter. Make sure you keep your receiver concealed in your car or a briefcase. Otherwise they're sure to spot you and kick you out. A report in *Popular Communications*, "The Monitoring Magazine" for scanner enthusiasts, revealed that "one televangelist was caught 'off camera' commenting to someone about how well he can manipulate his viewers. It was quite revealing."[11] This particular article gives a full-frequency guide to the "electronic church," disclosing the scanner bands that can be used to eavesdrop on each televangelist's wireless mikes, remote pick-ups, and walkie-talkies. The article was written in 1992, so the given frequencies may be out of date.

During the show you can analyze the action by paying close attention. Come prepared with a small pad and pen to take notes, and maybe even a miniature tape recorder (although you should hide that, as it is probably not allowed). A video camera in the theater will almost certainly get you kicked out.

We talked about lighting earlier. One might point out that darkness can be an effective aid to the magician too. As an article in *Spy* magazine alleged, David Copperfield uses a darkened stage to hide his incompetence. They claim that, "At least some of the time, he's not really working live at all. It seems he's just not proficient enough to carry off the more difficult feats of illusion. So, rather than screw it up in front of an eager, if gullible, audience, Copperfield will work in shadow onstage, with a camera on him, while a pre-recorded video of the trick plays out on a large-screen monitor. Anyone paying close attention to the show can reportedly see the difference between the 'real' magician's movements and those of his video counterpart."[12] Is Copperfield incompetent, as *Spy* claims? Many of his close-up effects I've seen televised were clunkily done, in my opinion. To his credit, Copperfield is probably on the road a lot, with little time to practice new illusions well enough to be as perfect as a less jet-setting magician would be. On the other hand, there was the time Copperfield cut off a fingertip while doing a rope trick. Blood spurting from his severed digit, the show ended early as he was rushed to the hospital. Is Copperfield incompetent enough to require a televised video double? Maybe he took it on advice of his physician.

It occurs to me that if one had some extra cash lying around they could purchase a night vision scope for better viewing of magic in a darkened theater, Copperfield's or otherwise. The scopes let you see clearly, even in a darkened room. They cost anywhere from $379 to $1,000 and up. Imagine watching a levitation effect in a dark theater with one of those babies, with all the supports and wires revealed for the eye to see!

If you're really frustrated in your quest for the truth, you might follow the lead of America's first famous magician, Harry Kellar. Kellar was astounded by the levitation effect performed by Maskelyne, the great British magician. Every night Kellar took to the theater to study Maskelyne's performance, but he could not figure out how it was done. Kellar approached Maskelyne and offered a large sum of money to purchase the secret of the effect, but Maskelyne turned him down. Kellar went back to studying the technique in his chair but after a few nights he became so frustrated and restless that he jumped out of the audience and climbed up on stage in order to see how the trick was done! After vitriolics were exchanged, the curious Kellar was forcibly ushered off stage. It's not known for sure whether his jump to the forefront helped his cause in any way, but in a few years, the jealous Kellar would mystify audiences with a levitation effect much more sophisticated than the one Maskelyne had devised. But I'd suggest you get yourself a good lawyer if you wish to attempt this method of analyzing the action.

REPEATED VIEWINGS

If you have the opportunity to see a live show more than once, you can make use of your knowledge from the first show to help figure out the tricks the second time around. You'll know all the surprises and twists on second viewing, so you know what to expect. In sucker tricks you'll know who's really being fooled. Magicians have a rule "never perform a trick more than once for the same people." By seeing the show twice you're helping the magician to break this magician's code of conduct—without the magician even knowing he's doing so! Here are some tips to guide you.

- The second time around you know what all the climaxes are. That means you can safely ignore them. In a fast sleight-of-hand routine, when an empty hand goes up to reveal that there's suddenly a grapefruit in it, remind yourself that you know about the grapefruit. It's more important to look at the other hand.
- In audience-participation tricks, you can see if the same people are used more than once, indicating that they're stooges.
- For that matter, you might try to be a volunteer yourself. It will be less stressful because you know what to expect, and you can try to do things differently than the volunteer in the last show.
- On second viewing you can try to sit in a different seat of the theater, perhaps gaining better angles that will help disclose the mysteries.
- Look for same outcomes. Some tricks may look random, but in fact always work out the same way no matter what. Does the volunteer always happen to pick the five of clubs no matter how many shows you attend? That tells you something.
- Are mistakes and blunders repeated from one show to the next? As we'll see below, what looks like a mistake may actually be intentional and has an ulterior motive!

Hello, My Name Is Pat Pending

Another way of "analyzing the action" is by ordering up a copy of a trick from the U.S. government Patent Office. If an illusion is registered with the Patent Office, you can send away for complete instructions, schematics, and comments by the creators of the effect. The next time you're in a magic shop, look around on the boxes to see if any patent numbers are listed. (Probably not, but it's worth a try, right?)

If an illusion or any invention is labeled "Pat Pending" or "Patent Pending" then you won't be able to dig up dirt on it. Pending patents have not yet been issued and the invention can be regarded as a trade secret if the inventor so desires. Patents may be in a "pending" state for up to three years. That, by the way, is enough time for a magician to widely perform and popularize an illusion, and then, when the patent is granted (and thus the secret publicized), to dump the trick from his show since at that point it's an old trick.

There are over seventy Patent Depository Libraries scattered throughout the United States, as well as the main patent office in Arlington, Virginia. These libraries contain a good deal of the issued patents, regular updates as new patents are issued, and complex indexes to help with a search. The larger libraries offer patents on a microfilm cartridge system, and some have the same computerized system as used in the U.S. Patent and Trademark Office. If you're interested in seriously pursuing this line of investigation, your best start would be to go to your local library and have them help you find information on the nearest patent depository branch.

SIMPLY ASKING

The most effective way of finding out how a trick is done might be to simply ask the magician.

You: "How did you do that?!"

Magician: "Can you keep a secret?"

You: "Yeah!"

Magician: "Yeah, well so can I!"

Well, who knows, maybe they will divulge something every once in a while. Definitely no magician will reveal secrets just because you want to know. You will have to ingratiate yourself with the magician first. Win their trust in you. Two illustrative anecdotes from the Feynman files prove the point that sometimes magicians do tell all.

Richard Feynman, Nobel Prize winner for physics and known to many as a raconteur with many wild tales to tell, told about his encounters with mind readers in the first of his two biographies. When Richard was a child, a mind reader had come to town and demonstrated an act where he found a five-dollar bill hidden somewhere—anywhere—in town. The bill was hidden by a banker and a judge. The mind reader took their hands and began walking through the town, "reading their thoughts" and ultimately locating the hidden money in a dresser drawer in somebody's house. Feynman's father happened to hire the mind reader as a tutor for the young Feynman, and after one of his lessons, his father asked the mind reader how he was able to find the money.

The mindreader explained that you hold onto their hands, loosely, and as you move, you jiggle a little bit. You come to an intersection. . . . You jiggle a little bit to the left, and if it's incorrect, you feel a certain amount of resistance, because they don't expect you to move that way. But when you move in the right direction, because they think you might be able to do it, they give way more easily, and there's no resistance. So you must be always be jiggling a little bit, testing out which seems to be the easiest way.[13]

Feynman goes on to say that he tested out this trick one day when he was a graduate student at Princeton. Although it didn't work 100 percent of the time, "it worked better than I thought. It was very easy." And that was his first time—with no practice!

Richard Feynman also tells how years later he went with his father to Atlantic City and saw a different mind reading act there. Both of them wanted to know how it was done. Feynman's father went off to watch the show again to figure out how it was done. When he came back, he told his son the whole code they used, a similar code to the one we discussed earlier. "Blue is 'Oh, Great Master,' green is 'Oh, Most Knowledgeable One,' and so forth." His father explained how he suckered the magician: "I went up to him, afterwards, and told him I used to do a show in Patchogue, and we had a code, but it couldn't do many numbers, and the range of colors was shorter, I asked him, 'How do you carry so much information?'" Richard concludes: "The mindreader was so proud of his code that he sat down and explained the *whole works* to my father. My father was a salesman. He could set up a situation like that."[14]

Like I said, simply asking may pay off, especially if you use some deception of your own. While interviewing magicians for this book I've found that the magicians were more willing to talk to me once I had shown them that I knew the parlance, knew how the tricks are done, and that they weren't particularly teaching me anything new, only talking to "one of them." Tell the magician you are a hobbyist and you've been practicing magic in your bedroom for years. That's one of the reasons a glossary is given at the end, to familiarize you with the jargon of magicians and to give you more of a backstage look at how they talk while amongst themselves. A little later in this book we will look at how to enter the magical realm, the clubs and organizations that magicians haunt.

The experienced magician, 90 percent of the time, can work it out so it looks like [a mistake] was part of the trick, and they just go on. And the audience doesn't know any better.—Matthew, Illusion Artist

The Accidental Tap and Other "Blunders"

The tightrope walker is poised a hundred feet in the air above a hard concrete ground. We raise an eyebrow as she takes one tentative step onto the rope. We take a breath as she puts her full weight down on that foot. And then she lifts her back foot, and struts out onto the ever-thinning wire. Our enjoyment of the spectacle is wrapped up in the suspense we feel. We know she is good at what she does, but deep inside we feel our own insecurities. We know that sometimes we fail at even the things we are good at. And this tightrope walker, though practiced, is as human as we. The tension in the rope parallels the tension in our hearts, as we wonder if this time will be different for her. If this time she will make a mistake.

We sometimes feel the same way about magicians. Other magicians, who know how the trick is done, and know where the hard parts are, are apt to be nervous for the performer, hoping everything goes right. The spectacle is in wanting to see the performer's training pay off. But there's also an element of nervousness that the performer does not project, but may be killing him inside.

And sometimes the magician does foul up a trick.

But sometimes that foul up is merely part of the show.

With all of that training and all of that practice, and all of that thinking that goes on in the magician's head, it is unlikely that he really will mess up. Sometimes they do, and you can catch the mistake. Other times you don't catch him, and still other times, you think you've caught him, but you're actually the one who was caught, because the mistake was intentional, meant to deceive.

This goes back to the many seeds of misdirection that the magician plants, to grow a tree of realism in the act. Some seeds are as unobvious as a particular choice of wording. Others are as noticeable as a pretend mistake. Mistakes really make us sit up and take notice. As such, they are good forms of misdirection, taking us off guard, showing us what we believe is a vulnerable, unprepared side of the magician. There is believability in chaos, because there is no control of it. The subtle magician creates his own chaos, and with it, his own control of the audience.

One time I was watching a show where the magician happened to produce a hefty brown bottle of whisky. As he brought it in front of him, the bottle happened to tap against the microphone stand with a solid thud. A bag was produced from somewhere, and the bottle went into the bag. As the magician continued talking, he casually crumpled up the bottle into a small ball and tossed it over his shoulder. Two young women in the front row looked at each other in surprised wonder. *How did he crumple up a solid bottle?!*

The "accidental tap" of the bottle against the microphone stand proved that the bottle was a large, heavy glass bottle. It proved this much better than any amount of explaining or demonstrating that the magician might do.

Of course, the entire bottle was actually made of a soft rubber that could easily be crumpled up. The whole bottle that is, except for the small section that "accidentally" tapped against the microphone.

You will often see magicians "proving" the solidity of objects—magic wands, boxes, buckets, and the metal slicers that will perforate an assistant's body. You have to be aware that some of these proofs are real, and some are fake. If the magician only taps some of the object, or does so "accidentally," you can start considering the "proof" as nothing more than proof that deceit is underway. (Or if the tapping is done absent mindedly. Any good magician will be in complete control of his gestures and movements throughout the show. If you see him tapping a magic wand, for instance, as a nervous habit, you can bet he is either a novice at this or is trying to subconsciously get it in your mind that the wand is made of metal, not a tube of tissue paper. Probably the only thing metal about it is the small white tip at the end.)

Intentional accidents are sometimes the basis of simple sleights. There is an old but delightful illusion in which the magician disappears a coin by rubbing it into her elbow, which makes use of an accidental dropping of the coin. This trick is as old as the hills, but I was still surprised by it recently when my sister presented it to me after she learned it from a book. She showed me a quarter and announced she would make it disappear by rubbing it into her elbow. She bent her arm, and started rubbing the coin against her elbow. It didn't go in, it was still there on the surface. She rubbed so vigorously that she accidentally dropped it. She picked it up and started rubbing again, trying so hard to push the coin through her clothes, through her skin, and into her elbow. After awhile she lifted her fingers to reveal the coin was gone.

The trick is in the "accident," when she "accidentally" dropped the coin. That was no accident! It was a carefully prepared part of the trick! After she drops the coin, she picks it up with her left hand, then pretends to transfer it to the right hand—but secretly keeps it in her left! Then she bends her arm again and starts rubbing her fingers, pretending that the coin is underneath. Actually the coin is in her left hand up by her shoulder, and to further dispose of the evidence, she drops the coin down the back of her shirt through the neck hole. (She makes sure her shirt is tucked in before starting.)

While we're on the topic of hands, let's regress to our earlier discussion of gestures. Earlier we talked about the intentionality of everything the magician does, down to the arrangements of fingers and placements of the arms, hands, and belly button. My sister's rubbing trick illustrates this perfectly. Here she has to hold the coin the same way when she doesn't have it as when she does have it (that is, she must cover the coin, not let it show). At the same time, the magician must "prove" there really is a coin in her hand, so she might start by showing the coin, then switch to covering it, then dropping it, then maintaining the covered pose before showing it finally gone. You can see how it's wise, if you're analyzing the action of a show, to make sure you analyze the mistakes as well as the "action"—they may not be the accidental blunders they appear to be.

Looking for Unusual Covers

Covers are necessary for most appearances and disappearances in magic. For instance, if Wanda Wizard says she's going to make a giraffe disappear, you can bet your life she's not going to make it disappear before your eyes. She will first cover the giraffe with a tube or a box, drop cloth, screen, or curtain. Other, more tricky, covers are used to cover objects. Bright lights can be shined in the spectator's faces, or smoke can be poured onto the stage. In one gory act, Penn & Teller splash a lot of blood around; it is part of the storyline and also offers diversion and cover for their sleight of handiwork. Covers are so necessary to magic that one anonymous magician blurted out in interview, "I can't do magic without covers! What am I, a magician?"

Some tricks rely on specialized covers that are incorporated into the illusions themselves, and can therefore be used only for that particular trick. Copperfield does a Death Saw illusion in which his body is sheared in two by a rotating buzz saw. You see him laying flat on the table; you see the saw slicing through his clean white shirt. No covers there. Or is there? Actually, the cover already happened earlier in the trick (time misdirection). What you don't see is the moment when he is strapped onto the table. Why not? Because when he lies down on the table, a robotic boxlike contraption forms around his waist, thus hiding the fact that Copperfield is slipping half his body into one end of the table, and an assistant is slipping his legs out the other end.

The shirt tail covers the crease between the two people, and once it is in place the box cover is taken away to reveal what seems to be a single David stretched across the table.

After the Death Saw strikes, Copperfield seems to be in two pieces. Now he must be made intact again. When Copperfield was designing the illusion he had a motivational problem: The box contraption is really suspicious and obviously is there to hide something. But it's also necessary for the restoration part of the trick. ("What am I, a magician?") How could he rationalize hiding his split body with the box? Because, you see, without a rational motivation, our minds realize it is only a trick. You can't have an effective illusion if the mind is disbelieving.

Copperfield solved the problem by interworking his cutsy dance routine into the functioning of the illusion. When it comes time to heal himself, Copperfield magically reverses the flow of time. We watch the dance go backwards in time. Part of the dance includes the suspicious covering of his midsection with the box, thus giving a logical motivation for covering him with the box a second time. It isn't that he's covering himself again—he's merely reverting back to that time a few moments ago when he was covered.

One way or another, magicians get to use their covers. In the best acts, the use of covers is covered up by a logical motivation stemming from the story of the trick.

COVERS AND EVANISHMENTS

Now let's talk specifically about vanishing objects with covers. Most vanishings take place under a cover of some sort or another. Often the cover is used to cover up a bit of time misdirection. In other words, the audience is sitting there looking at the thing that is about to be vanished. What they don't realize is that the magician vanished it ten minutes ago. Right now they are looking at a cover that has the appearance of the missing object.

For instance, there is an old parlor trick, Pushing a Quarter Through the Table, that involves a combination of covers, time misdirection, thought misdirection, and surprise.

This is an illusion done at the dinner table, preferably after a good Thanksgiving dinner when Uncle Urkel is heading off to the medicine cabinet to get the Tums and Grandma Edna is starting to loosen her belt. Instead of offering to help clear the table, you (the magician) realize you have a quarter in your pocket, a salt shaker on the table, an extra paper napkin, and an audience. You get the kids to gather round.

"I'm going to magically push this quarter through the table," you say. The kids wander off because they're sick of this shtick, but Grandma Edna is interested, so you continue.

You place the quarter down on the table with a *plunk*. Solid table, solid quarter. Put the salt shaker on top of it. Cover the salt shaker with the paper napkin.

Now you begin to squeeze the salt shaker onto the table, attempting to push the quarter straight through the table. "Hmm, it's not working." You move aside the salt shaker, pick up the quarter, and examine it carefully on both sides. "Oh," you say, "It's a bicentennial quarter. Those never work right with this trick." You replace the quarter, and the salt shaker on top of it, and continue with some more squeezing, pushing, and, preferably, piggish grunting noises, trying your hardest to push it through the table.

(Of course at this point the salt shaker isn't there any more. When you moved it aside to check the quarter, you let the salt shaker fall secretly into your lap. The audience didn't notice this move because they were too busy looking at the bicentennial quarter you were holding in front of your face and theirs. The quarter is back on the table, and it appears the salt shaker is on top of it, when in reality it's just the napkin conforming to the shape of the salt shaker on top of the quarter, because when you first covered the salt shaker with the napkin, you pressed the napkin deeply and firmly onto the body of the salt shaker.)

Now you are pretending to press the salt shaker firmly onto the quarter.

After some time, with one final loud bang on the table, you ram the entire salt shaker through the wooden surface as the napkin flattens onto the tabletop. You retrieve the shaker from under the table and display it proudly. "I guess I pushed too hard," you say. "It went right through!" Grandma Edna buttons her pants and walks away, mystified and amused.

David Copperfield used a few very different kinds of covers in his 1981 disappearance of an airplane. For this illusion, he had a group of audience members circle around the airplane and hold hands. There was no way for the plane to escape from this circle of people. These people were made to wear blindfolds. It's very rare to have a disappearance without some kind of cover.

This particular disappearance was televised, and Copperfield didn't have enough blindfolds to share with everybody on Earth watching the show, so he had his assistants build up a square of screens around the circle of people. Now the home audience had a cover as well, but we were somewhat better off than the studio audience, because Copperfield turned on a giant spotlight that illuminated the plane from behind. A shadow image of the plane was thrown up onto the screens, so we could verify that the plane was there until the very moment when it vanished.

The illusion is actually pretty similar to the salt shaker trick mentioned above. Even though one trick is a small trick involving kitchen items, and the other is a large televised affair, they have very similar properties. This is often true of magic, that once you know some basic facts about how illusions are created, the facts can be applied on small or large scales. In this case, the screens surrounding the airplane worked like the napkin in the salt shaker trick. In the salt shaker trick, the audience thinks the salt shaker is under the napkin, because they think they can see its outline through the paper. They don't know the shaker has already been removed. In Copperfield's airplane vanish, a similar ploy is at work. The audience thinks the airplane is inside the screens because they see its shadow outline projected on the screen. They don't know that the airplane has already been wheeled away long before. At that point it's merely a matter of suspenseful build-up and loud music until the screens are pulled aside to reveal the plane is missing.

So how did the airplane disappear? British magician Paul Daniels was interviewed on a talk show and was asked, "Why can't *you* make a jet disappear?" and his answer was something to the effect of, "because I don't believe in stooges."[15] An alt.magic poster explains: "For the vanishing of the airplane the crowd that was around where the curtain opened was in on the trick. The plane was actually pulled out of the curtain's area and moved somewhere else by Copperfield's crew. I know this because my dad was at a dinner for engineers and the owner of the plane was the guest speaker and he said how the trick was done."[16]

It should be mentioned that once again Copperfield makes exquisite use of camera angles. When it comes time to vanish the plane, the camera is nowhere near it. The camera is pulled far enough back so only the screens and shadow are visible. And we definitely can't see over the top of the screens. He does that because he has to hide the fact that the back screen is being taken away and some of the stooges are unjoining their hands and moving apart from each other to allow the airplane to be hauled away.

Another way Copperfield uses covers, besides the screens, is the loud music mentioned above. Loud music serves to cover the sound of the airplane being rolled away. And you thought it was just to build suspense! Copperfield's a master at using loud music for cover. At the end of his shows he occasionally sits in the foyer of the theater to say hello to people as they exit. Bigshot that he is, he doesn't want to have a meaningful discussion with anyone, so he makes sure to have his stereo beside him, loudly playing some cheesy Top 40 song.[17]

COVERS USED OUTSIDE OF MAGIC

The cover technique has been used outside of magic shows by advertisers. For instance, there was one television commercial in which a housewife picks up a newspaper from her favorite food store and excitedly reads all the special deals being offered that week. The advertisers had a problem when they produced this commercial: how could they show this ad week after week, when the prices and products would be changing from one week to the next? Their solution was this: the housewife picks up the paper, and with eyes wide and mouth agape, she brings it closer and closer to her face to study it. When her face is practically buried within its price-saving pages, she begins to chat amiably about all the weekly food bargains. With her face hidden in the pages of the paper, you can't see if her mouth is really moving or not. The weekly deals are dubbed in each week, so every week they could use the same basic commercial frame, but have "her" talk about a new set of food bargains.

The New York State Lottery uses the same trick in some of its ads. The prize money amount changes from one week to the next. The commercial features a meek little man who steps close to a huge microphone in order to announce the weekly jackpot. The microphone covers his mouth so you can't tell that his voice is dubbed in. Additionally, since he is supposedly talking through a microphone, any subtle change in voice due to the dubbing will not be as readily noticed (some echo effects are also used, further distorting the speaker's voice).

These advertising covers remind me of a billboard I saw recently while driving down Interstate 95 to Philadelphia. The billboard was for one of the casinos in Atlantic City and it featured a midnight blue background and the name of the headlining performer atop a bed of sparking yellow stars. It occurred to me that this billboard is there from one month to the next, and yet the performers come and go. I noticed that the background of stars, besides adding visual beauty and excitement to the billboard, also serves as a cover of sorts. Instead of having to repaint the entire billboard every month, they can simply plaster up the half of the sign with the performer's name on it. The difference in background helps hide any differences in the blue color from one month to the next. After all, if half the sign is new each month and the other half stays up year-round, there's bound to be a difference in coloration as half the sign starts fading in the sun and rain. This is exactly the kind of trick that makes many magic tricks work—exploiting what looks like an innocent feature or ornament on an object in order to create a deception. In this case the yellow stars evoke the tranquillity of the night sky—very few realize they also serve this ulterior, cost-cutting purpose as well!

COVERS IN THE MOVIES

Another use of covers is in moviemaking. Movie directors conventionally take miles of extra footage of every scene. For a conversation scene, it will be filmed first head-on, then over the shoulder of one character, then over the shoulder of the other, then in close-up of one character, and close-up of another, and perhaps even more variations. An unreleased film is previewed to preliminary audiences to gauge their reaction and to indicate how it should be edited or altered to better please the viewing public. If a joke doesn't work, or the director feels something will play better, they might decide to splice in an over-the-shoulder shot of an actor and dub in a different line. The actor's back covers the fact that the actor is not really speaking the line.[18]

There's a long scene at the end of Oliver Stone's *JFK* that similarly uses over-the-shoulder shots of Donald Sutherland. Stone had shot two scenes that needed to be included because they contained information essential to the movie's plot. The problem was, the movie was way too long, and having two similar scenes would unnecessarily prolong it. The editor's decision was to combine the scenes into one huge mega scene. However, a problem arose in that in one scene Sutherland wears a blue suit; in the other, a brown suit. The editor overcame the problem by using footage from the first scene but dialog from both. Whenever Sutherland said crucial information in the "wrong color suit," an over-the-shoulder shot was used.[19]

There are also times when an actor is not available for one reason or another, and so a substitute actor is used. The terrible *Plan 9 from Outer Space* comes a little too easily to mind. Schlock director Ed Wood happened to have filmed two minutes of Bela Lugosi for a previous project before Lugosi's untimely death. Not wanting the footage to go to waste, Wood frugally took the two minutes and beefed it up with a stand-in for the remainder of the shoot. Because the new actor's face couldn't be shown, we see the Lugosi character through half the movie only from the back, or with his cape draped rakishly over his features.[20]

Stunt work usually relies on covers as well, the cover being either the stunt person facing away from the camera, or sheer distance making it difficult to see the stunt person's face. In the movie *Speed*, there is one quick shot in which Sandra Bullock's stunt double is briefly seen driving the bus. This is a special treat to the sharp-eyed, as the stunt double is a gargantuan, brawny man wearing a woman's wig, and is somewhat *plumper* than Sandra herself. So that's a case where the cover was the actor's back plus the quickness of the camera. But the freeze frame definitely uncovers the cover on that one.

In conclusion, magicians use covers to hide an action or a gimmick from the audience. Often the cover is visible (such as a silk, box, or curtain). Other times, the magician wants to hide the cover itself. The cover may be "hidden" through a psychological motivation for its existence—such as the Copperfield's reversal of time, or the cover may be hidden because it is worked into the story of the piece (the housewife who is so surprised by FoodLand's great prices that she simply has to get a closer look at the circular). A cover doesn't always have to be an "official" cover either. In other words, if the magician purposely covers a box with a big red silk, then obviously that's a cover. But what about when one of Copperfield's dancing assistants "happens" to dance in front of the box at a certain time? Could the assistant be dancing there for a reason? It happens all the time in shows. What about the different panels and props and pieces that are carried around, casually placed here and there? Those don't look like covers, just pieces being moved around during the course of the trick. But the magician has carefully orchestrated control over the whole show—it's probable that the movement is not so random as it appears. In short, when you uncover the covers, you have often discovered where the heart of the trick sits.

6

Things to Look for
When Watching a Magic Show

You little devil you! You've been analyzing the action on tape, on television, and at live shows. You've been applying what you've learned about magic and misdirection to try and figure out how the tricks are done. Good for you! But what's that—you say you still feel like you're missing out on things? Well, here's the pill to cure that. Now we get to the real fun stuff. This here is an encyclopedic medley of special things to look for when the magician is on stage performing. Some of these items will help you figure out how the trick is done. Others will reveal special ways in which the magician is enriching and enhancing his performance. Others are just fun things to look for. See how many you can spot at your next magic show.

Things to Look For

Transitions

Transitions from one part of an act to another may be shaky, like when the assistant steps into or out of a box. I was watching one live show in which the magicians performed an illusion where a woman lies back on a sword and twirls around on it, perfectly balanced on its tip. Then the sword punctures her body straight through, and she continues spinning. After a while the sword retracts, she is lifted off and to her feet. During this performance, the magician made a minor goof while lifting his assistant off the sword: There was a small but visible up-then-down jerk as he disengaged her from the sword. If it had been legit you would expect him to simply lift her off the sword, but the sharp-eyed spectators could see he was actually unhooking her from the sword. In other words, that tiny jerking motion made it clear that she was wearing some kind of support under her clothes, and the support hooked into the sword. A neat thing to look for!

RED MARKS

In the same show, the magic duo performed a levitation in which the woman was first "hypnotized" and then leaning against a giant Chinese fan. She then lifted up her legs and was able to remain suspended in the air as if she were weightless and needed to hold onto the fan so she wouldn't float away. She danced graceful motions with her arms and legs, high above the stage floor, twisting and turning, suspended up there in the air. It was a fairly successful illusion. Throughout the rest of the show, every time the woman turned her back to the audience, we could see a red mark pressed into the flesh of her back, where she had been leaning against the supporting rod attached to the fan. My advice: "Don't wear a scoop back!"

THE MAGICIAN'S FACE

A careful eye may reveal a telltale grimace, frown, or suddenly strained smile at the moment that the magician is trying to cover up some secret maneuver. Does his eye shift to an unlikely spot? Does his forced smile revert to a frown at one point? That's telling. It's a way of knowing that something is going on behind your back—or his.

RUNNING OFF STAGE

Some vanishings are done when the magician secretly passes the item to an assistant who runs off stage. In a popular children's show effect, the magician borrows a kid's sneaker and puts it in his magic washing machine. The machine starts to smoke and make funny noises, and maybe even disintegrate. When he opens it up, the magician is horrified (and the kids are delighted) to find the sneaker burnt to a crisp and terribly ruined. Later, after comic relief whereby the magician tries to get the too-smart kid to accept the damaged sneaker, the magician says he will try to make amends with a gift. A present is brought out, which the kid unwraps to find his undamaged sneaker. The trick is funny and effective, and accomplished with a hidden compartment in the lid of the washing machine. When the magician tosses the sneaker inside, he's really placing it in the secret compartment. The thing starts to rattle and smoke, and when he opens it up, he hands the lid to his assistant, who runs off-stage with it as if running for a fire extinguisher. Now they have the sneaker backstage and can do whatever they want with it, like wrap it into a present.

THE CURTAIN SWITCHEROO

This is a technique used to switch one person for another. The first time I saw the Curtain Switcheroo was at an outdoor magic show at Cypress Gardens in Florida. The magician was doing a corny dance routine that involved a lot of twirling and toe tapping. At one point he swirled himself up inside a curtain, which then unrolled to reveal the lovely young assistant inside. The magician was gone.

The switch is accomplished as the first person is being wound up inside the curtain.

1. The assistant is hiding behind the curtain (see figure 17).
2. The magician approaches the curtain and steps behind it. (Now both of them are behind the curtain.)
3. The magician sticks his head out from behind the curtain and simultaneously the assistant sticks out her hand (figure 18). She either grasps the edge of the curtain or waves to the crowd. The audience sees the magician's head, so they assume it is the magician's hand as well.
4. Now the magician ducks his head behind the curtain and runs backstage.
5. The assistant starts wrapping the curtain around herself. The audience thinks it is the magician getting wrapped up.
6. The curtain unrolls to reveal the assistant inside (figure 19).
7. The magician can reappear from the back of the theater. This is called a *run-around* in theater parlance, because while everyone was focused on the stage, the magician ran backstage and around to the back of the theater.

The overall effect is that the magician was rolled up in the curtain, but the assistant popped out. And there was never a moment when you lost track of exactly where the magician was, because a hand or head was always visible. This same technique is used in many variations in many illusions, such as Metamorphosis.

Fig. 17. The Curtain Switcheroo begins with the magician on stage and an assistant hiding behind the curtain. The magician approaches the curtain . . .

Fig. 18. The magician ducks behind the curtain, then quickly sticks out his head, while the assistant sticks out her hand. She might wave goodbye or simply grab the curtain. The audience doesn't know she's there, so they believe it is the magician's hand.

Fig. 19. Finally, the magician steps completely backstage, and the assistant reveals herself to the audience. As far as the audience is concerned, this is the first time they are seeing the assistant, so to them it looks like an instantaneous switch!

THE OTHER HAND

When one hand is doing movement that is necessary to the show, the other is probably doing something sneaky. This often happens when you least expect it—during the *climax* of a trick.

HAND OUT OF SIGHT

Out of sight, out of mind. This is especially true in magic shows where if a hand is out of sight usually you're not thinking about that fact because you don't even notice that the hand is gone. The other hand is busy misdirecting you away from it. Or some bit of business is used as a logical pretext for taking that hand out of sight. For instance, the magician needs to replace the pen in his pocket. It is a natural gesture, but while that hand is in there, it is also secretly pulling out a coin, or dropping in something that will later be shown to have vanished.

Look for the magician's hands sneaking into pockets and jackets of clothing, underneath tables or into the magician's lap, or generally behind or into anything. After the hand is removed, watch to see how the hand is held, because it may very well now be holding something that was secretly removed from the pocket and the magician is now palming it there.

Another deception is to hide coins or balls underneath the bottom edge of a suit jacket. It is unobtrusive and natural for a man to fold his fingers underneath the bottom of a sports coat. But what isn't common is for the man to have a three of clubs clipped there.

THE UNSHOWN

I know you're not a computer, but the well-prepared magic analyzer will do his or her best to keep track of what's been shown and what hasn't been. Magicians like to choreograph lots of box-twisting and spinning, so it's hard to be sure if you've seen every side, inside and out, of each piece of apparatus as it's presented. But do your best to follow. If something is left unshown there's undoubtedly a reason for it. For instance Siegfried and Roy perform a variation on the Metamorphosis illusion in which instead of one of them appearing inside the locked trunk, a panther appears in the trunk. According to reportage by author William Poundstone the panther is in the box from the start of the trick, but the audience is never shown the inside of the box. In this case the surprise of the panther is enough to ease people into forgetting this very important fact. (And at the beginning of the trick there was no good reason to show the interior of the box, since the trick was purportedly one where Siegfried and Roy would exchange places, thus no need to show the box as empty.)[1]

For that matter, it's interesting to note that in most versions of Metamorphosis, they never show you the bottom of the canvas bag inside the trunk. What usually happens is, the bag is inside the trunk to start with. The assistant steps into the bag while it is still in there. For all you know, the bag might not have a bottom (which would explain how the escape is made). On the other hand, some versions use a bag whose bottom is held together with a loose thread, snaps, or Velcro. The bag initially does have a real bottom and can be shown to the audience fully. But once inside the trunk, the assistant pulls apart the bottom of the bag. Now she can escape, the magician can enter, and *now* the bottom of the bag is left unshown.

The famous "breakaway rabbit box" trick has been performed on small scale (with rabbits) and large scale (to vanish humans), but it all relies on the same principle. A box is shown. In goes the rabbit (or human). The box is twirled around. All sides are shown (except for one side of one particular panel of the box). And then, with a grand gesture, the box breaks open to reveal a big empty nothing. Of course, what the audience doesn't see is the bag hanging there.

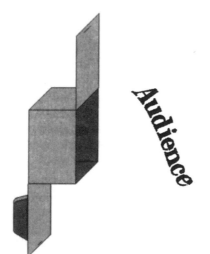

Fig. 20. The audience looks right through the box—it is obviously empty. They don't see the box or bag attached to the back lid.

Once when I was a kid I constructed a breakaway box like that out of an old wooden cigar box from my grandmother's garage, and a velvet bag I picked up someplace. It seemed obvious to me even then. I can't believe magicians still get away with crap like that. But they do.

Here is another illusion that relies on the "unshown" as the magician causes silk scarves to appear from an empty box. The illusion is created by misdirection, unthought of assumptions, and the unshown.

CREATE MAGIC!—SOMETHING FROM NOTHING

In this trick, the magician pulls objects out of an empty shoe box! The shoebox is sitting on a table with its lid propped up behind it. The magician shows the box on all sides, then shows both sides of the lid. but even when all sides are shown, looks can be deceiving. He puts the lid on the shoebox, says some *hocus pocus,* then pulls out all sorts of scarves and streamers from the "empty" box.

Here's how it's done. Fill a plastic bag with scarves, silks, etc. Tie a thread of a few inches to the bag. Then tie the thread to the inside of the lid, along one of its long edges. Place the box on the table. Place the lid on the table, with the top of the lid facing the ceiling. Hide the bag by letting it hang off the back of the table. It should be hidden from the audience by a table cloth. Figure 21 shows the layout of the table.

Fig. 21. The table is arranged to perform Something From Nothing. An empty box, and its prepared lid with a hidden bag hanging off the end of the table. The bag is hidden from audience view by the tablecloth.

To perform the trick, show all sides of the box, inside and out, to prove it's empty. Then show the inside of the lid by lifting it off the table. When you lift the lid, keep it on or very close to the table so the thread won't be visible (figure 22a). Now rotate the lid down towards the table so that the bag gets lifted up and is hidden behind the lid (figure 22b).

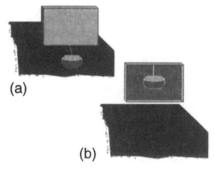

(a)

(b)

Fig. 22a and 22b. Prove to the audience that the lid isn't hiding anything. First show the inside of the lid (a). Then rotate it down and away so the bag is concealed (b). The audience has now seen both sides of the lid, so as far as they're concerned, it isn't hiding anything.

> The audience has now seen every side of the box and lid, and should be convinced there is no way to produce anything from that box. After all, the box is empty, and the lid is too flat and thin to conceal anything!
> Put the lid on the box, being careful to hide the bag from the audience. When you're ready to produce items from the box, remove the lid and prop it against the front of the box, with the bag dangling inside. Produce the items with much fanfare and swirling of silks.

Sometimes we are our own magicians, creating tricks that fool ourselves. For instance, a friend of mine wanted to show me a chart written in fine print on a videotape box. He picked up the box, looked at one side, then at the edges, pulled the tape out and examined both sides, replaced the tape, and did another search of the sides of the video box. He was getting increasingly frustrated because he was not finding the chart he was looking for. "I'm *sure* it was on this box!" he said. I pointed out that he had overlooked one side. Indeed, he merely turned the tape over, and there found what he was looking for. The point is that the magician on stage is merely exploiting limitations of our brains—limitations that are with us constantly as we step through our daily existence. Often the little frustrations, such as misplacing something, are due to a form of magic trick that deceives us into believing we've got all the bases covered, when really there's another side to the puzzle we have not yet examined.

Anything That Detracts from the Illusion

Anything that detracts from the illusion is there to make the trick work. All magic tricks should be straightforward and as easy to follow as possible. If something is complicated by rules, covers, or verbiage, you can bet there's a reason for it. Anything that distracts is most likely being used for either a cover or "proof" of the illusion.

For instance, when I was a kid I went to a show given by a supposed psychic. I'm ashamed to admit, before arriving I was pretty nervous that he would be able to read my mind. I planned to make my brain as blank as possible. When I got there, I lost all my fears. I realized right away that his psychic charade was nothing more than stage magic overlaid with a blanket of lying—his blanket statement that he had psychic powers when really all he had was a few practiced tricks and a stage presence.

One of the psychic's accomplishments was his ability to psychically receive a number that a spectator was thinking of. That was how he announced the effect: that an audience member would think of a number and it would be psychically transmitted to him. Now, that would be a good trick. I'd like to see that. Of course, the announced effect was far from what actually occurred. What did occur was that he had two audience volunteers submit two numbers, these were added together by a third volunteer, and a series of mathematical operations were performed on the numbers. After all that, he had one of the volunteers give him a piece of information that at that point, after so many calculations, seemed irrelevant and useless in helping him deduce the answer. He called it his "focus point." By focusing on this number it would help him read the mind of the volunteer.

Anyone with any common sense can see that this is all a big setup. If he can really read minds, then why doesn't he just read the person's mind? Why have them go through the whole rigmarole? In the case of number-manipulation tricks, the detractors are usually a reproducible set of steps that appear to generate a random number but which in fact produce a very obvious and easy-to-calculate number if you know the secret. Clearly the illusion would have been a lot more effective had he just "read their mind." Of course, that is impossible. And so we have the rule: *Anything that detracts from the illusion is a clue to how it's done.*

CREATE MAGIC!—THE MONEY ENVELOPE MYSTERY

Here is a trick that relies on the principle of number manipulation. An array of sealed envelopes are arranged across a table. The magician has an audience volunteer think of a number. "Make it a big number, three or four digits, to make it really hard for me to guess. Also make sure all the digits are different. That will make it nearly impossible for me to know—unless I use my psychic powers of course," the magician banters.

The volunteer writes down the number. The magician says, "Okay, now reverse its digits and subtract the two numbers. Subtract the smaller of the two from the larger value." When this is accomplished, the magician makes one final request. "Add up the digits in your answer, and write that number big on the paper, and hold it up so the whole audience can see. At this point, the volunteer might have something like this written on the paper. First the number he selected:

    6,405

Then, that number with its digits reversed:

    5,046

Then the two numbers are subtracted:

    6,405
    −5,046
    1,359

Finally, the digits of the answer are added up and written big on the paper, so everyone (except the magician) can see:

    $1 + 3 + 5 + 9 = 18$

The volunteer crumples up the paper and the magician goes into brain overdrive. His face becomes bright red as he strains to slip into the mind of the audience member. The magician picks up an envelope off the table, and tosses it off to the side. One by one he picks up and then discards envelopes, until finally only one is left. He rips it open and slowly counts out the dollar bills inside. Sure enough, there are eighteen dollar bills in that envelope.

The trick is embarrassingly simple. If the audience member follows the instructions precisely, the answer will always be 18. Take any three- or four-digit number with unique digits, reverse it, then subtract. Now add the digits together to produce 18. Some examples:

341	5,091	912	9,876
−143	−1,905	−219	−6,789
198	3,186	693	3,087
1 + 9 + 8 = 18	3 + 1 + 8 + 6 = 18	6 + 9 + 3 = 18	3 + 0 + 8 + 7 = 18

Presentation is key here, as the trick is so simple to unravel. The magician might throw in some additional calculations to obscure and hide the crucial subtraction within a mess of numerical formulations. The envelopes may all be filled with $18, or the $18 may be in only one key envelope, the location of which the magician knows. Another option is to force the $18 envelope, show all the other envelopes are empty, then rip open the selected envelope for the amazing denouement!

THINGS NEXT TO OTHER THINGS

Sometimes the magician, or one of his assistants, will put down a piece of equipment (like a lid) next to a cabinet or some other apparatus. That could be an innocent action, or the magician may be creating a secret hiding place for someone to hide behind. For instance, maybe someone was hiding in the cabinet. The person sneaks out and gets behind the lid. Now the magician twirls around the cabinet, and shows it empty. The person sneaks back in, the lid goes on, and *whamo*, now suddenly there's a person inside! A variation on this technique was used by magician Harry Kellar in his Dollhouse Effect, where he came on stage with the walls and roof of a grand dollhouse. All pieces of the dollhouse look innocent enough on both sides, but once they were assembled, a person pops out.

STALLING

Stalling usually indicates time misdirection, as in Metamorphosis. In some instances stalling merely indicates that the magician is waiting for some mechanical or chemical process to take place. David Copperfield used stalling in his evanishment and reappearance of the Statue of Liberty illusion (it takes time to move around the huge statue!), although the tell-tale stalling was noticeably edited out during a rebroadcast of the illusion during a subsequent special. And he might also be using it in his flying routine: "Immediately before takeoff, several minutes of silly old scratchy movies were shown, giving ample time to ready aerial props" reported the *Times*.[2] Remember, the ultimate goal of the magic show is to be entertaining, so if for some reason there's a drag or lull in the action, you have to believe that it is due to either the magician's ineptitude or that somehow it produces the trick.

HALTING

If the magician seems to be at a loss for words, chances are that he's trying to recover from some backstage catastrophe or on-stage slip-up. It is rare, but if the show halts for some reason, it is very likely that something went wrong, or the magician is trying to secretly "do something" but he's so badly unpracticed at it that he can't talk and do the secret thing at the same time. Therefore the show stops while he does the secret thing. It may look like he's not doing anything . . . that's because what he's doing is a secret. I'll give you an example. Earlier I mentioned a magic show where a magician was "practicing" on the small-town stage before heading off to the glitzy casino to perform a few weeks later. I told you how interesting it was to attend such an event, because it gave an opportunity to witness a magician slightly out of control, not as well-practiced as he would've liked.

One of his magic tricks involved a large, square box that had curtains and doors that opened in the front and the rear. The box was spun around, danced around, magic stuff was happening. Then came a climactic moment in the act. The magician's assistant undulated herself into the box, and she waved goodbye as he slowly shut the front door on her. He walked around one side of the box, continued to the back, slowly emerged from the other side, came around front, and continued to circle again, this time opening up the front door as he circled past, around the side, and once again slowing down immensely as he neared the back of the box. The show halted at this point. The audience didn't know what he was doing back there. He was clearly doing some sort of square-dance around the box, but we didn't see what the point of it was. He wasn't a very competent dancer. Finally he got the back door of the box opened as well, but kept the back curtain drawn shut. We could see that the assistant had vanished from the box, and then he closed up the front door, closed up the rear door, opened them again, and the assistant had reappeared inside.

What gave away the trick was the way he *halted* so obviously when he came around the rear. The halting looked like part of his dance around the box, but in reality I believe it was due to lack of practice. He was *doing something* back there that he didn't want us to see, so he invented the dance to hide the fact that he needed to be behind the box at certain points to work the gimmick without us seeing it. In this case, the gimmick was a hidden ledge that got pulled out from the platform on which the box rests. With the front door closed, the assistant had crawled out of the back door, onto the ledge in back of the box.

The assistant was not visible on the ledge because the curtain was drawn shut. One thing is unclear to me now as I think about the trick. I wonder if the audience was not supposed to see the curtain inside the box? That is, perhaps we were supposed to believe we were seeing straight through the box to the curtain at the back of the theater (similar to the tiger trick of figure 1, chapter 1). If that was the desired effect, it was not achieved—the curtain was very clearly attached inside the box. It occurs to me that maybe the trick didn't work right because the trick was being performed on the wrong stage—instead of being presented in the large-scale casino stage, it was being performed more close-up, without proper lighting, in the local theater. If that's the case, then the audience got less of an illusion than was intended. It was intended that we perceive ourselves looking straight through to the back of the theater. Instead, we saw an empty box. That in itself was still a pretty compelling illusion, for I'm sure most of the audience was fooled by the mystery of the disappearing assistant. But it goes to show you that sometimes even if something goes wrong in a magic show, you can still be amazed or fooled at the surprising events that unfold.

LOADS

The magician will show the top hat to be empty, then proceed to pull a rabbit out of it. What you didn't notice was the in-between part, called the *load*. The load is when the magician loads the rabbit into the hat. Another example of loads is in the Cups and Balls routine. Tiny sponge balls will appear and disappear, multiply and divide underneath a few metal cups. At the end, a cup is lifted to reveal a lemon or pomegranate or whatever fruit is in season.

These two cases are classic examples of spatial misdirection. During the course of the performance the magician reveals one climactic moment, and while so doing, prepares another one. For instance, the magician will turn over an empty cup and out will pour a dozen red balls. Meanwhile, as the audience oohs and ahs, the magician is loading a different cup full of blue balls.

Peter Nardi says, "What I find funny is I'm watching a magician, and most of the time I can see him load the last time (cause I know what to look for, I'm looking in a different place), and I'm saying to myself, "God! They must have seen them put that orange underneath that cup!" And then as soon as he uncovers it the whole audience gasps audibly. And again, that's one of the tricks of magic—to realize that people don't see it."

THINGS BEING PUT IN THEN REMOVED

This is related to the notion of anything that detracts from the illusion that is described above. The idea here is that we know that every move in a magic trick is precisely planned out in advance, thus if we see any extraneous movement it clearly has something to do with how the trick is done. In this case we're talking specifically about things being put in, then removed.

For example, here's a popular magic trick I remember seeing at a birthday party when I was about nine years old: the magician decides to bake a cake in his hat. Oh, he's not that dumb, first he puts a pan into the hat to catch all the ingredients. He's about to crack the eggs into the hat when something distracts him. Without thinking, he removes the pan (now the hat is empty) and he proceeds to crack the eggs into his nice clean magic hat. The kids start yelling. He ignores them, as he pours the milk into the hat as well. The jocularity continues for a while, until finally (after some mixing with the magic wand) he reaches into the hat and pulls out a decorated birthday cake (probably a small one, but it's clean and impressive enough to make its point).

The key lies in the fact that the pan is put into the hat and then removed. The cake starts out in a hidden compartment in the pan. The magician puts the pan in the hat, secretly loading the cake into the hat by this action. When the pan is "removed," it is actually just a metal shell that is taken out, while the rest of the pan (containing the cake) stays inside the hat.

Do-it-yourselfers can do a scaled-down version of this trick at home with two paper drinking cups. Prepare one of the cups beforehand by cutting off its rim. Cut out the bottom of the other cup. Now stack the bottomless cup *inside* the rimless cup. With the cups stacked like that they will appear to be a single cup. Get yourself a glass pitcher full of milk, and a hat. You'll also need an audience of children. Round up some nieces and nephews. Now you're ready to perform!

Tell the audience how thirsty you are. Pour yourself a cup of milk, then pour the milk back into the pitcher. (Now they know the pitcher is genuine, the milk is genuine, and the cup is genuine.) Suddenly an idea pops into your head: "I may be thirsty later also, so I might as well pour myself a glass of milk to keep in my hat!" Put the cup into the hat, then say, "Wait a minute, why don't I just fill up the whole hat with milk!" At this point you appear to remove the cup from the hat. Really you're removing only the inner cup, the bottomless cup, and leaving the rimless cup inside the hat. The audience doesn't know the difference—it *looks* like you're taking out the cup. Now you carefully pour the milk into the hat (really into the cup inside the hat). The children will start yelling and laughing and flinging boogers at you, because it looks like you're filling the hat with milk. Ignore their cries. Finally, when the cup is filled, look up and ask what they're yelling about. They will explain it to you in uproarious tones. "Ohh!" you say, coming to your senses, "you want me to put the *cup* in the hat!" So put the (bottomless) cup back into the hat, being sure to stack it inside the cup full of milk. The children still think you have a soggy hat full of milk. Remove the stacked cups and ask them what they're *kvetching* about as you pour the milk back into the pitcher. "I guess everything worked out fine after all!" you smile as you toss them the dry hat to inspect.

The whole point of this exercise is to illustrate the idea of "looking for loading." In this case, the rimless cup was secretly inserted into the hat by putting in, then removing, the two stacked cups. When you're watching a magic show, be on the lookout for things put in—and then removed.

SUDDEN MOVEMENT

The magician is scared that the audience will see something it shouldn't, so he acts fast to remove it from view. In one TV special a magician did a trick with an audience volunteer and a borrowed ring. At the end of the trick he suddenly reached out and grabbed the ring into his fist, exclaiming, "Doesn't this amaze you!" with a smile and a twinkle in his eye, and pulling the ring out of sight. Everyone laughed at his joke, but they didn't realize he was really, in his clunky way, performing a sleight of hand, because there was a gimmick he had to remove from the ring while it was out of sight in his fist.

FURNITURE

Notice any furniture standing around on stage, especially if there's no good reason for it. Magicians have been known to hide items by hanging them behind chairs, behind boxes, under tables, etc. Also notice the various pedestals and stands that make up the magician's apparatus. Things like to be hidden in the fringe of the tablecloth. If you never see the back of something, become suspicious of it. Notice if the magician comes close to a piece of furniture during a trick, whether he stands behind it, happens to lean against it, or happens to let his hand touch it. The most casual touching of furniture may mean he's swiping something attached behind or underneath it, or dropping something into a hidden basket hanging off the back of it.

SOMEBODY'S FACE IS COVERED

If the magician or an assistant's face is covered, either with a hood, helmet, sunglasses, cowl, or mask, look out for a switcheroo taking place. It's very likely that the face covering is more than just decorative. Probably the covering will fit it into the storyline and dance routine of the act, but there is probably also an ulterior motive as well, a prelude to a disappearance or torture trick, for instance. With the face covered they can sneak in a dummy head or a whole different person. This technique is often used along with the Curtain Switcheroo to vanish the magician or to transpose him with an assistant.

ABNORMAL CLOTHES

Anytime the magician wears abnormal clothes it is suspect. Some observers have pointed out that every time Copperfield does his flying illusion he wears the same loose sweater. We may not know exactly how it's done, but it's pretty clear he's wearing some sort of harness under there which a tight costume would reveal.

AMAZE YOUR FRIENDS!

When you're watching an action movie you can always predict which character will get kicked in the groin during a fight scene. If one character is wearing tight jeans, and the other is wearing loose slacks, you can safely predict the loose-slacks guy will get it where it hurts. The reason is, the stunt person wears a sturdy elastic band under his clothes. The band is attached to each ankle and runs up one pant leg and down the other. When someone kicks him, their foot catches in the band and is halted a few close inches before the crucial point of contact. The stunt person has to wear loose-fitting pants, otherwise the protective band would be pushed up against his groin. Wearing loose-fitting pants with a large inseam gives the band free room to move as it gets kicked up, while still remaining well-separated from the stunt person's body. There's not much separating movie stunt people from the stunt artist or escape artist that takes on challenges of physical danger. When this kind of deception is used to achieve a real-time effect, it only serves to blur the lines between movie magic and magic of the stage.

THE PROPS THAT ARE NOT PASSED AROUND

'Nuff said.

DISAPPEARING ASSISTANTS

One of my favorite magic techniques is when a magician "loses" or "gains" an assistant on stage. You have to watch closely to see this, especially look out when a complicated dance number is going on. You see eight dancers come out on stage, but one twirls behind a piece of equipment and stays there. The dancers leave—but that one is still hidden back there. No one notices her but you, because you're the only one smart enough to be on the lookout for such sneakiness!

One trick I saw involved a large puzzle, like one of those number puzzles with squares that move around. Instead of numbers, the puzzle had a drawing of a woman on it. As they were wheeling out the apparatus and setting it up, one of the assistants disappeared behind it and never came out. The audience was not supposed to notice that! An assistant stepped into the puzzle box and her body was broken up and moved around as the magician switched around the squares of the puzzle. Her face, hands, and feet were sticking out through holes in the box, (supplied in part by the second woman who was hiding behind the contraption). At the end of the trick, the puzzle was rolled away with the woman still hiding behind it.

APPEARING ASSISTANTS

The reverse of the disappearing assistants is appearing ones. Some amazing escapes are performed this way. The magician is manacled and steps into a crate. A team of uniformed workmen come out and start hammering it shut, wrapping chains around it, setting locks in place, etc. Amid this flutter of activity, the magician slips out and hides behind the crate. Hidden in the crate was a hat and uniform identical to the ones the workers are wearing. He dons this garb and pops up again at an opportune time, but he is lost in the gaggle of workers moving around. The crate is then dumped in the ocean or something to that effect. It's up to the magician to re-emerge in some ingenious way.

Smoke and Lights

These are used to obscure the stage. Often smoke and lights are used in conjunction with solid penetration effects (that is, the magician walks through a mirror, or through a slab of glass). The lights shine out at your face so you can't see if there really is a hole in the glass or not, and the smoke, while giving the stage a misty as well as mystical appearance, also contributes to the cover up of the mystery.

Anything That Looks Like a Prop Bought at a Magic Store

—probably is.

Which Tricks Are Done First?

As you know well by now, everything about the show is carefully planned out in advance, including the ordering of the tricks. But did it occur to you that the order the magician does tricks is important? It can be! For instance, imagine a friend tells you about a magician she saw: "Oh, he did this great trick where his hands were empty and he reached into the air and plucked out a full glass of wine!" That's pretty impressive. One thing that your friend will probably forget to mention is when during the show the magician performed this miraculous feat. My guess would be that it was his first trick, or close to the beginning of the show. The wine glass was hidden under his jacket (maybe strung there on a length of elastic), with the mouth of the glass covered tightly with Saran Wrap. When you see a magician perform a trick like this that involves liquids, usually it will be at the start of the show, before the Saran Wrap has had a chance to become undone.

Does the magician take off his jacket after a trick? Then ask yourself, "What was hiding in the jacket?" He may use the excuse that it's too hot to wear a jacket, but probably the only reason he had it on in the first place was because he needed it to hide something in. Now that the trick is done, he removes the jacket to make sure the incriminating pull or takeup reel doesn't slip into audience view.

We've mentioned briefly the standard magician's prop called a pull, which is a length of elastic that is attached to the inside back of a jacket. On the other end of the elastic is a clip or cup, into which the magician pushes an item that is to be vanished. The elastic is secretly stretched out from the back of the jacket and into the magician's hand. The magician will push a dollar bill or a magic wand or something into his fist (really into the clip). When he opens his hand, the elastic snaps the item under his jacket and so it appears to have disappeared. Wow! Magic! Sometimes the elastic is run up the sleeve. Other times it simply goes around the magician's body. Either way, the magician will most likely mention soon after how hot he is, and that he simply must remove his jacket. Of course he has to remove his jacket—he has a piece of elastic stuck with a safety pin and a magic wand dangling down his back! The jacket (and the revealing evidence it contains) gets flipped over the back of a chair, out of the way. Now you know that any subsequent trick that the magician does will not rely on a jacket pocket (remember what we said about pockets before!)

Order is important in ways that may not be readily apparent. Many live shows combat quandaries with creative ordering. "The amount of time it takes to apply makeup can determine the running order of the show," it was said of "Saturday Night Live," "with the most complicated pieces coming at the opening."[3] That's an interesting thing to look for the next time you're up late on a Saturday night!

People don't remember or think about the ordering of tricks because it seems irrelevant. Also, as discussed earlier, magicians have a magical aura about them; they give the impression that the tricks could be performed anywhere at anytime. If people do consider the ordering of tricks, usually what they are thinking about are the aesthetics of trick-ordering.

The magician is likely to begin the show with a bang—some uncomplicated but dramatic display of his power. This gets the audience in the mood, hopefully induces them to a magical mindset, and causes the audience to slip comfortably into confidence that this magician is a capable performer.

The opening will be followed by a good mixture of tricks. Most magicians, being semiliterate in their craft, will follow Houdini's model: "Always leave them wanting more." Now, I've seen magicians break this rule, but I've never seen a good magician break the rule. Any half-decent prestidigitator will have a few favorite illusions, know how to perform them well, and perform them in a way designed to stun your mind.

The close of the magician's act is symmetrical with the start—a dramatic display of power. Only this time, the effect is usually a more complicated one, often involving audience volunteers, a feeling of danger or suspense, and much hyperbole.

It is not enough that the individual tricks should tell a story; the show as a whole should follow the familiar plot triangle of opening → rising action → climax, and falling action lasting as long as the applause does. If the magician can manage this feat, he will have created a show that, even if it didn't amaze and stun, at least created some suspense and entertainment for the crowd.

INTERMISSIONS

What is new about the magician after intermission? New clothes? This could represent a new "glass of wine" or animals hiding in his sports jacket. New props on stage? Certainly this means new tricks (one would hope) but it may also mean that the props have been placed in a certain way to obscure a certain part of the stage, or to cover up an action that the magician will do. Coming back from an intermission means that if you want to analyze the action, you'll have to be on your guard in top form once again, because the performers have had time to relax and regroup, to set up new ways of deceiving you, and to get the rest of the audience into a state of relaxed submissiveness. Maybe you should stay in the theater during intermission to watch the stage being set up, walk up front and take a good look at the stage, and perhaps even get a chance to chat with a stagehand.

SLIP-UPS

As discussed earlier, intentional accidents and mess-ups can actually be intentional, meant to reveal some information or provide the gimmick that works the trick. In one embarrassingly blunt approach, magician Harry Blackstone Sr. made a live duck vanish before an audience by relying on the misdirection caused by an assistant who would "accidentally" stumble as he brought a pistol onstage, at the exact moment when Blackstone needed to divert attention away from the duck.[4] Remember what I said before about going to see a show twice!

RIP-UPS

Rips and tears always add a big dramatic finish to a trick, but, as is so common in magic, the very moment that you are being impressed by the magical effect, there is probably some hidden meaning going on that you're not aware of. Ripping it up is a wonderful way to destroy evidence of a very *un*-magical explanation for the illusion.

Here's a very simple but convincing illusion: The magician places a marked coin in an envelope, then immediately rips up the envelope into tiny pieces, throws them in an ashtray, lights a match, and burns the paper to a crisp. Amazingly, the same marked coin is then produced in some magical and startling way.

Rip-ups of this kind are almost always: (1) Very effective illusions—

Wow! How did that coin disappear?! and (2) Very often hiding something. When the magician rips up the envelope, he is probably destroying evidence while at the same time "proving" to you that the coin has "genuinely" vanished. In fact, the envelope probably had a small cut in it, through which the coin escaped into his palm right before he ripped it up.

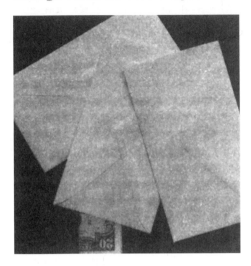

Fig. 23. These three envelopes look exactly alike, but two have been prepared. The top left envelope is completely unprepared. The middle and rightmost envelopes both have a tiny slit in the bottom. Notice the slit is undetectable, yet big enough to fit a bill through. The magician can insert a ring or money into the envelope, appear to seal it up tightly, and then destroy the envelope. The object has been slipped through the minute slit and into the magician's hand.

The rip-up has many variations. Very often a trick will involve a paper bag that is ripped open at the end to show that it is empty—the egg has disappeared, or that there are no extra scarves hiding inside, whatever the trick demands proof of. The ripping of the bag actually hides the fact that a false partition was used inside the bag, or a smaller bag within the bag was used to conceal something. The bag is proven to be unfaked, at the same time destroying the evidence that otherwise would have to be passed around for audience approval.

CREDIT WHEN CREDIT IS NOT DUE

Some mentalists take advantage of a situation by offering multiple predictions and allowing the audience to choose the correct one. For instance, before a show the mentalist's assistants go out scouring the crowd for possible volunteers. They happen to find a guy they can use. Now it's showtime. "We've never met before, have we?"

"No."

"I want you to think of your name—no, that's too easy. I can feel your name slipping from your mind as we speak." Dramatic pause. "But I won't reveal it just yet." He pulls a deck of cards from his pocket. "Now here I have a deck of cards, each with a category word on it, such as 'tree,' or 'animal', or 'food.' Now I'd like you to select a category, but do not show it to me.

"Now I want you to take the first letter of your first name. Do you have it? Now think of the category you selected, and think of something that begins with that letter and fits the category." The volunteer does so.

The mentalist concentrates, then writes something on a pad. "It would be amazing if I could read your thoughts and discover your name. But more amazing still if somehow it were possible to discern what secret item and what secret category you are holding in your mind." The mentalist reveals his prediction card. There are four words written on it: David, Flower, Daffodil, Daisy. The word Daffodil is scribbled out, as if the mentalist had first received the mental impression of one flower and then the other.

"Is your name David?"

"Yes!"

"And did you select 'flower' as your category?"

"Yes!"

"And was daisy your selected flower?"

"Well, first I thought of daisy, but then switched to daffodil. I guess you picked up both those vibes."

"You switched back and forth a few times, didn't you?"

David nods. The mentalist has proved his ability well enough to impress most audience members with his special powers. Surely he can't be faulted for getting the last one wrong, when David himself had trouble making up his mind.

There are many variations on the technique. As you've guessed, the flower card is forced on David (another way to do it is with a weighted die, with one word on each face). David was chosen specifically for this experiment because the pre-show scouts heard his wife mentioning his name, and there aren't too many common flowers that begin with the letter D.

The scribbled-out wrong answer is a common ploy amongst mentalists. Kreskin uses a numerical variation. He writes two number predictions on a card, with one prediction scribbled out. Most mentalists have a well-practiced routine that uses all sorts of the most popular colors, numbers from 1 through 10, animals, etc. When they know the common answers most people give, they are correct in their guesses most of the time.

Psychic Uri Geller used a similar ploy on a recent airing of the Howard Stern radio show (almost all psychics and mentalists use the ploy occasionally, because occasionally they're going to get something wrong). While Geller was in the studio, he tuned in his thoughts to the woman in the green room (a waiting room where guests sit before appearing on a show) who was drawing a picture on a pad. "A house," he announced. The woman came in and showed that she had not drawn a house at all. Then she admitted that earlier, before the show, she indeed had drawn a house. Ah ha! He did get it after all! Geller said that he must have been picking up her *earlier* thoughts by mistake. More likely, either Geller or an assistant had been sitting in the green room before the show and looked at the pad, or saw the pad laying around, and saw the drawing.

Given Stern's admitted skepticism of psychics and so forth, I was surprised that neither Stern nor any of the other denizens of the show picked up on this obvious and oft-used ploy, and especially that no one commented on the fact that Geller had *gotten it wrong*. In fact, after it was shown that some of Geller's other visions did not come true concerning what the woman was wearing and what she looked like, Stern consoled Geller by pointing out his successes, such as the house. This is another ploy that psychics (and regular magicians) rely on to a great degree: that after the show is over, the audience tends to think highly of a performer's successes, and forgets their failures (except in extreme cases, of course). That's why mentalists can use a technique like scribbling out the daffodil, or predicting the wrong drawing, because, in time, the audience will give them credit where credit is not due.

FLARES AND THICK PLACES

Any time someone steps into a box, bag, or basket, take a good look for places where the container flares out or where the walls tend to look thick. One of the classic illusions, the Indian Basket Trick, has a young boy hop into a basket, which is then penetrated by swords. The boy emerges unharmed. The trick is that the boy curls himself up where the basket flares outward, and the conjurer knows how to poke swords through without striking the boy. An additional illusion lays a hand in creating the illusion: the basket is oval shaped, but is shown with a short end facing the audience. The audience perceives the basket as circular. They don't realize how deep it really is. Modern-day illusions, such as sawing a woman in half, use similar optical illusions to try to make these hiding spots look smaller than they are. Thus we are led to believe no one could be hiding in there.

"TECHNOLOGY"

Let's say you're at a comedy club and one of the comedians fancies himself a comedic magician. You're sitting close to the stage and he makes you the butt of some jokes, and then offers you a chance to get back at him. "If I can't name your card, you can pour a beer over my head." You know you're no match against a practiced magician, even if it is just a comedian-magician, but peer pressure forces you into the gag. You pull out the four of hearts, show it to the crowd, and slip it back in the pack. The comedian moans and groans, and finally comes up with, "Two of clubs!" *Ha, ha,* the audience snickers. You're debating whether to let him buy his own drink-shampoo, or should you just go ahead and pour the watered down concoction they served you over his head, but your ruminations are shattered by the comedian's last desperate plea: "Wait! I've got a friend in Seattle! He's the magician that taught me the trick! Let me call him . . . please?" Okay, so you acquiesce. Funny Boy pulls out his cell phone and dials the digits. The phone rings—and rings—and rings! *It looks like the beer's going to be flowing tonight,* you grin as you reach for your mug, but then the friend's answering machine picks up. "Hi this is Marty the Magi. I'm not here right now, so leave you message after the beep. Oh, and one more thing, if this is some comedian calling, it's the four of hearts, you dope!"

Anytime you see technology in a magic show, it's almost certainly faked. For example, magicians will sometimes use televisions, "live" video footage, or computer readouts as proofs of their magical actions. You can pretty much ignore all this. It has been rigged beforehand. One trick that immediately comes to mind is the Disappearing Radio trick that is commercially available in magic shops. The radio (available in more modern guise as a boom box) is covered with a cloth and then vanished. It turns out the radio/boom box is a fake—a cardboard shell that folds flat with a flick of the wrist, easily hidden in the large cloth.

Some, though not all, mentalists use bunco technology in their acts. There are some devious calculators on the market that have hidden functions to aid the mentalist. The calculators look like normal calculators, and in fact they are normal calculators. But they have hidden functions to them. The mentalist hands out the calculator and has the spectator enter numbers, multiply, divide, etc, to arrive at a total. The spectator writes down this secret number, presses the Clear button, and hands the calculator back to the mentalist. The mentalist can retrieve the secret number from the supposedly cleared calculator.

One of these calculators has the sinister appellation Force-U-Lator. It can be programmed by the mentalist to give any number as the answer to a math problem. The idea is to have the audience volunteer go through a long, convoluted series of mathematical operations ("Your birthdate divided by your age times your Social Security number," etc.) then press the Equals key. By this time only a mathematical prodigy could have computed the answer in their head, and the audience member is satisfied with any answer the calculator gives her. Of course, the mentalist knows exactly what number that is since he has told the calculator beforehand to spit out that number. Pretty devious, huh?

Just as devious as the fake cell phone that picks the four of hearts. You don't *really* think some two-bit stand-up comedian is running up huge cell phone bills every night doing that routine, do you? The phone is fake. It has a recording device built into it. The magician recorded the fake answering machine message beforehand, and plays it back during the show. It sounds simple enough, but remember, the magician's ability to entertain with such a trick rests on much more than the gizmo. In this case, the magician had to be competent enough to force a card, and build an amusing routine around it. The ability to entertain with a single sleight and prop should not be underestimated.

David Copperfield is a great lover of technology. He uses his to enhance his illusions, especially on his televised performances, in a way reminiscent of Ernie Kovacs or early David Letterman playing with the very nature of TV itself. For instance Copperfield will often have a picture-in-picture on the TV. The small video rectangle will purport to be live video footage showing the inside of a box where miracles are transpiring, or otherwise showing inside where the audience cannot see. Of course, the video was taped beforehand and reveals nothing. In the Statue of Liberty evanishment, Copperfield used a fake radar display as proof that the statue disappeared. He also used cameras to capture the statue at its moment of disappearance. As William Poundstone points out, the cheap cameras would be ineffective from that distance at night.[5]

So, in short, whenever you see a magician introducing technology, either as the main attraction or as proof of an illusion, be very, very critical. In fact, ignore the technology as insulting to your intelligence.

LOCATION ON STAGE

Where is the magician performing? Is he near a back wall? Or up front and personal? Center stage or off to one side? For most tricks the magician will be in front and center for reasons of visibility. If the magician breaks that rule, you can bet there's a reason for it.

Smaller-scale illusions usually will be performed center stage, although the magician may create an artificial side or back of the stage by putting up a curtain or three-sided screen on the stage itself. The magic is performed in front of this prop, thus creating a way to introduce a trap door closer to the magician (that is, a trap door in the screen).

For large-scale illusions, if the magician steps to the side of the stage it might be that he needs to do a curtain switcheroo or secretly get something from off stage. An off-center illusion may indicate that there is a trap door in that part of the stage that must be used. Levitating a person can be done center stage, but is usually done close to a curtain near the front of the stage that hides the lifting mechanism directly behind the magician.

If the trick is done close to the back of the stage, be wary of things being slipped in and out through a slit in the back curtain. I've seen one magician (with the initials D.C. who has recently married a supermodel) who had a gridlike backdrop to his set. The grid was used to hide the fact that one of the many panels was removable, and thus created a hole where an assistant could be slipped through. D.C. used the same grid backdrop in two of his television magic specials.

Fig. 24. A Japanese-style gridded screen in back of the theater may look decorative—and it is—but it might also be used because individual sections of the grid can be removed under cover, to allow performers to escape backstage or to appear on stage. The entire storyline and character of an illusion may grow from a deception like this.

A magic book from 1897 describes an effect that uses a similar ploy. The effect, called La Strobeika Persane, was created by two Germans who produced it in Paris; it was later popularized by the legendary Alexander Herrmann.[6] The effect takes place in a dungeon. Not a real dungeon, of course, but on a stage made up to look like a dungeon, with a brooding atmosphere and walls made from large, gray, cement blocks. A prisoner is shackled and locked to a wooden board by audience members (who may even furnish their own locks for the purpose), and his neck is locked by a steel collar that is also padlocked to the board. These shackles and the neckpiece are firmly bolted to the plank. The plank is suspended in the air above the stage by chains and surrounded by a curtain. The curtain is closed (the audience can still see the empty space beneath the plank to the back of the theater) and in a moment the curtains are swept open to reveal the prisoner is gone. A female assistant is chained there instead—and the original prisoner comes running into the theater from the back of the room.

This is really a two-part escape. First there is the escape from the shackles, then comes the escape from the wooden board. The shackle escape is entirely mechanical. Audience members can supply their own locks because the locks are essentially useless. The metal shackles and neckpiece appear to be bolted to the plank, but in fact one of the bolts is a fake, it is merely the head of the bolt, with a nut underneath the plank giving the illusion that the bolt passes all the way through the plank. (Actually, the old magic book explains how all four shackles and the neckpiece are secretly connected by a complicated system of levers so that the prisoner need only lift one shackle, and the rest lift up as well.) It is as if the shackles are on hinges; they can be lifted off the board with the locks still in place. This leaves him room to slip free so that the woman can slip in.

This takes us to the second part of the trick, the escape from the curtained plank. This is where the location on stage and a gridded backdrop come into play. You'll recall that the stage is dressed to look like a dungeon, with drab cement block in back. The plank is hanging a few feet away from this back wall. One of the cement blocks (probably a fake) is removed from backstage, and a second plank is stuck out from backstage, to the curtained plank. The prisoner merely crawls along the plank, through the hole in the back wall, to the backstage area. The female assistant then crawls onto the curtained plank and lies down. The "escaped prisoner" leans over from behind the wall and shuts the shackles on her. All of this goes on behind the curtain that surrounds the plank. These actions actually go faster than it takes to describe them here, and I'm sure an element of time misdirection and stalling is involved as well, as the magician takes time front-stage to engage in histrionics. That's the other factor that comes into play here: the character and storyline of the trick. This is a prime example of how the story of a trick helps out with creating the illusion—the dungeon setting gives an excuse for having the gridded backdrop, which allows one of the squares of the grid to be covertly removed.

The fact that in the 1990s a world-famous magician is using the very same technique employed by a magician of the 1890s proves the point made earlier—that magicians have been using the *same techniques* to fool us for a very long time. Whatever the place, whenever the time, whatever the century—humans are humans and we will always be tricked by the same deceptions as long as we don't know to look for them.

LOOSENESS

If an escape artist is locked up in handcuffs, those can be inspected to ensure they are solid and hard. But anything loose, like cloth or rope, is suspect. If he is tied up in ropes, you're never quite sure if the rope is tight enough to really contain him well: there may be some slack in it. Even if the material appears to be taut, there can still be a hidden section that is loose. The mail bag escape is often based on this notion of slack in rope, where even though the bag appears to be tied tightly shut, extra slack has been kept inside the bag.

Omni magazine ran details of a smaller-scale, but equally puzzling illusion that worked on the same principle. In this case a small, zippered change purse was shown filled with some coins and locked with a padlock. A spectator holds the key to the lock. The purse is hidden under a silk for a moment and then handed back to the spectator, who unlocks it to discover it is empty. The coins re-emerge in the magician's pocket.

The trick works because the purse is cloth or soft, pliable plastic. Under the cover of the silk, the magician simply bunches up the sides of the purse and is thus able to unzip the purse even with the lock in place. As described in *Omni* magazine, this vulnerable design was being used by banks worldwide on their moneybags. After being alerted to the problem, the manufacturers of the bags eventually realized their product was not secure and re-designed the bags in such a way that thieves could not make use of the "looseness" principle of magic to illegally gain some wealth.

Sometimes a potentially loose item is used as a proof. Houdini used a drop cloth for proof in his Walk Through a Brick Wall illusion. A cloth was placed on the stage, then a thin wooden platform was rolled onto the cloth. Masons came out and built a wall, brick by brick, on the platform. Audience volunteers were brought on stage to witness the miracle first hand. Then two booths were set up on either side of the wall. Houdini stepped into one booth, and, moments later, emerged from the other. He had walked through the brick wall, surrounded by spectators.

The cloth was used as a proof that he didn't go through a trap door in the stage, but that's really what he did. It was a false proof, based on the looseness principle. Inside the booth, Houdini would pull aside the cloth, go down a trap door in the stage, and re-emerge in the other booth on the other side of the brick wall. Some magicians have used newspapers to prove to the audience that trap doors in the stage were not used. But it's always a false proof. No one counts on the looseness principle.

SQUISHINESS

Anything that is "squishy" is suspect, especially if it's involved in an appearance or disappearance trick. For instance, consider the sponge ball, a common magician's prop. If you squish two sponge balls together in the hand, they are indistinguishable from each other. It looks like you're squishing only one into the hand, and the audience will believe it's only one ball if that's what they've been led to believe. Objects made of rubber and paper may also be squished to produce startling effects. Here's a simple trick you can do that illustrates the squishiness factor.

CREATE MAGIC!—THE MULTIPLYING DOLLARS

Show your audience a flat, crisp, twenty-dollar bill and explain that one of the new anticounterfeiting measures being installed into money is a new kind of paper. Let someone inspect the bill to ensure it is genuine and quite ordinary. You take back the bill and start crinkling it up into a small ball as you explain that the new paper they're using to make bills is made from the skin of earthworms. And surprisingly, the dollars made with earthworm skins have some very unusual properties. For instance, just like earthworms . . . —at this point you rip the crumpled bill in half. Slowly you uncrinkle the two halves to reveal not two ripped-up twenty-dollar bills, but two *fully whole* bills. "Just like earthworms," you say, "if you cut them in half—the two halves are just fine."

This trick is best for a small, close-up audience of a few people. The trick is accomplished using the squishiness principle: When two squishy things are squished together, nobody can tell how many squishy things there are.

1. Before the trick begins you crumple up a twenty-dollar bill and place it in your pocket. Keep the other bill crisp and fresh.

2. During the trick you hand out the crisp bill for inspection. While that's going on, secretly retrieve the crumpled bill from your pocket and hide it in your hand.
3. As you're talking you start crinkling up the inspected bill. At one point during your talk you look up at your audience and explain a point to them. While they are thus misdirected by your face-to-face conversation, you squish the two bills together.
4. Now you have a ball of two $20 bills squished together in your hand (but it looks like one bill). Continue crinkling them together until you come to the appropriate spot in the patter.
5. When you're ready to "rip the bill in half," do it with a twisting motion. Twist the two balled bills away from each-other while pushing them together. The crinkled paper helps add a convincing sound of paper tearing.
6. Finally, unfold both balls and show how, just like earthworms, these newfangled bills have reproduced by being torn in two.

UNRELIABLE SILKS

Silks scarves are used as covers in many smaller illusions, but because of their looseness they may reveal as much as they give away. I remember one magic show I attended as a boy where as soon as the magician pulled out his bright yellow silk, I knew he was going to magically transform it into a bright green silk. How did I know this? Because I was sitting on the hard-wood floor below him, and had a wonderful view up into the silk he was holding in his hand, and I could plainly see that underneath the yellow silk he was hiding a green silk.

Some tricks such as the Zombie Ball rely on a stick that is hidden under the silk. In the Zombie Ball, a metal ball seems to float and fly around the stage. Depending on the miming skills of the magician, the illusion can range from wonderful to satisfactory to boring to utter dreck. The metal ball is hollow and not so heavy as it looks. The ball, while flying, is always hidden under a large silk. What's to hide? Well, plenty. The ball is attached to a rod the audience never sees. The magician's hands hold two corners of the silk. One of those hands also holds the rod, which is used to move and direct the ball, which appears to be floating about behind the silk. At times the ball may "fly upwards" so fast that the magician is almost pulled up off the stage by it. Of course this effect is accomplished with some pantomime, legs bent and then unbent into a slight jump. In the hands of an incompetent magician (and there are many incompetent perpetuators of Zombie) the stick can become visible, at times pressing its hard edge up against the loose silk for all to see who know to look. It's generally recommended that magicians use a foulard of heavier weight for such illusions in order to conceal the stick, but in many cases the magician's incompetence weighs too heavily on the covering cloth.

Another time when silks have been unreliable covers are with a certain mind-boggling effect where a borrowed penny disappears and then magically reappears inside a ball of yarn. The trick is accomplished with a flattened rectangular tube that is shoved into the yarn to the very core. The

whole thing is covered with a silk and sits in a glass bowl. After the magician vanishes the penny, he covertly slips his hand under the silk and drops
the penny into the tube. It slides down the tube, into the center of the ball
of yarn. The silk is pulled away with a dramatic flourish (and the tube goes
with it) to reveal the ball of yarn underneath. An audience volunteer un-
ravels the yarn to reveal the penny magically inside it. In another variation,
the penny reappears inside a series of tied bags and sealed boxes. In both
cases the tube is used, and the silk cover. And in both cases there have been
several times when I've been able to see this tube pressing through the soft
cloth of the unreliable silk.

DRAMATIC COVERS

Look for times when a cover is used for no reason whatsoever. (Usually
covers serve a function. The magician says he will make something disappear, so he covers it with a silk, and it vanishes. The audience may have no
idea how it's done, but they recognize that the cover is a necessary part of
the trick.) But sometimes it seems there is no reason at all for the cover, except perhaps to add a dramatic flourish to the show. One example is the yarn
ball trick described above. The audience sees the magician whipping off
the silk to reveal the yarn ball sitting in a glass bowl. They think he merely
used the silk for dramatic effect—to create suspense. *What could possibly be
under that silk? Oh that's what's under the silk!*

They think the silk was mere window dressing, when really it served an
ulterior purpose. In this case the tube is being removed with the removal of
the silk. In general, whenever you see a silk being used as a cover, even if
the cover only looks like it's there for a dramatic flourish, be aware that once
again the magician has carefully prepared this show in advance. The
flourish may be the only reason, but then again, perhaps something else is
going on as well.

UNRELIABLE CLOTHING

Clothing is used by the magician as covers, but just like the unreliable silks
and scarves we've discussed, sometimes the magician's clothing can be unreliable too.

- If the magician leans forward towards the audience, his suit jacket will
  open up. If you are sitting to the side you can peek in and look for topits,
  hidden doves, or extra pockets sewn in.
- In certain levitations and suspensions that involve laying down on a concealed rod, sometimes you can see a tent rising under the clothes where
  the support mechanism is hidden!
- From some angles you may be able to peek into a loose sleeve, or under

a dinner jacket as it flails around with the magician's movements. You might notice a supposedly "empty" pocket bulging with—something.

REPETITIONS

Usually you do not see repetitions in a magic show. The magician will perform the trick once, and that's it. He moves on to the next trick. Why aren't the illusions done more than once?

- It's one of the cardinal rules of magic: never perform a trick more than once for the same audience. After that the surprise is lost, and now that they have a headstart, they might be able to piece together how it's done.
- Artistic reasons. No matter how compelling the illusion, a show would quickly become boring if the magician kept repeating the same thing over and over again. Many professional magicians have such a large repertoire of tricks that they'll say, "Let me show you something even better!" and go on to dazzle the eager viewer with another trick instead.
- Sometimes gimmicks need to be reset, or the props become out of order, or a prop has been "used up." Some card tricks rely on the deck being stacked in a certain way. Other tricks rely on an accidental tap or other blunder. When I was a kid I liked to perform a particular trick that relied on a secret compartment in an envelope. In order to work the trick, I needed to turn over the envelope at a crucial time in order to get the compartment facing up. I wasn't too adept at sleight of hand, so I did the next best thing—I would "accidentally" drop the envelope on the floor and pick it up, subtly turning it over in the process. Needless to say, an obvious move of this kind prevented me from showing the trick twice in a row to the same person.

There are plenty of good reasons why magicians don't repeat tricks. That means: *if the magician ever does repeat something, you should question why that particular trick was chosen to violate the rule.* When a magician does do repetitions, there is some good reason for it and it's something that you should pay close attention to because it may give you a clue as to the working of the trick. Usually what happens in these cases is that the magician is not repeating the trick exactly, but making use of different techniques to achieve the same result.

For example, in the Miser's Coins illusion, the magician will begin by throwing some real coins into a bucket and showing the coin-full bucket to the audience. Later he will palm coins, only pretending to throw them in. The audience is confident that subsequent coin tosses are as genuine as the first, which the magician has proven to them were real. Nardi points out that con artists use the same technique to gain the spectator's confidence, by letting a spectator win a few bucks legitimately before cleaning them out for good (with trickery) when the stakes are high.[7]

SELF-WORKING, SAME-EVERY-TIME TRICKS

Some tricks can't be repeated because to repeat the trick would expose that the trick works the exact same way every time. For instance, suppose you select a card from the deck (it's the ace of spades) and then I magically predict the card you selected. Fine. Now we try the trick again, and once again it's also the ace of spades. You're going to start being suspicious that the entire deck is made of aces of spades.

The magic books available to the layperson in public libraries are filled with self-working, same-every-time tricks. Since they work the same way every time, they are easy for a layperson to present. Many such tricks are numerical in nature, or rely on a prearranged deck of cards. Because of the mathematics involved, the audience volunteer always ends up picking the same card, or arriving at the same number.

There are also the gags and bar-bet kinds of tricks that rely on the fact that most people are not encyclopedias of knowledge. Here are several of such gags you've undoubtedly seen:

- Circle a number: 1   2   3   4
- Name a country, any country in the world, that begins with the letter D.
- Name a red flower.

If Kreskin were in the room, he would have predicted you circled the number 3, gave Denmark as the country, and named a rose as the red flower. You may or may not have done these things. Most people, for whatever reason, give those as answers. A magician or psychic seer can rely on the predictability of the human mind and build an act around such predictions.

In fact, once I witnessed a performance by a so-called psychic who used a more elaborate variation of these bar bets in his show. On stage was an easel. The easel showed five strips of color. The psychic invited an audience member up on stage. The volunteer was instructed to think of one of the colors, then use her psychic energies to relay that color to us, the audience. She concentrated, concentrated, and we the audience were supposedly picking up her psychic signals. "Which color were you thinking of?" he asked her. Green. Gasps from the audience. "All right," he asked the crowd. "How many of you knew she was thinking of the green band?" Most hands were raised. Amazing! She had transferred her psychic thoughts to us!

A few months later an acquaintance of mine who happened to have an interest in magic, announced that he had seen another performance by that alleged psychic, and at that performance the audience *also* was "thinking of green." He said this sarcastically, as if some trick were involved and it were not a result of psychic forces at work. Of course a trick was involved! Anyone looking at the easel was immediately attracted to the bright green strip of color, for it was bright and lush, whereas the other colors were duller and not as attractive.⁸ Could such a simple thing sway the minds of two audiences of people? Sounds unlikely, doesn't it? And yet it happened. No matter how sophisticated we believe ourselves to be, we are fooled and we are led and misled by such simple provocations as one color being brighter than the others.

THINGS INSIDE—OR BEHIND?

When I was a boy, there was a tall kid in the neighborhood with a messy mop of red hair who was a thousand years old. His name was Krondor and he was from the planet Pluto. I did not believe him. My friend Robert believed his story. I told him he was crazy.

"But he has super powers!" Rob said.

"Like what?"

"He can run through trees!"

"What?!"

"He goes right through the trees. He can go through walls too, but he didn't show me that one yet."

Of course the kid wasn't going through anything. He was running *behind* the tree, and from a distance it seemed to an impressionable kid, that Krondor was actually penetrating the tree. Magicians use this same illusion sometimes, not as much as you might think, but occasionally they do. Usually they use the technique with envelopes. They borrow a crisp twenty-dollar bill, the spectator signs it, it gets shoved in an envelope, and the envelope is burned to a crisp. Later the signed twenty-dollar bill is pulled out of the magician's sock, very much un-burnt, crisp but not crispy. There are many ways to perform this miracle; one way is for the magician to *pretend* to slide the bill into the envelope, when really he's sliding it *behind* the envelope. The envelope is sealed and thrown into an ashtray to be burned, but the money is retained in the magician's hand.

TWINS AND LOOKALIKES

Along with the notion of repeatability comes the idea of widespread applicability of the magic. If the magician chooses a volunteer from the audience and levitates her, we all assume that he could have chosen *any* volunteers and levitated them just as well. If he makes a quarter disappear, we assume that any quarter (or coin) could have vanished just as easily. These assumptions may or may not be true depending on the method of magic used (maybe it was a gimmicked quarter). But what is invariable is that this idea is usually ignored, an unthought-of assumption by the audience.

One way in which the magician can break the assumption is through the use of twins. This method is so unexpected, so tricky, that it can be used without arousing suspicion. In fact, the idea of using twins to produce magical

effects seems so hokey and stupid that only a really naive person would suggest, while walking out of a magic show, that twins might've been used for
some transposition effect, for instance. Consider the doubting Douglas of the
New York Times who balked that one insider's "tale of watching Mr. Copperfield coach identical twins seemed like science fiction."[9] However, in reality,
the use of twins has been attributed to a number of well-known magicians.

In 1756, a young man named Jacob Meyer set out to claim fame as a magician. Meyer started by renaming himself with an appellation he decided
was far more respectable, magical, and mystical than any other he could
imagine—the name of his hometown, Philadelphia. As a magician, Philadelphia is not known for his ingenuity. He is known to us today because of his
advertising genius. As he traveled around the world, performing for kings,
queens, and sultans, he would put up lavish advertising posters. Often his
advertisements would announce that Philadelphia would somehow arrive at
the city through two separate gates at the same time. This he accomplished
with a man who resembled him closely enough to fool anyone who knew
Philadelphia only from his advertising posters. Philadelphia also used his
double in his stage act, to make himself magically transport between two
cabinets on stage. Incidentally, both Harry Blackstone and Harry Houdini
admitted to using doubles at various points in their careers. Houdini did the
same gate-entry trick with his brother Hardeen. Blackstone took on his
brother as an accomplice so that he could vanish off the stage and reappear
at the back of the theater.

Notice that all of these and other illusions that rely on doubles could not
be performed on television, what with live satellite hookups, close-ups, and
other technical marvels that would reveal the ruse in an instant. (Of course,
an untelevised performance in a smoky lounge could easily make use of the
technique.)

Other magicians have done tricks with twin animals, which are much
more easy to come by than twin magicians. The early 1780s had a magician
called Katterfelto who did an act where he cut off and restored the tail of a
black cat. As it turns out, Katterfelto owned two black cats, one of whom
was born without a tail. Currently Siegfried and Roy make use of twin animals in their show. After all, only a mother, and perhaps not even she, can
tell the difference between two like animals, especially from far away on
stage, amid the hustle and bustle of the show.

NOISE WITH NO SOURCE

If the magician covers something, and you hear it making noise under the
cover, then you can assume that the thing is long gone; the magician is producing the noise through some other method and is trying to trick you into
believing it is the thing making the noise. For instance, the magician puts a
borrowed coin in a box, shakes the box to prove the coin is really in there,

then opens it up to show the coin is gone. The coin was never in there to begin with. The box probably has a metal slug embedded in one of its hollow walls.

Sometimes it is the magician himself who is the thing that vanishes. Occasionally I have seen magicians on television who have donned a space suit, or a full-head helmet of some kind, and are then forced to speak through a microphone. Of course, their voice is not coming from under the helmet. By that time, the magician is long gone. The "microphone" voice is prerecorded, and the person on stage is someone dressed in the same clothes as the magician, plus the head-covering helmet. Copperfield has used this technique several times, as in his Going Over Niagara Falls illusion, and the Cameraman Disappearing illusion, both of which had a person get inside a covering of some sort and then speak out loud to "prove" they were inside, when they were really someplace else entirely.

On the close-up level, there are parlor tricks where a clink of glass is used to "prove" that a coin is being dropped into a water-filled wine cup under cover of a handkerchief. Later, to everyone's surprise, the coin is gone. The coin was never in the glass to begin with—the clinking sound was made by a transparent circle of glass falling into the cup. The glass circle, of course, is invisible under the water. As mentioned earlier, the illusion called Miser's Dream also uses noise where the source of noise is not seen, to produce the illusion that many coins are dropping into a near-empty metal bucket.

SOURCES OF NOISE THAT PRODUCE NO NOISE

Always be attuned to the way things would be in real life if this were not a magic show. And then try to figure out why there is a reality gap. For instance, in real life if someone wanted to show you a little box there is a certain unconscious way of presenting it to you, quite different from the showy gestures that would accompany a magician's showing you the box. That's the reality gap, and you should always be on the lookout for it. Is the magician doing something that in real life a normal person would not do? That's the question to always keep in mind, as it is a pointer to clues as to how the trick is done.

But the question can also be asked of props: Are the props behaving in ways that real-life props would not behave? When the magician tears a piece of paper in two, do you hear the tearing sound? When he walks around with a cup full of liquid, do you hear the sloshing inside? Be on the lookout for sources of noise that don't produce the noise they should, and you might find the conjurer pulling a fast one on you.

THINGS PARTIALLY OBSCURED

It is up to the magician to provide the proof that what he says is true, but ultimately the illusion is in the eye of the beholder. For instance, the magician might show you three cards—the aces of clubs, diamonds, and spades. With a flick of the wrist, the cards are collected and fanned out again. Now, instead of the diamond, there is an ace of hearts.

Fig. 25. Three diamond cards— right?

Fig. 26. Pull them apart and you can see it wasn't a diamond at all! Always be wary of things partially obscured like this.

The illusion occurs because we made an initial assumption based on a partial proof. We never really knew for sure that was a diamond in the center. Magicians do this all the time: they pretend to show you something, but really they're only showing you part of it. The part they're covering up provides some valuable clues as to the real identity of the object.

EXTENT OF FOLDING

Whenever you find the magician *unfolding* something, like a card or paper money, take a look at how folded-up the item was. That can sometimes give you a clue as to how the trick was performed. If the items were folded extremely tiny, they might have just emerged from inside a thumb tip or another secret hiding spot on the magician's person.

"TIRE TRACKS"

I was watching a car chase on a TV show. The "good guys" were driving a Jeep, and to escape the "bad guys" they took a sudden turn off the road and cut through a sandy area to a dirt path on the other side. I noticed as they were cutting across that sandy area there was a set of tire tracks in the sand in front of the car. The scene flashed by in a moment, but it was time enough to glimpse those tire tracks. Why were those tire tracks in the sand? Why, they indicated where the Jeep had cut through the sand some previous time—I was catching a sneak peek at the show's rehearsal. They must have driven there earlier in the day, perhaps even a few minutes before the filming, thus creating those tire tracks.

I don't have any specific magic example to give you, but it occurs to me that if your eyes are sharp, you may every once in a while notice some "tire tracks" that the magician has left behind from rehearsal. Maybe the tracks will indicate where the trick is going. Maybe they will only indicate that some prethought and preplanning has gone into the illusion. Whatever it indicates, I'm sure it will be fun to discover.

A Census of Senses

Our sense of vision is so strong that we forget to pay attention to other senses. But if you wish to discover all the secrets and mysteries of a magical performance, you'd best keep every avenue of data gathering open to you. With ears perked, nostrils flared, and fingers wiggling, make sure you keep the following in mind:

THINGS TO LISTEN FOR—BACKSTAGE SOUNDS

Sounds are subtle indicators of the method of a trick. Card sharks know this: dealing a card off the top of the deck sounds differently than one dealt slyly off the bottom. Listen for mechanical noises from backstage. Are they preparing the electrical winches that will hoist the magician fifteen feet above the stage by invisible wires? "Even with binoculars in about row 20," wrote an alt.magic poster who attended Copperfield's show, "there was absolutely no sign of any wires, though the equipment could clearly be heard being moved into position before the flying session."[10] Listen for carts and equipment moving around. Listen for footsteps. *Is that the sound of the assistant running around backstage? I thought she was supposed to be locked inside that box—guess she must've escaped through a trap door!*

THINGS TO FEEL FOR—PROPS

Get yourself a good seat right up front or on an aisle. Go on, don't be afraid! If you get a good close seat and make eye contact with the performer, he or she will know you're interested in participating in the show however you can. If props need to be inspected, make yourself available to do so. If volunteers need to go on stage, click your heels three times and go go go! Bang those boxes to prove they're solid. Feel the solidity of the rope. You probably won't find anything unusual (after all, the magician is controlling the experience so you won't find anything out of the ordinary), but maybe you can at least get a sense of what it feels like to be on stage before all those people!

Things to Smell for—Stage Odors

I'll admit this is rare, but some tricks have a characteristic odor to them that can give away how it's done. One magic enthusiast who sat close to the stage when watching Harry Anderson perform said that he smelled "something like rubber cement in the air" during a trick. "I knew right away what was coming next!" Rubber cement is a handy prop in the magician's arsenal, and is used in several effects. It is commonly used in newspaper tearing effects. The magician cuts a piece of newspaper in half, folds it up, then unfolds it to reveal one happy restored newspaper again. The trick is that before the show, the magician coated one side of the paper with a thin layer of rubber cement. The rubber cement is sticky, and so the two cut pieces stick together.

But that wasn't the trick Harry Anderson performed. Rubber cement is also used in Poke a Needle Through Your Arm. The magician shows a long, dangerous-looking needle that he nonchalantly pierces through his flesh. Blood may drip out, pitter-pattering the stage for the cleaning crew to mop up.

You may be wondering, "What the hell does rubber cement have to do with sticking a needle through your arm?!" The answer shows how tricky a magic trick can be! The magician coats the skin of his arm with rubber cement, then takes two folds of skin and pushes them together to create a "skin tunnel" on the surface of his arm. When the needle is poked through the skin tunnel, it looks as through the needle has been pushed through the flesh of the arm. The blood is an additional factor that comes from a sponge hidden in the hand.

You may never have thought to sniff the air to detect a trick, but if you're serious about this you will use every avenue available to analyze the proceedings on stage.

Things to Taste for?!—Fake Foods

Magicians tend to use fake foods and drinks for various reasons, which theoretically your sense of taste could help you unearth. I don't expect you to really try this one, but it's worth knowing for informational purposes. When a sorcerer turns wine to water, undoubtedly the wine is not really wine, and the water is not water (your sense of smell might help you out here too). Magicians of the past would sometimes pour "any drink desired" from the same vessel. People would call out their favorite beverages, but if they had been allowed to actually taste what was produced, they'd have found it tasted nothing like what it looked like, for the drinks were the result of surreptitious dyes and chemical mixings. Now suppose you're approached by a strolling magician in a restaurant. He vanishes your wedding ring. Then he hands you a salt shaker, asks you to remove the top and dump out its contents. You do. Out pours a pile of salt and your wedding ring! How'd that get inside? After he's gone, make a careful inspection of the salt grains on the table. Chances are it's not really salt, but sugar grains or finely ground glass. You still don't know how the trick was done, but you do know something fishy was going on. (Real salt would ruin the aluminum that makes up the gimmicked salt shaker.)

Thinking Is Not Knowing

Magicians are quick to point out that even if you think you know how the trick was done, you're probably wrong, because there are dozens of ways to perform any trick. Furthermore, if your knowledge of how the trick was done is based on sheer guesswork, then you're probably completely off altogether. That's what magicians say anyway.

With those thoughts in mind, you might wonder how you should react to the above dictionary of deceptions. Are the magicians wrong? Can their illusions be broken down to a few explanatory paragraphs as I've tried to do above? The answer is, "Yes, no, maybe so." Now that you know a few of the methods, you mustn't fall into the trap of saying, "I know how it was done . . ." merely because you are making a connection between the show and this book. If you made a connection between every book you read and your everyday life, you would end up believing that rabbit holes lead to wonderlands and a boy named Huck once rafted down the Mississippi.

This is the trap most people fall into:

1. Watch ABC movie of the week, in which a crazed magician chops ex-wife in half. During movie, get "behind the scenes" look at how Hollywood imagines the trick is accomplished.
2. Take trip to Las Vegas. See Siegfried and Roy perform the Chop Endangered Species of the World in Half illusion.
3. Make illogical connection between TV show and magic show. Think to yourself, Ah ha! I know how they do this, I saw it on TV. Smugly sit back and smile because you know how it's done.
4. As you are leaving the theater, say real loud, "You know how they sawed that pink panther in half? Fake feet." Spouse is agog.

Normally you will see at least one magician in the audience of every magic show who either noticeably cringes or spits out his drink upon hearing this sort of garbage from the crowd. The trouble, of course, is that the spectator has no evidence that the TV technique was used. The spectator doesn't have the brains to watch the stage for clues (like the clues I talked about in the previous section). Very often, after observing a magic show very carefully, I'll hear these loudmouths and I'll want to scream at them, because their solution to the mystery will generally defy all the evidence that I've picked up by watching the show. "You dummy! How could he have used 'fake feet'? The panther's legs were visible the entire time!" In other words, you must trust your own insight and observation in addition to anything I can tell you, or anything you read about in a book. Furthermore, you're certainly better off trusting yourself than some bozo who's blabbermouthing out loud about his or her theories. I've *never* heard a blabbermouth at a magic show who knew what he was talking about. As John Mulholland said, "When a man is fooled he has not seen all that has happened; all that he did see were a series of disconnected details."[11]

One example of this happened to me recently. I was watching a magician perform a "cut the woman in half" routine. As he rolled out the box in which the assistant would be severed, I realized that the entire trick was based on an optical illusion (see figure 27).

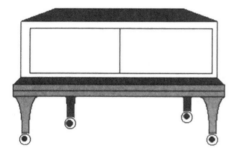

Fig. 27. Several layers and segments of platform give the illusion of thinness.

You see, the equipment consists mainly of a box sitting upon a rolling table. One of the common optical illusions with such equipment is that a ledge or table top looks really thin, too thin to hide a person in. This particular tabletop was made of three separate slabs of metal, each of which was thin-looking, and the top one slightly beveled to further give the illusion of slenderness. Sometimes this kind of equipment is made with a lens-shaped bottom that also looks smaller than it is. While appearing ultrathin to the audience, really about ten inches of space is available in the beveled bottom. These kinds of apparatuses, although appearing to be made of several separate sections, are actually unremovable from each other. Me in my smugness, I knew immediately as this thing was being rolled on stage exactly what was coming next. I knew immediately that the female assistant would lie down inside the box (but really be hiding inside that table top that was "too thin" to contain her).

The female assistant did climb into the box, and it was cut in half, the pieces separated widely across the stage. There are two open windows on the front of the box, so after the box is divided in two, we can clearly see the woman's head and neck on one side, and her kicking legs and feet on the other. I was sitting close enough to the stage to see that the legs and feet were fake—lifelike robotics wearing the same red dress as the woman in the box. Since the woman had obviously not been cut in two, she must have her real legs hiding inside that thin table top (which is not really thin, only an optical illusion of thinness).

After the two woman-halves were spun around the stage a few times, they were spliced together, the lid was opened, and the woman stepped out. Apparently I was sitting at a revealing angle because I saw something I should not have seen. As the woman was getting out of the box, I caught a fast glimpse of her legs uncurling inside the box in which her head had been.

It wasn't until days later that I realized what I had seen. All of my "knowledge" and suppositions about thin table tops and optical illusions had been *totally wrong!* She wasn't hidden inside the tabletop. She merely had her legs curled up in front of her in the box, with her. I realized then that my brain had been simultaneously harboring two differing explanations for the illusion. At the same time I had believed in the "thin table theory" while also believing in the "curled leg theory." It's funny how one's brain works, that even though I had two conflicting explanations, I chose to absentmindedly consider both as the truth.

COMBINATION PLATTER

One reason it can be hard to detect how a trick is done is because the magician has carefully combined multiple techniques into one effect. Eddie Gardner of Diamond's Magic, Inc., says that customers routinely buy ten or fifteen books on the same topic. They studiously compare multiple treatments of the same trick, and combine elements from each version to form one master effect or routine using the best pieces from each. Their master effect is harder to detect (because they have that many more ways to fool you), and if the trick happens to go wrong, they have alternative methods to rectify the mistake.

DENIALS

Magicians always deny that you guessed it right, which makes it especially tough to know if you're on the right track. Copperfield denies the use of stooges and camera tricks. Uri Geller denies anything but genuine psychic powers. Most magicians treat guesses with either a poker face or a joke, whether you've guessed correctly or not, even in the face of conclusive evidence that you've figured out how it was done. It's all in their nature of trying to fool you.

HUMBLENESS

But the real moral of this story is, you *can't* always trust your knowledge. And you certainly can't always trust your hunches. I thought I knew how the trick was done. But I was wrong. Completely wrong about the thin table top. (Although that method is used for other illusions, some even by that same illusionist. In fact his table might actually have been gimmicked and he might have used it for other illusions.) But if I had not, by chance, caught that secret glimpse at how the illusion was *really* done, I would still to do this day hold a false belief about the illusion. When analyzing the action, realize humbly that you may not be outwitting the magician. He or she may be outwitting you.

In Search of the Answers

Figuring out how the tricks are done is a combination of knowing what to look for, where to look for it, and when to look. It may also involve some thinking through of what you've just seen, which, as has been pointed out, can lead you astray. The magic act is designed to be fast and tricky, and much is designed to draw attention away from vital clues, or to obscure clues in a mess of other unimportant stage business. Ken Barham explains that magic "is for the most part very simple. You have to look at what happened and ignore the glitz to figure something out." Sometimes that can be hard to do, as a lot of that glitz is there specifically to overload the sensations and wear down one's attention. This is a trick that goes back decades and spans continents. It's been reported that Indian and Asiatic magicians rely on this technique of deadening the attention through the use of incense, garish colors, and extended swirling dances. The trick is to stay on guard and don't let yourself be lulled into a sense of security, for the trickery may be going on at any time!

Sociologist and amateur magician Peter Nardi recommends if you want to figure out how a trick is done, turn your thinking on its head. "You see, what people do when they start trying to figure you out is, they begin from the beginning, and try to recapture the sequence that way. I often tell somebody if you really want to figure it out, begin backwards. Go from the end to the front. And then begin logically." For instance, your thought processes might run like this: "Well, let's see, at the end of the trick, The Great Magini revealed that he knew what the card was. But people can't really read minds. He never saw the card, never touched it. . . . Ah! Insight! Magini must've known what the card was ahead of time. He must've forced the card!"

Whether or not your suppositions are correct will still be a matter of debate, but at least you will have come to a conclusion that is possible given the facts you have at hand, rather than working from a supernatural premise, or working from a premise based on total blind guessing, as the audience blabbermouth is wont to do.

Sometimes, no matter how skillful you are at analyzing the action, no matter how much knowledge you possess, you still don't know how the trick is done. Recently I found myself alone in a magic store, where the store owner started giving me a personal close-up magic act. He astounded me with wonderful wizardry right before my eyes. I watched each trick closely, and I felt sure he wasn't using any sleight of hand (although I had no idea how it was done). Sure enough, when he was through, he said, "These are very easy to do, no sleights, no skill." Then he quoted me a price and I skidoodled out of there since I didn't want to be suckered into spending money I didn't have!

But the point is sometimes you won't know how a trick is done, because there's no reason for you to know. These things are tricky! That's why they call them magic tricks! Magic companies are constantly churning out new gimmicks every day. Sometimes the best you can do is realize that it is some sort of gimmick and leave it at that. The only way you'll find out exactly what the gimmick is, is to buy the trick. On the other hand, be very careful when you label something a gimmick. That's no explanation. That's just saying you've given up on figuring it out for real.

7

Crashing the Clan

These are things you don't know about, because you're not sitting in with
the fellows or hearing the stories till 2, 3, 4 o'clock in the morning.
                                                            —Sandorse the Magician

Entering the Realm of Magicians—To Learn Their Secrets

Magicians have a lot of secrets to keep, and they keep them very well.
In the past, magicians held great power over the media, mostly due
to efforts by the Society of American Magicians to promote the secrecy of
magic. Will Hays, the "czar of the motion-picture world" in the late 1920s
ruled that no exposure of methods would be allowed in moving pictures.[1] The
great conjurer Mulholland also reports that magazines of his day like *Popular
Mechanics* cooperated with SAM to protect magicians' secrets. "Many editors
. . . believe that their readers are annoyed to discover the means by which
they were fooled, just as they are annoyed when a critic discloses a feeling of
hatred between the hero and the heroine of a successful romantic play. Audiences enjoy their illusions, and feel disgruntled when the illusions are shattered."[2] SAM also made a great effort to prevent magic publications from
being sold for less than a few dollars a copy; this allowed only those with the
dough to find out how illusions are accomplished. Early magic books required
a *written pledge* by all buyers that they would not disclose the secrets within.
Edward Marlo has written many magic books and manuscripts, some of which
can only be purchased after Marlo grants special permission to do so. Magician Will Goldstone wrote a series of books entitled *Exclusive Magical Secrets*
that were nicknamed the "locked books" because the buyer had to take an
oath that the books would always be locked up when not in use.

Today, the keeping of secrets is relegated to the lawyers. Contracts are written up to prevent unwanted revelations. Lawsuits have been waged against those who reveal magic secrets in print and elsewise in the media. Magician Herbert L. Becker had his book *All the Secrets of Magic Revealed* entangled in a lawsuit with David Copperfield's lawyers before publication. They didn't like the fact that Becker revealed some of Copperfield's secrets (although other authors had written about most of those secrets, and the information was traded publicly on the Internet). "I won the lawsuit," Becker explained in an e-mail to me, "and was allowed to publish the book as is. But Copperfield paid a secret bribe to the publisher allowing him (Copperfield) to rewrite the book. Dave had no such luck with the CD-ROM publisher." (Becker's book was also put out as a CD-ROM with the Copperfield illusions intact.) Becker sounds to be speaking caustically with words like "bribe" and "rewrite," but any bitterness is understandable.

Magicians feel a deep loyalty to their craft and often go overboard in their devotion to secrecy. Some magicians have said they find it "disturbing" and "wrong" that tricks of the trade can be sold to the general public. How, with this long and continuous history of secrecy, can you hope to crack the clan and become a magician yourself? (Or at least to learn more of their secrets?) As it turns out, it's surprisingly easy. Magicians are mostly very willing to help out someone new to the game, so long as the newbie is seriously interested in studying the art. There are plenty of books and videos available that truly reveal all there is to know about magic. And if that isn't enough for you, you can head down to a magic shop and buy the tricks outright.

DOGGY DOO AND YOU—MAGIC SHOPS

Why should magic stores sell gag novelties, like fake dog doo? Don't the owners—and more often than not, the owners are real magicians—know the difference between a gag, a trick, and an illusion? Sure they do, but they have to make a buck to keep in business, and selling whoopie cushions, ventriloquist dolls, and Fisher Price "My First Plastic Piece of Garbage Magic Kits" will pay a lot more of the electric bill than the neighborhood magic flunkies who come in mostly to strut and gab.

The owners of these places have built their business on a quandary! Their need to keep secrets battles their need to sell secrets to the community. After all, what you're buying at a magic store is basically a secret. Oh sure, you get the physical apparatus as well, but much of the advertising and selling of magical effects focuses on the secret, the magician's desire to know secrets that others do not know.

The owners guard their secrets. They value the secrecy in magic, and many will refuse to sell you a professional illusion until you've proven you are a professional magician, or at least a professionally minded one. One proprietor said he would not sell knowingly to nonmagicians, nor to anyone who wanted the tricks or books solely to reveal them, as some TV producers or radio disc jockeys have done.

If you're good, they may even let you in on the secret of a trick before you buy. Generally this is done in the interest of matching up your skill level with the demands of the illusion. Most shop owners will simply test you rather than divulge the trick. Some grill with questions. Others need a demonstration of your prowess then and there. One magic store owner admitted that sometimes he will "tip a gaff" to a potential customer when it will help the sale; for instance if the customer believes the trick is harder to perform than it really is, the store owner might show them it is not so.[3]

There are also mail order catalogs from which magical apparatus can be ordered. One thing I've noticed about magic catalogs is sometimes the ad copy panders to the very trait which magicians claim to despise in their viewers: wanting to know how the trick is done. For instance, there are catch phrases sprinkled throughout the magic catalogs such as, "The secret method will absolutely thrill you" or "You'll get a real kick from this new technique." On the whole, however, the tone of the catalogs is informative without giving away the secret. Sometimes they'll list off what methods are *not* used to achieve the effect ("No strings, wires, or batteries to run out.") In short, fun reading. But if you order these catalogs, be warned, you'll be tempted to buy a lot more than you can probably afford.

Hank Lee's bespeckled and bearded countenance smiles upon visitors to his Massachusetts mail order catalog. The catalog is currently eight dollars, which buys you a profusely illustrated tome and a spot on the mailing list. Tricks here range from small novelties to medium-size illusions to stage show extravaganzas. Most stuff in the catalog is, to my miserly mind, wildly expensive. The catalog also has top-secret blueprints of famous illusions such as Vanishing Birdcage, Girl to Lion, Mismade Girl, Sword Suspension, and Buzz Saw. To further up the catalog's coolness factor, Lee sells a wide array of machines that spew fire balls, smoke, and confetti for the surprisingly low price of forty to sixty dollars each. You can get the catalog from Hank Lee's Magic Factory, P.O. Box 789, Medford, Massachusetts 02155, (617) 482-8749, (617) 482-8750, or (800) 874-7400.

A slick but slimmer catalog of magic books and videos is the L & L Publishing catalog, which includes many nice photographs and product descriptions. You can get it at L & L Publishing, Quality Magic Literature, P.O. Box 100, Tahoma, California 96142, (800) 626-6572.

Diamond's Magic catalog has the look and feel of a homemade zine. The company supplies a full line of small-scale and larger-scale tricks and illusions, as well as books, videos, and all the rest of it. They'll stuff your box for free, and once you start ordering they'll keep you happy with plenty of flyers and updates on all the latest magic gizmos. You can reach the company at Diamond's Magic, Inc., P.O. Box 3335, Peabody, Massachusetts 01961-3335, (800) 330-2713.

The world's first virtual magic store can be accessed via Internet E-mail. The proprietor, Charlie Ellis, is usually willing to answer questions concerning the content of books and videos and make recommendations for those just starting out. Prices are discounted, especially, as Charlie says, when you say the magic words: "Here's My Money!" To subscribe to the once-a-month electronic mailing list, drop a note to emagic@universe. digex.net. The cyberly disinclined can receive paper copies in their mailbox by writing to Charlie Ellis, The Electronic Magic Store, 1498-M Reisterstown Road #337, Baltimore, Maryland 21208, (410) 358-8889.

Of course there are many more catalogs, Worldwide Web pages, and magic shops; these are just a few of the ones I've had pleasurable experiences with. Most cities have at least one magic store with a proprietor willing to show you some tricks and help you out.

COMPUTER NETWORKS

There are a number of local computer bulletin boards around the country devoted to magic. If you can't find any, the Internet has become a wonderful midway for meeting and greeting fellow magicians. The primary spot is the Usenet newsgroup alt.magic. Alt.magic is for magicians, and the magicians are mostly pretty closed-mouthed about blabbing secrets. However, most are willing to use private email to discuss tricks of the trade if they deem you worthy of the knowledge. A more recently formed group is alt.magic.secrets. This one is ostensibly devoted to the trading of magic secrets, but the very thought is so horrific to most magicians that none of any caliber post messages on that forum. There are a plethora of pages on the Worldwide Web devoted to magic, illusion, and related topics. The easiest way to find it all is by visiting the All Magic Guide web page at http://www. uelectric.com/allmagicguide.html. It lists everything.

Electronic Grymoire is a top-secret electronic magic club for people that are frustrated by alt.magic. Suzanne the Magician says, "They have you fill out an application and then everyone votes on whether to let you in or not. It seems a bit elitist, but alt.magic is starting to suck and I want to talk to people without having to wade through all the flaming." Sometimes you will see this secret club mentioned cryptically as EG. Now you know what that means.

READING BETWEEN THE LINES

Are you good at figuring out the words on the game show "Wheel of Fortune"? Sometimes it helps. When magicians exchange messages on computer bulletin boards and other public forums, they often try to disguise their intent by leaving out crucial letters. You might see an amateur magician asking his friends: "Have any of you bought the new f—ing coin yet?"

"I saw a great new I—— deck routine today . . ."

"My SOH failed me but luckily I had an out."

Sometimes they abbreviate simply because it's faster and easier (SOH for sleight of hand). But sometimes the abbreviation is to keep *you* from knowing what they're talking about! After all, they don't want to reveal to the general public such secrets as "the new *folding* coin" or "a great new *Invisible* deck routine." (A folding coin is exactly what you think it is—a gimmicked coin that looks real, but has minute invisible hinges that allow it to fold into three sections, thus becoming skinny enough to slip through the narrow opening of a bottle. An Invisible deck is not at all what you think it is. It's a specially prepared deck of cards that allows the magician to perform all sorts of miracles.)

So if you ever find yourself playing "Wheel of Fortune" when you thought you were reading a bulletin board message, now you'll know to pull out the glossary at the end of this book, and perhaps that will help you decode the secret meaning they're trying to keep from you!

MAGIC WORDS

There are two kinds of magic books: those for amateurs, and those for professionals. The amateur books, many written for children, do what they can to tingle your senses with the fascinating allure of the hobby. The tricks presented are often—disappointing. You come to the books expecting great miracles, but are given a few simple tricks, which very often you know already because you've seen them in so many other books.

However, when you start looking at *real* books of magic—the textbooks experienced magicians use—you realize something both reassuring and frustrating: you can't do the tricks. They're too hard. You don't understand what they're talking about.

It's reassuring to know it's not just tricks, there's skill here, there's many years of practice and error, there's impenetrable magician's jargon, and there is the understanding that the illusion isn't being taught—it's being shared. It's frustrating because if you couldn't do it before you still can't do it now. This magic—real, skilled magic—is not for the casual reader of *Boy's Life*. For this you got to be a No Wimp Wizard.

However, you should be aware that the simple tricks described in the beginners' books are more than they appear to be. We've said time and again that a magic trick is more than just a trick; what makes a magic trick interesting and entertaining is the presentation of voice, story, showmanship, etc. The beginner tricks may be simplistic, but they have the same power to inspire awe as any forty-ton cut-the-Statue-of-Liberty-in-half illusion. Perhaps more important is the fact that you have to crawl before you can run . . . the artist must be able to hold a paintbrush before the Mona Lisa can appear on canvas. The magician must first be well-practiced in the presentation of illusions, learn the simple sleights, and learn the simple techniques as pre-requisites to performing more advanced illusions later on. In fact, the simple beginners' tricks are often pretty much the same thing as what master magicians do on stage. The only difference is, they use expensive large-scale props while you use an oatmeal can covered in colored paper.

Another way the two differ is that the beginner tricks often have you making use of a gimmick or sleight directly, as the main focus of the illusion, whereas the professional magician might use that gimmick or maneuver as only one part of a larger effect. Consider all the rigged boxes and bags that you can buy at a magic store that have fake bottoms and hidden compartments in them. A beginner magician would use them directly to make items disappear. To the beginner, that *is* the trick. A more advanced magician uses such an item as a quick way to make an item disappear as a stepping stone towards some grand finale. The gimmick is not the whole trick, just part of the buildup to the real magic. While the beginner focuses on the gimmick, the advanced magician hardly mentions it at all. You can see how one of these "simple beginner" gimmicks is used to great effect when buried amidst a larger accumulation of glitter, glamour, aura, and dramatics.

MAGIC CLUBS AND ORGANIZATIONS

From ancient times there have been secret clubs where grown adults got together and discussed magic and mysticism in secrecy in one of the club member's basements. The symbols, handshakes and lore of the club were closely guarded secrets. The very existence of the clubs themselves was not a topic of dinnertime discussion.

Nowadays magic clubs are out in the open, although it may still require something of an initiation rite to get into the clubs (in the form of an oath, endorsements by club members, and, of course, a nicely penned check or credit card number).

If you talk to magicians, a lot of them give a bad rap to the magic fraternities and clubs. It's not the clubs themselves that are disliked, but the haughty attitudes, the one-upmanship, and the showoffism expressed by the club members. Still, magic clubs are one of the best way to meet a lot of other magicians, see them at work, and exchange techniques with them. The national and international clubs all have local get-togethers so you can mingle with magicians from your area.

The Society of American Magicians, founded in 1902, describes itself as the oldest "and most prestigious" magical society in the world. The club has its origins in a New York magic shop where magicians would meet till all hours of the morning to discuss their craft. Eventually the group decided to form a magic organization. Club members receive *M-U-M* magazine ("Magic-Unity-Might") monthly. One useful club benefit is the SAM libraries of magic books, films and videocassettes, which club members can borrow through the mail. SAM also runs the Society of Young Magicians, for wizards aged seven through seventeen.

Becoming a member involves an application that asks you to write a biography explaining your affiliation with magic, being endorsed by club members, signing an oath ("I am opposed to cheap literature wherein magical secrets are needlessly exposed . . ."), and sending in the required money.

You can reach these organizations by writing the Society of American Magicians or the Society of Young Magicians, P.O. Box 510260, St. Louis, Missouri 63151-0260.

When magicians talk about IBM, they're not talking computers, they're talking shop. The International Brotherhood of Magicians was founded in 1922 and boasts a membership of over 13,500 magicians throughout the world. IBM publishes *The Linking Ring* monthly. To join, there is an annual fee, a pledge to sign, and a form to fill out. As with SAM, the applying magician must be endorsed by members already active in the club. You can reach them at The International Brotherhood of Magicians, P.O. Box 192090, St. Louis, Missouri 63119.

Project Magic was started by David Copperfield as a way to bring magic to the lives of people with "various physical, psychosocial, and developmental disabilities." This is not a secret magic club but an organization dedicated to using magic off-stage for good purposes. Learning to perform magic gives the handicapped a skill that few people, even unhandicapped people, can duplicate. The effect is both mentally uplifting and physically rehabilitating. You can contact the organization at David Copperfield's Project Magic, The Kansas Rehabilitation Hospital, 1504 S.W. 8th St., Topeka, Kansas 66601-2446.

The Magic Castle is a private, members-only club for magicians, built in an authentic Victorian mansion in the Hollywood hills. Full membership is to experienced magicians *only*, and they must prove their skills before membership is allowed. Nonmagicians may still gain a partial membership to the club, but only after demonstrating a keen knowledge and interest in magic and magic lore. Membership fees range from $100 to $900. There are three theaters in the castle: the Close-Up Gallery, the Parlour of Prestidigitation, and the Palace of Mystery. These theaters show several shows a night, and visitors can wander freely into and out of any or all shows. There are no tickets for shows, and no reserved seating, meaning that long lines are the rule rather than the exception. Even though only member magicians can enter the club, it is not so hard to get in. Any magician who is a member of the club can bestow upon you a guest card. In the course of doing this book I've had a number of magicians offer me guest cards, attesting to the very friendliness and generosity of those in the field. The Magic Castle is a great way to meet and greet and learn from other magicians, as well as to catch a *lot* of live magical performances. The Magic Castle is located at 7001 Franklin Ave., Hollywood, California 90028.

For those of you truly interested learning the art of magic, a club can be an enjoyable way to submerge yourself in the hobby. If there are no clubs in your area, start your own!

Siegfried . . . taught me the logic behind the execution of the manipulations. He showed me how a magician has to build the sequences properly in order to arrive at the desired climax, how he has to think the opposite from his spectators, and, most important of all, that a good magician manipulates the minds of the audience.[4]—Roy, of Siegfried and Roy.

How to Become a Magician

First of all, if you're reading this book you're well on your way to becoming a magician, if that is your desire. I say that because the thoughts I'm sharing—the controls the magician takes in performing his illusions—these are the things that are barely mentioned in magic books you can buy at the mall. Nor are they described in the instructions to tricks, which often explain only how to mechanically operate the thing you've just bought. You don't become a true magician by buying a magic trick. Becoming a magician requires exercising the sleights, learning the language, practicing in front of a mirror, carefully scripting your lines, viewing the performances of other magicians, talking with other magicians, refining one's act, and sitting there with magic books in your bedroom until the wee hours. When your mind is completely glogged up with all this, then, and only then, will you be a true—novice.

And then you go back up to your bedroom and practice some more. Las Vegas prestidigitator Jeff Hobson said that a trick can take up to one or two *years* before he's sufficiently confident in both the trick and his ability to perform the trick effectively enough that he will make it a part of his show. That can be after as much as five years of thought and planning.[5] Other magicians have worked on a trick for much longer than that before going public with it.

One of the things I've noticed is that much of magic is not really as secret as people think it is. When you hear magicians and non-magicians talking, you hear a lot of conversations like this:

Audience member: "How'd you do that?!"

Magician: "Sorry, I can't tell you."

Audience member: "Well, how can I find out if you won't tell me? I want to be a magician!"

Magician: "You do! That's great! The best way to start is to go to the library. There are dozens of great books—"

Audience member: "Aw, pshaw! I've read those books, they don't reveal any real secrets! I want to know how the *really good tricks are done!*"

At this point the magician may try to convince the audience member that there really are few secrets of magic that you won't find by looking in the library. But the audience member won't believe this, figuring the magician is trying to throw him off the trail of the good secrets. But it's true. It's the absolute truth, and this is perhaps the biggest secret of all about magic: that most of magic is not as secret as people think it is. Most of magic *can* be found out by checking out some books at the library.

After writing these words just now, I did a little data gathering experiment: I called up the electronic card catalog of my local public library to find out how many books on magic are available. Fifty-one books and videos are listed! That's a lot of magical knowledge contained in one place. To those of you who say "Aw, pshaw! I want to know how the *really good tricks are done!*" then to you I will reply, What do you think is in those fifty-one books? Garbage? Those books contain all the secrets of magic you could need to know. In this book I can only touch on the many issues and secrets and techniques that encompass all of magic. Believe me when I tell you there are entire books dedicated to each and every one of the techniques that I mention herein. If you think you're not getting real secrets, then you are being fooled! No wonder magicians can fool you with their tricks so easily, if you're thrown off by such a simple ploy! For this is a little-known but highly valuable secret of magic—it might be that magicians *want* you to believe that their tricks are performed by such cleverness that there's no way those secrets could be revealed in a public place like a library shelf or a toy store magic kit. But, in fact, secrets are revealed in those places. The secrets magicians use are no different from the ones that are revealed. It's how you use them that counts. Those of you who believe that "no good secrets are revealed in those books" are participating in your own version of Robert Jay Lifton's "thought-terminating cliché" that will be explored later in the section on brainwashing. In a sense you have brainwashed yourself into believing that the books contain no truths and no secrets . . . therefore there is no way for you to learn anything from them, and thus the secrets remain safe and secret within those unread pages.

I have in my hand a slim pamphlet with the windy title *Prestidigitation* by Jon Koons. This is a twelve-page little handbook that I sent away for as a child from the H-O oatmeal company in Indianapolis, Indiana. The booklet was part of a promotion where they included instructions for simple magic tricks on the packets of oatmeal, and budding young sorcerers could mail away for this booklet that promised to teach the secrets of prestidigitation—magic. Well, when the booklet arrived I was not exactly thrilled with its meager contents. It offered such pearls as "The Secret's the Thing" and "Showmanship Makes the Difference." At the time I felt it didn't give me any good advice. It certainly didn't reveal any secrets. What I didn't realize was what most nonmagicians overlook—the fact that the secret may be "the thing," but it's not *everything*. And what appears to be not so important may very well be the most important thing of all. What I didn't realize as a child was that most secrets of magic are not so mystical/magical/wonderful when you find out about them. That's the point! There's no such thing as real magic, so magicians have to rely on tricks that are *not* mystical/magical/wonderful. Some of the most amazing magical illusions rely on a dab of wax that the magician got from his daughter's orthodontist. And that's quite a big secret—knowing that nonmagicians will overlook the things that don't seem so thrilling, and thus magicians can fool them with those things. The nonmagician will never learn how the tricks are really done because when they see the real secrets that are used, they aren't impressed by them. They think they're not finding out anything of importance, and so they believe the secrets are too well guarded to be discovered. Not true.

The truth is, if you were to show my little oatmeal booklet to a professional magician, the magician would smile and nod and admit, "Yup! It's all in these twelve little pages!" While the nonmagician throws it away, the real magician nods his approval. That's why people don't know how the trick is done—they ignore the secrets even when they're right in front of their face. It takes a magician to notice the magical value of the most banal stage direction.

Fifty-one magic books. Many of those, I'm sure, are in the children's books section of the library. Here again the nonmagicians wouldn't even bother to take a look, saying "Feh! That's for kids!" And once again they would be fooled the way only a magician can fool them, because those magic books for children contain the same advice as the adult books do, and many of the same tricks. The person who becomes a proficient magician is not one who ignores information because they think it's too childish or beneath them. Most of us looked through a magic book or two as a kid, or got a magic kit for a birthday present. Why didn't we all become magicians? Many of us were turned off because we wanted "real" secrets but we were presented with this seeming "kids stuff." (Those who recognized the value in it perhaps did go on to cultivate their interest in the art.) Another important factor, I think, is that most magicians were inspired by seeing another magician perform. As I've been saying, there's more to magic than just the trick; there's the whole performance of it—that's something you never get from a kid magic book, or a magic kit. How can you be inspired by seeing a trick spelled out for you in black ink? It takes seeing the performance, feeling the experience of magic, to become inspired.

How did I become interested in magic? As a child, by watching "The Magic of Mark Wilson" every Saturday morning at 7:30 A.M. before even the cartoons came on. I wanted to do the magic things that he, his son, and his wife did on that show. And I wanted to know all those secrets behind how he did those magic things. Every magician, whether professional or amateur, has his or her own "how I became interested in magic" tale to tell. One of the ways you build a magician's trust in you is by having a story like that of your own. By sharing it with another magician, you show that you are just like him in that regard, having had an early and passionate interest in the art from early childhood. This will make him more likely to share secrets with you.

If you want to become a magician, hang out with magicians. Build their trust. You won't get anywhere by rudely asking how a trick is done. They may refer you to a book or series of books that will get you started. The books might contain simpler tricks, but consider that many good tricks are really a sequence of smaller tricks put together. If you don't know a good method of making a cat disappear and a cat reappear, then you can't do a push-a-cat-through-a-brick-wall trick. In order to get secrets out of magicians you have to prove to them you are worthy of becoming a member of their circle, that you have the patience to practice, and the ability to keep your lips glued shut. The feelings of many magicians are expressed by one who said that he is happy to show anyone how any trick is done, assuming two things are true: (1) Some time has passed since the trick was presented; to allow the feeling of magic to fill the heart and mind of the student, and (2) The magician is convinced that the student genuinely wants to know how to *perform* the illusion, rather than just wanting to know how it's done.

When all is said and done, the way one becomes a magician is by loving magic, and being willing to work on that love to achieve proficiency at it.

PART THREE

PEOPLE, PLACES, AND THINGS

At this point we have explored what magic is, how illusions are created, what goes on in the mind of the magician, how to watch a magic show intelligently, and how to figure out the secrets of the illusions. With this knowledge behind us, I want to now go into greater detail about a lot of the things we've mentioned only briefly. This section is a hodge-podge of different facets of magic. I hope to provide a look at the art form in all its diversity, as well as tie up loose ends and present final thoughts on the art of magic and illusion. Here we will consider magic from the point of view of the audience, the assistants, and the animals. We will also sneakily trespass into the magician's studio, where we will do something that a magician would ordinarily never let us do—sneak into his trunks and cartons, and inspect closely all those props, gizmos, and gadgets that you see on stage but that magicians never let you go anywhere near. Are they trying to hide something? You bet they are! We'll sneak backstage later, but for now let's take our seat in the audience . . .

8

The Audience

The music is all timed, the words are all timed, so you get an emotional response as well as amazement. . . . It's a romantic thing, an emotional thing. You can tell a story and put it into a book. But not a written book: a living book.
—Matthew Dwinells, illusion artist

I want to make their sphincters tighten and their stomachs rumble.
—Harley Newman, escape artist

Emotional Effects of Magic

Well-done magic is often accompanied by an emotional effect—what feelings can the magician stir up in the soul of the audience? Some of the magical forms lend themselves directly to a particular kind of emotion (escapes and proving invulnerability). Other forms, such as evanishments and productions, are by themselves no more than the dictionary definition of the term unless the magician comes up with a storyline or plot to hook the audience into the mysticism of the event. Here we will take a brief break from the magician, and concentrate on some of the audience responses to illusions.

MYSTIFICATION

Obviously, the main effect of magic is to mystify. When I asked laypeople to describe magicians, the word most often used was "magic" or "magical." That may seem like an unintelligent answer, but it is both very proper and telling. People didn't use words like "tricksters" or "fakers." There may be individual cases of magicians who are seen in that regard, but the nonmagicians I spoke with viewed magicians the way magicians want to be viewed: "They make the unreal happen. The unexpected, the unbelievable, the 'out of this world' experience . . ." One longtime devotee of magic explained how as a child his father would try to explain how the tricks are done. But he didn't want to believe his father's explanations. He was more willing to believe the impossibilities of the magician than the explanations of his father. When the audience is in a receptive mode, they "contribute to their own entertainment, being able to experience at least briefly a sense of thrill or awe at 'seeing' the supernatural in action."[1]

That is the goal of magic, if one can say that magic has a goal. To install that wonderment, especially in a child, is a great achievement for a magician.

NOSTALGIA

The more poetic magicians will tell a story with their presentation of the magic, often achieving a sense of nostalgia. Copperfield does this often as he searches for memories and emotions from his childhood to incorporate into his shows.

DANGER AND AMAZEMENT

The swami-type tricks, where the magician performs some physically harmful acts, invoke a sense of danger, excitement, and often total gross-out in the audience. The performer may claim magical powers enable him to perform these feats, but the desired effect is not a magical one. The performer is more interested in invoking a sense of danger and amazement at his ability to shove a nail up his nose, or eat fire. Harley Newman, a performer of escapes, stunts, magic, and crazed weirdness, said that when he lies down on a bed of nails, "I'm assured the entire audience will go—*gasp!* I'm very aware that I strive to get that very effect from the audience." And if not the nails, the clincher is the concrete block being crushed by a sledgehammer on his stomach.

He says that he thinks of escapes in two general categories: "intellectually oriented" and "go for the guts . . . things which have major danger factors to them." As an example he mentions the escape artist who is tied up in ropes and flung into a cold ocean. "Right away it appeals to people's sense of their own mortality." We are fascinated that the escape artist has seemingly conquered his fear of death. How confidently he offers himself to the freezing waters in so helpless a condition. If an escape artist or magician can elicit such emotions from a person, then they are performing at a much higher level than the typical hobbyist who buys a few stupid tricks at a magic store.

SURPRISE

The best magic will elicit surprise in the audience. The worst magic does not. Consider the magician who says, "I'm going to make this rabbit disappear" then does it. The audience is left thinking, "Okay, that was certainly puzzling, but so what?" There was no feeling of pleasant surprise. No delightful "Ha!" Surprise is not only essential for enjoying an act, it is also an essential maneuver used to misdirect attention. The audience is so surprised by the latest climax, they are unaware of sneakiness happening elsewhere on the stage.

FEAR AND AWE

People who portray magic as real (psychics, fortune tellers) often try to exploit their audience into feeling fear. Con artists may use fear to scam people into letting go of their wallets. Both use awe in a way that a stage illusionist would not. As stated before, the magician tries not to put on a holier-than-thou attitude, for that promotes an unmanageable attitude in the audience. But people like the psychics and other con artists actually want the audience to be in awe of their powers because it increases their revenue growth.

STUPIDITY

If the audience feels stupid, the magician is doing magic wrong. It can't be restated enough: Magic is illusion, it is not puzzlement. A magician's illusions should make you feel good about the world, not angry at yourself for being stupid. That's why magicians are disgusted when they hear people using the words "magic trick." Magicians create illusions—hookers do tricks.

EMOTIONLESSNESS

Sometimes the viewer is so absorbed in the fantasy, he notices no magic at all. For instance, in some of the big name magic shows, they do such an enormous build-up to the illusion involving dance routines, costuming, and flashy lights that the magical feat is lost in the spectacle. This is especially the case on television. We are so used to seeing special effects on TV it is hard to recognize the "real thing," as magicians would like us to believe their magic is. This can also happen at stage shows. After seeing a magician perform a lovely act where dainty butterflies floated in the air above a gently swaying Oriental fan, my sister remarked, "That was dumb. I could do that if I practiced enough!" I explained to her that she wasn't fanning the butterflies to keep them in the air, that it was a magic trick, probably done with threads. She didn't seem convinced, and I felt incapable of explaining it to her. I felt dumb for having to reveal a secret merely so an audience member would recognize that the floating was illusion and not skill in fan-waving. "Well," I told her, "if you think you can do that, go try."

Magician John Bannon, who often offers intelligent commentary on the performance of magic in his books, has pointed out that certain kinds of magic effects have emotional problems built into them; and those problems are unavoidable. For instance, "One problem with many prediction tricks is that, once the prediction is made, it is presumptively correct. Audiences *assume* the trick will have a successful conclusion and therefore immediately accept that the performer's prediction will be right. As a result, the emphasis shifts immediately to the *conditions* of the effect as the audience tries to figure out *how* the performer will make the prediction come true. The trick becomes a challenge effect, and much of the surprise element is lost."[2] Along with the surprise, the mystification is lost as well. The audience won't be mystified and awed when they know in advance how the trick will play out. Bannon refers to the magical/mystical feeling he likes to induce in the audience as a "Twilight Zone surprise." He's not after merely proving to the audience he can pull off an impossible feat (that's taken for granted). Rather, he'd like to surprise them when the conclusion of the illusion is reached. This he does by putting a bit of a twist into the effect. Bannon illustrates with a simple example. Suppose the magician announces he will make a coin vanish. He flips a coin into the air, catches it in his fist, and then opens the hand to show it is gone. The spectator will be surprised, but is likely to ask, "Wow. How did you do that?" It's nice that the trick went off successfully, but it came across as a puzzle, not a *magical* event. Instead Bannon proposes a better way of performing the trick: Flip the coin in the air and catch it in a fist. Ask the spectator to guess whether it came up heads or tails. When the fist is opened, the coin is gone. Here the reaction is more likely to be, "Hold on a minute. How did that happen?"[3] In a sense the magician is continuing his misdirection right up until the very last moment of the trick—and even after the trick is over. In this case, the magician is misdirecting the spectator's thoughts and emotions. Instead of being puzzled and wondering how the trick was done, the magician has misdirected the spectator to feel something more emotional, more magical. Not only does that make for a better trick, it also helps keep the secret intact, because the spectator isn't probing to find out how the trick was accomplished.

SURPRISE, SURPRISE

Usually magicians don't reveal beforehand how a trick is going to proceed. Doing so would ruin the surprise. When they do tell you what they're going to do, it's usually for a reason, such as sensationalism or advertising. The magician has to weigh his options. Which will cause the bigger emotional response: the surprise of finding out what miracle will be performed, or knowing beforehand what he will attempt to do, and the suspense that builds up from watching the attempt? In the best case, if the magician has some tricks up his sleeve, the trick itself may have some twists in it, thus the magician isn't really revealing anything by saying what he intends to do.

Magician Marcus suggests that in addition to the mystical emotions being raised in the spectators, the magician should try to create certain feelings about the magical performance itself:

I'd say we must not only create a "feeling of magic," but also some "feeling of exclusivity." I mean, the effects you do should *never look* so simple that the audience thinks "Hell, my dog could do that if he only had the gimmick!" Now, of course, one could argue: "It is neither sleights nor gimmicks that create feelings, magicians do." That's right, but sometimes you just can't do the trick as clean as possible *and* convince the audience that it was *not* a gimmick that did the trick for you.

Marcus uses as an example the card cassette. This is a piece of magical apparatus that is so well known to laypeople that any magician caught seriously using it is just unbelievably silly and should be laughed at by his peers. The card cassette is a shiny black plastic case that snaps open and shut. You put a playing card in, shut it, and the card has mysteriously vanished when you open the case. The trick works in reverse too. Other effects that can be done are changing from one card to another, shrinking a card (actually you exchange the card with one from a mini-sized deck), as well as a legion of other tricks. The trick is accomplished by a black plastic "false bottom" to the case. After dropping the card in, you shut the case and secretly turn it upside down. The playing card is now hidden under the false bottom, which drops into position on top of the card. When you open the case now, the card appears to be gone. As Marcus explains, even if you do a card cassette trick in the most skillful manner:

the trick just *looks* simple, because, logically seen, there's absolutely no possible explanation other than the card still being in the cassette, but being hidden by something. Just what exactly hides the card or why exactly it can't be seen anymore, doesn't matter for the spectator, because he realizes that the cassette *must* contain the secret, whatever this might be. And you can do *nothing* to convince the spectator that it isn't so.

It's exactly this mistake most magicians make when using gimmicks: They think the secret can't be found and that's enough for the audience to gasp.

There are more elaborate versions of the box. Some are made of wine wood and leather. One version contains a hidden magnet that holds the false flap firmly in place, so it can not be discovered on inspection. However, the fact remains that the trick is so simple in appearance that the audience still can't get past the fact that box *must be gimmicked in some way*. Marcus advises:

Now, if you wouldn't do the trick as . . . [simply] as possible, but include one or two points that make the trick *a little bit* dirtier (don't overdo!), for example hide the cassette for a short moment with a silk, the trick not only becomes more interesting, but also much more difficult, because now the spectator also takes the skill of the magician into consideration (without the magician actually having used any sleight of hand).

By supplying a red herring clue (a silk that looks like it's being used as a cover) the audience will be diverted from the gimmick inside the box. They will see the clue and wonder how it relates to the disappearance of the card. Usually a magician tries to cover up all artificial and suspicious movements, but this is one situation where he might actually subtly showcase a suspicious move to divert attention from the real gimmick.

Would a magician ever use a trick that was so transparent that he had to point out another method of doing the trick?[4] Yes. The very fact that a magician has the ability to divert an audience's thoughts in this way is representative of the kind of mind control we've been discussing throughout this book.

Just today I saw two children playing with a deck of cards. One of the girls squared up the deck and announced she was going to perform a card trick. Her friend picked a card, looked at it, then slid the card back into the deck. At this point, the girl performing the trick looked up, realizing for the first time that she had no magical way to find out the card. She looked at her mother and asked, "How do they do this trick?" The stage magic we see is so smooth, so effortless, so realistic, that it seems obvious that we should be able to somehow defy the laws of physics and do it too. Truthfully, I've fallen into the same trap as the little girl. I've started performing a casual trick for a friend, then realized that because I didn't plan it out or think about it beforehand, I suddenly find myself not knowing how the trick should proceed. The idea of magic is that it is impromptu, whimsical, snap-of-the-finger. These ideas are mutually exclusive to the reality that careful natural planning must go into creating the illusion. And it's good we forget, because it makes the magic more realistic.[5] This same idea has been expressed for many arts besides magic. Renowned Hollywood director Billy Wilder said of the movies, "Audiences don't know somebody sits down and writes a picture. They think the actors make it up as they go along."

You may be wondering, "Why is it at all important to look at the emotional effect an illusionist has on the audience?" Well, it's very important. The emotional effect is the whole basis for magic as entertainment. Actually, the whole reason for watching or participating in any sort of activity is the emotion you get out of it. Theatrical productions are divided into comedies and tragedies (or dramas). Magicians have the option of performing serious (dramatic) magic, or comedic magic, as well as all the other kinds of emotional effects described above. You can see how a thoughtful magician would want to pay attention to the emotion of an illusion, because emotion is going to affect how the illusion is created and maintained in the audience's mind.

THE MODERN MIND

Another consideration was proposed by sorcerer Peter Warlock, who wrote that what a conjurer does is prove "he can accomplish feats of improbability or impossibility, and he is aided in this by contemporary thought or expression."[6] In other words, the impossibility is assisted (perhaps even created) by the "contemporary thought" of the audience. What a magician does must be seen as impossible in the eyes of the audience for it to be a magical effect. An audience composed of angels will find no mystery in watching the magician dance on the head of a pin.

As technology advances, it improves our ability to perform in a given field. Many large-scale magical effects are only possible because of technological advancements. On the other hand, our knowledge of technology has disabled many effects that performers could do at one time, but would now seem decidedly unmagical, or at least trivial. "Magicians often employ cause-effect relations known to science but unfamiliar to the layman. These encompass chemical effects (self-lighting cigarettes, color changes), topological and mathematical facts (knots, magic number squares), and even some psychological phenomena (sensory thresholds, visual illusions). With changes in the layman's knowledge and beliefs about science, the magician's problems have changed."[7]

- French conjurer Robert-Houdin used electromagnets in the 1800s to make an iron weight too heavy for even the strongest audience members to lift. Nowadays, with better education, science museums, and construction cranes that use electromagnets, the public would hardly be fooled.
- One of the magicians Robert-Houdin admired was Philippe, who performed an astonishing feat: the curtains opened to a dark stage. Philippe apologized for the darkness, marched down into the audience, pulled out a pistol, and *blam!*—hundreds of candles magically lighted themselves at the gunshot. Today the secret of that trick would be all too apparent, I'm afraid. Who wouldn't guess that Philippe used a shock of electricity to light his candles? Not the nineteenth-century audiences, to whom electricity was new and unfamiliar.[8]
- European explorer Sir John Mandeville in the mid-1300s reported seeing Chinese magicians perform amazing feats in what was to him the mysterious Orient. He wrote about enchanters who performed before the court of the Great Kahn with sorcery so powerful they could create a shining sun in the night sky. Mandeville wrote that the enchanters "do many marvels; for they make to come in the air, as it seems, the sun and the moon

to do him reverence, which shine so bright that men may not behold them. And syne they make so great murkiness that it seems night; and afterwards they make the light to appear again."[9] People who read these accounts scoffed. But it is possible (probable?) that Sir John was telling the truth. Recall that the Chinese had invented gunpowder long before the Europeans learned of it, and they used gunpowder to make fireworks of all sorts—the bright sun in the night sky.[10]

- More recently, Doug Henning was known for his Sands of the Desert routine, where dry sand was pulled from a bowl of very wet water. The trick was done with special sand coated in wax that made it waterproof. A variation of the effect was later incorporated into a children's toy. No one could perform the trick anymore when people could see ads for the toy on television, or go to a toy store and pick it up.

EXTENDING ILLUSIONS INTO THE FUTURE

There is one ingenious aspect of illusion routinely ignored. Believe it or not, an illusion can change, grow, evolve, and emerge in the days following a performance. That is to say, if the magician does a good job on stage, the audience members' perception of the show will solidify into something greater than the magician presented on stage.

In the days following a magic show, audience members are likely to talk about the show with their friends and family. As they discuss tricks, they will forget about covers ("He sawed her in half and *poof* she was whole again!"). They will exaggerate what went on ("And suddenly the stage was *filled* with tigers and leopards, it was incredible!") The illusion gets bigger and better, as does the reputation of the magician. Even magicians can be surprised at the incredible stories that emerge from their performances: "I was constantly hearing reports of wonders that I had performed—some were so extravagant that I began wondering if I had really performed them."[11] Richard Hodgson summed it up when he said: "The account of a trick, by a person ignorant of the method used in its production, will involve a misdescription of its fundamental conditions. And this misdescription is frequently so marked that no clue is afforded to the student for the actual explanation."[12] The one who relates the trick to others neglects all the sundry details—the covers used to hide a prop for a moment, the explicit exchanges between magician and volunteers. The storyteller certainly doesn't relate all the subtle details like location on stage and when a trick was performed. By leaving out all those important clues, the illusion is made far grander in fable than it was in reality.

You might call this "magic after the fact" or "continuing the magic." You might also label it hyperbole. Magicians have traditionally played up their acts, partially I believe in order to achieve this long-lasting effect. By overstating the illusion in advertising, posters, playbills, and interviews, the magician leaves behind a legacy of having done greater illusions than he actually did. When Copperfield's television ads announced he would vanish the Orient Express, I was excited! The trick itself was a let-down. He didn't exactly vanish the entire train, just one car. Still, the legacy of the effect lives on every time a reporter incorrectly writes that Copperfield vanished the Orient Express. Fake psychics use the same techniques; when you read about their exploits you walk away with eyes wide in wonder. The truth is often far less amazing than their unsubstantiated claims lead one to believe.

The Indian Rope Trick has benefited greatly from this effect of mind. The Indian Rope Trick is generally regarded as impossible to perform. In the idealized account, a magician is standing in the middle of an open empty field in broad daylight. He throws a rope into the air, and it remains suspended vertically there. A boy climbs up the rope and disappears into a cloud. The magician climbs up the rope after him. They begin to argue, and then fight in the clouds! The magician is heard to pull out his sword, and he starts slicing off the boy's limbs, which drop to the ground below. The whole trick, as it is told, is quite elaborate and hard to believe. There have been recorded cases of magicians performing *some* of the effect, but not all of it. It's one thing to throw up a rope and have it stay put *on stage*, quite another to do that in the middle of an empty field with no visible means of support! Researchers have found that reports of magic tricks like the Indian Rope Trick are exaggerated from one telling to the next.[13] In the original trick, the magician may indeed have been standing near a tree or building, which could have an invisible thread running from it to support the rope in midair. Explanations can be dreamed up for the various components of the illusion, but the main point is that our memories are infinitely fallible and cannot necessarily be trusted!

Purveyors of the paranormal, such as psychics and others who flaunt their supernatural know-how, have also benefited greatly in this way. True believers are willing to give psychics, dowsers, faith healers, and their ilk the benefit of the doubt—they're also willing to give them a lot of money for results that are doubtful. Again, much of the results obtained by these methods turn out to be imagined by the clients or the psychic themselves. Supernatural misinformation has also received a great boost by print media, especially books, which repeatedly print information that has been proven wrong years ago. For instance, certain fraudulent mediums, such as the Fox sisters, have made deathbed confessions of how they fooled others into believing their powers, but years later the ghost tales are repeated as if no confession had been made. Why do we still have believers in crop circles, when the guys who created the original ones have long ago confessed their *modus operandi*? The all-too-credulous authors all use each other's writings as reference material, and so their mistakes never get discovered. And the illusions and magic get perpetuated well into the future.

Conjurus Interruptus

Hecklers are people in the audience who bother magicians. They talk too loudly in their seats. They try to give away how the trick is done. They'll yell out that they know the secret, or make lascivious remarks to the females on stage. Hecklers are a pest to both the magician and the audience. Teller, the nontalking half of Penn & Teller, said about them: "Hecklers are boring. That's what's really the matter with them. They usually imagine they're helping the show by adding witty banter, but they don't understand that the show, free-wheeling though it appears, has a movement and they are derailing it. We rarely get them, because we play theatres, where people are usually sober."

Every magician I spoke with agreed with this assessment to one extent or another. James "The Amazing" Randi denied hecklers were a problem, "I don't get hecklers," he said decisively. "There's a point in your career where you don't get hecklers . . . you get the respect, you get the attention you deserve. And if you do [get hecklers], you ignore them. You move right ahead. The audience usually stops them."

Sociomagician Peter Nardi pointed out that hecklers are unlikely to appear at stage shows because the audience has paid money to be there and everyone is happy to be there. Hecklers are more likely to appear when magic is performed on the street or in less formal settings. When a heckler does make a comment, "Magicians have a lot of great one-liners to respond. It brings the power back to the magician. It helps put *down* the heckler." Notice Nardi's very deliberate use of the word "down." The magician needs to have total control or power over the show—he needs to be "on top." The magician can "put down" the heckler with a put-down. If you thumb through a magic catalog you can actually buy books of one-liners for magicians. "All them brother magicians always have a bunch of lines that we can *kill* the heckler with," said Sandorse, "we can kill 'em." Sandorse is wont to eye the heckler and say, "Hey I only have ten minutes to make a jerk out of myself. You have all night." Penn & Teller have a different approach: "On the rare occasions we get them, Penn gives them a quick, 'Shut up, stupid,' which ends the problem"—says Teller.

Most of the magicians pointed out that you don't want to be overly cruel to hecklers. Sandorse said, "Most of the time, unless you have to, you don't use them. Most of the time you're better off not killing the heckler." Harley Newman explained that audience outbursts are sometimes funnier than what he has come up with for his routine. He doesn't mind laughing at their joke ("I have to give them their fame, otherwise it sours the whole thing") and has even incorporated audience heckling into his act. Some magicians said that if they're using ungimmicked props they might hand over the props to the heckler and let them have a go at it. Ken Barham explained, "If they can do it (and one guy was able to do a cheesy card trick) I applaud them and then continue with my stuff. This gets them on your side. If they can't then they get embarrassed and shut up." Of course, when a heckler reveals crucial information about a trick, even if it's misinformation, that's hard to laugh at.

Magicians have techniques for spotting a heckler in the crowd. Ken Barham notes, "Hecklers are given away by two things. First, they are heckling you. The idea is to search and destroy *before* they become hecklers. Things to watch for are: Sarcastic expressions on their faces, leaning to whisper to a friend who then looks annoyed or shakes his head yes (and their neighbors look annoyed)." According to Dunninger, "Personally, I screen such characters beforehand, by learning something of their likes and dislikes, or sounding them out by working a test with a more susceptible person and watching their reactions."[14] The Great Sol Messler says,

If it's a small show, I try to have my assistant go through the crowd beforehand and find out what people are saying to each other. Sometimes you'll hear them deciding who they're going to "volunteer" to go up and help me if I ask for volunteers. Sometimes you hear them planning what they would do if I did ask them up on stage—planning what they would say to wreck a trick. Obviously, since my show is very audience-involved, I can then avoid those people. I can pick the people who my assistant decides before the show will make good assistants by her pre-scouting.

And Derreck says, "I'm always wary of people who really, really want to come up on stage with me. People who talk to me before the show, before I've even shown them how good a magician I am, if they're already in love with the whole idea of sharing the show with me, you know to watch out for them."

Female magicians may have another kind of heckler to deal with: the Don Juan. Suzanne the Magician said she gets hit on by male audience members all the time, especially the time she agreed to be "guest magician" on a cruise liner. I asked her, "Well, that's flattering, isn't it? Or just annoying?" She responded,

Yes, it's more annoying than flattering. I am obviously married (wedding ring and all) but you get people that want you sitting on their laps and want to kiss your cheek (the one on your face), things like that. What bothers me most is that if I was male, this wouldn't happen. Women wouldn't say, "If you're such a good magician, why don't you sit on my lap and see if you can levitate something." Do they really think they are being clever when they say things like that? How crude can you get?

Hecklers are bad for everybody, with their (often drunken) calling out of taunts and jokes and pointing out how the trick was done (or how they think it was done). They believe their interjected comments are funny, and perhaps they believe the whole point of the show is to reveal the trick—to catch the magician at his game. They're "helping" by playing the game as they feel it is supposed to be played. Thus they don't feel social pressure to shut up. They are bad for the magician because they take away the magician's total control of the show. Hecklers are bad for the audience, because they take away the audience's belief in the magic.

SIMULATED HECKLERS

There have been instances where a magician has planted hecklers in the audience for the express purpose of making their magic more believable. At a crucial time in the illusion, the heckler will yell out, "I bet that box is gimmicked. Why don't you show us the box!" which the magician will then proceed to do, thus garnering extra trust from the viewing audience.

More magicians will not actually place hecklers in the crowd, but as part of their patter they will "pretend" to hear a heckler, or they will anticipate a heckler ("Ah I hear some of you complaining that I haven't shown the box. Well, take a good look and you'll see it's completely ordinary.") The audience doesn't have to believe that the magician really did hear someone in the crowd complaining. All they need to know is that their innermost private desire (to get a better look at the box) is being fulfilled, and meanwhile the magician is perhaps directing attention away from the *real* gimmick of the trick.

Magic and Children

The magical art has been trivialized by many to the realm of kiddy birthday party, the magician seen as interchangeable with a horn-honking, red-nosed clown. I'm sure professional clowns are as bugged about it as magicians are. But we know better. We know that magic has the capacity to instill a sense of wonder, to elevate our souls, and to entertain in a way that no other form of amusement can. And who better to appreciate magic than a wide-eyed, wondering child?

Ha! *Anyone* would be in a better position to appreciate magic than a child! Children aren't wide-eyed in wonder! They're wide-eyed from too much television and video games. Grade school kids don't *want* to be awestruck by magic—and they're *not*. They've spent too much of their lives being impressed by people in authority, being taken places against their will, being taught and forced to sit through demonstrations of another person's abilities. The magician on stage is just one more example of all that the child is full of and sick of.

If the child shows any interest in magic, it's for the trick value. Children want to know how the trick is done. They're snotty. They're brats. They're pokey and nosey and the worst hecklers a magician can have, mostly because the magician can't reason with them. Children simply do not have the necessary mental capability to appreciate much of magic.

Remember, magic is based on illusions, and this is meant quite literally. An illusion is the mind's way of dealing with our complicated world. The mind cannot process every iota of information presented to it, so it (either consciously or unconsciously) selects pieces of the environment to pay attention to. The brain makes logical assumptions based on those snippets of information. It fills in the gaps where it has not collected information, assuming that what it does not know, it can figure out from past experience.

That's where magic slips us up. Because magic (and other illusions) arrange the information and the gaps, so that when taken together, the gaps cannot be filled in with what we know as reality. There *are* no rational explanations the mind can fall back on. It must assume magic has transpired.

Some of the best examples of these tricks are "sucker tricks," whereby the audience thinks they catch the magician screwing up or trying to fool them, and, in the end, the tables are turned and it is the magician who fools the audience. Notice that sucker tricks play perfectly to a child audience, who is more interested in figuring out the trick than in sitting back and experiencing the wonder of magic. Look at some of the staples of any birthday party performer:

- *Cake in Hat.* The magician haphazardly throws milk, eggs, flour, and other messy ingredients into his hat. The children scream that he is making a big mistake—but the magician prevails, pulling out a baked cake. The hat is shown to be pristine, clean, and empty.
- *Milk in Hat.* A variation on the above in which the magician pours milk into a hat, only then remembering he should pour milk into a cup, not a hat. So he places the cup into the hat, and removes it full to the brim with milk. The hat is clean.
- *Sucker Die Box.* The magician places an oversized die into a double-doored cabinet. He closes the doors, subtly tilts the cabinet to one side, then opens the "higher" door to show the cabinet empty. The audience protests. Obviously the die has simply slid to the other side. (Some versions of this trick come equipped with a fake sliding sound.) After much misunderstanding, the magician finally dismantles the cabinet, showing that the die has completely vanished.
- *Hippity Hop Carrot.* The magician shows two cards with drawings of a carrot and a rabbit. The cards are put under rectangular tubes (or, in a newer version, cloth covers). The rabbit and carrot switch places several times. The kids are too smart: "You're just turning the cards around!" they scream. Indeed, it looks like that's what the magician is doing. Finally he catches their drift, and offers to turn around the cards to appease them. He turns around one card, and it shows the green carrot tops. He turns the other around, and it shows the rabbit eating the carrot. The kids are stumped.

These effects emphasize the trickiness of magic, and devalue the mystical tingles that other illusions attempt to provoke. Magic here is reduced to a cat and mouse chase, only here the cat is an audience of brats, and the mouse is a magic one who escapes at the last minute through a trick even trickier than the one the cat had envisioned. At first the audience fills in the gaps with what it knows to be true about the world (that a die can slide, or that this absent-minded professor of prestidigitation has fumbled the hat trick) but at the last moment the magician shows that the way they filled the gaps to solve the puzzle is wrong. The die did not slide. The hat is not a mess. The audience is left with no alternate explanations, no recourse to fall back on. In a sense this may actually be a high form of misdirection. Any suspicious moves the magician makes are overlooked because the audience already "knows" how it's done. They're not looking for the trick—they realize how painfully obvious the trick is. Or so they believe.

The catch is in the gimmick. The audience is led to believe that a simple sliding motion accomplishes the effect. Then the tables are turned. The Hippity Hop lever is pulled, or the clean hat is shown, or the hollow die shell falls out of sight into its compartment—and the mouse suddenly catches the cat!

Suzanne the Magician says she likes doing sucker tricks for kids, as long as she doesn't get them too mad.

> I actually wouldn't even do sucker tricks for adults. The premise is that you do something so obvious that the audience would yell out, "Oh, you are just . . ." whatever it looks like you are just doing. Well, in my experience, adults, for the most part, are just too polite to yell anything out. They will just sit there and think you suck. Kids on the other hand will *say* you suck and then proceed to tell you why they think so. Then when it doesn't turn out to be what they thought, they get very quiet. That's when you know you got 'em.

Children do perceive the world in a less sophisticated way than adults. I remember being amazed as a young child, that I could hold up my thumb and pointer finger, and look at a distant car through them, and somehow that huge automobile was so tiny it could fit between my fingers. "That's perspective," Mommy explained. That's the mind of the child, who is in the process of learning rules about the world. Perspective was so ingrained in the adult brain of my mother—the way it is ingrained in my brain now, and yours—that she and we never stop to think about it. In fact, our brain has learned this rule of perspective, and it allows us to make sense of the world. Imagine how difficult it would be to function if every time we saw a faraway person, we assumed that person really was an inch or two tall? And as the person gets closer and closer to us, naturally her size changes too, right? Of course not! We recognize size constancy in fellow humans; we see an inch-tall person as "normal," even though an inch-tall person is decidedly not normal. The conflict is resolved by our unconscious reasoning that the person isn't small at all—she's far away from us!

Magicians use these sorts of principles as the bases for their illusions. We are fooled because we make these unconscious assumptions (that the person is normal sized and far away) but our assumptions are wrong—the magician has played off our assumptions in an effort to conceal the workings of the trick. There are lots of organizing rules our brains use every day. Like perspective, we are so used to using them unnoticed, that they are easily the basis of slip-ups. Children, who haven't learned these rules yet, run the risk of not being fooled by the illusion. Marvin Kaye, in his *Catalog of Magic*, describes one such illusion.

In X-Salted, the magician shows a glass salt shaker. Perhaps there is a small amount of salt at the bottom, which the magician promptly dumps out. He removes the lid, turns the lid upside down, and salt starts pouring out—of nowhere! (Another version has the salt pouring from an obviously empty shaker, lid still screwed on.) From thin air comes salt and salt and more salt! Kaye describes some of the psychological accouterments that perpetuate the illusion:

> X-Salted is my favorite opening trick. The method ought to be obvious to anyone seeing it—that the salt is somehow contained in the lid, but the only people unsophisticated enough to realize this are children. (Don't do the trick for youngsters!) An adult audience reasons that there is far too much salt produced to be contained in the lid. This is a sensible enough assumption. I made it myself when I first saw X-Salted done, in a TV magic act. (I thought the magician must have a hose up his sleeve which he inserted into the shaker lid.) . . . The magician who performed it let the salt pour directly from the top of the shaker. He put the glass bottom of the shaker aside. The orchestra played fast music, which helped psychologically expand the playing time. Further, he let the salt run onto the stage floor, so that the quantity looked greater because there was a longer line of salt falling all the way down from his hand. At the close of his act, he simply walked off stage with the salt still pouring.

Children simply don't have enough worldly experience to be fooled by this sort of illusion. It's why magician Ricky Jay has said that sophisticated magic is unsuitable for children.[15] On the other hand, the adults in the crowd are completely baffled. You see, the adult audience has a dilemma. They "know" the salt is coming from up the magician's sleeve. But the magician will roll up his sleeve to prove otherwise. Their other option is to believe that all that salt fell from a secret compartment in the lid—as ludicrous as the first idea! In the end, magic wins out over rationality, since the assumptions underlying rational thought have led to a contradictory conclusion.

If some magic doesn't work for kids because they don't have the experience to see the illusion, other effects don't work for adults because they have it all too well. For instance, Eugene Burger describes an illusion in which a playing card is folded and unfolded and slid through another card, and, during these manipulations, the card magically turns inside out and is turned around in ways it should not be facing. Burger reports that some spectators of the illusion are perplexed because they don't understand where the magic is.[16] What happens is their rational mind attributes the magical topsy-turviness of the card to the folding and unfolding that the magician does. Even though the folding is done slowly and in a way to make it obvious that nothing sneaky is going on, the adult mind rationalizes that some folding too complicated for him to comprehend has created the twisting of the card, rather than the simpler explanation that "magic" has caused the twisting.

We talked before about how an illusion is created when the audience "fills in the gaps" that a magician doesn't supply. For instance, you see the ball go into her hand. She closes her hand. When she opens her hand, the ball is gone. Let's say the ball never actually went into her hand in the first place. Thus there is a gap in your knowledge. You don't notice the gap because your mind says, "Ah, I *saw* the ball go into her hand," even when you really didn't see it go in because it definitely did not go into her hand. We are so used to seeing people take objects into their hands, that we have little doubt about what that action looks like. Of course, it can also very well be the magician's fault if the audience doesn't "get it." The magician may be going through the trick too fast, not explaining it properly, or showing a trick that is more confusing than entertaining.

X-Salted shows how an adult's logic can produce magic because the adult's logic cannot explain away the miracle he is viewing. A child's logic can be used as the basis of an illusion too. Piaget's famous experiment showed the limitation of *preoperational* thinking, when a young child has trouble distinguishing between items using more than one well-defined factor. Piaget's most well-known experiment involved pouring liquid from one container to another. When liquid was poured from a short fat glass into a tall skinny one, children responded that now there was "more" liquid because the liquid rose higher in the glass.

Other experiments have used checkers. The child is shown a row of five checkers. Then, with the child watching, the checkers are spaced out so that even though the number of checkers stays the same, the line is now longer. "Which has more checkers?" Invariably the children would answer, "The second line." Even when the children had the ability to see and to count out an equal number of checkers in each line, their perception overrode their logical abilities. That's very often the effect that magicians use to their advantage—letting the audience perceive a situation in a certain (wrong) way, and not taking any steps to correct that misperception.

Fig. 28. To a young child, the bottom row seems to have more checkers, even after the rows have both been counted and shown to have the same number.

I used to do an illusion, the Stretching Scarf illusion, for my young sisters when they were at Piaget's stage, where perception overrode logic. Here's the basic routine: Take a big red scarf and show it to the children. Hold it lazily. Even though you know it's a big scarf, display it loosely, and project a sense of smallness and unworthiness about it.

Say: "I'm going to use magic to make this bigger."

Notice that for this illusion, the magician announces beforehand what he intends to do. That gives the audience a preconceived notion of what to expect. It allows the audience to start creating the illusion for themselves.

Fold the scarf in half. Hold it in front of you with the four corners facing up. Hold the top corners and twirl the scarf in the air so it rolls up. Continued twisting will make it look even smaller. At this point you can wave your hands over the scarf, or say some magic words, or whatever fits the bill at that moment. Now comes the magic. Take opposite corners of the scarf between thumb and forefinger and pull them apart. The scarf will appear to stretch, since it was folded straight across, but you're pulling it on a diagonal. Do the stretching very slowly and deliberately. Attitude is everything. Project the sense that the scarf is growing before your eyes. As you are stretching the scarf, slowly raise your arms and widen your eyes. Once you've stretched it as "big" as it's going to get, display the scarf with a majestic flourish. Hold it big and taut and high in front of your face. The audience cannot compare the now scarf to the scarf as it was before you magically stretched it, but it's quite obvious that the scarf is now much larger than it was before. Your very manner suggests that it's bigger. They saw the scarf growing before their eyes. The scarf, like the spaced-out checkers, has stayed the same size yet magically grown.

A similar ploy is used in rope tricks. At the end of rope tricks (cut and restored rope, etc.) the magician will stretch the rope out tightly, raise up his arms to display it higher, and emphasize its bigness and tautness. During a rope trick, the magician often must cut off a few inches of rope, and so the rope actually ends up a tad smaller than when the trick started. So it becomes even more important to project to the audience the idea that the intact rope is a long piece of rope.

This business about stretching a scarf reminds me of an optical illusion (see figure 29). This illusion probably could not be done with a scarf (you would not be able to hold the scarf as in part (b) of the figure. However, it is interesting to ponder other ways in which a magician may make use of this and similar illusions.

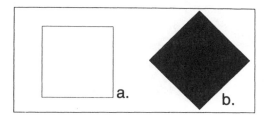

Fig. 29. The same size square looks much larger in (b). The illusion occurs because (b) has a greater height, which we mindlessly associate with surface area. Also adding to the illusion, (b) is closer to the bounding rectangle while (a) has a lot of blank space around its four edges.

Much of magic is derived from devilish folklore, satanic and ghostly rituals, deadly mysticism, and a frightening aura of doomful proclamations. Here's where you have witches performing magical acts of cruelty, and Satanic worshippers enacting ritualistic killings as part of their magical art. These are nightmares of magic, wholly unsuited for children. Much of the magic we know and watch today has its roots plainly visible in such ancient rites. The shaman tricks discussed earlier (drinking acid, eating razor blades), as well as decapitation and other torture tricks, are of this breed, one that would give many youngsters bad dreams for weeks after the show.

A more common magic show experience, yet still frightening if shown to the wrong audience, was described by nature photographer Piyush Patel: "The first time I saw a magician was probably in India. It was an interesting encounter . . . I was very young (probably five), he cut a person in half . . . that was a horrifying sight. I truly believed that the person was dead. I think I cried. Knowing the truth, of course, was comforting. At that point I probably compared him with god."

Other magic is just as menacing while seeming benign. Sandorse told me he stopped blowing balloon animals for children because his daughter, a nurse, warned him that little children are frequently rushed to emergency rooms after swallowing a piece of a burst balloon. The social conscience exhibited in so many of the magicians I spoke with is evident here. Also evident is one of the many good ways in which a magician's control of the audience is desirable.

And who can forget Cindy Brady on the "Brady Bunch"? After seeing a magician make his assistant disappear, the effect on Cindy was not magical but devastatingly scary to the frightened child, who insisted afterwards that she sleep with the lights on. Even children old enough to know better really are vulnerable to a convincing performance. Since they are in the stage of learning about the world, and learning about the rules that govern it, under the right conditions they may pick up on the idea that magic or supernatural forces play some role in their lives. After all, with all the rationalizing they try to do, if that fails (which it is bound to do, since the child—

as the adult—is unequipped to deal with the magician's full arsenal of illusionary devices), they may fall back on the rationale that it was magic after all. Hence Cindy's tears.

One night when I was around Cindy's age I was walking home from a lecture given by Daniel Cohen, who has written dozens of books glorifying every aspect of the occult and supernatural that he is capable of speculating about. Many of the books are for children, and I certainly had read a number of them. And walking home, as I was, through darkness, well past my bedtime, a child on the verge of believing some of what I was reading, and on top of that, having just emerged from a lecture given by this guy whose books I had read, and who had just delivered a very convincing lecture on why the Loch Ness monster must exist—my brain was ripe for the supernatural plucking it was about to receive.

I looked into the sky and saw a UFO. It was round, had red and green lights, and moved silently across the sky. I stared at it with my head tilted back, my mouth gaping open. And then I heard a voice call my name. It was my mother and grandmother: they had decided they didn't want me walking home alone in the dark, so they came to walk with me. Somehow they didn't notice anything unusual about that UFO in the sky.

Of course, after I started growing up and getting out more, I got accustomed to walking down that stretch of dark walkway around the same time on consecutive nights, and seeing the same airplane fly by with its red and green lights. Now I wasn't coming out of a scary two-hour lecture on the Loch Less monster, so I could think more rationally about the world and what certain objects in it represented. Instead of filling in the black gaps with an imagined circular image, I filled in the gaps with the more realistic body of an airplane. I have now no doubt in my mind that what I saw was a plane, and yet at the time, all my little brain could come up with was that lights soaring across the sky must be a flying saucer. Preposterous to look back on it now.

The magician has a power. That's the whole point of the show, to demonstrate, entertainingly, his power over his environment. Some magicians negate some of that power (they don't live up to the full responsibility it represents) by becoming "comedy magicians," the topic of the next section. Others play it to the hilt, by cloaking themselves in black garb, ruffling out their scrawling white beards, and intoning strange incantations under the flickering candlelight. Magicians know they are creating an image of themselves. They must also be aware that the image they create may live on in the mind of their audience, and that the image may be more frightening than mystical, especially to a child audience.

THE LOGIC OF THE AUDIENCE

The Amazing Randi once wrote, "All my efforts as a professional magician are based on the assumption that my audience thinks logically and can therefore be fooled by me if I work on that assumption."[17] As mentioned above, we are fooled because the magician leads us into territories of mind we are familiar with, yet the magician slips something past us, so that what we appear to be viewing is not entirely what we really are viewing. Our logical mind works against us. Magicians have performed magic to elderly people who have begun to act senile—and they found the magic as magical and bewildering as any "logical" and "rational" minded person fresh out of college. While they may be forgetful and they may have lost some of their faculties, they're underlying logical consciousness still remains humanly intact. In fact, psychologist Harold Kelley (who wrote an article on how attributional psychology can be used to explain magic tricks) told me about a friend of his who has Alzheimer's and yet still performs magic fluently and beautifully.

Other magicians have tested the logical facilities of animals. Psychologist Alfred Binet once wrote of the bewilderment caused when he "juggle[d] sugar-plums away before dogs," and a later writer "tested Binet's claim by performing sleight of hand for a gorilla at the National Zoo in Washington, D.C. The performance was rewarded with the gorilla's apparent expressions of amusement and puzzlement."[18] Animals are smart, no doubt about it, even if they do poop on the rug.

9

The Stage and the People on It

This chapter looks at the people who carry out the work of magic shows. It is here we begin to move away from the purist stereotype of a magician wearing a top hat and tails, performing on stage with turtle doves oozing from his sleeves and cards cascading through his hands. For in this chapter we start looking at some deviations from the norm. Not all magicians perform on a stage. Not all magicians are—magicians. Some magicians are ventriloquists, or escape artists. Some magicians are really the magician's assistant, helping out in secret ways that you never imagined. Here then I present to you the stage (or nonstage) and the people (not necessarily magicians) on it.

Venue

Not all magic is done on stage. Magic acts happen in restaurants, bars, hospitals, malls, and elsewhere. Magicians are often asked to perform in hospitals for sick children, in old age homes, and of course at children's birthday parties. To perform in such diverse surroundings, the magician's collection of effects must be one of two things: (1) angle-proof tricks that don't require special stage setups, trap doors, curtains, etc., or (2) self-working, gimmicked, probably store-bought items that can work anywhere at anytime. It is interesting to observe that books have been published specifically for the professional magician who works these kinds of gigs. These books teach the magician fundamental techniques of working surrounded, working bars and tables at restaurants. Restaurant magicians even have their own newsletter, *The Magic Menu*, dedicated to matters of concern to the professional bar-hopping magician. For instance, you know that magicians don't like to repeat a trick. Bartender and restaurant workers must therefore be prepared for the "regulars" and returnees who show up at the bar, or at the restaurant, every week. The material in these specialty publications covers not only the presentation of magic in these circumstances, but also the business end of it. They also touch on a hotly discussed issue: how to approach a restaurant table and offer to do magic without looking like an intrusive jerk. Once again, the magician is prepared for anything beforehand.

Angles and lack of backstage area are probably the peskiest problems in restaurant work. A restaurant worker once stopped at my family's table to do some tricks. He started with a sponge ball routine, then he took out a tiny purse and pulled a coat hanger from it. It was impressive to most of the table, except my dad. He was sitting at a bad angle, so he could see the coat hanger being pulled from out of the magician's sleeve. He told the rest of the table about it after the magician left! This is one way that the audience has control over the magician. When we do know how a trick is done, the magician can walk away feeling confident that he has entertained the crowd, though he might not realize the applause was done out of politeness, not because his magic was so thrilling. After he walked away my family watched the magician as he walked off to a corner of the restaurant and casually inserted the coat hanger back up into his sleeve.

CONTROLLING A CROWD

Street magicians have to be particularly careful of their effects, since anyone can be sneaking up to them from behind or watching a trick from a less-than-perfect angle. Unlike a theater, people are walking around in the street, and they're coming and going from all directions. Close-up magicians like to have a one-on-one, eye-to-eye relation with their audience, so they always know exactly where the audience is looking. But that's not possible on the street. To overcome this, the street magician must choose his tricks carefully. He might even select a spot near a wall or under an awning, any place that restricts viewing angles and turns light to his advantage.

Street performers in turn-of-the-century China had an ingenious method for controlling the position of the audience in a very clever and indirect way. They came onto the street and began beating a brass gong. Passers-by were attracted to the sound and came over to see what was going on. In this way a circle formed around the performers. When the crowd was large enough, they exhibited juggling feats using a weight on a string, which they whirled around themselves, drawing designs in the air. As they continued these acrobatics, they allowed the weight to swing out in ever-widening circles. Naturally the crowd starts to step back. The circle is maintained, but it widens. When the magicians decide the onlookers are sufficiently far from them, the magic starts. No words are spoken: just the bong of a gong and the twirl of a string, and the magicians have created a circle of people, controlled the dimensions of that circle, and the audience never suspects it was all planned that way.

Close-Up Magic

Large-scale stage illusions are flashy and attention-getting, but it is the close-up work that distinguishes a true magician from a mere buyer of props. For if a magician can effectively perform magic up close, in your face, under your nose, right in front of you, then that magician has truly created a marvelous illusion. After all, on stage the magician is playing a home game, on his turf. The audience is far away and bound by the magician's judgment as to stage setup, seating arrangements, angles, and everything else. With close-up magic, you gain an edge on the magician. Consequently the magician had better be pretty damn good.

Now this turns out to not always be true. Copperfield and bigwigs like him will perform close-up effects for his large stage shows in front of people in a crowded amphitheater. Sometimes he will sit on the edge of the stage. Sometimes he will travel out into the audience. The effect is made close-up (and visible) by on-stage video projection screens. Essentially the live studio audience ends up seeing the trick on television.

Many magic tricks rely on the distance between audience and stage to cover up gimmicks. It is surprising then how so often this same magic is performed as "parlor tricks," with the audience sitting or standing just a few footfalls away. Sometimes distance makes a difference, like the fake legs mentioned earlier. But sometimes not. "Take that simple handkerchief and thumb tip trick," Peter Nardi offers as an example, referring to the fake thumb worn by magicians that they use to conceal small scarves and other items. "I do that so many times to people, I often carry it around. *Right in front of their eyes* in broad daylight—and they don't see the thumb tip. And I'm astounded. In fact I have to learn to be more confident about it because I do it real quickly because I'm sure they're seeing it."

"But how could they *not* see it?" I protest.

"It's funny," Nardi says, "they don't know where to look."

I think this is true, and it's why the secrets of magic go unnoticed by the audience. After all, many of the secrets of magic are perpetrated right there before you, right in front of your eyes. If you are only looking there at it in the right way, with the right framework of mind, then you will see it.

Even the big boys of magic mess up occasionally. In the September-October 1996 issue of the Penn & Teller newsletter *Mofo Knows*, Penn says, "You Probably Didn't See This . . . It was the middle of the show, and, suddenly, one of the ways the trick works wasn't. It just wasn't working. . . . Teller didn't really know what was going on, but he could hear the cadence of my voice and had an idea something was wrong. . . . Teller knew enough to just pull pull pull. I found out later he was really pulling focus—what he was doing was the most interesting stuff in the world. . . . As the trick went on, I started to realize that we'd done it. It was going to be okay. . . . After the show NO ONE mentioned it . . . no one said anything fishy." Notice how Penn says "one of the ways the trick works" implying that normally they're prepared with many possible paths the trick can take, and many outs should it fail. The fact that monumental slip-ups can go unnoticed is a testament to the skill of the performers.

One time I was performing the Rising Card Trick for a friend. There are many ways of making a selected card rise out of a deck. My version used a gimmicked deck of cards. Half the cards are normal, and the other half have a rectangular hole cut through the center. The trick proceeds like this. I have my friend choose a card from the ungimmicked part of the deck. He memorizes it, then places it back in the deck. The selected card is brought to the bottom of the stack of ungimmicked cards, with the gimmicked cards placed under it. What you end up with is a full deck of cards, the bottom half of which has holes cut through the middle, and the top half appearing completely normal. If you stick your finger in the hole, you are touching the chosen card. The cards are placed into the card box, which itself has a hole cut in the back. Some magical words are spoken, a hand is waved liltingly atop the deck, and the chosen card begins to rise out. Actually, it is my finger pushing through the hole in the back of the card box, and through the backs of the cards. The finger presses against the selected card, magically raising it up and out of the deck.

Now, when I was performing this one time for a friend, I accidentally screwed up the trick. Not only did the chosen card get pushed up, but one of the gimmicked cards as well. There was a card with a large naked rectangular hole in its gut sticking out of the deck. For a few moments I stopped, looked at my friend, about to apologize for blowing the trick, when he said impatiently, "Well? Go on with the trick!" He didn't see the gimmick at all, even though it was staring him in the face. He just wanted to see me finish up and find his card. I'm always amazed at how very naive people are about this, that the very secrets of the illusion can be paraded before their eyes, and they are oblivious to it.

FINGER FRICTIONS

Magicians who work close-up magic have different sorts of problems from those of their big-stage counterparts. One problem is "sticky fingers." Their charmed fingers have to be dry and sweat-free to manipulate the cards and coins without the little buggers clanging to the floor mid-trick. Here are some of the methods magicians have come up with to take care of themselves in this situation:

- *Arrid XX Clear* roll-on deodorant.[1]
- *Listerine*

- *ProGrip,* made for bowlers and available at bowling alleys.[2]
- *Rosin,* carried by professional pickpockets (who are themselves magicians of a form) to reduce slippage when surreptitiously removing a watch from someone's wrist.[3]
- *Hairspray* will also do "in a pinch."[4]

Comedy Magic

We tend to associate comedy magic with children's birthday parties, don't we? Well, we don't want our living rooms infiltrated by a grim Satanic atmosphere on party day. But do we want buffoonery either? Eugene Burger, a very accomplished and intelligent magician, professes a disdain for the bumbling magi, for he says that magicians use the character as an excuse for tricks that don't work properly. Of course, they can also use bumbling as a diversionary tactic. The Amazing Kreskin, who professes to be psychic, has the appearance and agility of a bumbling numskull nerd. But that only goes towards clarifying for certain gullible people that he is the real deal. Get with it oh ye of little skepticism: his bumbling is all a part of his act. I agree with Burger and I say if you're going to use clowning to cover up bad magic you might as well say you're using magic to cover up bad clowning—you're neither a magician nor a clown, just under-practiced in both arenas.

But comedy can be used as a diversionary tactic. "Because an audience does not have the leisure to analyze the spoken word, as readers do the written, a speaker need not be precise or even particularly careful of word choice," noted Samuel Pickering Jr., the teacher that Robin Williams's character in *Dead Poets Society* was modeled after. "The wash from a comic story generally sweeps criticism and recollection of shoddy reasoning out of an audience's mind."[5] I've seen magicians use comedy many a time to "wash out" a mistake in their performance. In all cases I've seen, the audience laughed and accepted it, and the magician was able to move on to his next effect.

Other magicians are comedians who use magic in part of their acts. The ones I have seen are barely magicians, although they may be skillful in the tricks they have bought at their local magic emporium. I say "tricks" and not "illusions" because generally these are folks who've never bothered to distinguish the two, and whose act usually rests on the trickery of the magical effect. These are the kind of "magicians" who real magicians try not to be—the ones who take a holier-than-thou attitude toward their audience, the ones who equate jokes with patter, and the presenting of a trick with the preparing of an omelet—step by step, break an egg, pour the milk, just doing the steps right makes for an amazing feast for the mind or palate.

No, that's not the way it works, as you know by now. Real magicians use their patter not to demonstrate wit, but as further misdirection from their physical manipulations. And the manipulations themselves, both seen and unseen, are smooth moves, finely tuned, and as continuous as the circular curve of the yolk of the egg.

Escape Artists

Almost synonymous with magic is the name Houdini. And yet Houdini is not glorified for his magic. His escapes are remembered. When we say "escapes," what does that mean? Well, it means a lot of different things; as it happens, there are plenty of subspecialties within the specialty of escape artistry:

- *Rope ties.* The escape artist is tied up in strong ropes and may also be thrown in a river for added drama. Rope ties are often used in conjunction with containers. The escape artist might be tied up, locked into a wooden crate, and *then* thrown into the river.
- *Cuff escapes.* Handcuffs of varying forms are most often employed, but there are also leg cuffs and thumb cuffs. Cuff escapes are usually used in conjunction with a container, where the performer is cuffed up and locked in a box from which he must escape.
- *Straitjacket escapes.* The straitjacket is a restraint made of durable cloth, a staple of the escape artist's repertoire. Very often an escape artist will escape from a straitjacket while being suspended upside down in midair (a feat popularized by Houdini and later by James Randi). A skeptic might say, "Aw, but if you know how to escape from a straitjacket, it couldn't be *that* much harder to escape upside down!" But that skeptic would be wrong; as we'll see, being upside down does make the task somewhat more difficult.
- *Escape from containers.* A container might be a box, packing crate, or any other container that looks difficult to escape from. Escape artists through history have attempted escapes from all manner of sealed and locked packages.
- *Bag escapes.* The escape artist frees himself from a tied up or locked cloth bag such as a mail bag.
- *Jail cell escapes.* Popularized by Houdini (actually, Houdini popularized *every* kind of escape), the jail cell escape isn't done all that much anymore. But it was done frequently in the past . . . how? How is it possible to escape from a jail cell, of all things? (Especially when the performer has been strip-searched to ensure he's not carrying in any keys or tools?) This is a mystery whose answer bears explaining!

₊₊**₊**₊*

Escape artists are magicians, and yet we see the two in different lights. We feel that the escape artists use a worldly skill to perform their craft while magicians use an otherworldly skill (or at least, that's the impression we are left with). It's like the biblical story where Moses bangs his staff against the rock to magically produce water. Who produced the water—Moses or God? Who produced the effect—the magician himself or the magical forces of the universe? Does the source of magic come from within or without? Magicians use the "magical forces" while escape artists use their own skill. And yet the two very dissimilar effects are intertwined and often even presented during the same show. Why are escapes considered part of magic? Aren't these two different things? James Randi, a magician and escape artists argues, "Yeah, but it's the same kind of skill that somebody makes a woman float in the air—seems impossible. Somebody gets wrapped up in ropes and handcuffs and such, it *seems* impossible. It's the improbability of the thing. It seems to be something that can't be done. That's why it's similar."

Another reason escape acts are part of magic is because escapes fall into the "magician's dozen" we talked about earlier. An escape can be categorized as a "penetration through solid" as the escape artist seems to melt through the shackles and containers that pen him in. Some escapes are better categorized as transpositions, or as an evanishment from a locked room or box followed by a reappearance outside of that room or box.

Now, one of the differences between magic and escapes lies in what is revealed to the audience. In magic we believe we are seeing all the clues on stage. The bunny appears surprisingly from the hat. How did it get there? If we don't know the answer we have only ourselves to blame—we know that it was hidden somewhere on stage before its appearance. If the hiding spot is unfathomable, then magic has been done.

Escape acts, for the most part, are also done on stage before our eyes. But here it is a particular skill involved—lock picking? double jointedness? skinny arms? unimaginable strength?—that frees the man from his bonds. It is the skill that is kept hidden from us, rather than the physical arrangement of the stage. "Some of these things are done behind screens and such. It depends on what you're doing in the escape act," Randi points out. That was more true for vaudeville-age escape acts, like the kind Houdini performed. Nowadays audiences require visible action on stage, lest they get bored.

Escape artists have been known to escape from handcuffs, thumb cuffs, ropes, chains, jail cells, submerged steel cages, and straitjackets upside down. Houdini took this all one step further by escaping from a wooden barrel, a sewn-up football, a sealed envelope, a brown paper bag sealed with wax and signed by a committee of onlookers, and many other oddities. Escape artist Harley Newman escapes from Saran Wrap tightly wound upon the balled-up man inside.

The equipment can be faked or genuine. Handcuffs can be gaffed. Kellar performed a famous rope escape that relied on a twist of the wrists to make a tightly bound rope become suddenly loose enough to slip out of.

Straitjackets can also be purchased in genuine or artificial variety. One escape artist told me that the gaffed jackets usually have a means of gaining extra slack in the sleeves. A piece of the tightening strap can be held back inside the jacket, so the audience volunteers can never completely tighten it. The held-back portion is released during the performance. A gimmicked straitjacket can also have slightly wider sleeves, which is better for upside-down escapes. It is possible to escape from both kinds, the escape artist said, the only real difference being speed. It is interesting to note that this particular escape artist lamented the fact that his gaffed jacket actually looked more real than the real one! A brown leather strip on the gaffed jacket gave it a stiff, restraining look that the plain (but ungaffed) jacket lacked.

The escape from a straitjacket starts when the jacket is being put on. The escape artist will attempt to expand his chest and stomach to fill out the straitjacket as much as possible. Some performers use subtle resistance against the people tying them up in the straitjacket, as a way of ensuring it won't be so tight. This is another example of how the storyline can produce necessary motivations for the performer to behave in a certain way. They could use the story of an escaped convict, for instance, who is angry and resisting his captors. When the actual escape begins, the performer must first force an arm over his head. That's where having wider sleeves and some slack comes into play. The great escape artist Houdini was said to be double jointed, which made it easier for him to do this part of the escape. Once the arms are up, the fingers must be forced out the sleeve holes. They are used to unlatch the buckles on the back of the straitjacket. If you were one of those guys in high school who could never unfasten his date's bra strap, this line of work is not for you. By this time the arms are uncrossed, which means the extra cloth required for stretching the arms crosswise across the chest is now loose. The buckles themselves don't have to be completely removed, only loosened enough so that the performer can wiggle and wriggle his way out of its confines.

BAG ESCAPES

Bag escapes may be an effect to themselves, or used in conjunction with a larger container, such as a wooden crate. There are several means of escaping from a tied-up cloth bag. In one version there is a duplicate bag bunched up inside the outer bag. The escape artist gets in (the outer bag) and immediately shoves the duplicate up through the opening at the top. The assistant makes sure this duplicate, and not the outside bag, is the one that is sealed. The place where the inner bag emerges is covered over with a cloth or ropes, so the audience doesn't realize there are two bags.

Another version makes use of the looseness principle mentioned earlier. This requires a mail bag that shuts with a drawstring around the top. The escape artist gets in, and the bag is drawn tightly shut and knotted up. What the audience doesn't realize is that when the escape artist climbed into the bag, he drew down a few feet of the drawstring with him. Thus there is a lot of slack in the rope, which is the method of escaping. I heartily recommend that you try and procure a mail bag for yourself. The next time you're walking around in a busy city, look around under public mailboxes. Often you will see discarded mail bags sitting there. I picked one up in New York this past summer. It's too small to actually fit inside, but it offers a revealing glimpse at how this sort of escape can work.

Other methods involve a mail bag with a metal bar that seals the bag shut, and is then locked with a padlock. In one version, reserved for the highly skilled, the escape artist goes into the bag with a key and a string. Once inside he passes the key to the outside through a crack in the top of the bag, making sure to keep a good grip on the string inside so the key doesn't fall to the floor. He then grips the key through the cloth and uses it to unlock the lock. An alternative method simply involves a gimmick in the metal bar that allows the performer to take it apart from inside the bag.

ROPE TIE ESCAPES

In a typical rope tie escape the performer is tied up and thrown in the river and is expected to escape unharmed. But rope tying is also used in other ways. For example, there is a popular thumb tie trick in which the magician allows his thumbs to be tightly tied together by a volunteer. But then, whenever the volunteer's back is turned, the magician casually escapes from the knots. This can be humorously combined with a pickpocket routine. The thumbs are securely tied together, but the volunteer finds his wallet missing and his watch gone from his wrist. Another variation has the magician hooking hoops around his arm (impossible since the thumbs are supposedly attached together). While it doesn't look like a typical escape act full of danger and daring, it definitely is an escape act of sorts. It just happens to have a different emotional response as its goal.

In the 1800s, fake mediums and spiritualists used knowledge of rope escapes in order to induce yet another kind of emotion, an uneasy malaise as supernatural forces filled the room. The medium would claim to be able to communicate with ghosts. In order to prove her claim, she would be thoroughly tied up and locked within a dark cabinet. As soon as she was sealed away, strange things would begin occurring inside. There would be the ghostly ringing of bells and knocking sounds. Objects would start flying out of the top of the cabinet as if being cast out by angry poltergeists. The cabinet would be opened, but the spiritualist would be quietly sitting on her chair inside, still tightly tied up in ropes, and blindfolded. It seemed impossible . . . it seemed like ghosts. But it was really all a matter of knowing how to get a little slack in the rope.

A TWISTED EXPERIMENT

Here's a simple experiment that demonstrates one of the key principles used in all of these rope tie escapes. All you will need is a piece of rope and a friend. If you don't have a friend, take off your shoes and socks.

Lay the rope over your left thumb. Take the right end of the rope and wrap it around the thumb once. Put your right thumb on top of the left thumb, hiding the extra loop of rope. Now ask your friend to take the ends of the rope and tie your thumbs together as tightly as possible. (If you don't have a friend handy, you can do this on your toes.) Keep your thumbs (or toes) overlapped. Give a good tug with your thumb or toe. Try to pull it out. It's stuck good because the tactile pad on your fingertips adds a little bit of fat that keep your thumbs/toes interlocked together.

Ready to escape? Rotate your right thumb counterclockwise to the left. The extra loop in the rope will unloop itself, giving a bunch of slack with which to break free. Remember what I said in chapter 6 about looking for looseness? This is exactly the kind of thing I was talking about. Magicians and escape artists have built up entire acts on this principle. A knowledgeable escape artist knows countless ways of getting slack into the rope as it's being tied around his body. They know how to present their arms crossed at the wrists to get extra slack. And they know to push out their stomach and tighten their muscles so that later they can constrict themselves to loosen the ropes. They have such a large repertoire that they're not afraid to let anyone tie them up. They know how to exert control over the situation, even as the volunteer believes he's making all the tying choices himself.

Another way escape artists gain control is by directing the audience volunteers to tie them up a specific way. You've probably seen this before, if you've ever seen a rope tie being done. They think that with the escape artist's superior knowledge of ropes and knots, that he's giving them good tying advice. Hogwash! He's telling them how to tie a knot that's *easy* to escape from, one that provides a lot of slack when he uncrosses his arms!

A similar method of getting the slack was explained by David Charney, who, besides being a magician, is also an artist, science-fiction writer, ranking table-tennis player, concert flamenco guitarist, third-degree karate black belt, and the art director of a New York advertising agency. At least, that's the squib on at the back of his book *Magic: The Great Illusions Revealed and Explained.* How to get slack (if you still have your friend handy, you should give this one a whirl also): The escape artist presents a length of rope and instructs the volunteers to securely tie it around his left wrist. When they are satisfied that the knots are secure, the magician puts his hands behind his back and the volunteers proceed to tie his right wrist to his left wrist. The hands are pressed tightly together; no slack is visible, and, in fact, when they tug on the rope, it appears taut. At this point the escape artist is put into the box, cabinet, or wherever, and, mystery of mysteries, he is able to escape (or, in the case of the spirit cabinet, ghosts materialize). How is it done? It's done because the performer had control over the tying process—he instructed the volunteers in the creation of a "stupid knot," a knot that really is not all that tight. When he put his hands behind his back, he twisted the free ends of the rope before placing his right wrist atop his left. Now there is a hidden twist suspended between the two wrists. The knot that is made around the right wrist is ineffectual; all he needs to do is twist his wrists in the opposite direction to gain back all that slack and remove his right hand from the restraint. He can even go so far as to untie the left wrist completely.[6]

One final trick that allows escape artists to free themselves from ropes: thick ropes are hard to tie tightly. Thick ropes may be strong and sturdy, but they can also be difficult to pull into tight knots. And because the rope is so thick, it's easy to grab onto it in order to untie knots.

One time my grandpa was sitting at a magic show with a friend and the magician asked for some volunteers to tie him up. Grandpa was a brainy guy, a magic enthusiast, and a muscle-bound mechanic. He was happy to go up on stage with his friend, and the two of them proceeded to tie up the guy so thoroughly that he had to concede defeat. The magician simply could not escape from the ropes the way they tied him. They maintain that it was the tightness that did him in. Was it really too tight? Or was the magician not as skilled as he thought he was? Or had he made a mistake somewhere along the line? Perhaps a combination of all these explanations.

KEYS AND LOCKS

When you read about the great escapes by Houdini et al., you always read about how "the police searched his clothes, his hair, and in between his toes for any signs of a key or lock pick. Then they stripped him naked. Turned his anus inside-out, combed through his pubic hair. And then, only then, was The Great Escape Artiste allowed to go into the hermetically sealed quadruple locked death chamber." That's what you read about. But is that what really happens?

No! I'm sure it happens *sometimes,* but most of the time the performer is not searched at all. You can readily verify this yourself the next time you see an escape act. Modern escape artists are almost never searched for keys, picks, or tools. Often they are wearing a full set of clothes, sleeves, pockets and all! Houdini is said to have concealed a pair of nail cutters on his body when performing his underwater escape from a packing crate.[7] Furthermore, lately I've been seeing a certain kind of handcuff being used by a number of escape artists. These handcuffs have a foot length of chain between the wrists. With a foot of chain there is enough leeway for the performer to comfortably hold a key in one hand and unlock the other wrist with the other. Escape artist Harley Newman, casting a critical eye on the competition, explained that "most 'escape artists' are *magicians.* It doesn't look like an escape. It looks like a trick." This is bad, since the idea of escape artistry is to promote the idea that the artist possesses some special skill or talent to effect the escapes.

The whole thing boils down to a gritty paste of utter silliness when you realize that most handcuffs use the same key to unlock them. I personally own four handcuffs. Two from the same manufacturer, and the others from separate manufacturers. The two from the same manufacturer can use one key interchangeably, and the other two cuffs use a different key. Key-interchangability is necessary because police and security guards don't want to have to fuss around with ten different keys, never knowing which key goes with which of their cuffs. It makes life easy for law enforcement officials. And for escape artists. The escape artist will have a supply of handcuff keys at his disposal. Perhaps they are hidden on his person, or they might be hidden inside the container from which he is to escape. In some cases, a trustworthy assistant passes off a key to the performer after he's been strip-searched. (Many performers don't even bother with this extra bit of work. Handcuffs can be purchased with a secret mechanism that springs them open at a touch.)

Some escape artists will borrow locks from audience members. It is possible to pick locks, but it is unlikely that an escape artist would do such a thing. More likely the escape artist will position the borrowed lock at a nonessential place on his body. For instance, if he's being locked into a garment that loops through the legs and around both arms, the borrowed lock might be used to fasten one arm. To escape, the artist can merely ignore that lock, freeing himself from his own locks first and then slipping out of the sleeve with the borrowed lock still locked. He might then re-lock his own locks so as to not destroy the symmetry and ruin the illusion. To escape from chains, a similar technique can be employed. The tightest-binding chains are locked with locks the escape artist knows well. Any mystery locks borrowed from the audience are used in nonessential sections of the chain (the "looseness principle" again). The final question is, how does the magician escape from his own locked locks?

One plausible theory is that the escape artist uses lock picking tools to pick the locks. Escape artists are generally known for being fascinated by locks and the locksmithing trade.

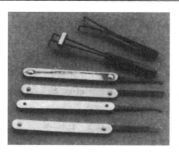

Fig. 30. Some lock picking tools from the author's collection. To pick locks, the lock picker must use a tension wrench (top two tools) and a lock pick (bottom four tools).

LOCK PICKS

For those of you who've never tried it, lock picking may seem as arcane and mysterious as a Bhali Moon Dance Worship Ceremony. But lock picking is not all that mysterious and can be learned by reading a short book on the subject and procuring the correct tools. Poke around on the Internet alt.locksmithing forum and you'll find plenty of free online instructional guides. If you'd rather curl up with a good book, I'd recommend *The Illustrated Art of Lock-Picking: An educational trade manual* by Mentor Publications with its simple and straightforward approach. There are plenty of other books on lockpicking available, and there are several online guides you can download from the Internet. A good source for cheap lock picks is Septon, Inc., a New York–based company that you can call or write for a catalog and pricing information: Septon, Inc., P.O. Box 9, Malden-on-Hudson, NY 12453, (800) 537-8752.

Houdini was renowned as such a good lock picker that one reviewer proudly proclaimed that Houdini was able to pick locks with a human hair. This would also explain how escapers such as Houdini and others were able to be strip-searched for keys and tools before an escape. With a skill and endurance such as Houdini possessed, all he needed was to not have his hair cut for a few weeks before the escape, and then he could enter the jail cell or lock box without a tool on him, confidently knowing all that was required was a little *pluck* to escape.

The problem with this theory is that it's complete rubbish! You can't pick a lock with a hair! As any lock picker will tell you, it requires at least two tools—the lock pick and a tension wrench. If you're going to conceal those things on you, you're better off simply hiding the key, which will let you out quicker. For whatever skill they have with locks, escape artists have no real need for lock picks.

The true answer is much simpler. They use the key to unlock the locks. As with handcuffs, it's a matter of hiding the key on or in their person, stashing it in the screen or bag or cabinet in which they are placed, or having it passed to them after the body search has been done. Jail cell escapes tended to be the same or much simpler: a publicity stunt set up beforehand between the escape artist and the local police departments.

COVERS IN ESCAPES

Visual and auditory covers are used in escapes. The escapes of yesteryear relied on a screen or curtain being placed in front of the container. Sound and music is also used. As mentioned, many escapes rely on the performer hiding a key or some other instrument on his person. If he accidentally drops the key while struggling to escape, he would rattle around the chains and handcuffs, creating a noise that would hopefully cover up the *plink* of metal as the key hit the ground. Houdini would play loud orchestra music during his escapes. Partially that was because nothing visible was happening on stage, but partially it was to cover up any sounds from behind the screen that would give away the trick.

Escaping from Containers

Larger-scale escapes will put the magician into a container of some kind—a crate, box, bag, mail sack, or other contrivance. During his heyday Houdini was being offered fluky stunts that, because of his flair for showmanship and egotism, may have been the only things Houdini couldn't get out of. A football team challenged him to escape from a giant football. He escaped from a sealed paper bag, from barrels, and from crates thrown in the ocean. No matter what the container or contrivance, the escape artist has four methods of escaping from the container: (1) a hidden trap door in the container, (2) careful destruction of a portion of the container, escape through the hole, and then careful reconstruction of the container, (3) never entering the container in the first place, and (4) never leaving the container—remaining hidden inside it.

HIDDEN TRAP DOOR

The most common method of escaping from a container is to escape out of some kind of trap door. When watching an escape act, look for the "proofs" the magician uses to prove to you there are no trap doors in the box. Perhaps he bangs each side of the box with his fists—but neglects to bang the lid. Perhaps he bangs only the outside surfaces while neglecting the inside surfaces—the trap door could easily be set up on a one-way hinge so that banging in one direction only forces the door to close more. The location of the banging may also come into play. As you gaze with careful scrutiny at the fast-moving action, maybe you'll notice that he bangs each side of the trunk squarely in the center—until he gets to the last side where he gets lazy and bangs it to one side, off-center. Could he be afraid to hit the hidden trap door on the other side of the side? Perhaps. Perhaps not. All of these banging clues are probably worthwhile to look at, if only to train your magic show visionary skills. However, most likely the trap door—if it exists at all—is built to resist any punch the magician could administer to it. For instance, there may be a nail or bolt in place that stops the trap door from opening up when the magician bangs on it. Later, when the magician is snug inside the box, he slides out the nail, allowing the trap door to open freely.

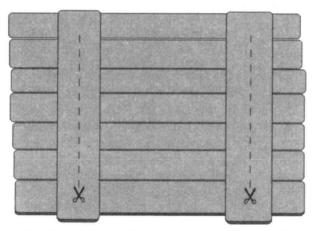

Fig. 31. There are many ways of escaping from a wooden crate. One technique is to prepare the crate beforehand by cutting through the horizontal slats in the lid, as shown here. The cuts are covered with the two vertical slats, which are attached weakly or with fake screws. To escape, the escape artist need only pull off the two weakly attached slats, push aside the cut horizontal slats, and squeeze through the hole. At this point the crate will look highly tampered with. To solve that problem, the escape artist will go hide somewhere. An assistant will feign worry ("What's taking him so long?") and smash apart the crate with an axe. The escape artist can then reappear, safe, escaped, and unharmed.

DESTROY AND RECONSTRUCT THE CONTAINER

Back in the golden years of magic, escape artists would go behind a screen to perform their stunts. While hidden back there, they could basically do whatever they wanted, including escaping from the container through any means. For a truly amazing trick, you want the container to appear unbroken after the escape is done. In certain cases the magician would escape by cutting a hole in the container, shimmying out through that hole, and then—hidden behind the screen—actually reconstructing or repairing the damage just done to the container. This is a sneaky trick that requires massive preplanning, and it was the method Houdini used for his escape from the paper bag. The bag was signed by a committee, and shut with wax and an impression made in the wax to ensure it could not be broken. But who would think of a duplicate seal? After the screen was set in front of him, Houdini sliced off the top portion of the bag from inside. The screen that concealed Houdini from view also concealed wax and an impressioning seal. He refolded the top of the bag, and sealed it with wax. The committee's signatures were made further down the side of the bag, so they were not cut off with the top of the bag. Another example of the magician controlling audience's participation in an event.

NEVER ENTER THE CONTAINER IN THE FIRST PLACE

One method of "escaping" from a container is to not enter the container in the first place. At one magic show I attended years ago, the magician/escape artist allowed himself to be rolled tightly into a carpet, which was then chained up, locked up, and thrown into a trunk. A giant red silk was brought out from one side of the stage while the wood lid of the trunk was brought out from the other side. The lid was pummeled a few times to prove its solidity, dropped onto the top of the trunk, and the whole thing covered over by the silk. The trunk was then raised high above the stage while female assistants danced around below. Then, in a sudden flash, the red silk leaped up and was tossed to the ground by the magician, who was standing proudly atop the trunk, shackles and chains gripped in his triumphant fists above his head. He smiled and accepted the thundering applause.

It was a remarkable escape, but one that relied entirely on some of the standard magician's tricks we've seen earlier in this book. It had nothing to do with double-jointedness or lock picking, or escape skill at all. When he was being rolled up into the carpet, a quick Curtain Switcheroo got him off stage—the carpet they rolled up was completely empty. While waiting backstage, the magician positioned himself behind the lid of the trunk. When an assistant carried the lid on stage, the magician was hunched over, waddling on stage, hidden behind it. He was further obscured by the dancers moving about, and our eyes were misdirected to the other side of the stage where the giant red silk was being brought out. When the lid approached the trunk at center stage, the magician sneaked out from behind the lid and took a position on a small shelf directly behind the trunk. Perhaps there were handgrips on the trunk, disguised as bolts, with which he could hang on as the trunk was lifted into the air by cables. The rest of the "escape" involved waiting for the rehearsed point when the music reached a particular crescendo, when it would be the preappointed time for the magician to leap up, fling down the silk, and show his handful of chains. Where did the chains come from? I cannot answer that. Perhaps they were extra chains, dropped by an assistant onto the shelf as the crate was being prepared to be lifted up. Or perhaps the magician himself brought them from off stage as he hid behind the lid of the trunk. We can't tell for sure, and that's why even the best analysis of a show still leaves us with the tingly flavor of mystery in our mouths.

REMAIN HIDDEN INSIDE THE CONTAINER

The final method of escaping from a container is sort of a sham—the escape artist never really escapes at all, but remains hidden inside the container. I would think this last method is infrequently used because it's so phony, but it's probably used more than we might expect. It is probably not used for the standard escape act that includes dangerous feats of derring-do and suspense around every corner. However, it could come in handy in more subtle ways. For instance, this method is sometimes used during a standard magic act in order to make an assistant or animal vanish from a box and reappear in another box or barrel elsewhere in the theater. The assistant or animal that is produced at the end is really a "twin," while the original assistant/animal remains concealed inside the container, behind a false partition or on a shelf suspended behind the opened box. You don't think of this as an escape (you think of it as an evanishment followed by an appearance) or perhaps as a transposition; but it is in fact an escape of sorts.

Ventriloquism

> Magician Harry Blackstone once said, 'Magicians are actors playing the part of magicians.' Ventriloquists, on the other hand, are magicians playing the part of two or more actors. The ability to turn a lifeless doll into a living creature is truly magic.'—Ventriloquist

I would add my own interpretation to the above epigraph: Ventriloquists are magicians who know one illusion—and know it very well. Ventriloquists seem related to magicians only in the sense that the two fall about on the same nerdiness level. But truthfully, as Stadelman points out, ventriloquism is more like magical illusion than one may initially think. Ventriloquists use various misdirections to direct the audience's gaze toward the dummy. They have a predefined patter that must be entertaining and funny, but at the same time the ventriloquist is always working on two levels: (1) presenting the show; and (2) presenting the illusion that life has been created in that lifeless doll. Just as the stage magician, the ventriloquist must simultaneously present an effect and work the underlying manipulations to make the effect take place.

Ventriloquism makes use of several principles to create the illusion of life:

- *The puppet must have its own voice.* Stadelman advises to go so far as to give each puppet its own character and personality.
- *Realistic movement.* The character should make eye contact. It might move its eyes, wiggle its eyebrows, and do other "lifelike" actions, but these should be kept to a minimum. In real life, when a person talks, they don't wiggle their eyebrows all that much.
- *Breaking the rules.* Contrary to popular belief, ventriloquists actually do move their lips sometimes when the situation warrants it. Stadelman explains that one of the punchlines in his show is, "somebody else's pants." The problem is, you can't say "pants" without moving your lips. No problem. As the puppet yells the punchline, its body movement is sudden and exaggerated, drawing attention to the puppet and away from Stadelman's moving lips. Misdirection at work!
- *Concealment.* Other times, the ventriloquist can turn his head slightly away from the audience in order to pronounce words where the lips must move.
- *Prethought and planning.* Most often, the ventriloquist will simply avoid such words (for instance, substitute "grin" for "smile," or "got" for the unspeakable "bought"). Or the ventriloquist will substitute one sound for another (instead of, "I bought new furniture," say, "I *got* new *thurniture*").

As you can see, the ventriloquist's job relies on a combination of magical illusion–creating stratagems. Some are designed to create the initial illusion (strategies to keep the lips from moving), while others are designed to perpetuate that notion (misdirection keeps the puppet looking alive). Finally, it's worth noting that a variation of ventriloquism is used by some spiritual performers. The Algonquin North American Indian tribes had shamans who would appear to converse with spirits by using a suitably frightening vented voice. Modern-day channelers, or mediums, also seem to have conversations with ghosts. Of course this is plain acting, with some aspects of ventriloquism thrown in for good measure. The only difference between that and ordinary ventriloquism is that in the channeler's case there is no doll—the channeler herself is the dummy.

Assistants

Assistants are often (but not always) of opposite gender to the magician, and yes, we can read a certain sexual suggestiveness into this. Consider this description of how a high school nobody named David Kotkin became the magical Davino, in order to pick up girls:

> He knew he had to do something, so he did magic, which was all he could do. In this way, he learned to dominate girls and make them like it. Magic, he realized, taught him sex, before sex was an option. "Men enjoy seeing a woman controlled, say, with levitation," he later explained. "Women, on the other hand, see magic as an act of trust—especially if she's going to let a guy do horrible things like stick swords through her body." Thus, his life would be spent wreaking out sweet revenge, having his way with women by skewering, floating, vanishing, and resurrecting them. And afterward, there would always be applause.[9]

Davino grew up to be David Copperfield, a magician whose grandiose illusions and deep pockets lined with gold allow him the luxury of working with many, many assistants, female and male. A female assistant is not chosen simply because she is a pretty woman. Other factors must be considered. For certain effects, a woman is chosen because of her smaller body size and weight. The assistant often ends up being crammed into little boxes and baskets, and a small figure (and flexibility) is essential. For levitation illusions you obviously want someone small enough to appear buoyant on air, and light enough for the wires to lift.

A lithe, sexy female allows for a sheer, slinky costume. Sex appeal aside, it makes for visual interest and contrast in the show, the same way a cardician might choose a two of diamonds and a king of spades as immediately distinct cards for a transposition effect. The tightness and sleevelessness of the costume also promotes a feeling of openness. Unfortunately, some criticize that women are chosen for assistants for the politically incorrect idea that women are less capable, less suited to performing magic than men, and certainly less powerful than men. (This is also one of the misdirections that supernaturalists use to substantiate their claims. "How could that charming little girl be deceiving us? She simply must be psychic!" This is just one use of magic techniques off the magic stage.) One magician I talked with explained, "Most [magicians] tend to use females because they tend to be more attractive and more willing to help. It's okay for a woman to be fooled in front of a crowd but a man may become offended and think you are making fun of him." The female assistant takes us off our guard, because she is "only" an assistant—all she does is move boxes around, so it doesn't occur to us that she is integral to the functioning of the trick.

Assistants sometimes have to sign nondisclosure agreements with the magician, usually in cases where there is no strong bond between magician and assistants. For example, David Copperfield picks up many new on-stage and off-stage helpers at every leg of the tour, many of whom are actors and not fellow magicians (actors to play the role of "audience member" for instance). Clearly by doing this Copperfield is supplying a lot of people with good stories to tell their friends! Nondisclosure forms are necessary, if not enforceable.

On the other hand there are magicians like Leigh Hotz, who form long-standing attachments with their assistants. He doesn't have to worry as much about assistants "kissing and telling" because these are fellow magicians acting as assistants, and they have a bond of friendship to keep their lips shut. Hotz says:

> While some magicians make assistants sign a nondisclosure form, most do not (including myself). I treat my assistants with respect and only a verbal agreement is needed. My assistants normally stay with my show an average of about five to seven years and I only need to replace them if they move out of state or something like that. I keep my assistants longer than most magicians for two reasons: (1) I pay them well. They get a third of my gross per show so the more money I make, the more they make. (2) I treat them as business partners. I take their comments and suggestions without the "boss-employee" attitude. In the event that one of my former assistants decides to expose my tricks of the trade, the number of the public would be so little I have little to worry.

Assistants are important simply in their roles of bringing props on and off stage—if done right it can provoke suspense as some odd piece of equipment is brought forth, and contributes order, as other props are removed out of sight when not in use. But the assistants need to be more than simple propmasters. Often the magician gives the appearance that *he* is controlling the magic, with his gesturing hands and knowing smile. But in fact it is the assistant, crammed into that suspicious box, who not only knows exactly what's going on but is performing the actions necessary to make the trick work. She also "helps generate the appropriate audience reaction by laughing, looking apprehensive, applauding, and making other gestures congruent with the effect called for by particular tricks. That is, she helps construct the anomalous reality among the audience striven for by the principal performer."[10] There has been at least one book written on the topic, celebrating the multifarious role assistants play in a magical performance. Called *The Magician's Assistant*, by Jan Jones et al., the book covers such aspects as makeup, poise, handling props, appearing on television, and a pictorial history with anecdotes of assistants.

Pull out your local phone book and read the ads for magicians. See anything unusual? Or rather, is there something you *don't* see on those pages? Usually you don't see any mention of assistants! Lots of animals, yeah—

show off the birds and rabbits and monkeys. But when it comes to people, you know who's boss. You know who's important. It's the magician, and that's that. But the assistants are important too! And surely a magician advertising the fact that he has scantily clad women showing off their ya-yas will help book club dates. But there are important reasons why the magician virtually ignores his gals in the ads: If you talk about people other than the magician, you are hinting that (1) magic isn't a special force confined to the magician (you are saying that the assistants—and maybe dozens of other people—share the power too) or (2) magic is done by trickery (which requires accomplices). With the first, there is a lessening of power, with the second, the elimination of it. Either way it does not bode well for the magician who is trying to create an illusion of mastery over his environment. Focusing on one person and the special powers he possesses is a good first step to creating the illusions that follow.

Women in Magic

"The threadbare vocabulary of the serial novels describing woman as a sorceress, an enchantress, fascinating and casting a spell over man, reflects the most ancient and universal of myths. Woman is dedicated to magic." So says Simone de Beauvoir in her seminal tome on the roles that women play in the world.[11] From the fertility goddesses to Earth Mothers, women have thousands of years of magic behind them. Why then are there so few women magicians? Well, for starters, there's something about the nature of magic that excludes women, whether it be discrimination, socialization, or something else. Sociologist Peter Nardi believes that in fact there are plenty of female magicians. But they are magicians of the supernatural sort:

> If you look at the *Enquirer* ("9 Out of 10 Psychics Predict the End of the World"), or whatever—they're almost all women. The Psychic Network TV shows. . . . The area that women are in, if you broaden the word magic to include (which I would) séances, palm readings, psychics (which are after all just magic tricks. . . .) Those seem to be the realm which women are in. And in a very traditional sense, they're doing what could be called "expressive magic." They hold your hand, they touch your palm. It's very touch-oriented. They're literally the *medium* through which they're channeling some alleged person from the other world. *Through them*, to the person. . . . They're not doing magic, but they are the conduit of magic.
>
> Whereas traditional magic is very male-oriented. Power emanates *from* the magician, rather than through the psychic. That's a much more masculine way of looking at it. And also just think of the imagery: sawing, swords, wands, all these phallic imagries. The ultimate example is . . . imagine a woman sawing a *man* in half—the castration imagery and all that.

Nardi contends that much of traditional stage magic is very masculine in nature, "both in the essence of what it is in terms of power, but also in its layers of tools and repertoire." When I spoke with Nardi I understood what he was saying, but I was doubtful. With my modern understanding of psychology and the human mind, could I rationally believe in such Freudian hoo-hah as phallic symbols and castration anxiety? No, I found that very hard to believe.

Then, the next night, I attended a magic show. This magician made me a believer in what Nardi was saying. This magician made Richard Speck look like Alan Alda. He did not use any of the techniques described throughout this book to make the magic believable, enjoyable, or anything more than a trick. His attitude was "ha ha, I'm cool." His stage presence was unnecessary as all that he did was shove a "girl" (that is, woman) into a box and penetrate her with swords, tubes, etc. Then he stood back, grinned, and put his hands out to his sides, a gesture indicating that he was ready for his applause. His entire act consisted of bought props (that is, no skill involved on his part). He performed fourteen of these "shove a girl in a box then penetrate her" magic tricks. One of these tricks involved a woman kneeling submissively on stage by the magician's feet; several had her caressing the sword that would soon penetrate her body. There was no variety in the act at all. In any case, this is a long tangent away from the issue of women in magic to illustrate the point that magic, when poorly done, is still rife with discrimination, sexism, male-dominated power, and, yes, much poking and prodding of symbolic phalluses.

Hypocrisies on Stage

Before concluding this chapter on "The Stage and the People On It," I'd like to dip the cup into the sour side of my psyche and pull out some observations of a cynical nature. Hypocrisies. Some magicians display certain hypocrisies. It's too often to be coincidence. I think it happens because they're forced to keep secrets. And when someone is forced to keep secrets of such magnitude (their livelihood depends on it), and from such a large group of people (all the nonmagicians), I guess it forces them into some convoluted ways of thinking.

For instance, magicians like to point out "there's more to the trick than just the trick—there's the atmosphere, lighting, story, mood evoked, music, character, etc." And yet, magic catalogs repeatedly sell items based on "A new gimmick!" "You haven't seen this one before!" "This method will absolutely tickle your magic bone!" And so on. More than one magician has commented how uncomfortable he feels to see certain magic items sold in toy stores, or that they can be purchased by laypeople. But if it weren't for the exciting gimmicks and gizmos and the easy availability of props, then almost no one would become interested in magic in the first place.

Furthermore, magic books repeatedly warn not to reveal secrets, Don't reveal secrets! I've even seen magic books complain that *other* magic books reveal too much. These statements can be found in books intended for professionals as well as laypeople. But what business do they have making comments like that, when the book that is making such a comment is itself revealing tricks to the public?!

It's true that magic secrets should not be shouted out at stage shows. They should not be whispered to those standing in line for a performance. They should not be discussed loudly on the way out of the theater. But it's silly to expect the kind of rigorous secret-keeping that some magicians expect everyone to abide by. The truth is hard and horrible to bear: Secrets are tempting and intriguing and infinitely interesting. The very fact that something is secret means that people are going to try and discover it, and hypothesize about it, and discuss the possibilities. Magicians can't control the actions of the entire world population. But I'm sure they will go on trying.

10

Grrrrrrrowlll!!! The Animals of Magic

The magician rolls up his sleeves, shows his hand empty on both sides, makes a fist, then opens his fist with a flourish. Out pops a red sponge ball. Boring! Stupid! Hum, what can we do about it? Okay, how about this: With a flourish, the magician opens his fist and a soft white dove spreads its wings and soars into the rafters of the theater. That's better.

If you think about it, producing birds should be no more difficult than making balls or scarves appear. But you don't think about it, and so the production of a live animal is more magical and more entertaining than the production of a red ball. Certainly there are difficulties in working with animals over objects. Before the object appears, it has to be hidden somewhere. Let's assume it is hidden on the body of the performer (although it could be in a secret compartment of some equipment). The animal has to remain fairly motionless beneath the magician's jacket or coattails. Luckily both birds and rabbits are used to remaining motionless in darkness for long periods of time. Of course they might not particularly *prefer* to stay that way. That's what dove harnesses are for. A dove harness is a cloth tube with a row of snaps or Velcro along the long ends to hold it closed, and a loop of wire protruding from the head end. A dove is put inside the cloth tube like a Birdie Burrito, with its head and tail sticking out from the ends. With the bird under wraps, the magician stuffs the silent creature into a special pocket in his clothing, letting the loop hang out discreetly. During the performance, the magician will casually link a finger or thumb in the loop, lift out the restrained dove, and conceal it in the handkerchief he just happened to pull out of his pocket with the other hand (naturally the material of the harness tube cleverly matches the material of the harness—they've even got dove harnesses covered in newsprint in case anyone wants to produce a dove from the *Times*). So now the magician has this dove confined in the harness, concealed in his hanky, and he will do something like suddenly rip away the handkerchief (while also ripping open the Velcro) at the same time. The dove goes, "Thank God!" and it flutters its wings and tail in a beautiful display (how would you like to be wrapped up in simulated newspaper and shoved in a sweaty guy's pocket all day?) before taking off in flight for the assistant in the wings.

Anyway, that's where those doves come from in case you were wondering.

But we were talking about the difficulty of working with animals over objects. The animals have to be restrained before being produced, but they've also got to remain quiet until the appearance. Well, what are the most commonly produced animals—talking parrots? No. Silent love birds and rabbits.

Notice also that birds can tuck their wings in and lower their heads, and basically roll up into a tight little packet and meditate. But when the need arises (as when a magician is throwing them into the air) they will outstretch their wings to create a wonderful illusion of *bigness* and flap their feathers and fly away. It is interesting to note the similarity between a small bird unfolding to show its wingspan and the rubber fruits and vegetables (and hot dog links and other goodies) that magicians can purchase. These rubber inedibles fold up into small loads that the magician can easily hide. As the item is produced, the magician covertly "unsquashes" it, letting the rubber body of the object come into full bloom. The audience wonders, "How did he ever pull such a big thing out of nowhere?" The answer is, he hid a little thing. Producing it created the big thing. With bird flight, the appearance is much more than the manifestation of an object, but the creation of beauty— a living being as alive and aware as any of us. In some ways the flight of the bird seems as magical as its strange appearance in the magician's hand. It makes for a thought-provoking juxtaposition of concepts—the real magic of life against the artificial magic of the theater.

Both children and adults love seeing animals as part of a show. It creates a slick professionalism and adds an element of realness to the illusion-filled proceedings. How much more real and innocent can you get than an adorable white bunny rabbit?

Sometimes tricks go awry. Magician Chris Roth pointed out on the Internet discussion group alt.magic the result of one sad and funny magic mishap: "Once, during the annual Milwaukee magician's conclave, a young man performed a dove routine. Usually there was a big stage show during one evening of the convention. This was in 1974 or 1975. Anyway, one of the doves was "produced." And this was done during an elaborate arcing arm motion. Rather than becoming airborne at the instant it magically appeared, the dove fell dead onto the stage floor. Either that or it was unconscious." Aside from the horror the audience must have felt at seeing the bird dead, it is a case like this which transforms the magical appearance of an animal back to the level of the appearance of an inanimate object. The dead bird, for its unwillingness to display its wingspan and take flight, might as well have been the red ball. At least the ball might've bounced.

BIRDS

Magicians have been using trained birds for thousands of years. Sometime around 3,800 B.C.E. the Egyptian magician Teta was entertaining the Pharaoh Khufu with his version of the cut-and-restore-the-goose trick. Khufu was the pharaoh who commanded the building of the Great Pyramid to be his eternal burial monument. In so doing, he wanted everything done right. Khufu was well-versed in the ancient legends, and he knew that Thoth, the Egyptian god of magic, had placed an *aptet* on the walls of his burial chamber. An *aptet* was a magical charm or verse (the exact meaning is now not known to us). The legends about Thoth were far more ancient than Khufu, and much of the magical lore had been lost through the ages. Khufu was anxious to know the exact number of *aptets* that should adorn his walls. So he said to his son, "Herutataf, bring me the finest magician—or interior decorator—in all of Egypt! And a Snapple!"

Herutataf set sail on the royal barge, forged up and down the Nile, and returned with Teta, a magician who some said was 110 years old. Khufu was discouraged that he was not living in the magical age of his forefathers. Khufu believed that the generations preceding him had attained true magical abilities. He knew that even though he was also a pharaoh, he was a mere man. Teta claimed to be a true magician, but Khufu was skeptical. He believed that Teta too was just a mere man. Khufu needed a test to prove that Teta had magical powers.

"Is it true that you can restore a head that has been cut from its body?" Khufu asked the old man. Teta excitedly replied that yes, he could perform that feat. The Pharaoh ordered a prisoner to be brought from the dungeon. Teta tactfully protested that he could not rightfully use his magic on a human being. They agreed that the magic should be performed on an animal.

Teta took a goose and sliced off its head. He placed the body on one end of a table, and the severed, bloody head on the other end. Under the spell of Teta's magic, the two pieces moved together, and joined as new in the center of the table. The goose got up, ruffled its feathers, and stretched out its perfectly intact neck, beautifully restored to life and wholeness. To further demonstrate his divine endowment, Teta performed the illusion on another bird, and then on an ox.

The legend does not say what became of Teta—or the Snapple.

When I first read this magical legend, I was very young, and the storybook that contained the tale was adorned by many fabulous watercolors. I attributed the story to storybook land. Certainly nothing like this could possibly have ever occurred for real. But as it happens, the illusion is one that has been performed repeatedly around the world throughout history. Unlike the meaning of the *aptet*, the trick to the trick has been passed down to us.

Geese (as well as many birds) will routinely tuck their heads under their wings before going to sleep. I've seen pet parrots that do this. While sleeping, the parrot looks very much like a headless green featherball. Many centuries ago, some trickster and bird watcher must have taken special notice of this unusual feature of birds, and he must have trained a goose, or duck, to tuck in its head on a command. A false head was carved from wood or soap, painted lifelike, and decorated with feathers. For added gruesomeness, some holes could be drilled into the bottom of the carved neck, filled with blood or red paint, and plugged up.

While performing the illusion, the magician would pretend to cut off the bird's head, while in reality giving it the cue to hide its head under its wings. The fake head was produced, the plugs opened up to allow a stream of blood to gush onto the stage and onto the bird as well, strengthening the illusion of a bloody stump where the neck was detached from the body. Later the magician restored the bird whole again by passing the carved head close to the body and then palming it or hiding it in his robes. The bird was cued to stick its head out again, and perhaps it was given a little pat on the behind to stoke it into some table-hopping action.

Of course, all of that is just one explanation and there is no guarantee that is the way Teta performed the miracle. However, magicians through the centuries have used that technique to cut off and restore the heads of birds.[1] One such magician was Giovanni Bartolomeo Bosco ("the Great Bosco"), an Italian wizard of the eighteenth century who seemed to relish decapitating a pigeon and letting the blood flow freely into a saucer.[2] Unlike the magicians before him, Bosco *actually decapitated* the birds to make the effect more convincing. Nice guy. Bosco's method was to use two boxes with false bottoms. Live birds were hidden under the false bottoms. Bosco would begin his trick with two pigeons, one black, one white. After slicing off their heads, he dropped the pieces into the boxes. Some incantations, presto chango, and Bosco would pull out the two live birds from under the false bottom. But Bosco had one more wily trick up his sleeve! When he pulled out the restored birds, he was surprised as anyone to discover he had accidentally reversed the heads—the black bird now had a white head, and the white pigeon had a black head. Perhaps this bit of dark humor helped the audience relax after the bloody decapitations, for the spectators might laugh to themselves, "Ah! So it was only a trick after all! He was fooling us all along!" A little levity to ease their concerns and to misdirect away from the true nature of the trick. The mixed-up heads were the result of dye applied before the show.

BUNNY RABBITS

The adorable white bunny rabbit is linked to the idea of the American magician as firmly as dalmatians are to firefighters. The cute and cuddly white rabbit has been popping out of magic hats since the late 1830s. Unfortunately, there is a darker side to the tale: for many years magicians were instructed to pick up rabbits by their ears, an action that causes the rabbit great pain. (Try pulling your own ears, buster! See how *you* like it!) The preferred method is to lift by the scruff of the neck, like a momma rabbit would, but magicians didn't know it, and the rabbits didn't complain much aside from kicking their feet in a lively display. This foot-kicking activity was greatly appreciated by the magician, since it proved the animal was feisty and real. Some old magic texts had instructions for "hypnotizing" a rabbit into a trance. The routines started with picking up the rabbit by the ears, to show how active it was, followed with other physical maneuverings to calm the rabbit into an apparent trance, and finally to snap it back into reality. The whole thing was fairly abusive, phony, and uncalled for. Hopefully it's not still done today, because most magicians are aware nowadays of the proper treatment of their animals. You can still sometimes see old black-and-white movies with magicians pulling rabbits out of hats by their ears. The little creatures are kicking and silently screaming.

Like the white dove, the rabbit makes a sharp visual contrast with the traditional magician's costume of black tie and tails on a darkened stage. Even folks in the back rows should be able to see the shiny little fuzzballs. Their other outstanding quality is their quietness, so they can be held hostage in bags, boxes, and under the coat for long periods of time. Maybe they don't like it there, but who knows? They don't say a word.

ZOO ANIMALS

Using large animals like jungle cats in a show adds extra danger and excitement to the stage. Most everyone recognizes that most of the "danger" has been taken out of the animals—they've been trained to be docile and obedient to their masters. And yet we all should be aware that that perception is not wholly accurate. After all, even the most well-trained jungle leopard does not have the heart of a pussy cat. Siegfried and Roy, the twosome best known for their long-running shows in Las Vegas as well as for their use of jungle animals, have had at least one bloody mishap on stage. After making a lion appear in his cage, Siegfried tried to rile up the lion to put on a good show for the audience. The lion swatted his paws and sliced his fangs into Siegfried's hand and arm. The arm was sewed up and bandaged after the show, but there was still a second show to do. In the middle of the second show, the stitches burst open and the throbbing, swelling arm poured blood through the rest of the show. Luckily bandages and elaborate costuming were there to sop up the moisture. At the end of the night, Roy describes the arm as looking like "a clump of raw, bloody meat."[3]

To be fair to Siegfried and Roy, they point out that this particular lion was not a usual part of the act, but rather a relatively new acquisition. Normally stage animals are carefully prepared with love and affection, to ensure that they know how to stay calm around people. Stage animals must be accustomed to being on stage in front of a bustling sea of faces, to have bright lights shined upon them, and to sit unreacting to the loud sounds around them.

11

Props and Gimmicks

What might you buy at a magician's garage sale? Boxes and bunny rabbits to be sure, but there would be a lot of other stuff there you wouldn't recognize—or you might think you recognize it for what it is, never knowing that it contains secrets codes, hidden trap doors, or false bottoms. Here we will open up the magic trunk and examine each prop the way the magician never lets you do when you're watching the show. In fact, a little later I'll tell you about a deck of cards I bought at a garage sale; they looked quite normal, but through a careful analysis of discovery I was able to reveal the secret workings of those magic cards.

There are different kinds of props. Some, like an ordinary handkerchief or coin, may be just what it appears to be. But for every real object there is its devious evil twin. The handkerchief may have a hidden pocket sewn into it. The coin may be two-headed, or be a hollow shell in which a different coin can be concealed. We then get into a different kind of prop, one which the audience never sees but is crucial in performing certain effects.

So let's open the dusty trunk, peer inside, and pull out all those props, gimmicks, utilities, and tools that make up the magic garage sale.

Props

Magicians set the stage with all sorts of suggestive and interesting props. Part of the excitement of the show lies in spotting some exotic equipment on stage and wondering what the magician will do with it. Much aggravation is caused when some thoughtless magician sets the stage with intriguing props he does not intend to use. He may see them as setting the stage with a mystical atmosphere; the audience remains only frustrated. The audience is supposed to leave "wanting more." These audiences leave with the unsatisfied feeling that they were promised more than was delivered.

Props may be exotic or commonplace. This goes along with the question of whether the magic is caused by the magician or happens around him. If the first, exotic props are used, such as gaudily ornamented tubes, scarves, and boxes. The magician whose magic "just happens" may be as surprised as the audience to find silverware bending, disappearing and restoring itself as he eats, or other standard items from the kitchen drawer begin dancing around the stage. But nobody's likely to be surprised when an obviously fake jewel-encrusted box with a genie painted on it starts to do mysterious things. Magician Tina Lenert has an act in which a few props become magically animated on stage. "You might say that I am not a woman magician at all, since the magic in my act happens *to* me, and is actually performed by the coat and mop that represents a man!"[1] Children are more likely to be delighted by the exotic pictures of pirates and Oriental mystery adorning some props, while adults eye such decorations suspiciously, as if the pictures hide some secret to the magic. As escape artist and stuntman Harley Newman quips, "You're gonna convince me that that's a box you got out of your backyard? I don't think so!" Less cynical adults may think of the designs nostalgically. With most audiences (the exception, perhaps, being an audience of other magicians) the flashy props are probably more anticipated than a deck of cards or some coins. *"Now we'll see some real magic!"*

Some props are gimmicked and others are not. The ungimmicked ones may be passed around for inspection. Actually, sometimes gimmicked props are also passed around, if the gimmick is concealed well enough. The magician must think through what he will allow to be inspected and what not. If every item except for one is inspected, attention is drawn to that object. Therefore the magician may ask the audience to trust him that many inspectable objects really are inspectable, even when he does not pass them around.

Passing around also slows down the momentum of the show, but, again, it does provide a dose of proof that children need, and the vicarious "we are not being tricked, this is real magic" that adults want to feel. It should also be considered that many props are as phony as a three-legged duck. The magician passes around a genuine prop, then switches it for a gimmicked one either before or after the trick is accomplished. Actually, passing stuff around is a good detractor, and magicians often use it to direct attention away from themselves for a moment. Look how tricky this is! At the moment when we believe the magician is being most honest with us, he is really exercising his right to sneakiness!

The most skilled magicians are often performing close-up magic. I say they are the most skilled because they have perfected the sleights that allow them to perform under close scrutiny. Because they know the moves so well, the props themselves are unlikely to be gimmicked—tricks are accomplished with skill rather than gimmicks. Still, a close-up audience may be suspicious of even ordinary-looking props (which very often are not ordinary at all). I have wondered if close-up audiences try to take the show "into their own hands" because they feel a sense of intimacy with the performer. Close-up artist Suzanne the Magician, talked about her children audiences: "As a matter of fact, they do grab. That's why I choose my material very carefully. I also can kinda tell, now that I have been doing this for a while, who will be the grabber and who will not. I may even say to the person that I think is a grabber 'Doon't touuuch the stuff!!' That gets the point across without challenging them. That is the last thing you want to do to a grabber." Magician Sol Messler added, "I think my adult audiences are worse than the kids. At least with the kids you can discipline them somewhat. Adults know it all, want it all, and most of all they understand that I'm just a big phony. Yeah they grab my stuff plenty." Grabbing may be annoying but "it's not really a problem," says Suzanne.

> I choose my material very carefully. If things can't be examined sometime between the start and finish of the effect, I probably won't do that effect. Even if it is a killer. There is maybe one prop that can't be examined, but it gets put away so fast that it doesn't really matter. I'm also kind of a purist. Most of what I do is sleight of hand. Coins, cards, Cup and Balls. Usually when doing that kind of stuff there is nothing gaff anyway.

Magicians let us examine only the props that are safe for passing around. That's where this book is different! Here, no prop is sacred from examination. In this chapter we shall explore these props from the magician's magic trunk:

- Bags
- Billiard balls
- Cards
- Choppers
- Coins
- Cups and balls
- Hats
- Paddles
- Rope
- Silks
- Screens and scenery
- Sponge
- Tables
- Thimbles
- Tubes
  and
- Wallets and purses

Bags

The egg bag is probably the most common type of bag used in a magic show. The egg bag is a simple cloth bag with a hidden pocket in it. The pocket is formed by one side that curves down into the bag until it reaches almost the very bottom. Items can be hidden in this slice between layers of velvet. It's called an egg bag because magicians commonly use it to cause eggs to vanish and appear.

One bad point is that the hidden pocket can easily be discovered if the magician allows the bag to be examined. The usual retort is to pass around an ungimmicked bag and then make a switch to the gimmicked one. De Biere, a magician well known for his outstanding egg bag routine, would conceal the gimmicked egg bag in the sleeve of his jacket. He would let the audience inspect an ordinary bag that was an exact copy. After they were satisfied, he would take back the bag. Before continuing with the trick, De Biere would remove his coat. As his hand slipped through the sleeve, he would exchange the ordinary bag for the gimmicked one with the hidden pocket in it. The jacket was tossed aside and he could continue the performance.

One good thing about this kind of reversed pocket is that when an egg is hidden inside it, you can shake out the bag to "prove" it's empty, and the egg will not fall out. Shaking the bag upside down only causes the egg to fall deeper and deeper into the hidden pocket, so the "proof" of innocence actually helps abet the crime! Sometimes the egg will even be inside the bag, in the hidden pocket, but the magician is holding the bag from the top with the egg held in place by his fingers at the top of the bag. He allows a volunteer to feel the bottom of the bag to ensure it's empty. The volunteer confirms that it is empty, and the magician need only relax his grip to allow the egg to slide out of the pocket and down into the bag. Magic!

Billiard Balls

Billiard balls are hard little balls that some magicians are fond of manipulating—making appear and multiply and so forth, with sleight-of-handi-work. The funny thing is, they're not really billiard balls at all. They're usually smaller than that, though they come in different sizes, and some are hollow plastic rather than wood. Arthur Buckley makes an interesting point: the balls come in two colors, red and white, but he prefers white because the bright color alone makes them look a trifle larger than red balls, making them a more impressive choice for manipulations.[2]

Beginners use a hollow half-shell. Snap the shell onto a real ball, and it looks like one ball. Hold the shell and ball combination between two fingers. Then roll them apart, keeping the outside of the shell positioned towards the audience. It will appear as if a second ball appeared out of nowhere.

More accomplished magicians can use only sleight of hand. There are various palms and moves the ball manipulator learns to achieve the effects. Buckley goes through about thirty pages of sleights ("Concealing a Ball Behind the Hand While Both Palms Are Shown," "The Strike Vanish," "Color Changes," etc.) before coming to his masterpiece: "The Production of Eight Solid Balls at the Fingertops Without a Shell." I can tell you that such a miracle requires having balls loaded beforehand all over the magician's body—behind the legs, in the vest, snapped into ball holders under the jacket. Oh yes, the magician will likely have a ball dispenser hidden under his jacket. Look for a free hand casually hanging by his side. If so, check out the fingers—do they seem to be curling up under the jacket, as if reaching for something? Hmm? Oh, well, you probably won't notice that action at all, since the magician does all that sneaky work while misdirecting with a flourish of balls in the other hand.

Cards

The first thing to know about cards is that magicians skilled in card manipulation and card tricks are called "cardicians." There is a love/hate thing between cards and magicians and audience members. "Pick a card, any card" may be the five most feared words in the English language! And yet a good cardician is certainly one of the most skilled of all magicians.

All sorts of unusual and cutsie-pie cards are on the market. There are round cards, jumbo face cards, tiny cards, wrong color cards (hearts and diamonds are black, spades and clubs are red), and decks that specifically depict the jack, queen, and king as African-Americans. Dozens of other variations exist. There are also decks that are gimmicked in some way. Magician Marcus Ludl from Vienna, Austria, summed up the thoughts of many magi on gimmicked cards thusly: "I prefer effects that I can do with a borrowed deck. . . . The only gimmicks I use are blank cards or double-backed cards or some other gimmicks that enhance the effect. What I don't like are gimmicks that just simplify the handling, like a stripper deck . . . with some practice you can do with a normal pack of cards everything that you can do with a stripper."

A stripper deck, he explained, consists of cards that are cut slightly "conical," so that one end is narrower than the other. "With some practice this deck enables you to do some great things, like riffle shuffling it together whilst keeping some setup intact." With no practice and some showmanship, you can arrange all the cards facing one direction, then have someone pick a card. As they are memorizing the card, secretly turn the deck around in your hands. Now when they replace the card, it will slide in reversed. Since the cards are narrower on one end, this selected card will be sticking out like a sore thumb—sticking out only a tiny fraction of an inch mind you, but enough for your thumb to catch the little ledge it provides and know instantly where in the deck the selected card is sitting. More practiced magicians don't need to use gimmicks like this, because they have learned how to do such sleights as to hold the card's position with their pinkie without using a gaffed deck. In fact, Henry Hay, in his impressive *Amateur Magician's Handbook*, describes how he can (usually) divine where a selected card has been inserted into the deck even when an audience volunteer picks the deck off a table and inserts the card, without the magician touching the deck until after the card is replaced.[3]

Most cardicians would tell you that they are proud of all the work they have put into learning to manipulate cards, and their skill alone is far more impressive than any trick deck they could pick up at the Quickie Magic Shop. We are going to mention some of these techniques that learned cardicians use, but first let's run through the gamut of card gimmicks that are available, starting with the marked deck.

CARDS CODE

When I was in elementary school, my mother bought me a trunkful of goodies at a yard sale. Sorting through the stuff, plastic binoculars, board games, some action figures, a few small magic tricks, a deck of cards, it all looked like the kind of stuff a boy might be getting rid of as he makes his way from being a little boy to a young man. Luckily I was still a little boy so I could appreciate it. The other day it suddenly occurred to me, for no particular reason, that the deck of cards was probably a marked deck. Quickly I rushed to my desk and pulled them out of their box. The box looks ordinary enough, a blue box saying simply, "DeLand's Automatic Playing Cards." I'd never before thought about what the word "automatic" meant. This is an old deck, and I guess I assumed the word came from some time in the fifties when automatic living was a novelty of the future that American manufacturers would gleefully apply to anything in order to sell a product, even something as ordinary as a deck of playing cards. On the back of the box is a pattern of circles inside circles on a meshy background. This is the same pattern that one finds on the back of the cards themselves. The design looks baroque and ornamental, complex enough that secret markings could easily be hidden in it. At the top and bottom of the design are the tiny words, "COPYRIGHT 1913 BY T.L. DE LAND." Ah, so that's who De-Land is, (of "DeLand's Automatic Playing Cards" fame). He's the guy who designed the back of the box. I pulled out the cards and spread them across the desktop to look at their backs. A quick glance showed what I had missed seeing for all those years. These cards are indeed marked.

Fig. 32. Look carefully and you can spot the differences between the card designs. Those subtle differences are a code that reveals crucial information about the card, its value, and its place in the deck.

The design on the card backs consists of circles and more circles. Twelve small white dots, forming a circle. And there are several of these circles on the back of the card; circles in each corner, and three larger circles down the vertical center of the card. My first instinct was that the marked part of the card, the part a deceptive poker player would be peeking at, would be the upper left corner of the card. I looked at a few cards in sequence, and it was easy to compare them and see that indeed, the upper left circle did differ between the cards. The cards use a sort of "binary code." Each white dot can be filled or unfilled. There are twelve dots making a circle, which of course reminds us of an analog clock, which acts as a further hint that the design was no mere accident of chance. These cards were specifically designed for fraudulent use. Depending on which dot of the clock is filled in, that represents the face value of the card. If the one o'clock position on the clock is filled, the card is an Ace. If the two o'clock position is filled, the card is a deuce, and so on. The king, the thirteenth card, is represented by altering the pattern for the right and left circles—no circle filled in on the left, ten o'clock filled in on the right.

But the markings don't end there. Inside the clock of dots are five more dots that remind me of a compass because they are in the pattern of a plus sign. Comparing the four aces, it was easy to figure out this part of the card code as well. The suit of the card is represented by the compass point—west (left) is spades, north (top) is diamonds, and so on.

By itself, this is enough information to make a killing in gin rummy if you were playing with these cards and had the requisite eyesight. Indeed, after a few minutes of practice it was pretty easy to determine which card was which just by glancing at the back.

Something bothered me though. Up to this point I had only looked at the circle in the upper left corner of the card (which is the same as the circle in the lower right of the card, so the cards could be held either way). But there were still plenty more circles on the card, and each of those circles is composed of smaller white dots, which sometimes are filled in, sometimes not. Clearly some more information was being imparted on the backs of the cards. Perhaps there was information in every one of those circles! Like a linguist tackling the Rosetta Stone, I set off on my quest to understand this mysterious pack of cards from a yard sale of long ago. I decided to look at each circle one at a time and try to make some sense of it. My first thought was what more information could possibly be given out? After all, we already know the suit and number of the card from the upper-left circle. Surely no more card information is available. Maybe the information is repeated, I considered. For instance maybe one of the circles indicates whether the card is red or black, a quick way for the magician to divine the color. Or perhaps the remaining circles are random dots, designed to throw card detectives off the trail of the real markings. Whatever the true story was, I was ready to find it.

I started by again picking up similar cards, but this time the markings did seem completely random. Some cards had no filled in dots. Others had all the dots filled in. Still others had a single filled dot per usual. It seemed that the only theory worth pursuing was the "completely random" theory. Still, I was not ready to give up. I decided the only way to really test the randomness of the dots was to completely chart out each card. This is the final chart for the top-middle dot clock. *ALL* means all dots are filled. A blank (—) means no dots are filled.

	♦ Diamonds	♣ Clubs	♥ Hearts	♠ Spades
Ace	ALL	7	4	—
2	4	1	8	—
3	8	5	2	—
4	2	9	6	3
5	—	3	ALL	7
6	—	7	4	1
7	2	1	8	5
8	6	—	2	9
9	ALL	—	6	3
10	4	1	ALL	7
Jack	8	5	—	1
Queen	2	9	—	5
King	6	3	ALL	9

At this point some patterns are emerging, but the meaning behind the pattern is elusive. The red cards have even numbers associated with them, and the black cards have odd. Is that meaningful? Useful? There does seem to be the beginning of a pattern: "ALL, 4, 8, 2, 6" and "3, 7, 1, 5, 9" are repeated a lot, but the meaning, if any, is unapparent to the uninitiated. The markings seem to be suggesting the Stebbins deck stacking. Stebbins worked variously as an acrobat, magician, and clown through the first half of the twentieth century (he died in 1950). He also published a few books on card tricks. He invented an influential card stacking system that today is known by his name. The cards are arranged in a seemingly haphazard fashion. The magician can show a fanning of cards to the audience, and they will see nothing but a mixture of pips and suits. They would never suspect that the deck was actually pre-ordered by the magician, and with this deck setup he can locate any card in the deck with a series of mental calculations!

In the Stebbins method, the top card is always a diamond, followed by a club, a heart, and a spade. Magicians use the word DuCHeSs to help them remember this set-up. Some magicians use CHaSeD by placing the club first. The cards follow a particular ordering: ace, 4, 7, 10, king, 3, 6, 9, queen, 2, 5,

8, jack. This ordering is repeated throughout the deck. Therefore, the first card is the ace of diamonds, the next is the 4 of clubs, etc. The untrained eye sees it as a random-looking deck, since reds and blacks and odds and evens and low cards and high cards are repeatedly alternated throughout the deck. (The trained eye might get suspicious of such a perfectly randomized deck.)

You can begin to see how the markings help the magician. The top card of the stack, the ace of diamonds has ALL dots filled in. The next card has nine dots. The next card has eight dots. Then seven, six, five, four, three, two, and one. The cycle repeats logically throughout the stack, as long as the cards were previously set up according to Stebbins' method.

So far this ordinary deck of cards was turning out to have a lot of secret properties to it! And I suspected it of keeping more secrets, because the back design was complicated and contained more circles-within-circles to conceal further codes. I next proceeded to look at the next large circle of dots on the backs of the cards, which was right below this one. Again the numbers were apparently random at best and meaningless at worst, but I filled in the chart as best I could, and got the results below:

	♦ Diamonds	♣ Clubs	♥ Hearts	♠ Spades
Ace	1	2	5	3
2	8	2	4	3
3	4	1	4	3
4	—	1	3	2
5	4	9	3	2
6	4	5	3	1
7	4	1	2	1
8	3	4	2	2
9	3	4	1	6
10	2	4	1	2
Jack	2	3	1	5
Queen	2	3	7	4
King	1	2	3	4

Some head-scratching and analysis later, I discovered the purpose of this code. If you look at the cards in their Stebbins ordering, you'll find that the first group of cards are all represented by a 1. The next group by 2, and so on. This allows the performer to know exactly which grouping a given card belongs to. For instance, if the deck has been cut a few times, the fourth group of cards might now be on top. Thus the performer knows the "top card" is towards the center of the deck.

Were there more secret codes etched into the back of that deck? Probably. My investigation stopped there.

As I was unraveling this mystery of the marked cards, I marveled at the complexity encoded on the backs of those cards with just a few dots. At first I had been ready to believe that *only* the suit and number were marked on the back, a reasonable thing to think. But, as we have been finding throughout this book's exploration of magic, magic is an onion of many layers. Additional complexity is built into the cards, a code to rival any World War II cryptographer. Not all marked decks are as complex as this, and perhaps some are full of even more telltale signs. Each has its own clever and fiendish way of broadcasting information about the card by a design displayed on the back.

PREARRANGED SETUPS

Some card effects rely on the deck being set up in a particular ordering before the show starts. Magicians have been known to buy a new deck of cards, carefully slice off the cellophane at the bottom, open the box from the bottom and remove the cards, arrange them in a certain order, then replace them in the box, regluing it shut. At showtime the magician needs only to conceal the slit in the cellophane with his very adept hand.

After removing the cards from the box, the magician will likely shuffle the deck a few times and perhaps offer it to a spectator to make a few cuts. The shuffles are false; they don't disturb the deck setup in the slightest. The cuts may be reversed by the magician, or they may not, since cuts don't affect certain setups. As mentioned, some setups order the cards in a rotating pattern where the top of the deck takes over where the bottom leaves off. In such cases, cutting the deck makes no difference at all.

What can be done with a pre-arranged deck? Lots of things. For one, if the magician knows the order of a deck, then he can determine if a card is out of place. That indicates a card that has been selected and replaced randomly in the deck. Another technique is to catch a glimpse of a card next to the chosen one. Since the magician knows the deck setup pattern, he can use the next card over to deduce the chosen card.

Some demonstrations of psychic powers also rely on a prearranged deck. The performer announces she will use her powers to discern the cards in a thoroughly shuffled deck. She has already glimpsed the bottom card, and from that she is able to calculate the top card, which she thus recites. The audience volunteer deals off cards in amazement as the mentalist guesses every one right! It's not that she's using psychic powers, merely that the cards only look randomly distributed. In fact, they follow a set pattern that merely looks confusing.

There are also numerous "counting" tricks whereby the magician counts out a certain number of cards, and the last one overturned is the chosen one; or he spells out a word or name, and the last letter of the word reveals the chosen card. These kinds of tricks also tend to depend on a prearranged setup.

SNEAKY DECK SETUP FOR SOLITAIRE

As a fun way to demonstrate the principle of prearranged deck setups, why don't you try out the setup below before playing a game of solitaire. Here's how it works. The first card is the king of spades, so put the king of spades *face up* on a table. Next put the 8 of clubs face up on top of it. Go through the rest of the deck in this way and you'll be ready to play—to win. Amaze your friends with your adeptness at the game! *Note:* When setting up the seven piles of cards prior to playing, be sure to set up the piles the standard solitaire way, where the cards are dealt one at a time into each of the seven piles, from left to right. In other words, deal one card into the first pile, one card into the second pile, and so on, until coming to the seventh pile. Then start dealing at the left end again, with one card in the second pile, etc.

1. King ♠	11. 10 ♠	21. Jack ♦	31. 7 ♠	41. 2 ♦	51. 3 ♥
2. 8 ♣	12. 9 ♠	22. Jack ♣	32. 5 ♥	42. 3 ♠	52. 4 ♠
3. 8 ♦	13. 9 ♦	23. Ace ♠	33. 6 ♠	43. 4 ♥	
4. 8 ♠	14. King ♣	24. Queen ♠	34. 7 ♦	44. 2 ♣	
5. 9 ♥	15. Jack ♥	25. Queen ♦	35. 5 ♠	45. 3 ♦	
6. Queen ♣	16. Jack ♠	26. Ace ♣	36. 6 ♦	46. 4 ♣	
7. 10 ♥	17. 10 ♦	27. Ace ♦	37. 7 ♣	47. 2 ♥	
8. King ♥	18. 10 ♣	28. Ace ♥	38. 5 ♦	48. 3 ♣	
9. 9 ♣	19. King ♦	29. 5 ♣	39. 6 ♣	49. 4 ♦	
10. 8 ♥	20. Queen ♥	30. 6 ♥	40. 7 ♥	50. 2 ♠	

OTHER MARKED DECKS

There are lots of other kinds of marked decks, and though they may be deceptive and sneaky and clever, none are impossible to notice or to figure out. This isn't the CIA here. If someone's using cards with a flowery pattern or geometric pattern on the back, simply take any two cards and compare their backs. Look at the little details and if there any minor differences between them, you've got yourself a marked deck. If you can get the whole deck away from them, simply square up the deck and riffle through, looking at the backs. The pattern should be exactly the same on all cards. If not, if there are jumps or differences between cards, then you should suspect a rigged deck.

Decks may be marked by having certain geometric shapes either clear or filled-in. Other decks are marked with a leaf or flower petal drawn too big or too small. Some very tricky decks have a plaid background. A close examination reveals the plaid design is carefully arranged on each card to represent its face value.

There are also edge-marked decks. To detect these, square up the deck and look for vertical black lines on the sides. Another kind of marking involves slightly discoloring the backs with enormous dashes and dots. The discoloring is done so boldly and yet so slightly, that only those in the know can see them. This is known as *juicing* a deck, since the markings are made with a liquid known as juice. (In earlier times, actual citric juices may have been used, the acid eating away the card ink to produce the marks.) Another trick, not much used now, is colored markings that emerge when the card shark wears specially tinted glasses. This trick is widely known in card shark circles, so its use has diminished. Still, if your poker buddy only sees the world through rose colored glasses, be wary, for his winnings might be less than genuine.

Most magicians don't use marked decks, but they do use their own personal markings during the course of a trick. A spectator's card might be crimped, nicked with a fingernail, bent, or smudged with some substance so the magician can later find it again. As always, such techniques are also widely known by card sharks to hustle their victims.

CARD SLEIGHTS

Card tricks are a good way of separating the men from the boys—the tricksters from the real magicians—because at heart it is very hard to take a card trick and turn it into a full-fledged, believable, mystifying illusion. There's too much claptrap in our minds about card sharks, riverboat gamblers, card counting, three-card monte dealers, and cheating at cards. Cards are associated with all that, and card tricks, if done wrong, are very obviously little more than an extension of all that. Besides, cards are just numbers and symbols. It's hard to engage the imagination with them, tell that magical story, instill a sense of wonder.

There are a few basic principles most magicians use to accomplish a card trick, but a trick may last several minutes on stage. The trick itself may take one second to accomplish. All the rest is padding put in to obfuscate that one second, and, in some cases, to tell that story, to instill that wonder. More books have been written about card tricks than any other form of magic, and there are dozens—hundreds?—of secret sleights magicians use to manipulate cards. That brings up a problem: ostensibly the purpose of this book is to help you understand how illusions are created so that you can use that knowledge to detect how and when you're being fooled. But I don't think that listing hundreds of card sleights would be helpful in any way. For example, I can tell you all about one sleight called a "break." A break is when the magician makes a slight break in a deck of cards with his pinkie finger, or the edge of his thumb, or by some other method. Okay. Now you know to look for "breaks." Is that helpful in any way? Not really. You still don't know how the break is used, or when it is used, or why. To fully understand these sleights would require a lot of studying on your part, and I have a hunch you're not prepared to do that. I will mention some of the basic card sleights, however, and perhaps the next time you're watching a cardician perform you will have a better appreciation of what's going on under the master's agile fingertips:

- *Biddle move.* The cardician is counting off cards from the deck, but one of the cards dealt off is secretly returned to the deck while another card is dealt out.
- *Breaks.* The deck appears to be squared-up, but the cardician has a "bookmark" in place so he can cut to a specific card in the deck. The bookmark might be a finger, or just a minute, undetectable, shifting of cards at that spot.
- *Double lifts.* The cardician picks up two cards, but holds them together so they appear to be one.
- *False shuffles.* The cardician seems to be shuffling the cards, but in reality they retain their order. The faro shuffle is the most prized by magicians: it is a perfect shuffling where cards from each half of the deck are alternately interlaced. Eight perfect faros will restore the deck to its original ordering.
- *False cuts.* The cards appear to have been cut, but in reality the top half stays on top and the bottom half stays on the bottom. There are variations of this, such as the *slip cut*, in which only one card's position is changed.
- *Glides.* The cardician seems to deal the bottom card of the deck, but really deals the second-to-bottom card.
- *Reversals.* A card is secretly reversed in the deck (while all the others are face up, it is turned face down).
- *Top change.* A card held in one hand is indetectably exchanged for the top card of the deck held in the other hand.

There are innumerable more sleights than these, and every sleight has many variations and styles. Each of these may seem not so impressive by themselves, but, when taken together and enacted within a practiced routine, the effects are astounding. You would never suspect that something as innocent-sounding as the glide, for instance, or the biddle move, would produce amazing effects, but that is why such sleights are so deceptive. These techniques can even fool other magicians. One named Jerry Andrus learned to handle cards without the benefit of previous publications. That is, he made stuff up as he went along. Some of his moves required the spectator to watch from a certain angle, and others required the magician to be seated at a table. When his book was published, the magical community scoffed that his moves were unworkable and too difficult for anyone to perform. In short, they believed he was scamming them. After some public performances he proved them wrong and won their respect.[4]

My point here is to impress upon you the complexity of card magic as it is studied and performed by the serious student of magic. One should realize that not only does such an immense multitude of sleights exist, but that many professional magicians (and swindlers) know many of these sleights—and most importantly, they know how to use them to achieve mysterious effects that might seem phenomenal or even paranormal to the uninitiated.

HIDING CARDS IN A STACK

Cards must at times be hidden from the audience for one reason or another. For instance, consider a trick where the magician deals out six cards, one of which will change from a having a blue back to having a red back. It's likely that red back was hidden in the stack all along, but the magician has gone to great pains to hide it from the viewer. Even when producing a seemingly impromptu fan or riffle through of the cards, the cardician is secretly hiding that card. Other sorts of gimmicked cards, like half-and-halfs, shiners, double-faced cards, or cards that are not supposed to be there (because supposedly you slipped it into your pocket earlier) may need to be hidden from audience view.

The magician must learn to deal out two cards as one, with one regular card concealing the gimmicked card underneath it. A practiced magi is so good at this that he can throw down the two cards on a table and they will land in perfect alignment. The magician can then flip over both cards as one, showing the previously hidden card.

There are literally hundreds of such sleights that an accomplished cardician can perform, and it's useless to go through all of them. The sleights are so many and varied that it's practically impossible for an onlooker to know which sleight is being employed, even when the onlooker is a fellow magician.

One sleight that is important to mention is the Elmsley Count. Variously known as Counting Four as Four or the Ghost Count, it is most often known by the name of its creator, Alex Elmsley. The Elmsley Count is often referred to as one of the most widely used "secret counts" and perhaps one of the most useful sleights employed in card magic. It is a lean base on which other "counts" and sleights can be built, and for that reason it is worth describing here. A "count" or "secret count" is a way in which a magician counts out cards. For instance, if I have four cards in my hand and want to show you four cards, I could merely go through each card one at a time, placing them on the table as I count out "One, two, three, four cards." But magicians often have an ulterior motive when counting cards. They may have five cards and need you to believe they have only four (in which case they might deal out two cards as one as described above). Or they may have a stack of three cards and need you to believe they have four cards in hand. The Elmsey Count may be used for this purpose.

The main purpose of the Elmsey Count is to count out four cards as cards without sharing one (although it can be used to count three as four also). Suppose I have a stack of four cards, one of which is gimmicked and therefore I must hide it until the climax of the trick. The Elmsey Count would be used to count out the *other* three cards as four (while the gimmicked card remains hidden beneath one of the other cards in the stack). I'm not going to go into the mechanics of how the count is accomplished, but suffice it to say that it relies on the principle of stacking cards, counting off two as one, and subtly deceiving the viewer as two cards are counted more than once to achieve a total of four.

Variations on the maneuver allow five or six cards to be counted as four, and it's easy to imagine some of the wonderful illusions that could be performed if that were done. Cards would seem to appear or disappear out of nowhere in the magician's capable hands.

A description of how the Elmsley Count is accomplished would take too long to describe here. (The truly interested can look up the method in a book on card magic.) What is important to keep in mind is that such an artful method exists such that when you see the performer doing even something as straightforward as counting cards, it is cause for suspicion.

Duplicate Cards

Some card tricks use duplicate cards. Consider the trick where a volunteer selects a card, rips off one corner and then burns the remainder. The magician then brings out a bowl of fruit, pulls out an orange, and slices it open to reveal the (restored!) remainder of the card inside. Of course, the torn corner fits exactly with the piece inside the orange. How is it done? One method is to prepare a *duplicate* card beforehand. Before the show, the magician ripped a corner off a card and hid the corner in his pocket and the rest inside an orange. At showtime the magician forces the same card on a volunteer, who rips off a corner. The remainder of the card is legitimately burned to a crisp. While attention is thus misdirected, the magician secretly switches the volunteer's torn corner with the corner he ripped off before the show started. Now all he needs to do is bring out the fruit bowl and slice open the orange.

It's a dead giveaway if the magician doesn't require the volunteer to sign the card. You see, if the volunteer had to sign the card (or otherwise provide "proof" it is his card) then obviously the trick would not work, because the duplicate card prepared before the show would not be signed. So that's one more thing to look for when watching a magic show—the extent to which the magician uses proofs. If a proof is not offered in a case like this, then you can expect a duplicate has been slipped in.

Oh yeah, how did he put the card in the orange? Find an orange with a stem on top, carefully pluck it off, and bore a hole straight down into the orange with an ice pick. Now roll up the card and insert it inside. Reattach the stem with a dab of glue, and *voila!*

* * * * *

Cards have been studied more than any other item used by the magician. A lot of tricks, sleights, and fakes have been devised. It's impossible to do anything here but barely mention just a few that have emerged from all that studious trickery. If you are truly interested in finding out more, there are a multitude of books devoted to the subject.

Choppers

Chop! Chop! Chop! Magicians love chopping off arms and legs, hands and fingers, and even heads! You know the routine. First they pull up an audience volunteer. She's giddy. He wheels out a guillotine. Her face turns ashen. The guillotine is big and wooden, with a steel blade. He punches the blade, and it resounds with a solid metallic clang. The assistant walks out with a cabbage. Lettuce would be okay too, but cabbage is better because with cabbage the magician can make cole slaw jokes. He places the cabbage into the guillotine and slams down the blade. It is sharp. It slices the cabbage clean in half. Now it's her turn.

The volunteer knows it's only a joke, right? She kneels down before the contraption. She inserts her head through the opening. He gives the blade one final check. And.... then ... *he slams it down.*

The woman is unharmed. Applause! She goes back to her seat with a half a cabbage.

I was fascinated by choppers as a child, because they seemed to defy very basic assumptions about the way the world works. How can physical matter pass through physical matter? Obviously it doesn't, but the apparatus seems so simple it's hard to tell where the gimmick is hiding. There are several different variations on the gimmick. In a typical chopper, the blade is encased in a wooden piece that the magician grabs hold of when he pushes down. The blade itself has a hole scooped out exactly where the person's neck rests. Why don't you see a big hole scooped out of the blade? Because a second blade covers it. This second blade will retract up into the wooden handle when it is pushed into the guillotine. The audience sees the two pieces of metal as one single blade. When the blade is pushed into the guillotine, it hits a ledge inside which pushes up the retractable blade into the wooden handle. The volunteer's neck becomes surrounded by the hole. (On wrist choppers there are two holes scooped out of the blade.)

Here's something to look for when watching a chopper routine: After the magician chops the cabbage (or carrot, or zucchini, or whatever), he has to flick a hidden switch on the guillotine. The switch makes the ledge jut out, so the fake blade will hit against it and retract. If you notice the magician casually touching the guillotine, wiping it with a handkerchief, or otherwise making an excuse to touch it, look more closely and you may see he's flicking the switch. It should only take a second, but you can usually catch him in the act of doing it.

Magicians have invented all sorts of kooky and scary variations on the chopper. Some actually show the hand (or head) falling into a basket after the chop. These are fake body parts, of course: the actual head or hand was never pushed through the opening. In these cases the magician will opt to use one of his own assistants, whom he can trust to keep the secret. There is also a wrist penetration that uses a slim knife blade to do the job. In this case, the magician uses his thumb to pull a lever, which retracts part of the blade into the knife's thin handle. Chances are the blood-frenzied magician won't let you inspect this contraption, since the lever is out in the open, merely facing away from the audience.

Coins

Coins are difficult props to master, but some magicians have become drawn to them and learn to manipulate coins through their fingers with enviable ease. Coins are nice props to work with, as they can be borrowed from the audience so as to ensure in everyone's mind that they are ungimmicked. Because coins are small, they can be easily palmed in innumerable ways, as well as hidden within the performer's clothing, all of which allows for a greater variety of effects that can be done with them.

There are gimmicked fake coins, like double-headed coins, and coin shells. A shell is a wafer-thin casing that looks like a coin but is hollow and can slip over a real coin to turn the two coins into one. Coin shells, unlike real coins, are magnetic, which allows the magician to secretly dispose of them by hiding a magnet in his hand and letting the shell cling to it. Coin shells are commonly used in such tricks as Scotch and Soda, where the magician places two coins in a spectator's hand. The spectator then opens the hand to reveal that one of the coins is missing and has been replaced by an entirely different coin.

There are as many coin sleights as there are card sleights. It is as pointless to list them, because simply reading about them won't add any great knowledge to your understanding of magic. Reading about these sleights, as with many of the gimmicks mentioned in this book, may seem awfully revealing, until you go to a magic show and realize you've been fooled *anyway*.

Cups and Balls

Three cups. Three balls. Or maybe there's four balls. Now there's five. Ten? Eighteen? Where'd that lemon come from? Cups and Balls is the quintessential magic trick. Maybe not from the audience's point of view, but certainly magicians know and view this as one of the oldest illusions, very well known and yet difficult to perfect. The props are simple and ungimmicked. The illusion requires that the magician create not only a combination of magical moves, but interesting patter, a rising tension in the routine, and a series of effects that are related yet not repetitive. The Cups and Balls dates back at least to ancient Egypt. An illustration from 2500 B.C.E. on the wall of an age-old burial chamber shows a magician performing the trick (sideways of course, like all those old Egyptian depictions). In modern times, the significance of Cups and Balls is twofold: (1) it spawned the crooked game called three-card monte, which fleeces money out of people to this day in major cities around the world, and (2) it was the trick that launched Penn & Teller's ascent into fame and fortune. As legend has it, the pre-fame Penn & Teller were sitting around in a diner (they were mainly performing on sidewalks and at carnivals at the time) and Teller was playing around with his Cups and Balls routine using clear drinking glasses and wadded-up paper napkins. This is a silly thing to do, because the cups are necessary to conceal the sleight of hand that puts balls into and out of the cups. With clear drinking glasses, all the sleights are visible for anyone to see. But Penn was watching closely, and he noticed an amazing thing: it didn't matter. Even with clear glasses revealing all the moves, the trick was still startling and surprising, and tricky. "Penn got very excited by the intellectual concept of doing something where the eye could see the moves, but the mind could not comprehend."[5] They worked up a "razzle-dazzle" routine and soon were performing on actual stages, not just sidewalk squares. The intention was to demonstrate, in a light-hearted manner, their failure at exposing the trick. It is a point that bears repeating: a well-performed illusion can withstand a knowledgeable audience.

Hats

Hats are not as omnipresent as they used to be—what was once a common, everyday object now looks phony, and so some of the original value in it is lost. Same thing with cane and tails. All of this formal attire has gone by the wayside, except perhaps on soap opera weddings. In fact top hat and tails or a cane are now recognized as magician's props. This will generally work against the magician, as the preconceived notion is that a magician's prop is gimmicked. Still, if the prop really is ungimmicked and can be passed around for inspection, there is no need to shun the most respected props of the magical trade.

Paddles

One time I was watching a magician performing the well-known paddle routine. In this routine, the magician shows a paddle with some polka dots on it. He then flips it over to show a different number of dots on the other side. He then flips it over again, and there is a completely different number of dots on the first side. More flips, and the audience becomes increasingly confused as dots seem to multiply and divide, give birth to twins and triplets and quadruplets and quintuplets, and then disappear with a blink of an eye. My neighbor in the theater whispered to me, "I can see how he does it. You see how the dots are raised above the surface of the paddle? He's sticking them onto the paddle." Now, we were sitting in just about the last row of the theater, and ignoring the fact that this guy seemed as blind as an umpire bat, it's unlikely he could have seen dots raised above the surface of the paddle, I would think. Some paddles do use magnets, and some have sliding parts or flaps that flip over, or the magician can push the stick in or out to change the color of dots on the paddle. But generally the paddle tricks are done with pure sleight of hand. Specifically magicians use the "paddle move," which is to flip the paddle over with the wrist and fingers simultaneously. What looks like one flip is really two, and so the audience ends up seeing only one side of the paddle, even when they think they've seen both sides.

You can try this yourself. Hold the end of a pen in your fingers so the logo is facing away from you. Now twist your wrist over to show the logo side of the pen. You have now legitimately shown both sides. No trick there. Start over. Again hold the pen in your fingers with the logo away from you. This time, twist your wrist over *while simultaneously rolling the pen in your fingertips*. If you time it right, it will appear as if you merely flipped over the pen, when really you flipped it and rolled it at the same time, and so it seems the pen has no logo.

If you were to now reveal the logo to the audience, they would be amazed, right? Somehow you have magically made a logo appear on the pen! Obviously a simple trick like this won't fool anybody. A true magician will employ all his methods of storytelling and planned routine to produce a convincing effect. Additionally, the trick becomes more impressive when two or more paddles are used in combination. Each paddle has a differing number of spots on each side, making for a variety of combinations with which to fool the audience.

So most likely extra stick-on dots are not being used. But even if they are, keep in mind it's not enough to explain the trick by such a pat answer. If I gave *you* a paddle and a pail of stick-on dots, could *you* fool an entire audience with them? Probably not.

Rope

Rope tricks are hard to sell in a magic store, because with rope tricks you are selling purely an idea. After all, the only props or equipment you need for rope tricks are a piece of clothesline and scissors. Typically a magician will perform a rope "routine" consisting of several rope tricks linked together. First he pulls out a rope and scissors. He cuts the rope in half, but it magically restores itself whole again. So the magician attempts to cut it in half again, this time perhaps slicing through a few thickness of the folded rope. He wraps the rope around his hand—and when he unwraps it, it has once again become whole. There may also be some "knot" magic. For instance after the rope is cut in half, the two halves are knotted together. But that looks too messy, so the magician slides the knot off the end of the rope and throws it away. The rope is one solid piece again.

These illusions are all intriguing and puzzling. How are they accomplished? There are a few basic principles that are the foundations for most rope tricks. Here we list the *modus operandi* underlying most rope illusions:

TWO ROPE X

The audience sees two ropes held in the hand. In actuality, the two ropes are there, but they are not hanging down as the audience supposes. The ropes are crossed in the middle. One rope has its ends sticking out the top of the hand, while the other rope has its ends sticking out the bottom of the hand. From the back it resembles a rope X. This technique is used in a very entertaining effect where three different-sized ropes all become the same length.

FAKE ROPE LOOP

This is sort of the opposite of the Two Rope X. In this deceit, the audience sees only one rope looped in the hand, while in reality there are two ropes. The "real" rope, the one that has been shown to the audience, has its two ends sticking out the bottom of the fist, while its top curve is hidden inside the fist. A short length of a second rope is sticking out the top of the fist, giving the appearance that it is the curve of the "real" rope. The magician will snip this short curl of rope with scissors, giving the impression that the "real" rope has been cut in two.

Penn & Teller used the Fake Rope Loop ruse when they appeared on "Saturday Night Live" on in 1986, but they performed the trick with their own sinister twist of blood and guts.[6] Instead of using a rope, they cut and restored a *snake*. It was a California king snake, to be precise, a nonpoisonous yellow and black reptile. After procuring the snake, Penn & Teller headed over to the butcher shop where they bought sausage of approximately the

Fig. 33. The audience sees two ropes hanging straight down.

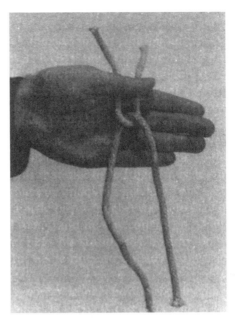

Fig. 34. It is two ropes, but they're not hanging straight down at all. There are many applications for this trick.

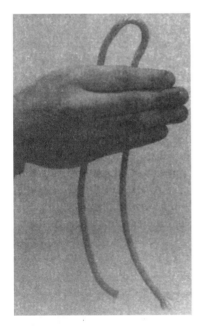

Fig. 35. The audience sees one continuous loop of rope.

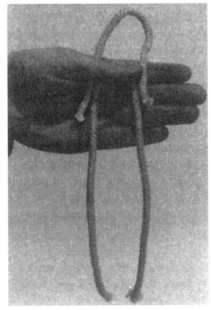

Fig. 36. It's really two ropes. The magician will cut the top loop in half, sparing the main rope from rope disaster.

same diameter as the snake's center. This sausage would be used for the fake loop. Before the show, they dyed and decorated the sausage with colored paper strips to give it the markings of the snake. To pump up the gross factor, they filled squirt rings with stage blood, and shoved the rings into the ends of the sausage section. When performing the illusion on stage for "Saturday Night Live," they brought out the snake, played with it awhile to show how real it really was, and then gently folded up its middle into one of Penn's big hands. The folded piece of snake could be seen sticking out of the top of the hand, looking a lot like a snake and not at all like a paper-stripped sausage. An audience member was commandeered to cut the "snake" in half with a pair of poultry shears (really cutting the fake loop of sausage). After a gasp of unbelieving panic from the audience, the squeeze bulbs were squeezed, forcing out a trickle of blood, and then again more forcefully as if a blood vessel has been severed. Penn & Teller then used the shears to remove the pieces of sausage and fling them into the audience. Anyone who bothered to pick up the discarded bloody pieces would find out what they really were, but no matter—the chance of discovery was a small price to pay for the larger effect achieved. Besides, it is necessary to "play" like this to build up the length of the time the snake remains cut in half. By doing things like squirting blood and flinging bloody snake bits into the audience, the viewer is diverted away from the snake, and from the fact that the snake has not really been severed at all. The final act was to show the snake fully whole again, which is a simple matter of waving some magic hands over the snake and showing it to be wriggling freely and alive.

FAKE KNOTS

Many rope tricks use knots for various reasons. For instance, a magician ties a rope around a volunteer's neck, and has additional audience volunteers yank on the ends. The ropes seem to jerk through the neck, but the ropes remain knotted. Magic books are filled with all kinds of tricks like these. The knot might be a slip knot (a genuine knot where one of the rope ends is pushed back into the knot, thus undoing itself). Or it might be not a knot at all, merely appearing to be one. In rope-through-neck, the rope is arranged so that when it is tugged the tugging will create a knot *in front* of the person's neck. The volunteers unknowingly tie the knot themselves!

THREAD

Thread is used to help make fake not-knots. The magician threads some wooden blocks and metal rings on two ropes. It's all solid. He knots them on there, and knots them again for extra protection. Then a volunteer gives it a tug. The rings and blocks penetrate the ropes and fall noisily to the floor, the knot still knotted. This trick (and many variations on it), is done with a slip of thread. The ropes appear to be threaded straight through the blocks, but really they only go halfway through and loop back to meet their ends. The two rope loops are tied together inside the center block with a thread. When the ropes are tugged, the thread breaks, and the blocks and rings fall through the hole between the two ropes. Because of the way the rope is folded, one knot will always disappear, so the magician will generally double- or triple-knot the rope. Then, when the ends are pulled, even though one knot slips out, the rest tighten into one gigantic and impressive knot. The audience is left wondering how the solid rings and blocks got through it.

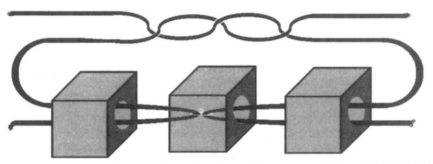

Fig. 37. A hidden thread can work wonders. Here, the audience believes that the blocks are solidly knotted in place on two ropes that run straight through. When the ropes are tugged, the thread will break, and the blocks will fall to the floor.

A Snip Off the End

Sometimes you see a magician cut a rope and tie the two loose ends together. It looks messy having the knot there, so he cuts *that* off, and now the rope is whole again. This effect uses some of the tricks we've already mentioned, but it also uses one more: he's not really cutting the center of the rope, but one of the ends. A typical routine has the magician presenting a rope. A volunteer points out the *exact center,* and the magician ties a knot there. But the way the rope loops on itself is confusing, and the magician cuts the loop of rope right above the knot. It seems he has sliced it in half, but he has merely snipped off a tiny segment from the end.

Those are some of the commoner ruses employed in rope magic. I encourage you to find some rope and give them a try. When you know about them you can usually detect which methods the magician is using on stage. If you don't know about them, the effects can seem miraculous. At a restaurant, a walk-around magician approached my family and asked if we would like to see some tricks. Yes! "Here is a length of rope—" Almost immediately he dropped his "extra" piece of rope for the Fake Rope Lope rose (described above). "Hee hee," he giggled nervously, scooping up the piece off the floor, "Sorry, I just bumbled the trick. I'll show you another one." I think he could have handled his mistake better. Usually spectators don't understood the significance of the extra piece of rope. If he hadn't been so nervous he might've said, "Tsk, where'd that come from?" and shoved it back in his pocket (really retaining it in his hand). I don't think the trick would have suffered because of it.

Along with these ruses are a few standard "proofs." You'll recall that a magician uses a proof in order to lead you astray. Proofs are used to prove to the audience that the rope really has been cut into two, or that it really has been restored whole again—but, as always in magic, appearances are deceiving. Here are the proofs of rope magic, and how to defeat them:

- *The proof of separate ropes.* The magician shows you two (or three) ropes. Perhaps they were formerly one rope that has just been cut in half. The proof is that you can see two ropes hanging down from the magician's hand. The reality is, it's probably a Two Rope X being employed. Usually you can see this if you look carefully. After all, the magician has to make the moves look natural, so he doesn't have a lot of time to straighten out the ropes in his hand and make them look like they're hanging straight down.

- *The proof of rope sturdiness.* When a thread is being used, the magician will want to prove that a thread is *not* being used. For instance, consider the case where two ropes are joined in the middle by a thread. To prove rope sturdiness, the magician holds the middle in his fist, and jerks on one end, looking at the end of the rope to draw attention towards the solid tugs he applies to the rope. Sure looks sturdy enough! The proof is false because it doesn't prove anything. The threaded joint between the two ropes is inside the magician's fist, so that jerking on one end of the ropes will not affect the thread at all. If a magician tries to prove rope sturdiness by tugging on a rope, look carefully to see how far down the length of the rope the tug will be felt.

- *The proof of false wholeness.* After cutting a rope in half and restoring it, the magician must prove that the rope is indeed whole again. This is done by simply holding the rope aloft and letting the audience see how big it is, as opposed to when it was previously cut up into two smaller segments. This seems straightforward enough, but there's a problem with it. Even though the rope looks big and looks restored, you don't know for sure that it's been restored to it's full pre-cut length. In fact, the rope is very likely a little bit shorter now than it was before the cutting began. The problem is that you have no basis of comparison. You can't compare the current rope with the pre-cut rope of five minutes ago. The proof of wholeness is a false proof that you cannot rebuke, only suspect.

Those are some of the secret principles underlying most rope tricks. But, as you can plainly see, to go from those mere tricks to a full-fledged stage routine takes a lot of effort, planning, timing, storytelling, and all the other things talked about in this book. For all of those "extras" added to the rope and scissors, most rope tricks end up looking pretty much the same from the audience's point of view. If you are a magician you would be advised to limit your use of rope tricks to just one or two in your show. Even better, don't use a rope at all. Instead, cut and restore a brightly colored scarf, a California king snake, or the head of a goose.

Silks

"Silks" or "scarves" is the magician's fancy way of saying "handkerchief." Particularly pedantic magicians may say "foulard," but not in polite conversation, in which case you have my permission to bop them one. Silks are colorful and garish and nice props to work with because they can be seen easily from afar and are quite versatile in their uses. Silks can be used to cover other objects, or they can be rolled out and used in ropelike tricks. Another handy property of silks is their squishiness. You can squish down a silk into a small ball, to be hidden easily somewhere on the magician's person. Some silks are gimmicked, like the ones with a hidden pocket in them. Some can be pulled through themselves to change their color.

Screens and Scenery

Screens and scenery are always used to hide things from the audience's view. The hiding may be for top secret magician's reasons, or it may be simply to reduce the clutter of the stage. In Houdini's day, a large screen was placed in front of the performer while he worked his escapes. Suspense mounted as the audience wondered what was going on behind the screen. Today's audiences demand visual illusions, but screens may still be used for other purposes. If the show is set up on a small platform in a gymnasium there may not be a backstage area to keep props, and so an ornamental screen serves as an on-stage storage closet.

Of course screens also serve their own impish purposes in tricks that rely on keeping something out of view from the audience. For example, sometimes Houdini would perform escapes by hiding tools inside the screen or curtain that shielded him from the audience. He would be stripped naked, frisked, searched, his body examined thoroughly for lock picks and other tools. Then he would set out the curtain or screen in front of the box from which he was to escape. While setting up the curtain, he would rip open the hem of the curtain and pull out the tools hidden therein.

One must always be on the lookout for times when the magician reaches behind a screen to pull out something. For example, there is the illusion called Confetti to Candy. The magician shows a glass full of confetti, which he pours out in a stream to prove it is genuine confetti. He dips the glass into a box of confetti to refill the glass, and then puts the glass behind a screen for a moment. As he's talking, he happens to reach into the glass and pull out a large pinch of confetti that he sprinkles around. He then pulls the screen away to reveal the confetti is gone and the glass is now filled with candy.

The effect is accomplished using two gimmicks: an envelope of confetti taped to the backside of the screen and a fake confetti shell that fits inside the glass and gives the appearance of a glassful of confetti. Before the show, the magician fills the confetti shell with pieces of candy, hides the filled shell inside the box of confetti, and attaches the envelope of confetti to the back of the screen.

At the start of the trick, the magician shows the empty glass to the audience and proceeds to dip it in the box to fill it with (real) confetti. He pours it out as proof that the confetti is real. Then the magician dips the glass in for a second time. This time, instead of scooping up confetti, the magician scoops up the confetti shell inside the glass. The magician shows the glassful of "confetti" and then places it behind the screen. This is where the rigged screen comes into play. The magician wants to prove that the glass is full of confetti, so he seems to reach into the glass and pulls out a wad of confetti that he sprinkles all around. Of course there is no confetti in the glass—he really reaches into the hidden envelope and takes the confetti from there. When the screen is lifted away, the magician is also lifting off the confetti shell with the same swoop of the hand. Left on the table is the glass full of candy.

CREATE MAGIC!—THE YARN BOX

Here's another example of an illusion that relies on a hidden device in a screen. You have three small balls of yarn colored red, white, and blue (or use whatever colors adorn your country's flag), in a box about the size of a children's shoe box. Give the shoe box to one audience member to inspect. Hand out the three yarn balls to three different audience members, and have them unravel the balls in their lap to prove they are made of genuine yarn. While this is ongoing, you do another short magic trick to pass the time.* When both you and they are done (and the yarn and box has been proven to be genuine), have them each bunch up their yarn and toss it into the box you hold in your outstretched hand. There is much laughter and comedy, because it's difficult to toss bunched-up yarn with any accuracy. Now the yarn is in the box, but the lid is missing. You put the box on the table and search around until you find the lid (additional comedy as you accuse the audience member who inspected the box of stealing the lid). Perhaps now you go into the audience in search of the lid, and while out there, manage to find coins and lemons and all sorts of things in the ears and noses of children. Finally the lid is found and placed on the box. Some words of hocus pocus are uttered, and then the box is opened to reveal the three yarns have woven together to become your national flag.

The trick is simple, and relies on humor and build-up to create an entertaining effect. The shoe box should be as close to square-sided as possible. By that I mean the sides of the box should be close to being a square. On the table there needs to be a three-sided screen that you can put the box behind for a moment. On the back of the screen, away from the audience, is a hidden ledge that contains the flag. The screen needs to be on the table from the very beginning of the act, so as not to provoke curiosity. The other piece that needs to be set up beforehand is a basket or box, open at the top, that hangs off the back of the table, away from the audience. The basket or box should be hidden by the table cloth.

After collecting the unrolled yarn in the box, walk back to the table and suddenly look up and announce that the lid is missing. Point to someone in the audience: "Did you see the lid?" Point to someone else. "Did *you* see it?" While this is going on, you quietly and unobservedly dump the yarn out of the box, into the open basket behind the table. All it takes is a quick roll of the wrist. The box is held in your hand, hidden behind the screen. The action won't be noticed because you seem to be preoccupied with the missing lid. This requires a degree of acting on your part to make it seem as though it suddenly occurred to you that the lid is missing. You are distracted. You put down the box on the table, directly behind the screen. "Where is that thing?" you mutter, as you begin looking around the stuff on the table. Pull the screen towards you, so that the flag drops off the shelf and into the box. The audience things you're trying to see what's on the other side of the screen. Put the screen aside on another table or on the floor, to get it out of the way. You can at this point go into the audience for some *shtick*. Every once in a while turn back towards the table and say, "Good, *that's* still there," referring to the box. Finally the lid turns up someplace, you put it on the box, and finish up the trick. Say your hocus pocus words before revealing that the yarn has transformed.

While the deception relies on some crude maneuvers, the effect is a good one. The combination of good acting and misdirection will take all eyes off the box at the proper time. A square-sided box will make it more difficult to detect the box rotating in your hand. It also helps if the box is decorated a single solid color on all its sides. If done right, it will look as though you've merely walked back to the table when suddenly it occurs to you the lid is missing. You pull back the screen to get a better look at your surroundings, and then go off into the audience in search of the lid. (Make sure the audience is lower-down than the box so that they can not see into it.) By the time you're out in the audience, the trick is done and you have nothing to worry about.

---

*If you're smart, you might hand out the yarn balls to audience members who have "bad angles" for your next trick. In other words, if there's a trick you want to perform that might have some bad angles to it (sitting in a particular seat in the audience will give away the trick) then hand out the yarn balls to those people. They will be somewhat preoccupied with their balls, and less able to make use of their bad angles.

Sponges

Sponges are common props, because they are lightweight, colorful, can be squished down small and spring back into shape again when released. Sponge balls are most commonly used for sleight-of-hand work, but there are all manner of sponge objects, such as sponge rabbits, available to the performer. One magic company is even marketing rubber cockroaches they say can be used exactly like sponge balls. The most important thing to remember about sponge and spongelike objects when used in a magic show is the squishiness factor. Two sponge balls can be squished together to appear as one. That's the main usefulness of sponge, and that's one of the main reasons sponge balls are used—to allow for sleight of hand that relies on squishing two balls together to give the appearance of only one.

Tables

The main purpose of the magician's table is to hold the small props that will be used during the show. But there are other, more nefarious purposes to which a table can be put. The tables of nineteenth-century magicians were constructed with spring-loaded trap doors in which objects could be made to disappear. Many other tricks are widespread:

SERVANTES

The *servante* is a ledge hidden behind a table. Servantes can also be a bag or box hidden behind the table, but usually they are thought of as a ledge. Servantes are not used in extreme close-up magic (because the audience seated around the table would notice the ledge!) But they are used when the audience is seated down below in an audience. Servantes are good to use at children's birthday parties where the children are sitting on the floor in front of the table. Their low angle makes it impossible for them to accidentally notice the servante hidden behind. The servante is used as a storage space. The magician may make something disappear by casually brushing it off the table onto the servante. Or things can be made to appear by taking them off the servante and placing them on the table. One example of a servante is in the yarn box trick just discussed.

BLACK ART TABLES

Black art, you'll recall, is based on the fact that matte black surfaces blend together because there are no depth clues—shadows, reflections, highlights, or visible edges—by which to identify outlines. A black art table is a small stand with a black velvet table cloth. The table cloth may be decorated with ribbon or embroidery, but only in such a way as to enhance the illusion. The black art table will have one or more holes in the top of it. The holes cannot be easily seen because they are lined with black velvet pockets. Generally a black art table would be used to make items disappear. For instance, the magician puts a hat brim-down on the table. He lifts it slightly as he rolls a ball underneath the hat. When he lifts the hat, the ball is gone. He might then produce a duplicate ball from his pocket or from across the stage, but the original ball has merely rolled into the black well of the table. Black art tables are used rarely nowadays, but if you're a budding magician looking for a craft project to do, you might find it enjoyable to build one yourself.

THE SCOOP BEHIND

Another way to gimmick a table is to hang an item on a hook behind it. This is often how a rabbit is produced from a hat: the rabbit starts out in a small satchel hanging down from the back of the table. Of course, the table has a table cloth on it to conceal its hidden bunny parcel. The magician shows the empty hat, and then subtly swoops it down and scoops up the rabbit-bag into the hat, from where he can then produce it.* This swoop/scoop requires a great deal of practice and skill to get right, and the magician must call upon every ounce of misdirection ability that he can muster to achieve it. At the moment of scooping, the magician might be in the middle of telling a joke, pointing to a child in the audience, and asking the child if she would like to see a rabbit. All eyes must be off the magician, the table, the hat, and the scoop.

THE UNDERSIDE

The table underside is probably the most frequently used component of the table, especially when the magician performs seated down in a dinner table setting, with family or friends sitting around the table with him. Perhaps the magician is making coins appear and multiply under drinking cups. You can bet that some of those coins were previously attached to the underside of the table with a daub of wax.

THE LAP

Another common use for the table is to hide things in the lap. Again, one must be sitting around the table, preferably one with a tablecloth so as to obscure the lap and the things it contains. A magician might go through an entire forty-five-minute routine with a grapefruit hidden in his lap, all so that at the end of the routine he can make a grapefruit appear under his hat.

---

*Look to see when in the show the trick is performed. Chances are the rabbit will be produced close to the start of the act so the rabbit doesn't freak out or suffocate in the dark bag. The magician will probably offer an explanation for doing this trick first, such as that he wants to start out with the "traditional rabbit trick" to "prove to you" he's a magician. The explanation is humorous, but it's bunk. The real reason the trick is done first is because the gimmick of the trick—a bunny in a bag—depends on it.

Thimbles, Tubes, Wallets

Thimbles are used by some sleight-of-hand artists the way other artists use cards, coins, or billiard balls. Thimbles are the normal kind of thimbles used in sewing. A skilled manipulator can make them appear and disappear on his fingers in startling ways. It's unheard of (as far as I know) for thimbles to be gimmicked, so if some magician is impressing you with his thimble magic, you can bet that a lot of fancy sleightwork is going on to make the magic happen.

Tubes were introduced earlier in the section on optical illusions. Tubes can be used to make items appear or disappear owing to their special nature. The magician can "prove" that a tube is empty without the audience getting a good look inside it. And the magician can use the cone-in-tube gimmick (see chapter 3) to provide a secret hiding place for streamers, silks, or flowers. The same illusion works with a rectangular tube with a diagonally slanting false bottom inside (see figure 38). The modern mind is so attuned to the geometry of boxes and perspective effects that it perceives the sloping false bottom as the flat bottom of the box. If the box is constructed properly it will be impossible to detect it, even if you know it's there.

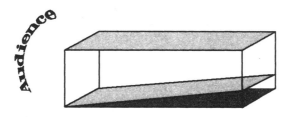

Fig. 38. An illusion of perspective creates a hiding place. The audience thinks they are seeing clear through an empty box. They don't realize that the box floor slants up. Scarves and silks can be concealed underneath.

Anytime you see a magician pull out a wallet, billfold, purse, or pocketbook in a magic act, you should be immediately on your guard. That wallet, billfold, or business card carrying case is almost certainly gimmicked, rigged in some way, so that it's less than genuine. If you want to be antagonistic you could ask the magician if you may inspect the wallet. Chances are you won't be allowed to do so. Or, if you don't want to embarrass the guy, how about saying, "Nice wallet. Is it Gucci?—or Himber?" Himber is a kind of gimmicked wallet that magicians have been using for decades. Wink at him to let him know you won't reveal the trick to the others. Con artists on the street use rigged wallets in some of their ploys, so it's helpful to be wary of this.

Rummaging Around

How are you enjoying the garage sale so far? We've picked through the big trunk of magic stuff and looked at the most common props. There are still some items remaining however, weird-looking things, many of which don't look very magical at all. Actually, they look like stuff you'd buy at a hardware store. Let's examine these secret gimmicks, utilities, and tools of magic . . .

Now we get to the seamy underworld of props. The props that you are not supposed to know about. These are items that are essential in any magician's bag of tricks, but you never get to see them because they're the secret that makes the trick work. It's important that you get a feel for all the rigging and connivery that goes on behind your back.

Whoops . . . make that right in front of your face.

There's a schism among magicians, those who like gimmicks, and those who don't. All but the most diehard purists will resort to using gimmicks at least on occasion. That is, all but the most skilled purists. The purists like to use pure sleight of hand. They believe that using hidden tools and gimmicks is not truly practicing the art of magic. They don't like the fact that other magicians break the trust of the audience by seemingly doing a trick via sleight of hand (skill) while really resorting to dime store gimmicks. Personally, I think they're jealous. They're jealous that they've spent all their lives practicing their sleight of hand, and here comes a newbie who can duplicate the same effect in a few minutes because they bought something from a magic store. They're jealous—but rightfully so—because the availability of such gimmicks tends to degrade the art of magic. Letting anyone perform certain tricks allows lesser-quality magicians to appear before the public. If a magician isn't well practiced, it makes all those skilled magicians look bad.

Another concern that professional magicians have is that they will spend all their lives perfecting a "move" or a "sleight" and then hear someone in the audience whispering, "I know how he did it . . . There's a trick you can buy at the magic store . . ." The magician is then caught in a bind. He knows he worked long and hard perfecting his skill. But to the audience, it's all the same. For this reason many magicians are appalled that secret magic items can be openly sold to the public in toy and department stores. (Other magicians reply that fledgling magicians have to start somehow, and that the open accessibility of such props helps to keep magic alive.) The debate rages on. While they debate, let's take the opportunity to investigate some of the top secret gimmicks, tools, and hidden utilities that make the tricks work. Here we shall examine:

- Hooks and holders
- Wax

- Roughing fluid
- Takeup reels
- Chemicals
- Key benders
- Hidden pockets
- Thumb tips

HOOKS AND HOLDERS

Different kinds of hooks and holders are used to secretly hang items out of view. For instance, there are all sorts of wire card holders and ball holders that can be constructed or bought to hang items under a sports jacket or tuxedo jacket. Often these are called droppers, because they drop the item into the magician's hand like a vending machine dispensing candy. There are also holders for small animals (for example, dove harnesses) to hold them still under the clothing or behind a table until they need to be produced.

A hook can be as meager as an paper clip formed into an S shape. One hook of the S is hooked onto a jacket that's been "carelessly" thrown over the back of a chair, while the free hook is used to hang a bouquet of flowers or a bag of streamers out of sight. A coin or card can be gimmicked with a hook that attaches to the back of the magician's pants, thus hiding it until it needs to be produced.

There are also products available such as the Michael Ammar Coin Clip. Michael Ammar is prominent in magician's circles as an accomplished performer as well as teacher of magic. He is known to have consulted for David Copperfield and Siegfried and Roy others. Ammar has lent his famous name to many products that magicians use, such as the Michael Ammar Invisible Thread and Michael Ammar Professional Topit Pattern. Judging by the photograph in the catalog, the coin clip looks like a metal bracket in a [shape, about an inch high. I'd like to quote from what it says in one magic catalog about the coin clip, to give you an idea about how these different gadgets, gimmicks, techniques, and methods we've been looking at all work together to make a trick:

> The clip is used to hold coins together silently so that they can be disposed of as a unit. Once in the Clip, the coins can be lapped, tossed into the Topit, dropped into a pocket, or sleeved. It can also be used with a Pull or to retrieve coins. It's a secret, small, light-weight, easy-to-load coin holding device that is easy to palm. It can hold 2 to 6 coins! Complete with a beautifully detailed instruction booklet. Specify dollar or half-dollar size. $10.00[7]

Right here we have mention of five different gimmicks and methods used to dispose of items (lap, topit, pocket, sleeve, and pull) and even that does not begin to cover all the options a magician has available. Most magicians will be good to greatly competent in most if not all of these methods, and will still have a few more techniques waiting in line. You can see why it's so hard to figure out what a magician is doing—they have so many options open to them at any one time. Even as you're looking for a topit or pull, they can be pulling a fast one with one of the many other methods at their disposal. Little gadgets like this clip and other hooks and holders only make the job of catching them in their trickery all the more difficult.

WAX

Wax is a sticky substance that magicians use to stick cards to ceilings as well as for more utilitarian purposes, such as temporarily attaching coins or cards to the undersides of tables. Wax is also used in animation effects. Magicians have trouble handling the thin, almost invisible thread they use to animate objects, so they will attach wax to the ends so they can work with it easier. One cute trick is to hide a dab of wax under a coat button. Before commencing a trick, the magician unbuttons and removes his coat, grabbing the wax as he does the unbuttoning. Now it is ready for whatever the trick calls for, such as secretly sticking a selected card under the table.

ROUGHING FLUID

Roughing fluid is a top secret magician's tool. It is used in card tricks to make the impossible happen. Basically it is a clear liquid that is applied to cards, causing them to stick together temporarily. The magician can separate the cards by sliding them apart, but if they are stacked up again, once again they will stick. This may sound rather benign and a little unusual, but magicians can make many impossible miracles occur by secretly using roughing fluid.

TAKEUP REELS

This gimmick is a small, spring-loaded device with a reel of thread or string inside. The magician uses it to dispense lengths of thread as needed, or reel it back in when done. Takeup reels are used when floating objects with invisible thread. When loaded with stronger string they may be used like a pull, to quickly yank an object into the performer's jacket.

CHEMICALS

In certain rare cases a gimmick may be a particular chemical that has some special property. You can't be expected to know about the chemical or its properties, but it does point out the modern-day magician's links to the wizards of the past, like Merlin and other sorcerers who were as much alchemists and chemists as they were magicians. For example, paper or string may be chemically treated to burn quickly in a fiery flash. Or they could be treated to burn slowly or not at all. Do-it-yourselfers out there can try this experiment: Find a nice big ball of cotton string. Now go to a safe place, take a length of the string and try burning it. It should burn nicely. Next take some string and soak it in salt water for a little while, then take it out and let it dry. The string will still look pretty normal, although perhaps a bit stiff. Now try burning it. Fun with household chemicals!

Chemicals are commonly used to fake out the audience. The conjurer shows a glass of water and says he will change it to wine. He pours the water from one glass to another, and suddenly it does turn to wine. (What the audience doesn't realize is that some of the water wasn't water at all; it was another clear, colorless liquid that, when combined with something else, produces a winelike liquid. One manuscript, *Valuable Tricks Exposed (Things You'd Like to Know),* informs us that phenolphthalein, ammonia, and water can be combined to produce a red liquid resembling wine. Another version uses diluted unsweetened grape juice, which the magician pours from a wine bottle, of course. When the magician then pours the glass of "wine" into a second glass, it changes to "liquid mint" due to the few drops of ammonia in the glass. To change it back, he pours it into another glass with a milliliter or two of white vinegar. It works because grape juice is an "indicator," like litmus paper, turning red in an acid chemical (vinegar is diluted acetic acid) and green in a base chemical (like ammonia).[8]

What I've described here is very straightforward chemical trick and not particularly engaging. Magicians generally won't do something as simple as pour liquid from one container to another. They'll use the gimmick, but they'll use it in a more complicated way. For instance, they might tell an amusing story about Prince Charming going door to door, trying to fit the glass slipper onto Cinderella's foot. The glass slipper is represented by a glass of "water," and the houses are represented by paper tubes. The conjurer places the glass into Cinderella's house (the tube), but when it emerges it has changed color, representing the blood of the big-footed woman who could not squeeze into the dainty shoe. The storyline supports further changes from red to purple to clear once again.

Tricks with chemicals prove the point that the magician has to be exceedingly careful about how he presents the illusion, paying attention to such details as storyline and logical motivations to involve the audience in the illusion. Otherwise the audience will just assume it's a chemical trick. In fact, one magic catalog describes a trick called P.O.W.E.R. where the water turns from clear to black and back again at the magician's command. The catalog describes it like this: "All visual signs of *chemistry* have been eliminated. It looks like real Magic! P.O.W.E.R. is self-contained. Easy to do; resets in 5 minutes. Completely safe chemicals."[9] Want it? Twenty-five bucks.

Key Benders

Key benders are an important topic to talk about, because they are gimmicks used by fake psychics to scam people. Some psychics prove their psychic powers by causing keys to bend in their hands. As with any magic trick, there are several ways this is done, one of which is called the Bongo Bender. It's a small tube that is concealed in the hand. The psychic places the key into it, and it puts a bend in the key. The device can then be nonchalantly dropped into the pocket. Another gimmick is called the Key Warper. Both of these are extremely inexpensive and can be purchased by anyone who wants to go around bending keys.

Key bending (and spoon bending) are magnificent examples of how a gimmick alone does not make a trick. To really create a sense of magical awe in the spectator, it's necessary for the magician to have good sleight skills and misdirection ability, so the audience will believe they have kept their eyes on the key at all times (even when they have not). Furthermore, there are plenty of nongimmick ways of bending keys, and the psychics are well versed in all of them. They're hard to catch because they switch methods depending on the situation. They might come to the show with a variety of common keys, all bent. Let's face it, most keys look pretty much alike, so it's not too hard to switch keys without anyone noticing. The psychic scouts out the audience's keys beforehand. He tries to solicit keys that match those he has brought with him to the show. A variety of subterfuges, misdirections, and sleights are used to substitute the volunteer's key with the duplicate bent key, which is revealed on stage.

Incidentally, spoon bending is an even easier feat, since spoons can be easily bent with one hand. It is generally a matter of showing the straight spoon, misdirecting the audience while secretly bending the spoon, and then revealing the bent spoon. More complicated versions of the trick use a duplicate spoon that was twisted before the show and substituted in. The psychic might also prepare a spoon beforehand by bending it back and forth until it's almost at the breaking point. At showtime, the psychic needs only to apply slight pressure to break it in two.

You might ask how a key or spoon can be made to bend *visually* in the psychic's hand. It's due in part to time misdirection. The psychic bends the object *without telling the audience she has done so*. The audience doesn't realize the key is bent, and they assume it is straight. They don't realize she is hiding the bent portion in her hand. The psychic then focuses her mental energy, and slowly reveals the bent portion, making it seem as if it is bending right then and there. It's simple time misdirection—the audience thinks it's bending *now*, when really it was already bent five minutes ago! Another method is to hold the key at an angle where it will appear foreshortened to spectators, and then rotate it so they get the full impact of the bend. The result is that the bend appears to visually increase right before the spectator's eyes.

If these explanations sound too simple to be true, I don't blame you. To offer these explanations so simply is to gloss over all the skill involved in performing such a feat. Even when people know how it's done, they still sometimes doubt the methods. Can it really be as simple as substituting one key for another, or using a store-bought gimmick to bend the key? *Yes.*

Once someone protested to me, "Yeah, but I saw a psychic on TV. He did his stuff with no tricks! He was just too good to be a magician—he *must* be real!"

"Keep in mind," I told him, "that performer you saw was not just some guy who walked in off the street. That's a guy who has been performing on stage for thirty years! He's good? Of course he's good! He's had thirty years of practice! Believe me, if you knew all the tricks and were doing them for thirty years, you'd be good too!"

If this book teaches you anything it should be that magicians have myriad ways of fooling you. If you are fooled, don't take it personally, for that's their job. And if you're tempted to believe in telekinesis or psychic powers, then it's because they have done the ultimate job of fooling you— not only fooling you with the trick, but fooling you that it's real. No matter how real it may look, remember, it is not a matter of mind over matter—but of performance, practice, skill, and patter over matter.

Hidden Pockets

We've already seen one example of a hidden pocket, where the pocket is in a screen set up on stage; it's used to hold escape tools or confetti for various tricks. Other pockets may be hiding in the magician's clothes. Eliaser Bamberg, a magician of the eighteenth century, was known by the stage name The Crippled Devil, because he had lost a leg in an explosion while serving duty on a warship, and replaced it with a wooden leg. The wooden leg contained hidden receptacles in which props were kept.

Another common pocket is in silk handkerchiefs. The magician creates a hidden pocket in a silk by sewing on a matching swatch of cloth. The pocket is effectively hidden from view by the hand, and perhaps also by a design on the silk. The most obvious use of a handkerchief pocket is to cause items to appear or disappear. Wrap the object in the handkerchief, casually slipping it into the pocket as you do so. Then say "Abracadabra" as you shake out the cloth, thus showing that the object has vanished. Objects can be made to appear by reversing these directions. Those are very obvious and dull uses of the hidden pocket, and a professional magician would never use a simple trick like that in a show by itself. If a handkerchief vanish (or appearance) is used, it would be used as part of a larger effect. A lot of times the magician needs a quick way to make an item disappear so that he can make it reappear in a very flashy manner. For instance, maybe the magician borrows someone's wedding ring from the audience. He makes a big show of the borrowing, swearing on his mother's grave that he won't lose the ring. Then he loses it in the handkerchief. He makes a bigger show of trying to find it. He goes into the audience—"Oh *there* it is, in your ear . . . *(pluck!)* Whoops!" And he starts pulling a procession of silver dollars, candy, and who knows what else out of all sorts of unusual places. "Sorry lady," he says. "I guess that ring is gone for good. Let me make it up to you. How about a birthday cake?" A chef in a white hat wheels out a silver cart with a birthday cake and flaming candles atop. The magician leads the audience in a rendition of the Happy Birthday song, and then the chef proudly hands over the knife to the woman with the missing ring. "Why don't you cut over there," he offers, pointing to a pink sugar rose. She slices in and takes out a piece of cake, revealing a plastic baggy inside. She opens the plastic baggy to find—her wedding ring!

This is a monumental trick, vastly entertaining, and hugely effective; but it all relies on a tiny little pocket in a scarf. The trick itself takes only a twinkling of an eye to perform. The magician merely slips the ring into the cloth pocket, and shows it has vanished. Even though the trick is over in a mere instant, the act itself continues on for the next fifteen minutes with the magician trying to find the ring and eventually the cake being wheeled out. When the magician went into the audience he covertly slips the ring to an assistant who is ushering the show. The usher hands off the ring to the "chef" backstage, where it gets put in a baggy and planted inside the cake. The cake is left partially unfrosted, and a hole is cut out of the top. The chef drops the ring into the hole, replaces the plug of cake, and then covers over it with frosting. Then he lights the candles and rolls out the cake at the proper time. This is a perfect example of how magicians turn a "molehill into a mountain" using storyline and humor. The trick is a simple one relying on a stupid gimmick like a fake pocket in a scarf. It takes but a moment, but it is turned into an amazing masterpiece of entertainment by a magician who knows how to please an audience.

THUMB TIPS

Some of the tricks you'll see magicians performing are so inexplicably baffling that you feel they simply must have been done by real magic. There doesn't seem to be any other explanation for them. The thumb tip is a tool that accounts for some of these most mystifying illusions. If you wish to remain at least partially in awe of magic then you should skip this section, because it explains how some of those most marvelously magical effects are done. Those of you who don't mind being further defiled, come along for the fun!

The tool in question is the thumb tip. A thumb tip is a fake thumb that fits over a magician's real thumb. Fake thumbs are usually made of plastic or metal. They come in different shades of flesh color, and the magician attempts to find one that most closely matches his or her skin tone. A wealthy magician might contract a magical "tailor" to custom-make a premium thumb tip, but most magicians get theirs off the shelf. The fake thumb doesn't look exactly like a real thumb, but, amazingly, it is incredibly difficult to notice the fake plastic thumb even when the magician keeps it in plain view of the audience.

Fake thumb tips have been around a long time. An English magician named Professor Herwinn was using a thumb tip as far back as the mid-1880s. The thumb tip was popularized at the turn of the century, when magicians realized they could use this devilish prop to duplicate Ching Ling Foo's famous torn and restored paper strip effect.[11] This is one of those amazing magic tricks that is simple and involving, and seems impossible to do, thus inspiring a great reverence in the spectator. The effect is simple. Ching Ling Foo would show his empty hands to the audience. He picks up a small strip of paper, and proceeds to rip it up into tiny pieces. He places the pieces in his fist, and then opens his fist. The strip has been fully restored whole again.

The effect is so simple it's jarring. It's amazing! There are no suspicious boxes or screens on stage. No assistants fluttering around. It's just a paper strip! A common little slip of paper! The trick is so effective and so mysterious because of the simplicity of it, and the ordinariness of the single prop. Earlier I mentioned how the audience can sometimes "feel" the magic as it happens (as in the linking rings, when you can *feel* the solid metal rings slipping through each other as if they were made of air). Here is the same feeling. You almost feel as if you can duplicate the feat by closing your fist around some torn paper. But then, you realize abruptly, no, you can't do that at all. It looked so simple when the magi did it, but it remains a fully unexplainable mystery. You can see why magicians everywhere were anxious to try and replicate Ching Ling Foo's "simple little" effect.

They did so by using a false thumb tip. Before the trick, the magician slips the thumb tip over the real thumb (he probably did this during the climax of the previous trick—breaking the limits of the trick as mentioned earlier—so the audience is misdirected away as he sneaks the thumb tip from his pocket and onto his thumb). Now he's ready to do the trick. The paper is ripped to shreds, and then the magician makes a fist. When he makes the fist, he puts his thumb in it, letting the thumb tip slide off his thumb and remain inside the fist. (Often the thumb tip starts on the opposite hand, and the routine is arranged in such a way that the two hands come together, with a sleight used to steal the tip into the palm of the other hand.) Now there is this hollow container concealed in the fist. A duplicate slip of paper was concealed inside the fake thumb, and that is drawn out by the action of removing the thumb from the thumb tip. The magician uses a finger to push the shredded paper into the fist (really into the hollow thumb inside the fist). The magician then surreptitiously re-inserts his thumb back into his fist, pushing the false thumb tip onto his thumb again, and making sure the restored duplicate paper is in the palm. Now when he opens his fist he can show the fully restored slip of paper.

The amazing thumb tip can be put to many uses. Back in the 1940s, magician Milbourne Christopher wrote a slim, handy booklet called *50 Tricks With a Thumb Tip* that shows off much of the versatility of this fascinating little prop. Back in chapter 1 I mentioned that Penn & Teller taught an audience to vanish a silk scarf using a thumb tip. The scarf vanish is much like the paper restoration, basically concealing the scarf inside the false tip that the magician wears on his thumb to prove his hand empty. This is another illusion that is incredibly mysterious, and it is one of the staples of magic. Think of it: the magician can roll up his sleeves, show his hands empty before and after the effect, and can even allow the audience to examine the silk scarf prior to it disappearing. The whole thing looks completely on the up-and-up. It appears to be gimmick-free and completely unsuspicious, and can even be shown in a close-up on television. That's the power of the thumb tip to baffle an audience. That's why many professional magicians were horrified that Penn & Teller would reveal such a useful gimmick to an audience. There's some tools and tricks that magicians don't really care about and wouldn't mind having revealed because it doesn't hurt the working magician. But to reveal the thumb tip is so crass and juvenile and damaging to the craft of magic, that it was inexcusable of them to do so, they said. It would be worse than Colonel Sanders handing out his recipe for fried chicken. The thumb tip is one of the most secret of trade secrets of the magician, and is not something that should be discussed freely with an entire lay audience!

On the other hand, the audience is likely to think because the thumb tip is so *obvious* that no real magician would use it. That sort of modern-day critical thinking is what accounts for much of the mystery of magic, as we've seen here and with the salt shaker illusion. But that brings up an interesting point that may have occurred to you already: It *does* seem rather obvious, doesn't it? To wear a fake plastic thumb in full view of the audience? Many people are incredulous when they hear such a ridiculous thing, especially if they know that most thumb tips are bought "off the rack." Especially when they see an amazing illusion such as the vanishing scarf on television close-up. You can *see* the hands in full view the whole time—*in close-up!*—and no fake thumb is visible at all. The idea of using a fake thumb is itself so crass and juvenile that you would think it would be obvious to the audience that the magician is wearing one. When we watch *Star Trek* we can easily see where the actor's face ends and the latex mask begins. The whole idea of wearing a false thumb is absurd, especially considering that it is right out in the open. (To make the notion more absurd, consider the false finger. That's right, some magicians wear a false finger on their hand to hide scarves and other items in. Usually the false finger does not slip over a real finger, but rather is used as an *extra finger on the hand*. That's even more absurd than a false thumb!)

So how can a magician wear this obviously fake thing on his hand and nobody notice? Well, there are several reasons:

Nobody thinks to look for it. Who in their right mind would think to look for a false thumb tip on the magician's hand? Consider this: Many of the tricks that rely on thumb tips also use other props such as scarves, envelopes, string, and other objects. Christopher gives an example of a trick where the magician fashions a dollar bill into a cone, drops in a knotted string, and then closes up the cone. The dollar (apparently containing the string) is handed over to an audience volunteer. The magician then takes another dollar bill, fashions it into a cone, and promptly pulls out the very same knotted string. The bamboozled audience member opens her cone to find it empty. In a trick like this there are two dollar bills, string, knots, and one audience volunteer. All of these are the things the audience sees, and so those are the items that become suspect. The audience isn't thinking about things they can't see, because there's no reason to think about "other things." Everything about the trick is so straightforward and unassuming that the audience is focusing on the props, all of which are readily visible and in plain view the entire time. There's no reason in the world for them to think of something as absurd as a fake plastic thumb or extra finger.

Quickness. Most of these tricks are fast, and the magician gets rid of the thumb tip as soon as possible by slipping his hand into his pocket, or by casually looping a thumb in his pants and allowing the tip to slip off. The trick itself is over so quickly that the audience doesn't have time to fully examine the magician, especially considering that they're not looking at his thumbs (of all things!)

Quality workmanship. The third reason the thumb tip is invisible is because the thumb tips themselves are quality items. If you go to your local toy store and buy a kiddy magic kit, it might include a thumb tip. But the tip can be of such poor quality that it would be difficult to get away with using it. When I was a kid I knew about thumb tips, but I was still amazed by thumb tip tricks because I never suspected they were used by real magicians in real life. After all, my entire experience with thumb tips were poor quality, cheap, shiny plastic thumbs that looked nothing like real thumbs. Besides, the fake thumb in the kiddy kits were always too big for a child magician to wear. For all these reasons I discounted the usefulness of a thumb tip, and was surprised to find later in life that magicians actually do use the thing. But the thing they use is of high-quality workmanship. My thumb tip is intricately detailed, with fingerprints, natural-looking wrinkles, and an uneven fingernail. There is no visible seam and the skin has a realistic, soft, fleshy appearance.

Foreshortening. The fourth reason the thumb tip remains invisible is foreshortening. The magician keeps the thumb pointed towards the audience, thus offering a limited view of the thumb while still keeping it in plain view. This is quite interesting and tricky of the magician! It seems he is being completely honest when in fact he is doing this tricky thing of reducing the amount of surface area visible to the audience. Keeping the thumb pointed towards the audience also helps hide the telltale seam where the thumb tip ends and the thumb begins. Another technique is to present the hands with crossed thumbs. The fake thumb goes behind the real thumb, thus covering the edge where the thumb tip ends and the real thumb begins. Once again we have a magician's technique that is so absurd that no one would think of it. You see an empty hand with a wide-open palm and you assume the hand is empty! No one thinks about such an odd concept as foreshortening of the thumb!

Volume of production. Even if someone imagines the magician wearing a thumb tip, they might change their mind when they see him producing items that appear to be too large to fit into the tiny thumb. "There's no way that could fit!" they might gasp to themselves. But magicians can pack a fairly large 9" silk scarf into a thumb tip, or a couple of $20 bills, or even a pack of sugar. There are special loads on the market that allow the magician to fit three feet of silk and streamers into a thumb tip. Magicians have become ingenious in finding ways to pack large items into the small space at the tips of their thumbs.

Those are the reasons why the thumb tip remains invisible. It *looks* like a thumb; the magician doesn't let you get a good look at it (while seemingly being completely honest and open); no one thinks of a fake thumb to begin with; or they think of it but discount it as a silly idea. That's how such an absurd tool can be used in plain view to achieve such magical effects.

A Stage Full of Stuff

Although I've just explained away the gimmicks behind many of the most common magician's props, it is worth remembering that props are just instruments. They are not the illusion in and of themselves. Utility props, like Foo Cans, gimmicked cards, chop cups, and the like are not illusions—they're not even magic tricks. They're just gimmicked props. It is up to the creativity of the magician to bring the props to life, the way an artist will turn a dab of white into a highlight, or a drop of dark paint into a ghostly shadow. So too the magician colors his stage with the emotions and magical story of the show.

PART FOUR

OFF STAGE AND OUT OF THE THEATER

The first three sections of this book have explained stage magic and how it works—how illusions are created in our minds, and why we are fooled so often by some very simple tricks. Part Four looks at magic from a different angle—off stage and out of the theater. If magicians are so good at fooling us during a show when we *expect* to be fooled, how much more effective magic and illusions could be when used to influence us outside of the theater, in real life, in the real world. Part Four thus takes the lessons learned from the preceding sections and applies them to the real world, out of the theater. Here we will learn how people in everyday life use techniques of magic to manipulate and influence others, and what we can do to protect ourselves from such real-world magic.

12

Illusion Outside of Magic

Illusion abounds in the world around us. Illusion is used in art, architecture, and music to create images in our minds. What is television and movies if not an illusion of motion? When we are watching a Meryl Streep movie, how do we know her words are coming out of her mouth? If you stop to think about it, the words *aren't* coming from her mouth—they're coming from the speakers on the walls of the theater. And yet it *seems* like the voice comes from the actor's mouth. Only by an illusion, only by the knowledge we have, because we know how to match up the sounds of speech with the visuals of mouth movements, do we hear voices from a movie screen. And it is a very hard illusion to get rid of. When we see a moving mouth, and we hear a voice, we put the two together . . . naturally. I'd go so far as to say that almost all nonparticipatory activities that we engage in are based on illusion. The activities we engage in are either responding to a physical need (hunger, lust, thirst), or to an emotional/intellectual ones—which are fulfilled by theater, magic, art, various kinds of performance art, poetry, movies, music. These forms all rely on illusion.

This section takes a brief look at illusion in the world around us. It's important to remember that the existence of an illusion does not necessarily mean that magic was used or thought about in creating that illusion. For example, in the next section we'll discuss illusion in art. There are probably few or no artists who think about magic when they create their illusions of landscapes and three-dimensional portraiture. I am not saying that artists think about magic when they create their art. What I am saying is that illusion exists in the world outside of magic, and because it is there we, and magicians, can look at it, study it, and learn how to improve our understanding of magical illusions. After looking at our world of illusions, the chapters that follow will show how the same techniques of illusion and magic are put to use by people in our everyday lives.

305

Illusion in Art

In high school I visited a lot of art museums. One time I was wandering through a museum with a friend. We stopped at a very ordinary painting of some noble personage—some duke or bishop or saint—and she said, "How adorable, the first fly of the summer." A big horsefly was perched delicately on the saint's neck. She raised her rolled up museum map to flick it off the painting when the guard came over and chased us away. Anyway, later we were coming back through that same room and noticed the fly still perched on the painting. Taking a closer look we realized it was not a fly at all, but a lifesize painting of a fly on the canvas. Welcome to *trompe l'oeil*.

The whole point of classical visual arts like portraits and landscape painting was to create an illusion of three solid dimensions on a flat canvas. *Trompe l'oeil* (literally, "fools the eye") goes beyond that. In a traditional painting, no matter how beautiful it is, you know it's a painting. *Tromp l'oeil* fools you. You don't know, at least at first, that it's not real.

Trompe l'oeil can be whimsical. For instance, if an artist paints a realistic painting of a piece of paper lying on a hardwood floor, every visitor to that house will stoop to pick up the paper—and find themselves scratching at flat wooden floorboards. *Trompe l'oeil* can be practical. Painting a picture of open windows and doorways with wide lush landscapes onto the walls of a cramped apartment may lend an expansive air of bigness to the room.

Formica and other "Space Age" home materials decorated with fake wood patterns are more durable than the real thing, but just as pretty. Vinyl floor coverings that look like stone paving are softer to walk on, and easier to sponge spilled jelly off of. Faux furs and imitation animal prints spare the lives of animals while allowing us to wear the beauty of their skins.

Tromp l'oeil is a more recent invention than illusion in art. Artists have always strived for the illusion of literal reproduction of reality in art. However, what they did not always realize is that faithful reproduction is not always the best way to convey the illusion of reality. Extremes in perspective and foreshortening, stark contrasts between light and dark regions, and artificially arranged still lifes may all exist in the real world, but carried over into a painting they are immediately suspect. Traditional illusionistic artists would therefore paint their art in ways to reduce these unrealistic portions of life. A modern example is the false perspective used on Sleeping Beauty's Castle at Disneyland. The castle (and the top portions of the quaint storefronts along Main Street USA in Disneyland), were purposely created with incorrect perspective in mind. The perspective makes the buildings appear cartoonishly taller without being menacing, hulking structures. In this way, Disneyland attempts to convey a particular carefree frame of mind. Similarly in art. For instance, *The Apotheosis of St. Ignatius*, a ceiling decoration in Rome, shows a three-dimensional rise of arches and angels floating to the heavens. The viewer is expected to stand on a particular spot marked on the floor to look up and get the best viewing angle of the ceiling painting. In contrast to the Disneyland perspectives, "No deception is attempted or achieved" with the St. Ignatius painting. "More importantly, the viewer is thus made aware that the painted scene is merely an incentive to his own imagination. Far from being passive, he must place himself not only in the right spot, but in the right frame of mind."[1] Upon reflection you'll find this is true of most realistic artwork. You can look at it skeptically and say, "Bah! I see the brush strokes!" Or you can welcome it with an open mind and say, "Ah! I see myself standing in that beautiful Fauvistic landscape."

So let's turn the subject back to magic. First of all, we can see there are two kinds of illusion represented in art: (1) The illusion that the unreal is happening, and (2) The illusion that the real is happening. The illusion of the *un*real is a magician performing a levitation—or a very realistic painting of a fantasy land. Both require the viewer to be in the right frame of mind, because both are obviously phony. Both of these illusions are fragile, breakable, destructable, given an unwelcoming frame of mind.

The illusion of the *real* is when a magician pretends to pass a coin from one hand to another (but secretly keeps it in the first hand). It is a very real, common everyday occurrence, and yet illusion is used to produce the effect (rather than actually transferring the coin over, which would be detrimental to the outcome of the trick). Illusion of the real in art is any realistic, illusionistic, or *trompe l'oeil* artwork. For example, the "fly" perched on the portrait.

Illusion of the real and unreal, illusion of deception and surprise, and "fudging the facts" to produce an illusion of reality, are all major parts of the illusion of art, and the art of magic.

Illusion in Music

I was minding my own business, listening to a compact disc, when suddenly there was an elephant in my room. I think there were a few of them actually. I heard their monstrously large bodies thundering across the plains. *That sounds like elephants.* I checked the compact disc. It was *The Carnival of the Animals Suite* by Camille Saint-Saëns. Yes: track seven was the music of elephants as played by a symphony orchestra. When the elephants were gone, a new song started. The sound bounced and hippity-hopped like the strong, tall bodies of kangaroos. "Kangaroos?" I asked myself. Sure enough, track eight on the CD was kangaroos.

How can an elephant and kangaroo emerge from the same orchestra of brass instruments and drums? It has to do with the illusion in music. It can be said that all music is illusion. After all, "music is nothing more than different frequencies along a vast range," explained musician and maker of miracles Patricia Ju. "A 'sound' or a note is comprised of this frequency, and timbre(s) that give it more character." Instruments are distinguished by their "attack waves," which can be seen on any digitizer or signal analyzer. However, she goes on, "None of it actually matters in a piece of music. You don't think of frequencies, attacks, or timbres. You think of melodies, of harmonies . . . and you feel it. Music is an illusion. The illusion is that most of us perceive a coherent, cohesive work among the masses of notes and instruments." We hear discrete notes as a continuous blur. We feel suspense in our stomachs as the gods prepare for battle in Holst's *Mars, the Bringer of War.* We feel elated by the pulse of a fast-moving road song. Our hair gets soaked listening to Debussy's *Jardins Sous la Pluie* (Gardens Under the Rain).

Music also induces us to feel other illusions, such as a passage of time that doesn't jibe with the hands on the clock, but rather "the rate of a particular series of pulsations that we select from among our perceptions."[2] That's an aspect of time that magicians, moviemakers, and the theater use in their own performances. Music theorist and composer Lewis Rowell has pointed out that music may appear to contain more or less temporal control than it actually has. Although Western music tends towards precise timing, he says, "we have come to prize the apparent spontaneity and freedom that we infer in fantasias, toccatas, preludes, cadenzas, recitatives, and the like. At times it seems as if the pieces are improvised on the spot"—an illusion of spontaneity much like the one a magician wishes to project. "At other times the sense of freedom is an illusion: the ambitious opening of Wagner's *Parsifal* is under complete temporal control but deliberately contrived to avoid any implication of strict metric organization."[3]

"Other compositional techniques or "tricks" are used to make the listener think something is the case, when it clearly is not," Ju explains.

> For example, Bach's fugues and 3-part inventions make use of several "voices" . . . all meant to be played with the two hands. As a listener, you might think there are three hands . . . you might think there are actually four or five different minds, one handling each "voice" but in fact the prowess of the performer is to be able to "multi-task," separate himself into these three, four, or five "different minds" and successfully sustain the illusion. That is what mastery of the piano and of music is—practicing and possessing the skill to sustain these illusions, making the audience feel they are listening to an orchestra, not one man at the piano.

Music can also present us with an illusion of volume, mass, weight, energy, and the feeling that it occupies space.[4] By itself music is an illusion, so it is that much more amazing to discover that an illusionary frequency in the air can provide illusions of illusions . . . of illusions!

Illusion in Landscaping and Gardening

As a magician wishes to control the natural forces of the world, a gardener seeks to control nature. Nature normally abhors straight rows and columns and would never think to grow a bush in the shape of a perfect sphere or Mickey Mouse head. The Marine and Coastal Sciences Building at Douglass College has its front lawn shaped into the crests and troughs of rolling waves. Nature is what the gardener wishes to control. But we're going to talk about something more than just gardening here. Landscape design is an artform in which the land is designed to achieve some ulterior purpose, to cause the viewer to think about the landscape in a certain way, to create an impression in the viewer's mind. This is architecture of plants and dirt. Like architecture, we can say the viewer is more than just a viewer, but a participant in the final product, because it is only with people walking through, touching, and using, that the carefully designed landscape becomes what it was meant to be.

Illusion has been used for centuries in gardening and landscape art to create the appearance of increased depth and space, and even to fool the observer into believing that distant landmarks are part of one's garden. A "perspective effect" can increase the sense of space "by contrasting dark foreground forms with lighter, less distinct ones farther away."[5] One horticulturist from Sussex, England, recommends painting the garden with flowers the way an artist paints a canvas. She says fiery reds, oranges, and yellows should be planted close by, soft pastels just beyond that, and, finally, layer the back edge of the garden with dark blues and purples and "misty mauves." The effect leads the eye to a conclusion of depth. Instead of seeing random colors (beautiful, but random), the eye sees a progression of colors that indicates enhanced perspective. If the distant view includes open sky or water, she recommends allowing the colors to trail off into "glaucous grey" so one's garden will appear to recede far into the distance.[6] Naturally the illusion is done in order to please the eye and to impart a sense of expansiveness. One doesn't plant a garden in this fashion to maliciously deceive people. The illusion is merely an additional way of enhancing the beauty of one's planted patch of ground.

The Japanese have made an art of capturing distant features of the landscape into their *shakkei* gardens. *Shakkei* means "borrowed scenery" or "borrowed landscape." A distant waterfall, mountain, woods, or lake may be captured into the garden by use of framing and covering devices. Some *shakkei* gardens have even captured the nighttime fire lures of fishermen on the water. The gardener must first decide what features of the landscape he would like to borrow into his own garden. Trees may be planted in the garden so that when a person gazes through their trunks she looks out to see a mountain. The mountain, though far away, is linked to the garden by this framing device. Without the frame, the mountain would seem just like any other distant object. With the frame, it appears to be under the control of the gardener. One gardener used a clever technique to capture a scraggly hillside into his garden. The hill itself was plain, amorphous bulges of shrubbery that didn't particularly stand out or detract from the landscape, but the gardener captured it by placing a single stone lantern in a strategic place. With the lantern there, the hill appears to be an extension of the garden. "The garden has been given greater depth through the incorporation of borrowed scenery that would otherwise have been nothing more than an unintegrated background."[7]

Illusion in the Movies

Earlier we mentioned some uses of sound effects by magicians. In the Miser's Dream, the magician shakes a near-empty pail, but the audience believes that it's full of coins because they hear the coins rattling around inside. One magician generated the feeling of drops of water falling from the ceiling by the plink of a stringed instrument. Such sound effects are very effective in creating illusions. In movies, a sound effect can be used in place of a visual image. It costs too much to show a spaceship taking off? Then keep the camera focused on a spectator's glowing face as she looks up, while overlaying the sound of a spaceship rising off the surface. Filmmaker Robert Rodriguez couldn't get the machine guns in his low-budget shoot-em-up *El Mariachi* to fire more than one shot at a time. He solved the problem by overlaying the staccato of machine gunfire over quick cuts of the guns. An illusion is created because the mind knows enough to link the visuals with the sound, even though in reality the two don't necessarily match up. Nicholas Negroponte, the founding director of the Massachusetts Institute of Technology's Media Lab, reports that when one of his scientists was testing a new model of high-definition television, he set up two televisions that were identical except for sound quality. One television had "better-than-CD-quality sound with excellent loudspeakers." He had subjects watch the same videocassette on both televisions, and, astonishingly, the subjects reported a much better picture quality on the television with the better sound setup. Why should the "viewing experience" be "considerably better," as Negroponte puts it, on a television that is in reality *not visually better at all?* Negroponte asserts that, "We tend to judge our experiences as a sensory whole, not by the parts." He gives the example of tanks designed for the military with virtual reality displays. The engineers went to considerable trouble to fine-tune the displays as much as possible, but they later realized there was no need to "go all the way" with the visuals when they could add another sensory element to the illusion. They introduced "an inexpensive motion platform that vibrated a little. By further including some additional sensory effects—tank motor and tread sounds—so much 'realism' was achieved that the designers were then able to reduce the [picture quality]; they nonetheless exceeded the requirement that the system look and feel real."[8] The engineers wanted to reduce picture quality to both save money and allow for faster update of images.

Blurring the Lines

Illusions, illusions everywhere! All around us, everywhere we look, what we see may not be what we think we're seeing. What we hear may not be what we think we're hearing. More and more illusion is becoming an everyday part of our daily lives. That's what I wanted to show by this chapter's small departure from the stage—how illusion is everywhere, in our entertainment, our technology, our gardening, throughout our lives. We used to be able to see magic as separate from other forms of entertainment, but that is no longer possible for the well-informed. We should see the magician as part of a larger continuum that includes everyone and everything from actors to mimes to faith healers to the computerized voice on the telephone. All of these are master illusionists of one form or another.

We have different words, different categories, for each of these people (or machines), but they're all illusionists to some degree or another. A magician is different than a pickpocket, and yet some magicians also do pickpocket acts. Some magicians are adept at performing the three card monte scam, and yet we don't call the hustlers on the street corner "sidewalk magicians." The lines are blurring between all these different practitioners of magic!

13

Translating Magic into Desires

At this point we've temporarily waltzed away from the magic stage, talking about illusions and the "real world." We're not ready yet to come back to the magic stage—let's take a look at some random people in the audience first. These are fictional people who have come to the magic show. Let's pull some people out of the audience and pick a little moment of their lives. Remember as you read, that while on the surface we are talking about Billy or Ed or Neal, we are really talking about you and me . . .

Let's start with Neal. Despite years of financial planning he is cold and cash dry after a series of unfortunate occurrences that ate away the money he had saved to send his last kid to college. Then he finds out his wife is expecting a baby. Neal feels spiritually crushed beneath his financial burdens, present and future.

Meanwhile, his brother Ed is walking down a city street, passing a mirrory skyscraper, and keeping his face turned staunchly forward to avoid catching a reflected glimpse of himself. Ed is ashamed of his body, of his fatness. *Maybe this walking will help,* he sighs, knowing in his heart it will be as ineffective as the stack of diet books in his closet, the skin creams, and the plastic wrap designed to melt away what he sees as ugly fat.

You might be remembering a time in your life when you felt like Neal, or like Ed. These, or similar situations, have afflicted us all. Here's a tale that happened to *me:* It was moving day, moving to a new place. As I was unstacking some boxes off the top shelf of a closet, one box fell out and landed on my toe. Excruciating pain! The box was a shoe box, and contained my heaviest, clunkiest, strongest pair of shoes. As I was hopping in agony, I thought back to the beginning of the day when I had to choose which shoes to wear. The choice was between the strong clunky shoes, and the shoes I actually did select—a comfortable, soft, thin-leathered pair. *Amusing,* I

312

thought. *If I had chosen to wear the hard shoes instead of these soft ones, I wouldn't be jumping in pain right now.*

One audience member is stuck outside in the parking lot. It's pouring rain, and the night is dark, and she is locked out of her car. She pounds on the door. "Damn!" Her frustration is interrupted as she begins to sneeze. Her cold hands tug the door handle uselessly, and she shivers.

Ah, you didn't even make it to the show. Under the comforter, you are almost asleep, snug in your bed, the television on. Through the flicker of your heavy eyelids you glimpse the remote control on top of the television. Oh! If only it could float over here and rest beneath your finger, so the only muscle you would need to move was that one little finger muscle, to press that one little button, to shut off that one annoying machine!

Another audience member is a little boy, who also wants to stay in bed. Billy doesn't want to go to school today, and he has convinced Mommy to take his temperature. *If only* . . . he begs his stubbornly healthy body . . . *if only I can be sick just this one day!* But his temperature reads normal, and it's off to school for Billy.

In a hospital bed across town, a woman kneels beside the sleeping body of her own little boy. This boy wishes, as he feels the intravenous solution dripping into his punctured hand, that he *was* in school—or anyplace else for that matter. His bones ache. He coughs, and the movement of his body shakes the creaky bed.

Even the pain of injury seems minor compared to the utter distress our next man feels. His wife of decades, many happy decades, has passed away. He can not even feel his sorrow, his mind is racing with distraught thoughts to distract him from this horror he must live with, the loneliness that he must feel forever. He sighs and wonders and wishes and prays and *hopes* . . .

A toddler feels with almost equal remorse the sharp *pow* of her balloon as she bites into it, and the pieces go flying everywhere around the room. "Balloony bye bye!" she sobs to Daddy.

This audience is diverse and encompasses all of us. Two more spectators sit close to the back of the theater. One is a preteenager, aloof and angry at the world. He wants a car, man. He wants to drive and explore and *live* finally! Get out of this town, man! And behind him one business-suited fellow three times his age thinks about the people in his life, wonders who is out to get him, who is jealous of his success, whom he can trust, and who knows secrets about him that he would rather not be made public. He wants to know how to deal with them, but he doesn't even know who is against him.

This is our audience then, a sampling of it anyway, and the problems that are going through their minds. You'll notice not all of these people are sitting in the magic theater. That will be important to us later!

Some of these situations are comic (such as the frustration of the faraway TV remote, which has happened to all of us; or the fallen shoe box, which ouchfully happened to me). Other situations are very serious—the tragic mourning for a departed loved one . . . *How will I survive without her?* All are dramatic when you are experiencing them (and you have just now felt the frustration of being locked out of your car, the distress of a broken toy, the loneliness, the despair, the emotional—and sometimes physical— pain.) These are things we all feel and have felt.

What has this to do with magic? Reread these situations and look back to the list of eleven magical forms listed at the beginning of the book. Do you see a connection?

A magical illusion may be a production (like Neal's much-needed cash) or an evanishment (like Ed's fat). But money isn't the only thing we want produced—there are myriad other things personal and profound we desire, from a lost childhood memory to someone to love. And there is plenty of badness in our lives that we would also love to be rid of. Similarly down the rest of the list. The magical form of transposition (darn, I wish the hard shoes were on my feet and the soft shoes were in the box!), may be desired in many cases and many ways. Changes in form, size, color, weight, or in this case temperature, can also be commonly desired. ("You painted the house *that* color!") The need for physical penetration of two solid objects is here represented by a need to enter a locked car, but, again, a need for magic may enter our lives in many ways. Down the list we go: invulnerability tested by a boy in a hospital bed. Animating the inanimate is longed for by a surviving widower. That toddler would like nothing more than her balloon to be restored whole again. The preteen would like to see a natural process accelerated (his life). And boy, wouldn't that middle-aged businessman like to have psychic powers to see into the minds of his colleagues!

Each magical form can therefore be expressed as a *desire*—a wish. Sometimes the wish is fleeting or trivial (the preteen's desire to grow up faster so he can drive). Other times the wish is serious and may be tragic if not fulfilled. How many tearful suicides have resulted over a longful wish for a dream that can never be made real?

As the perpetually sullen Woody Allen said, "I feel that the only way out of things is magic. Everything is so glum, so really depressing, that the only hope you have is . . . it would require magic . . . There's no way, short of a magical solution. All the rational solutions . . . are finally degrees of workable but not thrilling."[1] People want to—need to—believe in magic, because the alternatives are too hard to bear.

"If only my wife could be restored to life. . . ."

But sadly, no magic is forthcoming.

Wishes may lead to destruction, or they may lead to wishful thinking. That's where magic comes in. Magic comes at us in many forms every day to try and assuage our wishes. We don't call it magic—we call it advertising, or politics, or con artistry, or peer pressure. But here we will call it magic, because here we are looking at what happens when magic is taken out of the theater and into our lives. If we have a wish—a desire—and another person has the ability to deceive us the way a magician deceives an audience, we may wrongly believe that he has the ability to fulfill our wish. And the result may be comic, serious, or even tragic.

We've already seen how the magician has us buying in to his tricks by exploiting off-stage arrangements in seating, lighting, or clandestine before-show events. But what if we slide the magic even further away from the stage. What if we take it out of the theater altogether? If these techniques have been used effectively by stage magicians for countless years to deceive people, doesn't it seem probable that they have been used off stage as well, to manipulate us at home and on the streets?

After all, look at how often during the course of the day we meet up with folks who are trying to persuade, influence, cajole, and otherwise manipulate us:

- Advertisers
- Politicians
- Salespeople
- Religious figures
- Cult leaders and members
- Propagandists
- Many public speakers
- Agents
- Public relations people
- Doctors and psychiatrists
- Friends, boyfriends, girlfriends, parents, acquaintances
- Me

All have a vested interest in our minds, and in getting us to believe certain things about their products, ideas, or themselves. Face it, aren't there a lot of times when you wish you had the power to control another person? To make them believe there was something special about you, or simply to maneuver them into handing over some cash!

Okay, even if you're not interested, perhaps that's because you don't believe stage magic can be used against you in real life. Consider this, however: look at that list of people who want to control you to some degree. Could all those people be wrong? Could the methods they use be so ineffective? Or could it be that they are using subtle magic on us, and we are so blinded to the possibility that the idea seems this ludicrous?

Hmmm . . . could be!

Some people don't see magic as ludicrous at all, but, rather, very influential. In March 1993, during the Branch Davidian/David Koresh crisis in

Waco, Texas, members of the FBI were seriously considering using a Russian mind-control device. The device was supposed to subliminally implant thoughts in people's minds and thereby control their actions. A top FBI scientist—not just some rookie punk or secretary—but a *scientist*—deputy chief of the FBI's technical services division—suggested using the mind-control device on Koresh as he spoke with FBI agents on the telephone in an effort to alter Koresh's behavior.[2] It is clear that negotiations with terrorists are themselves an attempt at mind control, one that is decidedly imperfect. The need to believe in magic is strong when times are tough. The FBI considered relying on telepathic magic, while the Davidians relied on the magic they were being taught by their magical leader, David Koresh.

A sweeter story of magic being used in the real world was told by a building contractor who was fed up with his boss. The builder had been hired by an overbearing, cheapskate attorney to renovate an old bank to be used for the attorney's new law firm. The builder almost blew a fuse one day when this aggravating attorney started arguing with his crew, made lewd comments to one of his female workers, and accused him of overcharging on a recent invoice. Well, our hero decided to take some revenge on this jerk, and he did so using some magic.

He waited a few weeks (time misdirection), until they were working on the electrical wiring in a wall. At a moment the attorney was looking over his shoulder, the builder pulled out a crumpled, dusty, ten-dollar bill from the wall. Then he pulled out a twenty. "Look at this! There's money hidden away in this wall!" he called out to the lawyer. The greedy lawyer reached over and began pulling out more bills. "Open this wall up," he demanded, wiping drool off his chin. Our hero explained that opening the wall would cost a fortune, but the lawyer told him, "Just do it."

So, with his halo glowing brightly above his head, our hero set to work ripping apart the wall, very carefully looking for money that, of course, was not there. It was all a magic trick, the Miser's Dream come to life, designed to get revenge on the attorney. It also had the bonus of adding some significant dough to the builder's pockets. This is a clear case of a desire (greed), overriding the sensibility of a rational man.[3]

* * * * *

Whether the magic is based on scientific principles or absurd logic, whether it is presented by a cult leader or a vengeful building contractor, every day people in the world try to manipulate us the way magicians do in the theater. When we are unprepared for the magic in the theater it fools us. It is hard to imagine how truly lost we must be in detecting this other magic, which is designed to not only hit us every day but to do so without our knowing that it even exists.

To add to this, we are often hit with magic (or magical principles) when we are at our weakest, for instance, when we are suffering a need, as our fictional audience members were a few pages back. When they—or we—have a wish that needs fulfilling, we may start engaging in wishful thinking, which will enhance the effects of the magic being worked on us. And what happens when the wish is not fulfilled as promised? Or worse, when the hope is repeatedly shattered? This usually is accompanied by a complete loss of whatever the person (you?) is trying to regain—money, self-esteem, love, or, most generally, happiness. When the techniques of magic are used by manipulators, a sorrowful desperation may be the unfortunate result.

Thankfully, the principles of magic can also be used in a good light with good intentions. Let's explore now magic out of the theater, the dangers it presents, what we can do about it, and perhaps how we can work some good magic on our own.

14

The Use of Fakery and Magicians' Psychology Out of the Theater

There are many fakes in the world. Fake psychics. Fake faith healers. Fake people with fake special powers. Most of the time these fakes use simple magic tricks, and magicians' psychology to fool the gullible. For instance, consider the X-Salted trick discussed earlier, where an inexhaustible supply of salt is produced from a small container. It would be a boring show if the magician stood there for *years* with salt pouring from the tiny lid. How else can he prove that he really *can* produce an endless stream of salt? Really he just stands there for a minute or so, producing an undeniably large amount in that short time. The implication is, "I *could* stand around forever producing salt if I wanted to, but let's move on to something more interesting."

Of course, the *real* reason magicians don't stand around forever is because after that initial minute or so, all the salt is used up. Variations on the trick include Foo Cans, Keg of Plenty, and the Lota trick, in which gallons of liquids (sometimes different kinds of liquids) are poured from one vessel. The point is, once the liquid truly is poured out of the container, there is no magic in the world that will replenish the gimmick. The magician *pretends* he could go on all day producing liquid, while in reality his decision to stop the trick at that point is because he has used up the entire trick. Psychic charlatans use the same tactic when their powers are being tested.

Sometimes psychics undergo scientistic testing to examine the extent of their powers. The psychics employ a magician's psychology to work the tests in their favor. James Randi has reported that under poor testing conditions, psychics will decide to continue or stop a test of their powers based on how Lady Luck is treating them that night. If statistics are in their favor, they'll quit while they're ahead. If they're doing below average or average, they'll keep going at it, until they can either up their score, or, at the very least, end on a psychologically pleasing big kill.

Table 1 shows the same experiment as it may be handled three different ways. The experiment consists of ten trials. On each trial, the psychic must predict the color of a card drawn from a deck. If the psychic guesses correctly it is a "Hit." A wrong guess is a "Miss."

The first column shows the experiment done under controlled circumstances. The experiment called for ten trials, and thus the experimenter allows only ten trials to occur. Any more or less would disqualify the experiment. The second column shows an uncontrolled experiment in which the psychic decided it was time to cut short the experiment because her powers were apparently not working quite right that day. After a run of three misses, she (and the experimenters) are gratified to see two hits, and the psychic pleads fatigue and is allowed to quit. This is the psychologically pleasing grande finale. In the third column, the psychic is not exactly pleased with her score after the ten trials are over, so she has the experimenters extend the run for a few more trials. When her percentage is pleasing again, she decides it's time to quit.

TABLE 1		
Controlled	Stop Short	Continue the Streak
1. Hit	Hit	Hit
2. Hit	Hit	Hit
3. Miss	Miss	Miss
4. Miss	Miss	Miss
5. Miss	Miss	Miss
6. Hit	Hit	Hit
7. Hit	Hit	Hit
8. Miss		Miss
9. Miss		Miss
10. Hit		Hit
		Hit
		Miss
		Hit
		Hit
		Hit

If the psychic can control the amount of time she spends "on stage" in front of the experimenters, then she can, like the magician, control the amount of magic that she outputs. It is pretty clear that when someone is being tested, they should not be allowed to work an X-Salted on the experimenters. And yet this breaking of the principles of basic scientific inquiry happens all the time.

Consider this quote by George Kresge Jr. Don't recognize the name? Kresge has renamed himself Kreskin for our entertainment benefit and proclaimed himself to have otherworldly powers, such as these: "I found myself beginning to shake too. I'd opened up her mind as well as my own. We were mentally locked onto each other. I stopped immediately. Yet . . . I'm certain we could have gone on for two hours. However, I vowed then and there to limit . . . such adventuring to a few single thoughts. No person is prepared for an extended mental exchange when it does happen. It is eerie only because it is not customary."[1]

Kreskin is a performer who purports to have fabulous mental capabilities, among them the ability to read minds. In his book he takes what I believe to be nothing more than a before-show working of the crowd and turns it into a feat of mental dexterity. He had selected a volunteer from the audience and read off a litany of personal data from her brain (reality check: refer back to our chapter 1 discussion for methods used to perform such "miraculous" feats). Kreskin reports that this instance of mind melding, like all his telepathies, are exactly that—some kind of psychic connection between him and the volunteer. Oh well, I don't suppose we can get him to change his mind about that. In any case, magicians have noticed Kreskin resorting to magicians' tricks over and over again to perform his mentalism. One, who asked to remain anonymous, said, "Oh yes. You always see him using the same things that other magicians use, and . . . these are the kinds of tricks used by fortune tellers, gypsies, to make you believe they are psychic, and to take your money. These tricks are old." When Kreskin talks about his magical performance, he ascribes the effect to himself, his own special abilities. And he ascribes his stopping of the effect not to his running out of facts he swiped about that person but to his generous desire to cut off communication so as not to intrude on the poor girl's thoughts.

Kreskin, it should be noted, ups his believability factor by admitting, "I am not a 'psychic.' I'm not a *mind reader,* because that implies I could totally penetrate the processes of the human brain and receive chains of thought . . . Above all, I'm not a 'medium.' "[2] Kreskin has built a quandary for himself because he seriously wants to fight off the supernaturalism in the world (one of his pet projects is to inform all the world about the nonreality of hypnotism), but at the same time he is performing under the pretense of being a psychic (who claims no psychic powers). This, folks, is called underselling. Like much of good magic, you don't tell the audience what you want them to believe. You display your little trick, then let them make of it what they will. Their minds fill in the gaps, and if the gaps happen to say, "Oh yes, psychic forces are involved!" then who are you to argue?

MAY THE BLACK CAT HAVE NINE TIMES NINE LIVES

Katterfelto is sorry to find that newspapers have several times asserted that he and his Black Cat were DEVILS. On the contrary, Katterfelto professes himself to be nothing more than a Moral and Divine Philosopher, a Teacher in Mathematics and Natural Philosophy.

Neither he nor his Black Cat bears any resemblance to Devils. He assures the Nobility and the Public that the idea of him and his Black Cat being devils arises merely from the astonishing performances of Katterfelto and his said Cat, which, both in day's and the night's exhibition, are such as to induce all the spectators to believe them both Devils indeed. The Black Cat appearing at one instant with a tail, and the next without any. This has occasioned many thousands of pounds to be lost in wagers on this incomprehensible subject.

In the late 1700s, the warlock Katterfelto was pulling the same advertising gimmicks that Kreskin is today. Katterfelto denied vigorously that he and his cat had supernatural powers. The denials were designed to be unconvincing—and they worked.[3]

The most primitive underselling occurs when the spectator simply misinterprets the magic as requiring supernatural abilities to perform. We can excuse the many people who fall for Uri Geller or Kreskin's acts, because Geller and Kreskin are magicians who encourage their audience to believe, for the purposes of the feat, that their illusions are based on supernatural powers. But what of people who insist that other magicians use "real" psychic powers? Houdini had more than one person comment that his escapes could only have been done through ghostly dematerializations. Even such an obviously phony duo as Penn & Teller get it, as Teller explained:

> We are very up front, as you know, that there is *no such thing* as "real" magic. There will always be nuts who deny this (Arthur Conan Doyle did it to Houdini) but that can't be helped. I myself can't recall anybody believing we were doing anything but tricks, unless you count the kook who, when years ago we did a Non-Believer's Séance in which we *told* the people we were just doing tricks and then "read their minds," told us she knew *some* of our stuff was trickery, but "the mind-reading part—that was real—I know it." We strenuously denied it, but the experience still creeped us out so that we stopped doing the séances altogether.

I have heard similar reports about David Copperfield and Siegfried and Roy—"They are possessed by demons," said a woman behind a Las Vegas

7-11 counter.[4] Matthew Dwinells has also reported people who believed his magic was real. Sandorse the Magician said he has even gotten phone calls from people wanting advice on how to concoct a love potion and the best kind of crystal ball to buy. Can we simply write off these people as kooks? "Well I don't think they're very smart," says Randi. Maybe not, but I tend to think there's something other than intelligence at work. After all, many of the most brilliant minds of history have been taken in by all sorts of supernatural "real magick" hocus pocus. Perhaps it's less an issue of stupidity and more a matter of a bad choice: the people choose to focus their beliefs in an illogical manner. Every choice has a motivation behind it, so if someone chooses to believe in a logically undefendable position, we must assume that they have some good reason for doing so. Of course, their reason for believing is itself an illusion. As always with magic, an illusion has been created in their mind that a particular belief system is best suited to their emotional needs. Consider the following case from about the 1920s or so, described by a former chief inspector of Scotland Yard.[5] A woman visits a fortune teller. The fortune teller tells the woman her husband is keeping several mistresses. The woman is skeptical:

Client: "When was the last time he saw her [his mistress]?"

Fortune-teller: "Oh, my dear, he sees her every day."

Woman: "How can that be when my husband is always home to his time at night? He does not go out in the evenings."

Fortune-teller: "You see his work is out-of-doors, and he goes to see her on the pretense of going out to a job."

Woman: "But he hasn't money enough to keep another woman."

Fortune-teller: "She supplies him with money, and he keeps a child with it."

Over the course of the next few visits, the fortune teller's story grew more elaborate. The home was eventually broken up over it, even after the wife had much tangible evidence that her husband was faithful to her. Chief Inspector Berrett concludes his discussion of these scams with a rhetorical question that I wish, so many years later, we would have the sense to answer: "Knowing as I do the harm these people bring about, is there any wonder that I decline to think fortune-telling an amusing pastime that should be ignored by the police?"[6]

Bullets and Bloody Hands

Psychic surgery is a cruel example of magic tricks used to steal from people not only their money but their lives as well. In psychic surgery, the patient (usually suffering from a terminal illness, especially cancer), visits a mystical, magical faith healer in a foreign land who claims to have the power of removing tumors and foreign objects from the patient's body—without surgery. The patient lies down on a table, exposing her belly for the "doctor." The faith healer rubs her flesh, kneads it, plays with it until a state of communion is reached, at which point the faith healer's hands penetrate the surface of the flesh and plucks out the tumors. There is blood, but no pain. The patient is fully awake and can witness the miracle of the surgeon's hands reaching into her belly and extracting infected bodily matter. The terminally ill pay dearly to travel to the Philippines where psychic surgeons flourish. Many go back for repeat visits when they see that their first visit has not had the effect they wished it would. Some go because they've exhausted legitimate medical abilities. Others have forsaken legitimate medicine in favor of the false surgeons, whose healing often involves a ritual highly flavored by the icons of Catholicism.

Psychic surgery is one of the more ludicrous of supernatural beliefs. Most people realize that the real world does not allow matter to penetrate matter. But believers in psychic surgery have very pressing needs—desires, as we discussed earlier, that are a matter of life or death—that serve to override their normal ability to reason about the world. These people *need* psychic surgery to work, because if it doesn't work, *they will die*, or their loved one will die.

The magic tricks of the psychic surgeons have been exposed most thoroughly by magician James Randi in his book *The Faith Healers*. While psychic surgery is not something you're likely to encounter in your everyday life (as opposed to the magic tricks of advertisers and TV commercials, let's say) it is a tragic example of the extreme to which magicians' tricks are used off stage for evil purposes.

Although there are (unfortunately) many psychic surgeons, they all use pretty much the same techniques of deception. The psychic surgeon comes to the operating table as prepared as a magician comes to the stage. The sleight-of-hand magician may have tucked coins and cards into pockets and pant hems before the show, and the psychic surgeon does the same with pieces of "tumors," animal matter that will be "removed" from the patient's body. The tumors are all fake, of course. The faith healer or his assistants have previously visited a butcher market to obtain cow and pig livers and intestines. They pick off small glands and cysts from the animal parts and put them aside to be used in the operation. They take these pieces and wrap them individually in cotton balls for clean holding. Clots of blood are also wrapped up in cotton. These "bullets," as they call them, are concealed on the surgeon and his or her assistants in their pockets, stockings, belts, cigarette packs, and wherever else is available. "I observed one of the female psychic surgeons take one from her bra—any place on your body which would be or could be a hiding place," explained one former assistant.[7]

At the surgery site, the patient lies flat on the operating table and is given what she believes is a clear view of her psychic surgery down the front of her body. The surgeon uses methods of palming to bring the bloody bullets out of hiding and to pull them from folds of flesh on the person. The patient is told that these animal membranes are her tumors being removed. An assistant can pass along water-soaked cotton balls that drench the blood clots. As the blood gets wet it starts running and dripping, and the patient becomes convinced that the surgeon actually has penetrated her body with his hands. Another technique is to simply fold the fingers behind the hand and press the knuckles into the skin. The impression is given that the fingers are inside the body, looking for tumors to pluck out.

The faith healer has what every stage magician dreams of—complete control over the audience, an audience that has a very restricted view of the stage. The audience is lying flat on her back, and all she sees is straight down the line of her body. There are no bad angles to this magic trick. Some simple palming, using fat as covers, and a well-practiced exploiting of the patient's gullibility make for a sad state of affairs. The patient believes in magic—has to believe in it—and yet, unfortunately, the kind of magic she receives is not the kind of fantasies, but of the stage.

* * * * *

I make my living as a systems manager/analyst, and folks tend to get a little leery about who's managing their expensive equipment . . . So for my perspective, my "psy" is a personal fact of life, and not a professional thing. I would not discuss [my psychic powers] in my normal workplace."—John, a computer consultant who believes he has psychic powers.

It is apparent that it is a matter of blind belief, rather than actual proof, where such issues are concerned.[8]—James Randi

Self-Deception

Why can magic fool us? Because it is easier and more spiritually satisfying to believe than to delve into the truth behind the magic. I agree it feels good to believe in magic, but some people so need to believe that when their hope is shattered they will allow any garbage to fill the empty space left by what they once felt.

James Randi, who is well known as an investigator of the paranormal, relates a story about Yasha Katz, Uri Geller's longtime partner in his "psychic" feats. After awhile Katz finally got fed up by Geller's trickery. Katz had long believed that Geller had special powers. When he finally realized Geller was manipulating his audience, Katz allowed the relationship to terminate, but he still felt the need to vindicate his belief in psychic powers. Katz called Randi and said he had discovered "a *genuine* one-hundred-percent psychic young fellow who was obviously the real thing, since he denied that he wanted to become another Geller."[9] When Randi visited the psychic he found a magician who was baffled by Katz's reaction to his illusions. The new psychic had never *claimed* to have any supernatural powers at all! "I am not psychic, merely a magician, a showman," he said. Katz's need to believe outweighed the plain English that was being told to him.

Yes, it feels good to believe in the reality of an unreal magic, and some people do, to the point of disbelieving a reality that should be self-evident. Let me tell you a story about my own journey to the edge of evidence and the way I pulled myself out of the pit of psychic nonsense. When I was younger I was extremely skeptical of such phenomenon, but on the other hand, my head was so full of books on UFOs, psychic mumbo-jumbo, witchcraft, and other spookiness that it was hard not to believe in it. Besides, my young mind did not have the capacity to explain away all the weirdness I saw in the world.

One book I read gave exact instructions on how to create dowsing pendulums. It said to take a length of string and tie a weight to the end. Hold the pendulum above various objects and start it bobbing back and forth in a straight line. A pendulum of eighteen inches would start circling if held over gold or yellow, "femaleness," or water. A twenty-one-inch pendulum string would circle over "maleness" and diamonds. I made up two pendulums using exotic-looking pieces of coral and colored yarn, and set out to test them. HOLY MOLY! IT WORKED! Anytime I held the pendulum over something yellow—sure enough, the circling would begin! And when I moved the yellow away, it would stop. Magic! *Real* magic.

I showed this to a friend, who also got promising results (although I thought he might be shaking his hand a little). And even that friend's mother agreed, "No, you're not moving your hand," she told me, convinced that occult forces were at work. She looked carefully and knew that this dowsing was genuine. Other tests followed, blind examinations of the pendulums' powers. A deck of playing cards. Without looking I would hold a card in hand, and slowly recite numbers until the pendulum started swirling. Sometimes there would be a hit—the pendulum mysteriously knowing the face of a card, sight unseen. But usually this resulted in failure. A more productive test involved using the pendulum to guess "red" or "black" for the color of the card. Here the magic forces were right about half the time! Impressive!

I would stare at these miracles and would feel the reality of it and know that there was truth to it. But I also knew that there was something wrong in my tests. I was just too young and unmindful of rationality to figure out where I was going wrong. One time I held the coral and yarn in my hand and asked my friend, "Don't you want to figure out how it works?" No, he wanted to lie on the bed and read comic books. So I was left to my own ponderings.

Finally I came up with a way to test the marvels of ancient engineering. Instead of holding the pendulum in my hand, I tied it to a ruler. I had tried this one before, theorizing that subtle hand movements could not transfer through the ruler and to the string, and still the pendulums had functioned—proof for the mystic! But this time I would try something different. This time I tied the yarn to the ruler, and propped the ruler so it was sticking out off the edge of my desk. Without holding the ruler, I gave the pendulum a push of power, and held a bright yellow magazine underneath. The pendulum kept right on going straight, back and forth, straight as an arrow it went. It did not detect the yellow. A few more tests and I knew I was through as a sorcerer. When no human hand was touching the pendulum, no strange behavior ensured. This supernatural was quite natural after all. I was disappointed that I had discovered that the magic was nothing more than self-deception. But I was happy in myself for I had found the answer I had sought for so long.

Others may not be so lucky. My investigation into the supernatural was nothing more than me playing a game. But some take this very seriously. They have to. They're at the end of their rope. They have a great desire that needs to be fulfilled and they'll go to any length to fill it. To that end, we have self-proclaimed psychic detectives working for police departments. One of my sources spread to me the (unverified) story that a well-known "psychic" has teamed up with a former New York City cop and the two of them will sell you a secret word for $300,000 that you should think about if you are ever kidnapped or in danger. The psychic could then supposedly pick up on your thoughts, locate you psychically, and alert the proper authorities. Can you image the false hope that is generated amid the horror of a homicide or kidnapping and the immense disappointment when a charlatan is trusted and fails, or the agony a family must face when they realize their police department is so incompetent as to seek out help from such people. It's the deluded leading the deluded! The way psychic detectives find their criminal is sometimes by working from the clues the police have already dug up and other times just blind speculation. Often the psychic detective doesn't really contribute to the case at all, but provides cryptic clues that only later, after the case is solved by routine police work, are "retrofitted" to the actual crime.[10] In one case a psychic said she saw a vision of a red door. "That information did not help," the police chief said later with deadpan irony. "Our area of search was the south Bronx and there are thousands of red doors." Later a red door actually was found by the police in their investigation, but remember, it was one of thousands of red doors; one can hardly take credit for solving a crime with such a vague prediction as that. She might as well have predicted the victim would be found in a building with a wall.

As I'm writing this, a "news" story is on television extolling the virtues of a Psychic to the Stars. The alleged psychic has just told the story of how he made predictions such as the death of John Lennon and the rise to fame and wealth of clothing designer Perry Ellis. Even *I* can make predictions about things that happened in the past, especially considering that the people are dead and can't confirm that these are the predictions I gave them years before. But let's be trusting for a moment and feign gullibility for this psychic's claims. That still doesn't interfere with the probability that he has made these same predictions to others. To how many people did he predict success who never did succeed? How many failures went unreported? Plenty, I'm sure.

I'm also sure that the psychic in question is sincere. He truly believes he has special powers, or in any case, that such powers exist in the world. This can be useful to a person. It makes someone feel gifted while at the same time giving them zero responsibility for their actions. The stage magician who messes up feels embarrassment and anger. The "psychic" who messes up doesn't have to blame himself because it wasn't he who is at fault, but the cosmic structure of the universe. Something was not quite right with the universe while he was performing (bad vibes or astrological nonsense). Psychics have their cake and eat it too!

In the same way, they have their magic and magick too. Here I'll use magic to refer to stage magic, and magick with a "k" to refer to "real" magick—the supernatural, occult, psychic kind of magick. Unlike stage magicians, who must draw a line before what is trick and what is reality, real magickians need not fear this distinction, because they have an idea to proselytize. Even if the magickian is not actively trying to convert others to his way of thinking, he has an obligation to the magick to believe in it and defend it within his own mind. Any means to that end is fine. Max the Mad, a practicing chaos magickian from San Francisco, California, explained that even though he believes in the power of real magick, he might use a magic trick against "the kind of jerk who asks an [ignorant and mocking] question about magick" possibly by "dropping a quick illusion that (hopefully) makes him/her look like a fool, deflates their ego (doing them a service, really) and turns the tables on them in an amusing way—and *that* in itself is *real* magick, eh?" You can see how at odds this viewpoint is with that of stage magicians who try very much not to alienate their audience.

Magickians often talk about using magic tricks in their rituals to create a sensation of awed reverie. The need to believe and spread belief outweighs doubt about the righteousness of such trickery. Max the Mad explained to me his feelings about using "trick" magic within a supposedly real magick ritual:

> Though it is not something that can be proven conclusively, I'm quite sure that "stage magic" was quite important to ancient shamans and medicine men/women. Being able to do a little prestidigitation would certainly put people in the proper "mood" to be able to invest the necessary belief in "real" magick to make it work! Even in certain real "magickal orders" such things were practiced. In the Ritual of the Neophyte of the Order of the Golden Dawn there is a part where a simple chemical trick is used to make a vessel of water appear to turn into blood. This transubstantiation is an

important part of the symbolism of the ritual, and the use of the *magic* trick to put the point across to the new initiate was not beneath being used by the *real* magickians!

Personally, I'm all for the use of such things in magick ritual (though there are many who would disagree with me on this point). Hell, I'm all for using smoke machines, pyrotechnics and lasers! Invoking the "sense of wonder" is what makes *magick* work in the first place! In my humble opinion, of course.

The Ritual of the Neophyte of the Order of the Golden Dawn is a complex and inclusive initiation rite that involves as much prethought and planning as we've seen goes into a magical illusion. The difference is that the illusion being created is the aura of magick itself, whereas in stage magic, the aura is merely a byproduct of the magical goal.

In the Ritual of the Neophyte, the stage is set in a prescribed way, with pillars and banners and an altar and assistants standing in specific places throughout the room wearing ceremonial robes. The ritual is filled with occult words, incense, water-sprinkling, and sword-brandishing. Finally it is time to turn water into blood. The neophyte is given a dish of clear water to hold. Kerux, an officer of the Golden Dawn, intones, "If the Oath be forgotten, and the solemn pledge broken, then that which is secret shall be revealed, even as this pure fluid reveals the semblance of blood." At that point, Kerux pours more clear water into the neophyte's bowl. The water, swishing around, turns to blood. "Let this remind thee ever, O neophyte, how easily by a careless or unthinking word, thou mayst betray that which thou hast sworn to keep secret."[11] Water turned to blood by magick! The neophyte is convinced!

The mystery is explained by a mixture of chemicals: a small portion of sodium salicylate in one of the water dishes, and a small amount of ferric ammonium sulfate in the other dish. Both containers of water will remain clear until mixed, when the liquid will turn blood red. One editor of *The Golden Dawn* recommends, "A little experimentation beforehand [to] assure the best shade of red and avoid such disconcerting experience as having the fluid change back to a clear fluid (for example, when there is too little of one of the two ingredients)."[12]

Ancient shamans and mystics are not the only ones who have used physical deception to induce belief in an ethereal spirit world. I am reminded of how the twentieth-century Christian missionaries proselytized peoples of the rain forests away from their indigenous beliefs. In the words of one tribesman: "My people were very sick with the white man's diseases and our medicine men could not cure us. The whites said that they brought the religion and the medicine of the one true God. We accepted both. . . . The . . . shamans lost their powers because of the missionaries."[13] It wasn't because of the inherent superiority of Christendom that the tribespeople were converted. Rather, as the tribes had more contact with the white people they began contracting the white peoples' diseases. Their medicine men knew nothing of these new diseases, even with their thousands of years of knowledge, and could not stop them. By introducing Western medicines to cure the Western diseases that the missionaries themselves had inflicted upon the people of the rain forest, the natives saw their own native beliefs being one-upped. They weren't being cured *because* of Christianity—but they didn't know that. A lack of knowledge on their part, a body of science on the part of the Westerners, and an illusion of an almighty Christian God was created. Just like any magic trick, there is always a scientific principle underlying it, whether that science is physics, optics, psychology, the chemistry of the Golden Dawn, or, in this special case, biology—the biology of wonder drugs. The tribes simply weren't informed that the "wonder" in wonder drugs is not the Christian God but the mortal humans who developed the drugs.

So we have ancient shamans, mystics, and missionaries using science to buoy a belief in the spirit world. Modern-day psychics and faith healers do the exact same thing. Even the staunchest of believers must admit that their favorite psychic has used magic tricks from time to time, in order to keep up the illusion that they have constant, unstoppable psychic powers. Self-deception may not be so bad if it is kept to itself. Unfortunately, self-deception of power provides the opportunity for the gifted to share that power with those less fortunate, like rain forest tribes helpless against the influx of Western diseases. The world has rapidly lost out on much of the knowledge those tribes had collected over the years. The world will suffer for it.

Lack of Thought

Magic works because the magician thinks for you, or, at least, the magician provides answers to the questions your mind poses. For example, if you see a levitation being performed, the magician will pull a steel hoop around the floating subject to answer the question "Is she held aloft by string?" The hoop makes your mind answer, "No, she couldn't be held up by strings. Some magic must be involved here." Many stage illusions are also performed intentionally quickly so the audience doesn't have time to reflect on what has transpired.

These are the sorts of things that faith healers and other charlatans have to be able to do to collect your money. Religious cults do it to collect your soul. Cult members are cajoled into taking part in round-the-clock cult activities—prayer sessions, charity work, parties, get-togethers—so that the underlying "deck manipulation" cannot be spotted. They're always living in the present moment, perhaps looking toward the future but certainly never contemplatively, never wonderingly, because the answers are all spelled right out for them and thrust into their brains by others. One faith healer warned his congregation against the dangers of asking too many questions: "Let God fight your battles. . . . You just spend your time witnessing to your neighbors and to your friends about the power of God and don't try to answer agnostics and atheists!"[14] They don't want you to think for yourself because if you do you might realize you're being lied to and stolen from.

In some ways our brains are naturally lazy and welcome the opportunity to have thoughts thrust into them. I wave to my friend who's a block away—I can't recognize her face that far away, but I sure recognize her flaming red jacket and motorcycle helmet. My brain doesn't need proof positive that it is my friend; it only needs those few subtle clues and the question is sufficiently answered. What lazy brains we have. If our brains are so easily satisfied with these trivial issues, no wonder they can be fooled on monumental scales with the stakes so high, such as when people waste fortunes on frauds, or plunge all their time and effort into pursuing crazy notions. One author has theorized that not only are our brains particularly receptive to incoming thoughts, but they are naturally inclined "to believe that something else 'out there' is controlling us: a soul force, a mind force, a God force, or simply the force of our own wills, whatever that is. . . . The brain appears programmed to mask its role in our lives . . . It's as if it doesn't want us to know that it's up there, controlling us with computer-like techniques."[15] I'm not sure that I buy into this notion, but it certainly is true that many people's brains do act that way—unthinking, never self-reflective, and more attuned to what people tell them than what they tell themselves. That's when they get deceived. That, after all, is the basis of magic.

Evolving Thought

One reason we humans are so good at deceiving ourselves is our fallible memory. The phenomenon of exaggerating illusions was presented in chapter 8; now I'd like to touch on it again, as it is a significant factor in our daily lives. Here is a typical (true) example. A co-worker comes back from a business trip in Washington, D.C. "We saw a shooting!" she exclaims. I press her for details and after a while I get the whole story from her. The cops had their arms outstretched with guns out while arresting someone. "Did they fire?" No. "Did the person they were arresting, fire?" No. "Then you didn't see a shooting!"

This is the sort of picture that can build and change in one's mind over time. Even people with exceptional memories will at times insist that untrue events occurred because they've convinced themselves of the reality. Fraudulent psychics use this technique extensively to become more powerful in the eyes of their admirers, as time passes away from the events they claim prove their special powers. I'm reminded of a quote in *The Geller Effect*. The author is waiting for Uri Geller's psychic powers to swing a compass needle, but nothing is happening. " 'Yes,' I said. 'It moved a little.' It had not, but I felt that some false feedback would encourage him, as indeed it did."[16] We're supposed to trust the reportage and memory of someone who isn't truthful even to the psychic he supposedly admires? (And why didn't the psychic Geller perceive his lying?)

On a more down-to-earth scale, have you ever argued with a buddy over the terms of a bar bet made the week before? Or have you disagreed over exactly how much money you owed your friend? Or vice versa? I swear I owe my friend $7, but he insists it was more like $12. Isn't it funny how we remember things in our favor! The solution is to take careful notes when money or friendship is on the line. And when extraordinary powers are being claimed, it's important to document exactly what went on so future researchers cannot distort events.

Would a person who's well-dressed, well-mannered, and well-spoken lie? The answer is: *Yes.*[17]—James Randi

Con Artists

The con artist, with fast speech and reassuring smiles, has much in common with the magician. Both are out to deceive you, perhaps to manipulate your mind. Like faith healers and psychics, con artists use a lot of the same tricks as magicians, often right out of the box. The first notion that comes to mind is the con artist as smooth talker, or fast talker. Certainly it is true that the con artist carefully devises patter that will further his devious career. Patter is combined with a look that fits the part. Most con artists don't look like the greasy, seedy characters you might expect them to be. There are little-old-lady pickpocket teams[18] as well as young men and women who run their own brands of scam. You wouldn't expect a con artist to look like a soccer mom, nor would you expect a well-groomed valet parker to swipe your car. And yet people are taken all the time by cons playing these roles. If they looked like a con artist, you wouldn't be fooled, would you? You wouldn't be fooled because you wouldn't get involved with that seedy-looking person in the first place.

Another common deception is the use of confederates. Just as a magician might plant a stooge in the audience, the con artist often plants a shill in the crowd to help entice a victim into the swindle. In one scam, a woman stands outside a shopping center collecting charity for a local shelter. If a passer-by hesitates, a couple walks by and adds $20 to the collection can.

"They're a great organization," they say as they walk off, "it would be a shame if they close down." The victim is now assured this is a legitimate charity, so she adds her money to the can. It's important to remember that any legitimate charity does not need your funds *this instant,* as you're stepping out of a shopping mall. If you want to give charity, call the organization directly to find out how you can best contribute. In this case, one of the women exiting the shopping center happened to be in charge of fundraising for the shelter. She excused herself, grabbed a cop, and came back to find the scammer had vanished.[19]

Reading about scams makes it instantly apparent the great extent to which con artists rely on the same tricks as magicians to outsmart their victims. Techniques of confederates, costuming, poise, patter, and props are all used to dupe those who believe themselves city savvy. Let's look at some other kinds of cons, how they relate to stage magic, and how they use the magician's tricks:

Three-card monte is a corrupt game that's played in cities so often you would think by now people would have caught on to it. Before this three-card version the same con was the pea and walnut shell game, and before that it was the Cups and Balls. The three-card monte purveyor uses a cardboard box or lightweight folding card table as his stage. Three cards are shown: one's a queen, the others ain't. The cards are turned over and moved around on the table; it's your job to pick the queen. If you do you can win some cash. But you never can pick it, because the monte man is conning you every step of the way.

The dealer's repertoire of sleights is limited, but he doesn't need more than two or three moves since there's only three cards to deal with. The dealer picks up two or three cards at a time, stacks them up, and rearranges them by an *underthrow,* letting the bottom card drop back onto the table in a new place. The catch is, the dealer has a sleight, called the *hipe,* that snaps the *top* card onto the table. Both the hipe and the underthrow deals look the same in competent hands. Consider how these two deals alone can make the game impossible to win: The dealer might start out by switching positions of the cards, and then turning over the queen to make all the bystanders feel at ease—"Yes! I followed it okay! This isn't that hard!" Lulled into certainty now, just a few more of those, and the betting starts. This is when the dealer starts with the hipe, the fake deal from the top that looks like a deal from the bottom. The spectators think they know which card is being put down, but they're wrong. Some more adept monte dealers have been known to also use a fourth card in their game. The fourth card stays hidden and palmed, until the crucial moment when it's switched for a card the spectators *think* they have under control. If money's on the table, chances are that money's staying with the dealer.

Monte dealers usually work with partners. They'll have stooges or *shills* in the crowd who place bets to encourage the *real* crowd to lay down money.

Of course the stooge always wins—he makes it look easy to win. The hipe only starts when a stranger steps in to play. Stooges and dealers usually have a code system set up between them, either verbal or gestural. The dealer might keep a toothpick or cigarette in one side of his mouth to indicate the location of the queen. Other code systems use the placement of the dealer's hand, money, or other factors. The monte team might have lookouts in the crowd watching for the cops as well, with a code system in place to relate warnings as appropriate.

There are all sorts of con men and women, all sorts of cons, and many of them use magic. Short change artists use a fast pace, practiced routine, and sleight of hand to turn twenty-one dollars into thirty-one dollars in just a few minutes. The short change artist first locates a young or inexperienced cashier at a busy store or restaurant. He or she makes a small purchase, less than a dollar, with a twenty-dollar bill. He hands over the bill and begins some misdirecting patter about some news story, the weather, or even a personal comment about the clerk's hair style or jewelry. The clerk is listening to the rap while counting change and placing it on the countertop, and the con artist then asks to make another small purchase, like a pack of cigarettes, which the cashier has to reach for. While the cashier is occupied, the swindler produces a one-dollar bill from his pocket, and exclaims in surprise: "Oh wow, I had that all along!" Now comes the sleight of hand. As he reaches for the nineteen dollars in change, the one-dollar bill is folded and palmed in his hand, while almost simultaneously he folds up the ten-dollar bill (from the change on the countertop) and hides it in the rest of the change from the original purchase. (These moves are further covered up by his continuing compliments and chatter.) Now he apparently has ten dollars in his hand (one dollar from his pocket, and nine dollars change.) He asks the cashier if she would like the stack of singles in exchange for a ten from the register, and since it is a busy store and change is always in demand, the cashier agrees. When she takes the money from him, she will notice the extra ten-dollar bill and figure he made a mistake in giving her the ten instead of the one from his pocket. (If she doesn't, the con artist will "suddenly realize" his "mistake.") So the con artist takes out the one-dollar bill that he had palmed, and places it with the other nineteen, and again offers to give her the change, this time for a twenty-dollar bill. He walks away ten dollars richer. If you have trouble following the flow of money here, you're not alone. Con artists have been known to make three hundred dollars or more a day with the scam.

The short change artist, like most con artists, is as slick as any magician, but the "slickness" will not be evident. If he *looked* slick, the clerk wouldn't trust him. Unslickness is also a big concern of salespeople. "I stuttered in one of my infomercials," said TV pitchman Ron Popeil, "and my producer wanted to edit it out, but I said leave it in. People do stutter when they're not scripted. And I think the audience responds better to a less slick presentation."[20]

Once I was working behind a counter and had an exchange eerily familiar to me as a short change job. The guy must have noticed suspicion on my face because he said, "Don't worry, I'm not trying to short change you or nothing." He meant it reassuringly, but it got me even more panicked— *Oh no! He knows about short changing, so maybe he's doing it!* At that point I very carefully counted out his money and for the rest of the day I was doing mental calculations. He had produced a transaction so complicated I could hardly deconstruct it in my mind. I *thought* he got the correct amount of change, but I was never fully convinced he hadn't swindled me.

PROOFS IN THE CON

Magicians are presenting the illusion of the impossible, and in so doing they must make every effort to "prove" the impossible is occurring. The proof might be that they let an audience member inspect the props, bang on the side of a trunk, or show you both sides of their empty hand. The point is that they try to avert suspicion before it starts. "You think I hid it up my sleeve? Then I'll roll up my sleeves to prove otherwise." They attempt to prove to you that no trickery is involved (at least none that you can detect) and to ensure that you are awed by the experience of magic.

Con artists must also use proofs to show that they are genuine, trustworthy souls. One example of con artist proofs is called the "mirror play," where the con artist disarms the victim's suspicions by bringing the victim's innermost suspicions out to the surface. "You don't trust me enough to hand over the money? Well, just call my manager . . . here's the phone number." Most victims don't want to appear rude and suspicious, so they won't call the phone number (which is probably made up or bogus). Very often they don't call the phone number until after they've handed over the money and the con artist is long gone.

In one case a noted con man walked into an office in City Hall and explained that he was there to pick up a clock for repairs.[21] (The clock was extremely valuable and of course no repair had been ordered.) The alderman was suspicious and didn't want to hand over the clock, but the con artist pulled the mirror play, mirroring the alderman's internal thoughts. "Of course I realize the clock is valuable," he might've pointed out. "That's why I came *in person* to pick it up and insure it was handled properly!" The con artist used the victim's own doubts to create an illusion of acceptability.

A retired police inspector from the Oakland, California, police department wrote in his memoir about a particular forger who used this method.[22] The forger was going around to appliance and furniture stores buying items with bogus checks. The checks were always made out to a price a little higher than the cost of the item being purchased. The police department sent warnings out to the stores. At least one riled-up merchant said, "If he ever comes into my store, I will close the doors and call you up immediately." Two weeks later, the police inspector received a call from that very same store owner. He had been taken in.

The police inspector traveled to the store and was greeted by a roomful of smiling store clerks and one owner with a flushed face. The clerks were smiling that their boss had been duped so easily by the con man, while the boss stood there mystified. "Well, Inspector," he said in a deflated tone, "I done it; I waited on him myself, and when he produced the check, I gave him $6.00 change." He explained that he had been extremely cautious with the man, whom he suspected from the start was the con artist. First the owner asked the man for his home phone number. The owner wanted to call his wife at home to verify the purchase. Surprisingly, the con artist willingly gave him his phone number, which the store owner dialed immediately. The operator informed him that there was no such telephone number.

At this point one might think the jig would be up, but no. The con artist was using the mirror play to prove his case by mirroring the victim's internal thoughts. What's troubling the clerk is there was no such telephone number. Well then, feed that right back at him. "Oh yes there is such a phone number! It's a new house, we were recently married, and we just moved in." This line was smooth, but the store owner was suspicious anyway. In fact, now he was convinced that this man was the con artist the police had warned him about. He said to him, "You look just like a man the Police Department is looking for who is passing checks."

"Is that so? Why don't you call them?" the wily con artist replied. The owner stated that he was so dumbfounded at the replies he received to every question that he was completely disarmed, and, turning to the man, said, "Well, it is only $6.00 in change, so I will take a chance on the sale."

You can see what is happening here. Again and again the store owner is confronted by his own internal worries. The con artist so convincingly lays bare the owner's internal suspicions that it seems highly unlikely that he's doing something wrong. Surely a con artist would try to hide from suspicions? Surely a con artist would try to lie and talk his way out of each confrontation, rather than inviting the owner to phone the police? In this way the con artist adds layer upon layer to his proof, and the charade ends with a masterful stroke of misdirection—the paltry six dollars in change. Six dollars seems so small an amount. The word "change" seems even smaller. The con artist purposefully writes his forged checks a little bit higher than the actual amount so if the store owner is suspicious, the owner can reckon, "Well, it *is* only six dollars in change, maybe I'm being stingy about it. Maybe I'm maligning an innocent man." The owner never thinks that it's really six dollars *plus* the value of the appliance being purchased!

After the con artist left the store, the owner called the bank and found out that the check was bogus. He looked up and down the street and the man was long out of sight. Police Inspector Sternitzky explains that that's what most people do—they wait until it's too late to call the bank for verification. Isn't that what happens in a magic show? The magician presents all these proofs—roll up the sleeve, empty the pocket, show the empty hand—he shows you all these proofs, neglecting to show you the one essential proof that would blow his case. Sure it ain't up the sleeve, in the pocket, or in the hand, but maybe it's hidden behind his neck or under his tie. The skilled magician or con artist is convincing at bringing to light so many of your suspicions that you don't notice he's leaving out the crucial one.

On a happy note, the forger of this last story was eventually caught and brought to trial. The store owner, and all the other store owners who'd been bamboozled by him, had the pleasure of seeing the con man sent to prison.

Playing to Win

Another use of magical techniques is in games and sports of all sorts. Here the magic comes in two varieties: (1) Magic used to *cheat*, such as when a con artist employs sleight of hand to bring bogus dice into a craps game, and (2) *Magic used to deceive the other team while staying within the rules of the game* (such as a deceptive football play that makes use of misdirection).

Let's look at some ways in which magic tricks can deceive and cheat in games and sports. First of all, consider a football play. One deceptive play is the fake option reverse. As described by coach John Robinson of the University of Southern California Trojans football team:

> This is a deceptive play. The quarterback takes the snap, steps back, then heads right, like he's running the option. The running back is trailing behind. Meanwhile, the receiver on the right side takes one step forward, then turns around and runs left between the quarterback and running back, taking the ball from the QB. The play leaves the defense surprised because the action all flows right, while the ball actually goes left.[23]

The football team uses aspects of misdirection, building up false expectations and surprise in much the way a magician does, in order to fake out the opposing side. They also use sleight of hand, as when a player pretends to throw a ball he really doesn't have. It's entirely within the rules to deceive the opponents, so they do what they can to "work their magic" on the field. In the popular book and movie *M*A*S*H*, the surgeons of the 4077 Mobile Army Surgical Hospital play a game of football against their arch rivals, the 325th Evac Hospital. The 325th's team consists of specially picked and trained professionals, while the 4077 is stuck with a teamful of out-of-shape doctors. But they do have one formerly pro player, Spearchucker Jones, and he has a plan that includes all of the above deceptions: misdirection, build-up of certain expectations, and surprise, and adds to that one more magician's tool—the cover.

"We're gonna make the center eligible," says Spearchucker. Vollmer, the center is surprised. "I can't catch a pass," he says. "You don't have to," comes the reply. Trapper takes the snap and hands the ball right back to you between your legs. You hide it in your belly, and stay there like you're blockin'. Trapper, you start back like you got the ball, make a fake to me and keep going. . . . Meanwhile," Spearchucker says to Vollmer, "when your man goes by you, you straighten up, hidin' the ball with your arms, and you walk—don't run—toward that other goal line."[24] Deftly combining these illusionary tools, the play was made and it turned the tide for the 4077 (at least in fiction).

In elementary school I made use of my primitive ability to perform sleight of hand during a game of "paper football." Paper football is a kid's game of stealth that uses a "football" made from an ordinary sheet of paper folded down into a small packet. The two teams huddle and discuss their game plan. One person gets to hold onto the tiny paper football and run towards the goal with it hidden in his or her hands. The other team has to tag the person out before the goal is reached. The ball is hidden, so the other team doesn't know who has it. I don't remember much else about this game except for one glorious day when I was chosen to run with the ball. At first I hid the ball in my hand as I ran up the field. But then I saw the ever-enlarging shadow of a classmate growing on the grass beneath my feet. Someone was overtaking me! Glancing back I saw the kid. I didn't know him well, just that he was the bullying kind and two heads taller than me. Thinking fast, I slipped the paper football into the crack between thumb and forefinger, so that the packet extended out behind the back of my hand. "I don't have it," I said, showing him my empty hands. He looked at my clumsy back palm and demanded to know who did have the ball. "That guy there," I lied, and the bully took off after him just as I was crossing the goal line with the ball.

BASEBALL MAGIC

The game of baseball, with its small ball and big gloves, is ideal for all sorts of sleight of handwork, such as palming. One of the oldest tricks in the book has the runner at first with the pitcher acting like he has the ball, getting ready to throw it the moment the runner leaves the bag. But the ball's still in the first baseman's hands. When the runner moves off base, the first baseman tags him out. An entertaining combination of acting, misdirection, palming, and covers—don't tell me that's not a magic trick!

The batter can also use fake-outs to his advantage, with such techniques as the bunt and hit: appearing as if he is about to bunt, then instantly switching to a hit past the infielders, who should be on their way in. A play called the hit and run allows one team to control the actions of their opposition, much in the way a magician controls audience volunteers' behavior. In the hit and run, a situation is created where the second baseman moves onto base in advance of the first-base runner. The batter attempts to slam the ball into the empty space that the second baseman just vacated. The second baseman therefore has his actions controlled by the other team. He has to cover base, and he thinks he's making his own decision on how to move, but in effect it was a decision made by the opposite team's batter and coach. Even if the second baseman is wise to the play, which he surely is, he might not have any easy way out of it, and so he is still caught.[25]

Baseball also has its clever systems of secret signs and signals reminiscent of telepathy codes used by mentalists and the card codes of three-card monte dealers. The ball players and mentalists share a problem—how can they convey information secretly to their comrades in front of a watching audience? Mentalists use a combination of words and gestures. Baseball players and coaches tend to use gestures, although words are also sometimes spoken. The coach yelling "Come on, let's get a good pitch!" may sound like he's making an innocent comment, but in fact he may be alerting the batter that a particular pitch or sign is on the way.[26] Coaches signal their players with subtle and not-so-subtle signals: a touch of the belt-buckle, a tap of the cap or elbow. The actual sign, or "hot sign," is hidden inside a mix of phony signs so that the coach might be touching and tapping and rapping for ten minutes, but the signal itself is conveyed in a few moments. Like the magician, the coach must *"make certain all of his gestures and touches are given in a steady, continuous motion even after the sign has been given."*[27] Likewise, "even if there is no play called, they should go through some routine on every pitch, being sure in the first couple of innings that they touch every area of the package."[28] It is a combination of skill and acting, not only on the coach's part, but the players'. The players must act like they're interested in *all* the signs, even when the signs are not conveying any information, otherwise sign-stealers from opposing teams will be able to break the code. Maybe baseball coaches can give tips to the magicians, hobbyists, and skeptical audience members who try to break the codes of fraudulent psychics!

GAMBLER'S MAGIC

Magic techniques are used by gamblers in many ways to numerous to detail here. All methods from sleight of hand, crimping and marking cards, forces, mirrors and shiners (to glimpse other players' cards), fake dice, misdirection, and stooges are employed by professionals to fleece unwary victims in poker and craps.[29]

A professional crap crew will come to a game with a suitcase of *a thousand* rigged dice, which they keep out in the car. Each die is unique in its own way, with variations in shape, colors, transparency, markings (painted or concave) and roundness of corners. There are different kinds of rigged dice. Some are "sure things" that are weighted on one side to come up on top, but usually the crews will use percentage dice, which favor certain numbers over the long haul. A variation of time misdirection is at work here. The hustlers make sure to earn their money over an extended period of time, so as not to arouse the suspicions of the other players. They'll go into the game with about five dice hidden on their person, in concealed pockets throughout their clothing. Various sleights and misdirections are used to switch a game die for a rigged one. A member of the crew might act drunk and fling one of the dies wildly. When the rest of the players go off in search of the other die, the "drunk" one calmly puts it in his pocket and takes out a matching rigged die. More subtle sleights are also used, like reaching into a pocket for a cigarette, and pulling out a percentage die. The hustlers work in teams, so sometimes they use their partner as covers, or even use a sucker to cover their moves. It's all the same stuff as the magician uses.

Like any magician, the craps hustlers have to worry about setting up their tricks and angles beforehand. Some will try to push the table up against a wall and stand near it, so they will be in the right position to pick up the dice after every shot and toss them back to the shooter. Naturally they use their opportunity to switch dice. "Once you're against the wall," brags one hustler, "who cares how many people are watching you, because who can see anything? They can't see through your hand. No one can see what you're doing because you're against this wall."

BOARD GAMES

Another unseemly (but cute) way of using magic outside the theater is in board games. Board games offer all the usual magic apparatus: stacks of cards, dice, round pieces that are like coins. To a sleight-of-hand artist, playing a board game could be more fun than a day at the beach! A United Kingdom magician named Robin Allen, whose interest lies mainly in gambling scams but who also lists as one of his sparetime pursuits the making of crop circles, has recently started investigating the use of magic techniques to cheat at board games. He's quick to point out, however, it's "not because I desperately want to win (I only tend to cheat in them when I'm certain to lose in any case), but because I like to find opportunities to practice in strange places."

As one example, he gives the game Clue (known as Cluedo in the United Kingdom). Clue is a board game in which the playing board represents a mansion. A character is murdered in the game, and one of the players is the murderer. The winner of the game is the one who can deduce who was killed, who the killer is, and how the murder was committed. All of these factors are represented by playing cards that are kept hidden from the players, face down and in an envelope, until the end of the game. (This is starting to sound like a mentalism trick, isn't it?) Indeed it is, only the other players didn't know that any trickery was involved. While shuffling the pack of cards that would determine who the murderer was, this magician "glimpsed the bottom card of the 'murderer' set, shuffled it to the middle, classic forced it on my brother, and with that advantage won the round." He points out that he could have used the same card force to give himself special knowledge of the murder weapon and victim, "but that would have been a little over the top."

On dice, he says,

> I've found Monopoly to be perfect for practicing controlled dice shots. How do you avoid Mayfair when someone has two hotels on it, and you're five spaces away? You have two dice: use a slide shot, with the lower die set on five or six, and you can't fail to avoid it. I lasted probably a good dozen rounds extra in a game by saving my skin this way (I had no chance of winning).

There are probably ways to apply magician's skills to almost any game. The magician Allen made a few intriguing further speculations on how the techniques could be applied: In Monopoly, the banker could short-change players, or use a false count to give the wrong amount of money. A double lift or false dealing, or false shuffling could be used on the Community Chest cards to give yourself the card you want. "Would it be worth 'stripping' them?" he asks. Or why not go all out and apply secret markings to the back of Clue cards, "and note them as they're selected." One might do a French drop switch with Scrabble pieces, the "Elmsley Blank Square Visual Switch" he terms it. "Are there false-count methods for moving extra spaces in Snakes and Ladders? What about chess or checkers? If your opponent isn't in the rocket-scientist class, or just inattentive, could you secretly palm some of his pieces off the board, and/or replace some of yours?" The possibilities for deception, it seems, are endless!

15

Misdirection Magic in Everyday Life

This chapter continues our look at how magic techniques are used off stage and in everyday situations. Particularly we will look at varying forms of misdirection: misdirection of emotions, vision, time, and the sense of touch. When I asked one magician, the Great Sol Messler, whether he uses magic out of his magic show, he replied with a resounding "Yes! I *do* use sleight of hand in my everyday life! For one thing, it makes it easier to get the last olive from the bottom of the jar!"

Emotional Misdirection

We can use a knowledge of magic to understand how we are fooled, deceived, manipulated and connived against, because the techniques that magicians use pop up again and again in all sorts of contexts. Later I'll explain how I used magiclike psychology to shape my sister's mind into wanting to do the dishes for me. I may not have been thinking of magic at the time, but I was certainly thinking of techniques identical to those used by magicians when they shape our minds from the stage.

A magical technique doesn't even have to be intentional for it to be effective. It is often the chance happenings in life that become the great discoveries in science and technology. Or, in this case, mind control. One summer I attended one of the many carnivals that were popping up around my hometown with the coming of warm weather. One of the attractions—a silly little ride called Lost World Explorer—made such effective use of spatial misdirection, visual and auditory effects, and, most prominently, sucker tricks, that the contraption itself would rival most kiddie birthday party magicians in skillful presentation of magic.

The ride went like this. You and your loved one get into a little roller coaster car on a track and head off into a dark tunnel, apparently on your way to Exploring Lost Worlds. Every once in a while the darkness and solitude is shattered by a monster appearing before you, accompanied by a blast of a foghorn. This all is entertaining and even mildly hair-raising, but you basically know what to expect, and it isn't all that frightening.

Then comes the part where you and your loved one start grabbing each other. The car climbs up a hill and you find yourself outside on a ledge overlooking the carnival. It's a pleasant view and somewhat relaxing. The car then re-enters the darkness. You turn a corner and—another one of those stupid papier-mâché monsters. Unrealistic, unconvincing, and, by now, old hat. Nothing to be frightened of. Then, out of the corner of your eye you notice a human running up in the darkness . . . *someone is in the tunnel with you!* Is it one of the delinquents in the car behind you? Is it the crazy ride operator, the one with a tattoo of a butterfly on his tongue who was casually licking his peg leg as he sent your car off into the tunnel? No! It's worse! It's a ghoul that sneaks up behind you, sticks its hideous face in yours, grins wickedly and whispers in your ear: "*Scary . . . scarrryyyy!*"

It *is* scary! And at first you're not sure what happened. Then you come around another corner, and *blam!* there's the foghorn again, signalling another papier-mâché beast. There's the monster in front of you—not scary, you expected it to be there—but then, there is the ghoul from behind you, pressing it's hideousness right against you and whispering in your ear. You actually have to turn your head to see it, and when you do, it's *right there* in your face. Again and again this happens, and each time you jump up in fright. The papier-mâché creature before you is so phony and so unscary and so *expected* that when you are presented with a second monster it is just the opposite— realistic, frightening and unexpected. In addition, the second monster pops up not in your face, but near the side of your face. Your attention shoots to the side on reflex, as you try and figure out what nasty thing is floating by your head. The fact that it is not directly visible to you, but that you have to turn your head to see it, only makes the effect more striking. After all, in the real world things that are presented to you neatly for your inspection are the things you know have been set up for you to inspect. The things that you happen to come across by chance are more "real" and more unprepared.

Two forces are at work here. One, your eyes and ears have been conditioned by the first half of the ride to expect these dumb papier-mâché creatures to pop up at regular intervals. The fact that they continue to pop up makes you feel relaxed, because what you expect to happen actually does happen. But at the same time those monsters are directing your gaze ahead. The second force is an unintentional one: the utter phoniness of the monsters. Because the ride starts out so fake, you are lulled into a sense of security. There couldn't possibly be *two* monsters, certainly nothing to be afraid of! This ride is too cheap to show you two monsters at one time. The very fact that during the second half of the ride a monster pops up predisposes you to believe that the scare is over for now. But you are fooled, because the ride is not as cheap as you thought it was! Now you're getting two monsters at a time, and it becomes rather frightening because your mind knows the first one is fake and therefore the second one is relatively real, at least for a few moments.

Isn't this what clown magicians do, and "bumbler" magicians and comic magicians? They present themselves as unskilled or unlearned, and so when you are fooled by them you are doubly surprised. The Lost World Explorer was like one big sucker trick in which I got suckered into believing I had figured out the trick—and that in itself was the trick! My belief told me that this was a cheesy ride and I had no reason to be frightened. Yet it was this very belief that induced a bigger fright.

One of the trademarks of a Steven Spielberg film is the sucker trick effect (or perhaps we should call it a relax-startle effect). Spielberg will have a character smile, laugh, make a little joke, put a little levity into the film, and *that's* when the shark comes out of the water with fangs set to devour.

There is certainly nothing new about putting people at ease. That's the basis for many cons and scams. Most of a con job involves setting up the sucker to believe that the con man is friendly, honest, perhaps wealthy, perhaps a sucker himself. Putting people at ease is one reason magicians try to get their audience to like them, as we will discuss below. It is in essence *emotional misdirection*. In the case of the carnival ride, my emotions were misdirected toward feeling amused by its hokiness, which greatly heightened the surprise I felt when it wasn't.

Influence and Misdirection

There is a classic psychology experiment with an easily predictable outcome. Some graduate students stood on a street corner and looked up at the sky. What was the result of this? People walking past also looked up. Right away you can see the eye of the magician peering down on all this with amusement. Isn't this what he has been doing for centuries to misdirect his audience into looking at an innocent area of the stage? Isn't this what we did when we wanted others to believe a flea was in our fist?

Magic works so well because humans always do look to see what's up in the sky. If there's some people standing around looking up, our brain gets the clue that something interesting must be going on up there, more interesting than anything that could be transpiring here on earth. It's a survival mechanism. It protects us from danger and helps us learn interesting things about the world.

Where magic comes in is this: because we do have the tendency to look where others are looking we may be tempted to believe that what we find there really is more interesting than whatever's on the ground. In the case of magic, we may see the magician holding aloft a twenty-dollar bill that he had burnt to a crisp a moment before. Meanwhile you're ignoring the hand that's reaching into the pocket and slipping off the false thumbtip. In the case of real-world magic, we often find what we believe are magnificent solutions to our problems. We are misdirected from where the real solutions lie—in our own minds, in our lives here on earth. Such is what religion is made of, as well as much occult thinking, propaganda, and politics.

While we are looking up at the lofty visions being presented to us, we are ignoring the trivial solutions that abound aplenty in the real world. We are also being worked on in other ways. Psychologically it is pleasing to us to know that we are like other people—that we aren't weird. Eric Fromm commented that, "Most people are not even aware of their need to conform. They live under the illusion that they follow their own ideas and inclinations, that they are individualists, that they have arrived at their opinions as a result of their own thinking—and that it just happens that their ideas are the same as those of the majority."[1] In other words, we find an idea or solution that feels right to us, something we want to believe in. If we can also look around and see other people believing it, we have a set of supports that prods us happily on our way to the sky. And as we journey there, fortunes are lost; self-esteem is repeatedly battered and healed and battered again; hopes are crushed; and the bad guys not only win out, but retain the controlling hand.

One technique that politicians (and occasionally advertisers) will use is to argue slightly against their interests. This promotes a sense of honesty in the speaker while allowing him to recoup his losses and explain his position in a much better light than the opposition would. Magicians will act similarly when they purposely accidentally mess up a trick, only to outdo themselves in the finale. Propaganda and politics are things meant to influence us, and it is often done without our awareness of the fact. Looking at the psychological and sociological literature on the subject of influence and mind manipulation, one interesting fact reappears over and over again: when subjects are asked to predict what they would do in situations where influential tactics are being employed against them, invariably the subjects underestimate their vulnerability. This implies that we often don't realize we are being influenced to behave in certain ways, to believe in certain ideas, and to act with certain motivations. Some of the influencing tactics described by Robert Cialdini are listed below. Notice how they all relate to magic to some degree, as well as to outside interests attempting to convert you to their ways of thinking:[2]

- *Likability*. We are more susceptible to influence by those we like. Magicians follow this rule by trying to induce awe, not frustration; they try not to be a smart aleck.

- *Good looks.* While not every magician is good looking, it is often said that power is sexy—and who has more power than a magician?
- *Authority.* The magician takes noticeable control over the stage, over the props, over his assistants, and over the audience. We respond to this authority.
- *Direct commands.* Tell people exactly what to do or what to think and those thoughts and actions will more readily be absorbed into their minds (as opposed to merely presenting ideas and allowing the audience to form their own conclusions).
- *Wearing a uniform.* People in uniform seem to have particular skills, knowledge, or power.

All of these factors help influence one's perception of the communicator; they are some of the fundamental building blocks of deception. When I asked Harley Newman, an escape artist and doer of weird stuff, if his knowledge of illusion helped in his prior career as a therapist, he answered, "Yes. It's both the same, you're trying to turn around their perceptions." Newman offered an example of a paranoid schizophrenic patient who would sit home alone in his "dumpy little room" and have conversations with the doorknob. The doorknob would rattle and shake and talk to him, putting evil thoughts into his head. Instead of disagreeing with the patient, Newman helped him work with the problem, convincing the patient that the doorknob was actually *his friend*. It wasn't so much of a problem when the doorknob said *nice* things to him! "As a showman that's what I do," he says, "Guide the way people think." He also admits he got a lot of reprimands from his boss. Go figure.

"Beliefs are very powerful things;" instructs Richard Bandler, a therapist who uses neurolinguistic programming to help people to better themselves and overcome their fears: "When you change one [belief] it can do a lot of good, but if you install the wrong one, it can do a lot of harm, too. I want you to be *very* careful about the kinds of new beliefs you go around installing in people."[3]

Brainwashing and Magic

Brainwashing has traditionally been used by totalitarian governments to reform the thought processes of subversives. Robert Jay Lifton wrote a classic analysis of brainwashing and thought reform after interviewing numerous victims of Chinese Communist brainwashing in the 1950s. After the Communists took over China in 1948–49, some of the Westerners who remained in China were deemed to be problematic by the new regime and taken into custody in order to undergo "brainwashing." Lifton talked with some of those Westerners about their ordeal, as well as a number of Chinese who had also undergone the brainwashing treatment, and he came to the conclusion that brainwashing is based on a number of characteristics: milieu control, mystical manipulation, the "sacred science," "loading the language," and "doctrine over person."

Milieu Control

The most basic feature of brainwashing is the control of the victim's human communication, not just with the outside world, but also with what Lifton calls the "penetration of his inner life—over what we may speak of as his communication with himself."[4] An atmosphere is created within which the victim has trouble distinguishing between his own thoughts and the thoughts of his captors; between what is right and wrong and what he formally believed to be right but now is being led to believe is wrong. In being denied the ability to think, the victim is forced to rely more and more on data given to him by his captors. This is the kind of action a magician takes in a fast-moving show that does not give the audience a chance to think for themselves. The audience must rely totally on the clues and cues provided by the magician.

Mystical Manipulation

The brainwashers continue to exert their control over their captive, and do so in a way that "seeks to provoke specific patterns of behavior and emotion in such a way that these will appear to have arisen spontaneously from within the environment. This element of planned spontaneity, directed as it is by an ostensibly omniscient group, must assume, for the manipulated, a near-mystical quality."[5] Brainwashers have complete control over their subject's place and placement. Some of that control is obvious (such as the fact that subjects are forced into prison) but other forms of control are more subtle. For instance, the brainwashers may restrain the subject in metal shackles that force the subject to sit in a submissive or humiliating position lest the shackles dig painfully into the skin. It seems merely an accident that they are forced to assume a degrading posture—but it is in fact quite intentional. Magicians do the very same thing!

First the magician controls seating in the theater. When someone leaves their seat (such as to volunteer to go up on stage), the magician continues to control the person's viewing angle and behaviors. The magician carefully controls audience volunteers in ways that seem accidental but are in fact done purposefully to achieve a certain effect. Magicians call this *restricted choice*. They appear to be giving complete control to a spectator, when in fact the magician is in control all along. Consider the card trick where the magician riffles through a deck of cards, imploring the volunteer to shout "Stop" at any time. The choice of cards appears entirely random and in the control of the spectator. *Au contraire!* Notice that the magician is speaking *while* he's riffling. Therefore the volunteer can never yell "Stop" at the topmost cards in the deck. Almost certainly the magician has placed a special card at the top of the deck that the spectator can never select and which helps in accomplishing the magic. Another example of actions secretly controlled by the magician is the escape artist who offers his arms to the volunteers so that they can chain him up. It appears the spectator has complete control over how the shackles are applied but in fact the escape artist presents his limbs in a certain way so that no matter how tightly the chains are applied they can be made loose. "When someone in the audience does not respond correctly," notes legendary sorcerer John Mulholland, "there are ways to control his actions."[6]

THE "SACRED SCIENCE"

The "sacred science" facet of brainwashing holds that victims must be made to feel reverence towards the ideology being thrust upon them. For instance, the Chinese Communist ideology is made to seem wholly logical and complete unto itself, with no room for error, and certainly no room for Western capitalism. "While thus transcending ordinary concerns of logic, however, the milieu at the same time makes an exaggerated claim of airtight logic, of absolute 'scientific' precision."[7] Magicians do the same thing as they set up a system for the audience and then proceed to show every aspect of the system, demonstrating that there is no room for gimmicks, tricks, or sleight of hand. For instance, the magician will take actions such as showing every side of a box and letting an audience member examine the box to prove there are no trap doors in it. The magician then somehow vanishes from the box. How did he do it? You believed there couldn't be a trap door because of the way the box was inspected, but it's very likely that a trap door was used after all! The magician carefully led the inspection in such a way that the trap door was not discovered. In this way, the audience is brainwashed down a path of "airtight logic" only to have that logic backfire on them because now they cannot explain how the illusion was accomplished.

LOADING THE LANGUAGE

When brainwashers "load the language" they are using language to direct the victim's thoughts towards one unavoidable conclusion: that the brainwashing ideology is "correct" and everything else is either wrong or evil. The brainwashers use a lot of what Lifton calls the "thought-terminating cliché. The most far-reaching and complex of human problems are compressed into brief, highly reductive, definitive-sounding phrases, easily memorized and easily expressed."[8] Whenever the victim attempts to reason his way out of the logic of the brainwasher's ideology, his struggle is torn down with a swift and succinct phrase that goes in place of actual thinking.

The brainwashers don't want the victim to think, so they continually tell him: "That's just capitalist thinking." They will shake their head disapprovingly as they mutter, "Bourgeois! Bourgeois!" The victim cannot reason his way out of the brainwasher's ideology because they do not allow him to. Their answers seem to explain away his dissensions, but in reality they provide no explanation at all. They're just name-calling, judgmental, abstract, academic, all-encompassing categories that the brainwashers use in place of rational thought. Lionel Trilling called this "the language of nonthought." The link to magic is a clear one. Magicians frequently create illusions based on clichés and nonthought. The magician uses the spectators' intuitions about the world to fool them, because if the spectators were given a chance to really think about the illusion, they would be able to discern the truth behind the facade.

DOCTRINE OVER PERSON

The theory of "doctrine over person" is that the brainwashing victim must be made to feel nothing—and must be made to feel confused over what he or she feels. If the victim feels the ideology is wrong, the ideology has a reason why the person is wrong for feeling that way. It is "the subordination of human experience to the claims of doctrine."[9] Brainwashers use such methods as loading the language, blaming wayward thoughts on "capitalist imperialists from abroad" or "the bourgeois" and other faraway mythical characters, and "when the myth becomes fused with the totalist sacred science, the resulting 'logic' can be so compelling and coercive that it simply replaces the realities of individual experience."[10] There are several ways in which magicians use this technique. Occasionally a magician will tell an outright lie that he needs the audience to believe in order for the illusion to be effective. Invariably the audience will believe the lie because of the feeling of doctrine over person—in this case, that the magician is an authority figure of some sort, given to such traits as honesty and a moral character. Even when the lie flies in the face of what the audience knows from personal experience, they are likely to go along with it, much as the victim of brainwashing goes along with the lies being fed to him.

It may not be a lie *per se,* but rather an irregularity or something somewhat unusual that the magician ignores. If the magician confidently ignores it, the audience members assume it is nothing to pay attention to. For instance, suppose the magician is handling an empty box (but it's not really empty; the magician has secretly snuck some candies into the box, but the audience believes it to be empty) and the box starts to rattle a bit as it's moved around. Chances are that if the magician keeps talking, remains confident, does what he can to minimize the rattling, and ignores the sound, the audience will ignore it as well.[11] For a magician, confidence is golden. The confident actions of the performer cues the audience as to how it should behave.

A good magician can rule small countries or vast religions.—Mark, a magician.

Magic in War

Magic has been used time and time again during wartime in order to counteract some of the evilness in the air. When lives are at stake, the deception that magic provides is necessary in order to protect oneself and win the battle. Let us take a short walk through the history of warfare, as seen by the eyes of a magician.

PENETRATING CITY WALLS

The Trojan Horse is an early example of a wartime magic trick using a *very big prop*. From out of nowhere came the magical appearance of Greek soldiers within the gated walls of Troy. (Come to think of it, the Trojan Horse may also have been an early example of the circus "clown car.")

LOTA POISON

It has been speculated that a magician's prop similar to the Lota bowl discussed earlier may have been used to poison one's enemies. A trick cup much like magicians use today was dug up in Greece. The sides of the cup were thick and hollow. Near the top of the inner wall was a secret slit. The assassin would fill the main portion of the cup with poisoned wine. He would take a sip from the cup with the slit facing his mouth. As he tilted back the cup, the wine would flow through the slit and down into the wall of the cup, rather than into his mouth. By this method he could "prove" to his enemy the cup was safe to drink from. He could then pass along the cup, making sure to position it with the slit *away* from his enemy's mouth. One big gulp of the stuff and the enemy was flat on his back, dead.[12]

THE BLACK ART OF WAR

Black art, you'll recall, is the magician's use of black-on-black settings to hide things on stage. For example, in a seance show that takes place on a darkened stage, assistants dressed in all black will lift luminous objects around the room, seemingly causing the objects to float of their own accord.

One such use of black art in wartime took place during the War of 1812. The small town of St. Michaels, Maryland, had been building ships for many years and was a source for many of the ships that were used by Americans to capture or sink over five hundred British merchant vessels. The British decided they needed to strike back. On the foggy morning of August 10, 1813, the British began their assault with an attack on a fort in the St. Michaels harbor. They huffed and they puffed, but they could not blow that fort down. After much frustrated shelling of the fort and town, both of which were immersed in the thick morning fog, the British realized they were inexplicably not hitting their targets. In fact, the town's lights remained lit and the townsfolk seemed to be ignoring the artillery fire. Finally the British gave up and departed.

The British did not know that during the night the savvy Marylanders had used the black art principle. They first darkened the town to conceal it in the night and then hung lanterns high up in the trees to misdirect British gunners into aiming their fire high. The deception worked perfectly except for a single house that was hit (and thus named "Cannonball House"). The town of St. Michaels is now known as "The Town That Fooled the British."[13]

THE WAR THAT WASN'T

One of the world's most renowned magicians, Robert-Houdin, was once called upon to use his knowledge of magic to prevent a war between the Arabs of Algeria and the French Foreign Legion.[14] It was June 1856. France had occupied part of northern Africa several years earlier and the holy men, called *marabouts*, were not so keen on the invasion of their land. They were trying to goad the Algerians into a jingoistic, bellicose frenzy—by using magic tricks to prove to the superstitious Arabs that they had supernatural powers that could protect them in wartime from gunfire. ("If you help us fight, we will use our magic to protect you from bullets.") One of the tricks used by the *marabouts* was to keep a gun from firing. One of these holy men would hand a loaded gun to a spectator, and ask the spectator to shoot at him. Of course they would refuse, since Allah would be pretty upset with someone who went around killing holy men. But the *marabout* would insist and finally the spectator would pull the trigger. Nothing. The gun refused to fire. The *marabout's* supernatural powers were in full swing. They would then take back the gun from the bewildered spectator and instantly fire it into the ground, to prove the gun was indeed genuine and loaded.

The French government asked Robert-Houdin to swoop in and put a stop to this. Robert-Houdin realized the *marabouts* were doing a magic trick to stop the guns from firing. In fact, the trick was very similar to the Lota bowl trick mentioned earlier! You see, these old-fashioned guns contained a small air hole bored into the side that allowed oxygen to make contact with the gunpowder. Without the air hole, the powder would not ignite and the gun would not fire. The *marabouts* would secretly plug up the hole with a small wooden peg, to disable the gun. After taking the gun back from the spectator, they would remove the peg and show the gun in working order again.

Robert-Houdin thought it best to not expose the *marabouts* outright, since he didn't want to upset the belief system of the superstitious natives. Instead he decided to prove that French magic was stronger than the holy men could deal with. He went down to Algiers and performed feats of illusion designed to impress the holy men and the natives with the strength of French magic. He used his electromagnet tabletop to fool the Arabs into believing he had power over their strength. The strongest Arab couldn't lift a weight off the table, while Robert-Houdin had no trouble at all. To conclusively prove France's power, he also provided a small electric shock to the burly Arab attempting to lift the weight. Electricity was unheard of then: to receive a shock of pain from nowhere must have seemed a miraculous feat, as if Robert-Houdin had shot invisible lightning from his eyes.

Robert-Houdin also performed some other feats of magic—appearances, evanishments. The topper came when he showed that he could one-up the *marabout* gun trick. Instead of merely causing the gun to choke, Robert-Houdin allowed one of the Arabs to fire a gun at him. More precisely, Robert-Houdin held an apple before his heart, and the Arab shot at that. After the shot, he sliced open the apple to show he had caught the bullet inside. Apparently the Arabs were being swayed by this more impressive display, because the incensed *marabouts* challenged the Frenchman to perform his magic off stage—and out of the theater! Would Robert-Houdin agree to the bullet catch on *their* terms? "No problem," he said (actually he said it in French).

The next morning, the *marabouts* took Robert-Houdin to the center of the town to have him shot. The magician asked to see the guns and bullets that would be used to shoot him. The holy men watched carefully so he wouldn't plug up the air holes. They were undoubtedly surprised to see he left the air holes open. Robert-Houdin said the guns looked fine to him, and he had the holy men mark the bullets so they could be identified later. He then held up the bullets, and he himself loaded them into the very gun that would be used to kill him. The *marabouts* stood him up against a mud wall, aimed carefully with one of the guns, then fired. The magician fell backwards against the wall.

Then he stood up. He grinned to show the marked bullet caught between his teeth.

Robert-Houdin had prepared for the illusion the night before. He stayed up all night fashioning fake bullets from candle wax colored with soot. The next morning he used his world-famous skills of sleight of hand to substitute his wax fakes for the real bullets. With these deceptions, the natives were convinced that French magic was stronger than any their own people could come up with, and the threat of revolt dissipated. Robert-Houdin is credited with using his knowledge of magic to halt a war before it ever started.

WARTIME DECEPTIONS

During World War II, illusion was used to hide an entire United States airplane factory. Fearing that the factory would be bombed by the Japanese, the Lockheed Corporation covered over its Burbank, California plant with a tarpan decorated with houses, bushes, and other indicia of suburbia. The camouflage made use of knowledge about human perception of objects at a distance. The flat paintings of houses looked realistic from the sky because human beings are unaccustomed to looking down from that perspective.

The British magician Jasper Maskelyne used his knowledge of magic while working as a camouflage artist during World War II to hide the Suez Canal and Alexandria Harbor from the Germans. His book on the subject is called *Magic—Top Secret*. Maskelyne ended up on the Gestapo's blacklist of undesirables.

The Axis powers had their own magic to deal out from up their armbanded sleeves. Before the war Hitler's air force commander invited the chiefs of the French Armée de l'Air to a friendly inspection and showing-off tour of the German air forces. The French readily agreed and they were taken up by General Ernst Udet in his personal courier plane. While cruising along, the pilot brought the airplane to near-stall speed (as slow as a plane can go without plummeting to the ground in a tailspin), unbe-

Fig. 39. A view of the Lockheed Corporation from the air. The industrial setting includes airplanes, factories, smokestacks, parking lots—all tempting targets for bombardiers. Photo courtesy of Lockheed Corporation.

Fig. 40. The same view, now with camouflage in place. It seems to be a rural suburban area, filled with private homes, shrubbery, open fields, and grassy backyards. However, the careful observer will note some clues to the deception: lack of shadows, airplanes in someone's front yard, and the road that doesn't lead anywhere! Photo courtesy of Lockheed Corporation.

knownst to the French officer on board. "Suddenly a Heinkel He-100 streaked past at full throttle, a mere blur and a hiss." After they landed, one German general turned to another and casually asked Udet how far along production was on those planes. "Oh, the second production line is ready and third will be within two weeks." (Actually that was a lie, a bit of pre-planned patter. Only three of the He-100 aircraft were ever built.) Later the French general would sadly report to his headquarters the disheartening news that the Luftwaffe was unbeatable.[15] Now that's a magic trick that makes use of a deception of speed, preplanned patter that seems impromptu, and two gigantic props!

The old standby of misdirection is widely used on the warfront. During World War II, the attack on the Normandy beach began at three o'clock on the morning of June 6, when the Allies launched a fake attack against Isigny, Cherbourg, to divert defending forces away from Normandy. The fake attack consisted of three British paratroopers coming down with hundreds of dummy explosions, chemicals churning to create gobs of thick smoke, and a battery of Victrola phonographs playing loudly the sounds of gunfire and soldiers talking and moving. The trick worked its magic as the Germans moved their 916th infantry regiment away from Omaha Beach. By

Fig. 41. A view under the camouflage netting at Lockheed. Note the fake shrubbery planted on top, and check out the vintage cars in the parking lot! Photo courtesy of Lockheed Corporation.

the time the Germans realized they'd been duped, the United States 1st Division had mostly taken over the Normandy beach. This mini magic trick was actually part of a larger misdirection tactic designed to lead Hitler into believing the attack was due to come at Pas de Calais. The Allies created the misdirection from propaganda by double agents and by placing submarines, turbo boats, and minesweepers in the waters around Pas de Calais. Like a con artist who tries to point out the proofs before his victims become suspicious, one British agent, code-named Garbo, was even authorized to reveal to the Germans some of the plans to attack Normandy, but he revealed them with the indication that those plans were merely a diversionary tactic designed to throw the Germans off. Later it was found out that Hitler himself had heard of the Garbo lie—and believed it).[16]

Sandorse reports that when General Norman H. Schwarzkopf (himself an amateur magician) addressed a meeting of his magic club, he explained how he used misdirection during the Gulf War. He said that he was "waving his left hand," creating an illusion in the media that forces were heading north to Kuwait. Since Iraqi commanders watched CNN as much as anybody, they were suckered into his misdirective tactics. Meanwhile Schwarzkopf's "right hand" was steadily and slowly working troops hundreds of miles west, heading them into Iraq in an outflanking maneuver. The westerly movements went unnoticed because of the diversionary misdirection up north. The rest is history. As Schwarzkopf put it, "Magic won the war."

Time Misdirection

War is hell. Let's get something to eat.

The grease trucks are a staple in my town, a parking lot of food vendors who have the market cornered on twenty-four-hours-a-day Fat Cats, chili dogs, gyros, and . . . grease. One night I was strolling through the area with a hunger for a falafel and I was aiming for one truck in particular, because I'd never tried it before. But before I got halfway into the parking lot, a young woman leaned her head out of a rival truck, looked me in the eyes and said, "Hello, what would you like today?" Well, I looked into that woman's big brown eyes and her smile and I knew what I wanted today, but I figured she was asking in the food-service sense, so I regained my composure and started walking towards her truck. I knew what she was doing: she was using impressionment, trapping me with her friendliness, putting the force on me but at the same time giving me my choice of food options—a form of restricted choice. I knew what she was up to, but I decided to go with the flow, go with the force. Besides, these trucks are so competitive, there really is little difference from one to another, except for the personality of the owner and maybe what kind of cheese they use on a cheese 'n' chili dog. Like the magician who suggests the assumption that the volunteer will choose one of the forced options, this woman put forth the assumption that I would buy from her. Her confidence, her good looks, and the fact that she was providing me with some action to perform—all techniques used by magicians—were additional helps to her sale. When it came time to pay for my sandwich, she made another assumption—that I would want a drink as well. This time I wouldn't be suckered! "I don't have enough money," I told her truthfully. She eyed my three bucks. "Fifty cents for a soda," she shrugged, quickly adjusting the price to meet my needs. These magi are versatile. How could I resist this niceness, her accommodating nature, her kind caring for my welfare?

Since that night, when I come back to the grease trucks I've noticed this vendor working the same tricks again and again. Unlike the magician who can control who his assistants are and what props they use, this woman has to practice her magic on the fly under a variety of circumstances. She has her arsenal of subtle misdirections, and the skill involves not only performing them in correct sequence, but choosing which to use for the situation at hand. Actually, that's what magicians have to do too.

One of the other tricks of the trucks involves keeping their customers happy using time misdirection. The trucks want to give the impression that they are comparable to fast food joints but with a greater variety of food. Fast food places are fast because their limited menu allows them to prepare and wrap extra food items even before the customer comes into the store. The wider menu of the grease trucks doesn't allow this preparedness, so the customer must wait while the food is being prepared, as in traditional restaurants. But unlike restaurants, the truck owners use misdirection of time to shorten the wait. To hide the preparation time, the truck owners make directed banter with the customers. Almost all of them do this, even the less friendly ones. They feel they have to do it, even if they don't understand the reasoning behind it. Their directed chatter fills in the time between order and service. Sometimes as you are giving your order they begin the cooking process. As they are finishing the cooking, they are handling the business of whether you want a drink and napkins and figuring the cost. So let's say the entire transaction involves three steps: ordering, cooking, paying. The cooking is the long, boring part, the part where the customer is free to walk away (there is a bus stop nearby; often students order food while waiting for a bus), leaving the vendor with half-cooked, unsalable food on his hands. By having the "paying" step overlap the cooking step, that tedious middle process has been psychologically shortened.

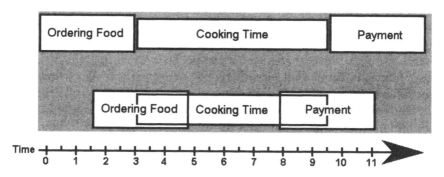

Fig. 42. You're standing on your feet waiting for food the same length of time, but it seems shorter because of the psychological scissors shearing off the ends of the cooking process. You stick around to receive your food, and to pay the chef.

Each of these things shears psychological minutes off the preparation time. Many times I've heard a grease truck owner say, "Thank you for waiting." They realize it takes a while to prepare the food and they are somewhat surprised that a person would wait through the long process. I have a feeling that these chefs' use of time misdirection and squeezing is unintentional—but they certainly know they're doing something right. And you can see that it does work: students develop brand loyalty to their grease trucks. College students make friends with the truck owners, who are the least likely people for the students to make friends with (contrast the stereotypical image of the grease truck worker—foreign, way uncool, greasy, lower-class—with the middle- or upper-class, educated university student). And yet, their friendliness works and their use of magic psychology works, because students come back to the trucks time and time again.

Another example of real-world time squeezing was done by a company that received numerous complaints about the slow elevators in their skyscraper. The options were either too costly or too unrealistic (build a new elevator? upgrade the existing lifting mechanisms?) The company ended up reducing complaints by simply hanging up a few mirrors in the elevator waiting area. Now people had something to do while waiting for the still-slow elevators. They could look at themselves and steal glimpses at the other people waiting with them. The complaints diminished. See for yourself when you visit large office buildings. Very often there are mirrors or other objects of interest placed strategically near waiting areas in order to eat up mind-time. The very fact that you're now going to be sitting there searching for this stuff will itself eat up time, confirming its purpose for being there!

There is one lesson in time misdirection that I learned from magic that I apply to my business dealings. In fact, it is a lesson I learned from the master Houdini, who knew the value of keeping the audience in suspense. After being shackled up and locked in a trunk, a screen would be drawn in front to conceal Houdini's supernatural dealings with the devil as he bargained his way out of the locked box. Often it would take Houdini just a matter of minutes to escape, but he would stay behind the screen for much longer than that. He was known to sit backstage reading a book as the audience got more and more worried. "Let him out!" "He's gonna suffocate in there!" they would scream. When they'd had enough, Houdini would emerge triumphant and to great applause.

If it only took a few moments to escape his bonds, why not step out as soon as he was free? Wouldn't that impress the audience with his skill? Perhaps, but probably not. If he had stepped out immediately the audience would mutter, "Oh, no one could escape that fast for real. It must be a trick. He must have the key." By waiting and waiting and waiting, Houdini made it look like great effort was going into his escape. (In fact, very often he *did* have the key.)

I've found that in the world of business we must be like Houdini. If the boss asks us to look into a problem and try to solve it, we should not come back in a few minutes with the answer. That makes it look too easy. You want praise and recognition for your work. Take a day or more. Hold off. Stall. Perhaps gain some sympathy by explaining all the difficulties you're going through trying to get the problem solved. But don't come back immediately with an answer, because then it'll look like just a trick. No skill involved. "He must have the key."

On second thought, perhaps I learned that lesson from Richard Feynman, who in his wonderful first autobiography tells the story of how he found a "trick" to unlocking the safes at Los Alamos during World War II. In order to impress the guys, he'd use the "time management" of Houdini on them: "I'd open the safe in a few minutes . . . then sit around, reading a magazine or something, for fifteen or twenty minutes. There was no use trying to make it look too easy; somebody would figure out there was a trick to it! After a while I'd open the door and say, 'It's open.' "[17] Feynman also used classic magician's time misdirection in order to pick open the locks. You see, the other scientists at Los Alamos thought he was opening the locks from scratch, then and there. In reality it had taken him two years of research, playing around with the locks, and learning about locksmithing to get to that stage. Each lock required preparation beforehand to learn. He figured out a trick way of reading two of the numbers from the combination if the safe door was opened. He would keep lists of these numbers as he figured them out. Weeks or months later it would take him minutes to open a lock only because, unknown to others, the trick had started those many weeks in the past. Surely you can see how this relates to the stage magician's use of time misdirection—the trick begins before the audience thinks it does, sometimes even before the show begins.

Coming back to the business world for a moment, I have a friend who uses similar time misdirection to impress his boss. He will start a project and get halfway through with it. Then he says to his boss, "Say, I have a great idea . . ." and pitch the project he has already started. The boss agrees, and then he has a lot of freedom to do as he pleases. If he wants, he can quickly finish the project and impress his boss with how fast he accomplished it. Or, since most of the project is done already, he can sit around all day at work not doing anything while his boss thinks he's starting this new project. After a few days of mini paid vacation he can finish it up and present it to the boss for accolades!

Time misdirection is used by some upscale doctors and dentists. The less prestigious doctors need to squeeze in as many appointments as they can each day to make more money. You're stuck waiting in the waiting room for a half hour or even an hour or more. Just think of the waiting rooms in any big city hospital or clinic. Very low-class and lots of waiting. On the other hand, you may have to wait only five or ten minutes in an upscale doctor's office. The difference is—you had to wait a month to get the appointment! Because the upscale doctor is well-to-do, he can afford to schedule less patients per day. You have to wait a month for the appointment but then you get ushered in almost immediately, and you're impressed with the speedy service. It's not speedy at all—you had to wait a month for it! Time misdirection in action: you disregard a month of waiting in order to praise a five-minute wait.

Spatial Misdirection

Spatial misdirection is largely the magician bringing certain actions to the forefront of importance and downplaying the importance of others. In other words, playing with the importance of visual cues that enter the audience's eyes. The magician Sol Messler explained that he frequently plays with the importance of visual cues not only on stage, but off stage as well:

> Once I played a venue in France. The first day there my pocket was pick-pocketed. Since then I keep a special eye on my money. I know that pick-pockets (and bums) are likely to be around the bank and money machines. What most people do is they take their money from the machine and stick it directly in their pocket. No! Can't do that! The pickpocket is looking for that. He sees which pocket you put your money into.
>
> What I do is I take the money from the machine, then do a quick French drop. The pickpocket thinks the money's in my left hand, but it's really still in my right. I can then pretend to put the money into my left pocket. When I take my card from the machine, I take it with my right hand (where the money is palmed) and that all goes into my right pocket. There's also other times I'll use a maneuver, or use a sleight, just in case . . . because you never know when someone's watching. You never know when some lowlife's up to no good!

(And you thought magic outside the theater was only for charlatans, crack-pots and thieves! See, us innocent folk can use deceptions to protect our-selves as well!)

Messler advised people to always be careful about how they handle money in public, whether it's at an automatic money machine, store, or food stand, and he commented that knowing some simple sleights can therefore be beneficial to people in real life. He also said that he has recently started using a similar misdirection when typing in his PIN number and passwords, and when typing in his telephone calling card number on public pay phones:

> If I'm pressing the keypad number with my pinky, then I'll make as slight a movement as I can with the pinky, so they can't see my number. Mean-while I'm making an exaggerated movement with my index finger. And the other way 'round too. If the number's a 1 or 4, those are under my index finger to type, so I press lightly with my index finger, but press hard with my pinky. Misdirection. It's no different than the movements I use in manipulating coins or cards. Manipulating the hands and muscles so they look like they're moving opposite to how they really are moving.

Messler, who has been heavily into sleight of hand since his grade school days, said that he's been able to pick up these habits of money transfer and digital dexterity pretty rapidly, and he attributes that to his fingers' familiarity with magicians' sleights. He concluded, "It doesn't matter if you're performing on stage for an audience, or just making an illusion on the street so your wallet don't get stolen. It's the same thing. It's creating an illusion in order to deceive the onlookers."

CREATE MAGIC!—THE PUSH-TUBE MANEUVER

This is another variation on a way to use magic to foil thieves at the automatic teller machine. This uses a technique similar to the one where a coin is slipped through a tiny slit in a sealed envelope. The procedure:

1. Spend all your money.
2. Okay, now you have to go to the ATM machine to get some cash. Go there now.
3. Put in your ATM card, make a withdrawal of twenty dollars.
4. When the money comes out, remove it from the slot with the right hand. While the left hand continues punching buttons on the ATM machine, the right hand casually folds the bill in half to make a square, then in half again to make a tight little packet.
5. By this time you should be pulling the paper receipt out of the machine. Pull it out with the left hand and bend it in half. You don't have to make a perfect crease, just get it folded in half (not lengthwise, the other way), enough to make a sort of tube.
6. Bring the right hand to the left hand and insert the folded twenty-dollar packet into the creased receipt. With your index finger, secretly push the twenty dollar bill out the bottom end of the receipt and into the palm of your hand. The twenty dollar bill will be resting on the bottom part of your palm, opposite the thumb.
7. Take the receipt with the right hand while turning down the palm of the left hand. To an observer it appears as though you have the receipt and the money in your right hand.
8. Now you have some choices. Generally if you're getting money from a money machine it's because you're going to be spending it soon anyway. What I do at this point is simply put both hands into my pockets. It appears as though the money and receipt are going into the right pocket (and so becomes the target of thievery) but in fact the money is safely hidden in the left.
9. If you have a money clip in your right pocket, you can clip the empty receipt into the clip. When you return the clip to your right pocket, also casually put the left hand into your left pocket, depositing the money there.
10. Another option is to place the receipt into your wallet. When you return the wallet to your pocket, also put the left hand into the left pocket, nonchalantly dropping the twenty bucks therein.

Another conjurer of sorts who used magic in a real-world situation was Michael Knox, one of the jurors on the O. J. Simpson jury. Before being sequestered, the jurors and their luggage were searched, and they all had to pass through a metal detector to ensure they wouldn't be bringing weapons into the courtroom. (One of the jurors was found to have bullets in his suitcase; he had absentmindedly left the bullets in his suitcase after a recent hunting trip.) Knox relates how a little magic helped him out: "I managed to smuggle in one piece of contraband—my little pocketknife. I'm a great believer in the tradition that red-blooded American boys should carry a pocketknife at all times. I didn't feel a shred of guilt for beating the system that day. How did I do it? Like any good magician, I'm not going to reveal my tricks but the hand IS quicker than the eye!"[18]

I showed this quote to a friend and he said, "Oh, well, that guy's not really using magic. He's not really a magician, he's just using the word 'magician,' but that doesn't make him a magician. Just because he uses the word, doesn't mean he's really doing magic tricks." I understand that point, but I don't think it's a valid argument. It doesn't matter whether or not Knox is a magician. It doesn't matter whether he smuggled the knife in using a thumb tip, front palm, back palm, thumb palm, pinch palm, tucked into his sleeve, into a topit, or whatever. All that matters is that somehow he used deceit to get the knife past the guards and through the metal detector undetected. That makes it a magic trick. After all, that's what magic is: using trickery and deceit to make the impossible happen. If you had asked the guards if they did a thorough search of the jurors, they'd say, "Yes! We sure did! We even caught someone trying to bring a bunch of bullets in with him!" So they would be proud of their good work. Now if you asked the guards, "Is there any way anyone could have snuck something past you, a knife for instance?" They would reply, "No! Of course not! We passed them through a metal detector! We searched their bags thoroughly!"

And then Knox could pull out his pocketknife and show them they'd been had. Yes, I'd say that magic—whether performed by a skilled magician or a mischievous red-blooded American boy—is still magic. It's doing the impossible for one reason or another. In Knox's case, he "resented being 'locked down' like a common criminal. . . . Hiding that pocketknife was my personal rebellion."[19]

CLICHÉS

Preachers and politicians have always known the value of a fist pounding on the podium. No matter how many times we hear the clichéd rap of the fist rapping the wood, it draws us towards the speaker, it is audio iconography representing our need to pay attention to what is being said. The noise, like a thunderclap, draws our attention to the lighting in the speaker's voice, and, hopefully, the meaning behind the words.

Magicians too know the effectiveness of the sudden rap to get our attention. It takes a sulky person or an autistic one to ignore the pounding of the podium. In fact, the way our attention turns to the noise is instinctual and hard to suppress. Clichés, though trite, are often effective for the very reason that we know instinctively how to respond to them. Think of some of the clichés of magic—showing empty hands, letting a pack of cards be inspected for gimmickry, broad and showy gestures, ostentatious presentation. All of these are expected and gladly eaten up. The magician plays his role, and the audience is directed into theirs. Like when we looked at the flea in our fist, like the stooge who stands on tiptoes to draw passers-by into the three card monte game, the magician directs the very way we interact with him and think about his magic, down to the way we respond to the clichés he provides.* The pounding fist will always draw our attention, either by instinct or because we force ourselves to look at it—because we know that this is when the important stuff is going on. We don't want to miss the important stuff as it happens.

When people don't use clichés, when they become creative and produce their own ways of doing things, they require a thoughtful response from the audience or observer. No, that's not what we want in magic, politics, and advertising. In these fields we need a group mentality, a zero mentality, a follow-the-leader intellect, otherwise illusion won't be created—skepticism will be. Skepticism is the death of any illusion that a magician or advertiser wants to create in your mind.

Clichés are good because when you encounter one, you know what's expected of you. We know how to react at restaurants, gas stations, on dates, at funerals, because of the clichés involved. A clichéd first date, dinner and a movie, is probably more effective than something creative like a picnic or a special trip somewhere. Both know what's going on and what's expected. The couple can go into typical "date mode" and see if they are compatible within that mode. But going on an unorthodox date is creating the situation on the fly. Without preconceived notions of how the get-together is supposed to proceed, both may leave feeling uncertain about what has transpired between them. Even if they walk away from the date feeling great, that uncertainness is there because they have built their relationship on uncertainty. Like the skeptical audience member, they are led to ask questions of the situation—what did it all mean, and where are we going?

Movies often use clichés about people, or stereotypes (the mad scientist, the strict school teacher, etc.) as a way to quickly get a point across. A screenwriter for the movie *Sleeping with the Enemy* relates how he needed to quickly make the audience take a liking to the character that Julia Roberts would fall for in the film. He did that by having her spy on him out a window as he waters the grass and sings a song from *West Side Story*. He looks up to catch her spying, and he's totally embarrassed. "In that moment, you like him. Instantaneously. It's just a gimmick."[20] Commercials use clichés even more frequently because they have a shorter time in which to tell a story and sell a product. Even video games use stereotypes where necessary to involve the player into the story by making the player feel the same things as the on-screen hero feels.[21]

---

*And don't forget that Art History 101 class in college. Remember how artwork is structured with a certain balance and composition? Remember your kooky teacher showing you how this mythological character's spear pointed toward another character, whose arm led your eyes to another grouping, which pointed you along. . . . It sounded overwrought at the time: I remember more than one disbelieving student in my classes. "Aw, he didn't think about all that when he painted it!" Ah, but he did!

Clichés are good because they're common. But very often it is the commonplace that we ignore. If I put up a sign in Times Square, you are unlikely to notice it. If I put another person in Times Square, you are unlikely to notice him or her amid the hustle and bustle of the city. There is, however, one person I've noticed every time I've been to Times Square: a boy standing on tiptoes in front of a religious, cultlike soapbox. The orator stands beneath the fire of a giant menorah, spouting out the tenets of his conviction, a messianic Christian cult. The boy stands in front of the preacher, leaning forward like a downhill skier. His back is straight. He *pays attention* to the preacher. Like the psychology experiment in which people looked up at the sky, this lad shows us passers-by where to look amid the hustle-bustle of the cityscape. A human figure—one of us—is so much more meaningful and so much more effective than neon signs, giveaways, or an attractive display.

CONSTANCY

The constancy principle is used by magicians to create a cliché that can be exploited, and it is used by others off stage as well. An example of constancy is the magician who tosses a ball in the air several times, and the last time it vanishes. In truth, the final toss-up never occurred. The magi merely mimicked the tossing action and retained it in his hand. The audience follows the imaginary toss as if it were real, and are fooled into thinking it vanished in thin air. Constancy is used to great effect in many tricks, and it is used by tricksters off stage as well. Researcher Paul Ekman offers the example of a poker player who deliberately coughs every time he's bluffing over the course of a long game. After awhile the others catch on to his habit and they start taking advantage of it. But don't worry about the guy, he's setting them up for a big kill! When he's satisfied they're all taking advantage of his cough, he drums up the pot, coughs, they think he's bluffing—but this time he's not! He cleans them out.[22]

Constancy is a ploy used in many ways. "I was doing shows when I was in high school," said one young magician. "In college I used my knowledge of moves to do things like sneak bottles into my room when we had a party. The R.A. [resident adviser, a person who oversees a college dormitory] was this nosy jerk. The first time I'd pass the lounge where he hung out, with some text books. Then I passed again with my girlfriend's books. The third time, it would be a box with the bottles underneath and another book on top. I told him I was pre-med to explain all the books and he thought I was hen pecked from my girlfriend bossing me around—but it got the job done. He never suspected the third time was different."

COMPUTER MISDIRECTION

Even the most modern technological advances in computers can make use of the age-old devices of magic and illusion. One magician/computer programmer at the Massachusetts Institute of Technology is researching how magiclike misdirection can be used in the design of graphical user interfaces. A GUI is a visual way that a computer program collects information from its users. Microsoft Windows is a GUI. The Macintosh uses a GUI interface. The user may have checkboxes on screen that can be checked on or off, input fields where text or numbers can be typed in, and pushbuttons that can be pushed with a click of the mouse.

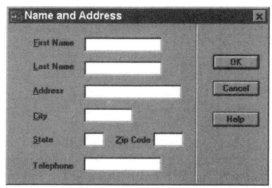

Fig. 43. An example of a computer program that uses a graphical user interface. Techniques of attention-direction might be employed in certain GUIs to better help the user navigate through the software.

One problem with GUIs is that the user is in charge of what course of action he or she wants to take next. All of the choices are available on screen, but if you're new to the software, you may not have the slightest clue which is your best option at that time. The MIT researcher is investigating how his knowledge of magical misdirection can be used to nudge a new user into making more correct choices. Colors can be strategically placed to highlight certain areas on screen, or to camouflage areas where only experienced users should dare to tread.

Another practice is to place the most commonly used controls closer to the top of the screen, or closer to the left side. Studies have shown that when we look at an image (in this case, a computer screen) our eyes tend to scan it in a Z shape, starting with the upper left corner. This natural tendency, seen even in babies, is made even more deeply entrenched in our minds by a lifetime of reading left to right and top to bottom. Thus, when given a choice of how to place controls on the screen, default controls should be toward the top or on the left side, depending on the screen layout. If an action is potentially dangerous (delete, clear, reset), then that control should be downward or toward the right.

A magician might learn from this to misdirect using his right hand (because his right hand is to the audience's left) and therefore that is the first place the audience will look. On the other hand, he should hide things downstage right, because that's the last place the viewer's eyes will rest (and hopefully their eyes will be distracted before they can get to that point).

In addition to misdirection, the researcher says he hopes to enhance user interfaces by incorporating other aspects of magic: "navigation of users' minds through sub-climaxes" (inducing emotion by playing the brain like a piano), "adapting to the situation," "identifying the target audience," and "seamless transitions and fluid motion."

VIRTUAL REALITY

All of virtual reality is based on an illusion of cause and effect, where the viewer (the computer user) is both audience and unknowing magician. You see, when you strap on the virtual reality helmet with its eye goggles delivering pictures to each eye, you see before you a graphical world that appears to be very real. As you move your head, you see the landscape very naturally, from differing perspectives. (Why shouldn't you? That's what happens when you turn your head in real life.) But virtual reality is merely an illusionistic sham. As explained by Nicholas Negroponte, a leading computer researcher at MIT's famed Media Lab, "Each display delivers a slightly different perspective image of what you would see if you were there. As you move your head, the images are, in principle, so rapidly updated that you feel you are making these changes by moving your head [versus the computer actually following your movement, which it is]. You feel you are the cause, not the effect."[23] In other words, you feel you are exerting a control over your environment. It feels as if you have the ability to turn your head and see "what is over there." Of course in reality there is *nothing* "over there" to see. The image does not appear in view because you turn your head to view it. It appears in view because the computer figures out what your next move will be and presents the proper image that corresponds to your movement. It's like a gigantic card force, the computer dealing out displays from a deck of cards with a billion possible world views, and all the while you feel you are the one controlling it.

COVER OF DARKNESS

One more illusionistic technique that has been used by game designers: darkness. Magicians use darkness to hide details from the audience; in the same way some computer game designers have purposely created a dim, shadowy atmosphere because they can't afford to fill in all the details of the fictional game world. One lone-wolf game designer who programmed and designed a game in his own home said that a "darkly lit design sets the mood . . . The darkness also helps by masking areas where there should be more detail but I couldn't afford to put it in."[24] It's a perfect example of using a logical motivation with an ulterior function to achieve an illusory effect—a fictional world that seems complete and real.

SOUNDS IN COMPUTER MISDIRECTION

Finally, it should be mentioned that just as a magician can use sounds and music to create illusion and misdirection, so too a graphical user interface can use sounds to direct the computer user. If you input correct data, or shoot your way through the tenth level of Phaser Blazers, you will be rewarded with a pretty melody or at least a pleasing note. Error conditions, getting shot at by an enemy soldier, or invalid data may be punished with a computerized razzberry. I have gotten so accustomed to the sounds made by certain software that I don't even look at the status bar for data. I rely solely on the sounds being made to judge my next move or action. If the computer were to suddenly go crazy without issuing the wrong sounds, I could easily go on using the software blithely unaware that anything was wrong, for quite some time, much like a touch typist who accidentally puts her fingers down one key right of the home key, therefore typing up the entire document in gibberish, each keypress one key to the right of where it should have been.

Earlier we discussed how magicians (and advertisers and movie makers, and . . .) use sound and music to make us feel a certain way, like the magician who played boisterous, suspenseful music that had me on the edge of my seat, even though nothing was happening on stage. The same technique has been used in video games to manipulate the player into action. As explained by Jonathan Knight, a producer at Viacom, one facet of a good video game is that the player identifies with the on-screen hero, and not only feels for that hero, but believes that they *are* the hero they see on screen. The first step in creating that unity is to have the player's actions coincide with what is best for the on-screen character. Knight explains the diabolic way in which this is accomplished:

> Because stories are so psychologically complex, and the distance between what the hero and the players want is so great, I think we need to use animal conditioning on our players, and basically reward and punish them psychologically, right in line with the objectives of the story for certain behaviors.
>
> If you think back to Asteroids, if you didn't destroy the rocks like you were supposed to, if you just sat there and cruised around and didn't go after the objective, then they started playing this music. It makes you really nervous and you get really scared. And if you go after the rocks, it stops. They're conditioning you.[25]

The music Knight is referring to is the same sort of booming, threatening music that the magician used on stage to get my heart racing and to induce a sort of mood. "The goal is . . . to reward and punish emotional responses.

Emotion is what is deep down and subtle, and that's what the player is not going to be conscious of." If we didn't know this was a video game designer we might think it was a cult leader talking! Another technique Knight mentions is to have other characters in the game "goad the hero in certain ways." (I swear he's not a cult leader!) Part of the reasoning behind this is that the player wants to stay within the boundaries of the game so he doesn't break the spell of illusion. If the player plays along as he's supposed to, he will get a realistic view into the fictional game world. But if the player goes against the grain, tries to do things the designer never anticipated, the reality of the game will be shattered. Like the magician who controls prop inspections and views of the stage, these game designers create the game world so as to direct your thoughts and actions along *their* lines, not yours.

It is clear that the human animal responds to certain kinds of psychological pressures, and it doesn't matter if those pressures are being applied by a magician, video game, cult leader, or advertiser. We are all likely to be influenced by them, react to them, or at the very least notice them, to some degree or another.

PICKPOCKETS

We've been discussing different kinds of misdirection, and now we turn to one more kind: physical misdirection. Pickpockets use a kind of physical misdirection of touch to ply their trade. Instead of visually leading the subject to look in the wrong direction (as in classic misdirection) or using sound to attract attention, the pickpocket allows himself or herself to come crashing into the victim with the hope that the great shock of the blow will negate the feeling of a hand slipping into the pocket. Who would feel the slight sensation of a hand touching the pocket when their whole side of the body is stinging from being jostled against? My dentist informs me that dentists and doctors use the same trick when administering shots to patients. They first use the fingers to pinch the skin, rendering the patient a bit less sensitive to the needle to come.

There is an amusing anecdote told by one valiant author who spied a woman emerging from the restroom at the public library with a trail of toilet paper streaming from her waist. As any Captain Kirk would have done, the author set out to destroy that Klingon. A few subtle efforts left some paper still trailing out of her skirt, so the author made one last ditch effort as the woman neared the front door. "Permit me to get the door," he said. "Thus positioned on her left as she went through, he released the door prematurely so that it slammed into her left hip, momentarily distracting her and providing him with a split second to take this one and only remaining swipe at the toilet paper tail. Excalibur! He had the trophy!"[26]

Magicians use touch misdirection only rarely. Since most magic is performed for many people, a physical tap or brush or crash of misdirection can only work wonders on the recipient. The rest of the crowd is left to see how it's done. (Although one is reminded of the pickpocket acts that presumably do make use of physical misdirection on stage before a crowd.) The point is, we are all alone as we set out in the real world, and we normally do not have an audience or camera crew following us around. The real-world magician, pickpocket, thief, scam artist, has many more opportunities for misdirection than the stage magician, because the real-world magician needs only fool one person, and not a whole group. Therefore we must take precautions. Traveling women should place a metal screen or netting at the bottom of their purses so that a cut-bagger can't cut out the bottom of their bags. Men should place wallets in their front pocket, not the rear, as that is a slightly more difficult place to pick from (and men, where would you rather have a bulge—in the back of your pants, or the front?) Or wear a money belt hidden under cover of clothes. Even these precautions may not be enough to foil the professional pickpocket, who is just as well-practiced as any on-stage magician, and in fact, the professional pickpocket uses many techniques that a stage magician would feel right at home with: assistants, misdirection, patter, and proofs. An excellent source of information on this subject is Wayne B. Yeager's comprehensive *Techniques of the Professional Pickpocket*. Some of Yeager's major points:

Assistants. In a magic show the assistants appear to be mere accessories, especially when they're dolled up in revealing, skin-tight, costumes. It looks like they're there just to be pretty. It doesn't occur to you that they might be helping out with the trick also. Pickpockets use helpers in the same way: the assistants appear to be merely innocent bystanders; you would never suspect they were working together as a team. To this end, pickpockets and their assistants have been known to dress as priests or act as drunks. Well-endowed female pickpockets might rub up against a male victim and make him think about things other than his wallet.

Misdirection. Whether they use assistants or not, pickpockets will always use misdirection. They might use a clumsy approach, where the assistant accidentally spills ketchup or coffee on the victim, and while the victim is thus occupied with the mess, the pickpocket is sneaking the wallet out of the pocket. Or they might go with the less infuriating "bump in the crowd" approach mentioned earlier. Some pickpockets have been known to run headlong into a victim so as to grab the wallet from his inside coat pocket at the time of collision. If working alone, misdirection might be as simple as pointing out *"Over there!"* while sneaking a hand into a pocket as attention is diverted.

Patter. The patter must fit the persona and storyline of the "act" being created. Some pickpockets pretend to be drunks and will sally up to a victim, swing their arm over his shoulder, and describe a very fulfilling encounter they've just had with a prostitute. This is a particularly good bit of story and patter to use since it allows the pickpocket to use a lot of hand gestures (as he describes her hourglass figure and large proportions). And hand gestures, as we know, are a useful prerequisite to misdirection. The pickpocket who pretends to be a drunk will take a drink right before "showtime" so he'll have some alcohol on his breath, a subtle clue to the victim that he's dealing with a drunk. This brings us to the next trick—proofs.

Proofs. In magic, proofs are used to prove to the audience that a particular method is not being used to do the trick (showing an empty hand "proves" that it's not holding a card). It's a false proof because while it may prove that one method isn't being used, it doesn't prove that *all* methods aren't being used (the hand looks empty, but maybe the magician is using a back palm). Similarly, pickpockets will offer proofs that show they are not picking your pocket (when in fact they are). As an example, consider the pickpocket technique called "pushing." While waiting on a long line at an amusement park, the pickpocket slowly nudges a wallet up and out of the pocket of the person standing in front of him in line. They have a long line ahead of them, so the pickpocket can use his hand or knee to very slowly push it up while waiting on line. But, as one ex-pickpocket explains, "You got to push it ever so slight, and show him your hands after every push. You don't want to say 'Hey look at my hands,' but you have to let your hands be seen, so he don't get suspicious."[27] Clearly this is very similar to a magician rolling up his sleeves and showing his hands empty.

Misdirection is probably *the* most important tool that a magician uses. Appropriately, it becomes equally important when looking at off-stage magic—if someone is trying to deceive you, they are in essence trying to "slip something past you," as the saying goes. In order to slip it past, they need you to be looking in another direction (or listening in another direction, or feeling in another direction). Misdirection can be used for good (such as making a computer interface easier to use) or it can be used for evil (as a pickpocket may do). Perhaps the best thing we can do to detect misdirection, deceit, and deception, is to *look the other way*. Dare to be different. Pickpockets can slip a wristwatch off your wrist in a few seconds while they shake your hand. They can do that because they are well-practiced, but part of it rests on the fact that they are talking to the victim and looking into his eyes—so of course the victim is returning the look, staring directly back into the watch-grabber's eyes. Dare to protect yourself; if someone comes out of nowhere and introduces himself to you with a big handshake, you'd better watch your wrist, and don't be scared that you're going to offend.

As we saw before and will see again, much of magic rests on the audience's willingness to act as sheep to the slaughter. People react in certain ways because they want to look "normal" or they want to be "polite." Many scams are pulled on polite people who stop to aid a pretend cripple; many robberies are pulled on strangers who kindly pull over to pick up a hitch-hiker. My advice to you is don't be so caught up in what other people think, and rather, do what seems smart. For you see, if you do what you think will look "normal" or "polite" or "correct," you're not doing it for the benefit of others, you're doing it for yourself, your own benefit, to make yourself look good. And when your attention is focused inwardly like that, you won't be looking outwardly, and thus con artists and magicians will be able to fool you. To overcome misdirection we must pay attention to the world outside our heads, and we must pay attention to the right things, not necessarily the things we are being directed to see. Not everyone can do that. It requires being a little different, a little creative, and a little bold.

16

Magic in Selling and Advertising

> Almost every advertisement you see is obviously designed, in some way or another, to fool the customer: the print that they don't want you to read is small; the statements are written in an obscure way. It is obvious to anybody that the product is not being presented in a scientific and balanced way. Therefore, in the selling business, there's a lack of integrity.
>
> —Richard Feynman[1]

I was watching one of the home shopping channels on television—(please forgive me, it was an accident . . . I was, uhm, merely rewinding a video at the time!)—and there was a demonstration of a newfangled miracle mop. This mop would pick up any mess that spilled onto the floor. They were putting this mop through the wringer, literally, and it was doing its stuff superbly on nationwide cable TV. They did one demonstration of the amazing mop's capabilities when they dumped a load of human hair on the floor, wiped the mop over it, and then turned the mop over to show how the hair had all been picked up by one short sweep. Ready to buy yet?

What interested me in the mop demo (really an ad for the mop, you know) was that the ad was actually a magic trick. It was an amazing trick. We might call it the Picking Up Human Hair Off the Floor Effortlessly and Easily trick. The *illusion* was that this mop could handle the job as well as they showed it could. Am I doubting what I saw with my own eyes? In a word, yes.

After dumping the hair on the floor, there was a barrage of verbal build-up as the demonstrator explained what a tough job it is to pick up hair with an ordinary mop. I could go into great detail about the similarity between the build-up of the mop demo with the build-up in a magic trick, but I trust you get the idea. There are also parallels of believability—we must believe the magician is basically honest even though he's generally not honest (remember the big fuss I made in chapter 1 about how magicians break the rules?) Advertisers must appear honest too (an actor pretending to play the role of an everyday user of the product, thus imparting an air of honesty and a bond between the actor and the viewer). These apparently honest advertisers and people who demonstrate products have their own code of ethics that they break. For instance, ads that show toy airplanes that fly (when the real toy does not). Or, in this case, a mop demonstration that appeared completely straightforward but was in reality a magic trick.

For you see, after the mop was pushed across the hair, it was turned over to show all the hairs that had been picked up by the mop. The mop filled the screen and we could see that it was covered with hair. But we couldn't see the floor—the mop filled the entire frame—so we at home could not see the state of the floor. Sure it had picked up hair—but did it pick up *all* the hair as the demonstrator claimed it did? We would never know, because they never showed the floor! They immediately cut away to a spokesperson, whose patter concentrated our thoughts in one direction (how wonderful the mop is) while concealing less profitable matters from public view. For all we know they could've planted the hair on the mop before the cameras rolled.

The entire demonstration may have taken less than five minutes. This is a small example of a magic trick being used to mislead and deceive the viewer into believing the product is not what it is. You can see how many techniques of magicians were crammed into that one minute: patter, build-up, betrayal, covers, verbal misdirection, incorrect logical conclusion, and a camera trick thrown in for good measure.

Yes, magic tricks, illusions, are being foisted upon us in advertisements. In this chapter we will look closely at how techniques of magic are used in selling and advertising. Advertisements are aimed at a particular target group (for example, "housewives" or "beer drinkers"). But magic has to be aimed at an audience of anybody and everybody. So if we are to compare the techniques used to influence us to buy, we must compare either broad ads or broad techniques. Most advertising consists of: (1) Showing people having fun with the product (or showing them in an exotic locale, or "being cool" because of the product), and (2) dispensing information about the product. A commercial may have one or both of these elements. These elements don't exist by themselves of course. They exist within the story of the commercial, the tale that is told, the catch phrase or jingle. The whole nature of TV and print commercials is to form a concept in your mind, the concept that "this product is necessary," or "this product is better than any other one like it." That concept that you have about the product is an illusion. If you believe a commercial then we can say that your mind has been manipulated in such a way that an illusion has been created. Sometimes the mind manipulation is deceitful (as when the advertisement tells a lie).

Other times, the mind manipulation is misdirecting (a political campaign will tell you all the soup kitchens the governor has visited, but forget to mention the crack dens and brothels). Sometimes the mind manipulation is very honest, and you may be persuaded to believe in a company that really does have good intentions at heart.

Magical Results

Advertising often appeals to the consumer's belief in magic, or to their *wish* for real magic to be possible. Certain food ads treat the food as a magic potion that will transform one's life into a wonderful new realm of sensory enjoyment. Switching to a new butter will make the difference between an ordinary plate of asparagus and a *ButterWonderful!* plate of asparagus. A little drop of Lea & Perrins will turn a plain casserole into a masterpiece. It's a magic potion, and we can be the magician, the alchemist, who transforms our ho-hum life to gold.

We see the wish for magic in split-screen ads that show before and after shots simultaneously. At once we feel like the sorry, sad person at left, with a frown on her face and downcast eyes—and at the same time we feel optimistically giddy at the prospect of the right side of the screen: the smiling, shiny, post-product-usage consumer. Oh, we want to believe so badly in the magic!

Part of the problem, according to ad decoder Judith Williamson, is that modern consumerism society turns us into passive, unproductive people who barely know how to get by in the world. Look at how many people pay other people to do their taxes, iron their shirts, or put spark plugs into their cars. Hardly anyone grows the food that they eat, or knows even rudimentarily how to repair the machines they use in daily life. Certainly almost no one could actually *build* one of the things.

> We are always users, not creators; manufactured goods make up our world, removing the need for any action from us. In advertising it is essential to compensate for the inactivity forced on us; hence advertising's Romanticism, its emphasis on adventure and excitement. . . . But the only thing we can *do* in fact is to buy the product or incant its name—this is all the action possible as *our* part of the excitement offered. Such minimal action inevitably creates a "magical spell" element: from a little action, we get "great" results (or are promised them).[2]

That "minimal action" we can take is the purchasing of the product. Williamson points out that magic is "the production of results disproportionate to the effort put in."[3] This makes sense. Any professional wrestler can smash two linking rings together and join them. But only a magician can slide them together with minimal effort. So advertisements claim to make us all magicians of a sort, with magic control over our world. Ads offer to work magic on us: we can be transformed into new people, by changing our hair color, losing weight, putting on pounds, learning to read faster, becoming invisible to disease—anything we want to be or do can be accomplished by magic means. After all, the people in the commercial took only thirty seconds to do it!

SKIPPING STEPS

A magic trick is a sequence of steps the magician takes to get the trick done. Some of those actions are secret. When The Great Doodini makes a sausage appear in his empty hand, the sausage had to get there somehow. That one crucial step, where he put the sausage in his hand, is kept from you, because that is the secret step that would reveal the trick. Advertisers also use this "skipping steps" maneuver.

> Feeling fat? Flabby? Try the new GUTBUSTER 3000! It's the only exercise machine guaranteed to help you lose weight or your money back! Here's what Joe has to say about it: "I was so fat I could touch my toes—with my belly! Then I got the GUT-BUSTER 3000! I followed the program and lost over 200 pounds! Now I'm so popular, Hef comes to my house to party!"

This is a common sort of advertisement. It offers a Before and After shot of the satisfied customer. There's no question the customer is satisfied and the product did work. It worked as if by magic! A magical quality is imparted to the product because the advertisement failed to show all the steps. Just as a magician hides important steps/actions, the advertisement hides many important steps and actions too. We don't see Joe actually following the program, as he claimed to do. We don't see him scheduling time to work out twenty minutes a day for the next six months. We don't see him making careful food choices at the supermarket. We don't feel his anguish when he tells his friends he can't join them at the bar because he has to stick to his diet. All of those crucial steps are missing: "since magic is instant, it just 'happens,' metaphysically, and does not *work, materially*."[4] The "Skipping Steps" technique is used in much self-improvement advertising such as liposuction, face lifts, and other plastic surgery. They don't show you the black eyes, the pain, or for that matter, the medical bill. When you find yourself drawn to the magical aura of a cute little nose or a flat, hard tummy that seems to spring like a genie from a bottle, take a moment to consider all the hidden steps and actions that they might be hiding from you.

LOGICAL STEPS

Sometimes advertising makes claims with a series of logical arguments that lead step by step to form an illusion: "Three out of four dentists recommend sugarless gum to their patients who chew gum. Our gum is sugarless, so why don't you take the dentists' advice and try some today?"

Here we have the magician's two hands coming together to make a false exchange that never gets made—the logic seems to connect one argument to the next, but the two arguments are really as unconnected as the two hands. For years and years I unthinkingly thought (and I'm sure many other people thought) that dentists recommended *that brand* of sugarless gum. The illusion is created that they do from the sequence of arguments, because of the words and confidence of the speaker. Advertisers, like magicians, also use the professional, knowledgeable, and higher-up look of a spokesperson to plead their case. The magician practices magic, and so he will take the appearance of a wizard or devil. The advertiser will take the knowledgeable-looking appearance of a dentist, dental hygienist, doctor, mother, pharmacist, or whoever else has the visual appeal necessary to substantiate the illusion.

Extending the Sizzle

Earlier we discussed the magician's technique of first using hyperbole to boost up a trick and then allowing the illusion to simmer in the spectator's mind a while, changing and growing with each retelling (for example, the Indian Rope Trick gets more exaggerated each time it's told). Advertisers have a similar concept called "selling the sizzle, not the steak." As Elmer Wheeler points out in his classic sales manual of 1940, even the sizzle has some down points, but if you're selling steaks you keep the mind focused on the good points and save the bicarbonate for later. To update ourselves to the current age a bit, there are some restaurants now offering gourmet steaks for $100 or more a pop. The steaks are cut from Kobe cattle, Japanese cows that are massaged and cared for and fed beer and chocolates as they stroll to the slaughterhouse. The steaks are delicious, no question about that, but they can also be nauseating. The steaks are so rich and fatty, some people's stomachs just can't handle it. Furthermore, some people have a reaction to aged beef that further sets their tummies on a slip 'n' slide ride. So why are people willing to put up with this? To shell out big bucks for something that is liable to make them sick? Well, they want to taste it, of course. They want to perhaps impress whomever they are eating dinner with. They want to create an ambiance of wealth and power. All of these things are illusions of one sort or another. In selling, an advertisement must put across these kinds of illusions—the sizzle, the glamour, the grandeur—while playing down or ignoring the upset stomach in the middle of the night (that is, misdirecting away from it). Wheeler-dealer Elmer Wheeler advises salespeople to, "Find the illusion about you that people like and admire, the part of you that is as individual as your thumbprint. . . . That's your *illusion*—your *sizzle*."[5] One example Wheeler uses is the woman who beautifies herself with a curling iron. "The illusion of a curl in the moonlight won [her beau's heart], even though he later found that the curl cleverly covered a wart on her neck."[6] Her sizzle was her looks. Her sizzle was an illusion built of makeup and hairdressing.

A quick look at a few minutes of TV commercials show that advertisers take sizzle to heart. Commercials for restaurants show an atmosphere of fun and excitement to such an extreme that you easily forget that it's just a restaurant and not a tourist attraction. Toys for children, especially dolls and action figures, are shown not as molded pieces of plastic, but integral components of a larger realm of fantasy and melodrama. This is exactly what a magician does when the crucial moves of a trick are buried within the larger illusion of dance, staging, costume, and performance. A simple card force becomes a mega-event.

A different kind of commercial, movie trailers, must condense two hours of film into a few short minutes that convey the essence of the film— or an essence the studio wants the audience to believe represents the film. Like the magician who selectively shows or does not show some of his movements, the producer must decide how to best "sum up" the movie from the available film. It's one thing to pack all the great jokes or action sequences into a trailer. That's not illusionistic, merely deceitful, as the audience attends the movie later to find that they've seen it all. More illusionistic are some of the subtle stratagems employed to manipulate the viewer's thoughts about the movie. The owner of one company that produces movie trailers said that for the *My Girl* ads, Macaulay Culkin's voice was used to "make him a more important element in the movie."[7] Culkin, who was a big box office draw when the movie was released, was only a supporting cast member of the movie, but viewers could go to the film and perhaps even walk away from it thinking they had seen a Macaulay Culkin movie. Not so: then it would've been called *My Boy*.

Another trailer producer points out that music is the most potent way to jazz up a weak movie. "Notice how much you hear Motown or opera in trailers these days? Ten to one, the audience doesn't follow the story but simply thinks, 'Ah, it's a movie about the way this music makes me feel.' "[8] This is the same technique magicians use when selecting a pulse-pounding score to highlight undramatic action on stage. Human beings are lazily led by clichés into the easiest reaction to any stimulus. Especially when we are relaxed, being entertained, or not suspecting trickery, we will succumb to having our minds led by the magician's or advertiser's finger slyly leading us exactly to the conclusion they wish us to make.

Space, Size, and Illusion

David Ogilvy was chairman and CEO of the Ogilvy Group, a fantastically successful and world-renowned advertising agency. In *The Unpublished David Ogilvy,* a collection of previously private works by the man, one begins to see many ways in which the magician's creation of illusions is important in advertising. Consider this excerpt from a sales manual about the Aga Cooker. Ogilvy advises, when a salesman is demonstrating the cooker to a customer: "Before you open the top oven door, either actually or by description, forestall the inevitable observation that it 'looks very small.' It is an optical illusion. . . . Demonstrate with exaggerated groping how far back the oven goes . . ."[9] Very often in selling it is up to the advertiser to plant thoughts in the buyer's head. The potential buyer can plainly see that the cooker is small. Thus it is up to the advertiser to create the illusion that the buyer is wrong. A stage magician would probably welcome a box that appeared smaller than it actually was. That way he could hide larger items in it and no one would suspect.

Sony, the electronics company, used a magic trick of its own when promoting the first pocket-sized transistor radios in the late 1950s. The radios were too big to fit into standard shirt pockets, so Sony ordered custom-made shirts with larger pockets for its salespeople to wear. Like the magician's table top that is *just* thick enough to contain the legs of the sawed-in-half woman, Sony's shirt pockets were *just* wide enough to accommodate the extra space the radios required, but not big enough (presumably) to tip off the consumer that they were being hoodwinked. "We never said which pocket we had in mind," Sony's head honcho explained coyly.[10]

Give 'Em What They Want

Many business leaders and other professional manipulators have stressed that the nice way to get ahead is to find out what people want and then give it to them.[11] In stage magic, the illusion often works because the audience comes in wanting a sense of mystery and magic, entertainment, and the execution of mind games, and the magician delivers that up to them. The Great Kellar, master illusionist of the late 1800s, advertised his shows with billboards that depicted him performing chilling feats of magic, surrounded by the spectre of devils and sometimes Mephistopheles himself. "The people who came to the show expecting to see devils generally did see them, or thought they did. All over the stage and even in the theater lobby, when they were on the way out."[12]

Lest you think that this superstitiousness is restricted to audiences of decades ago, consider a story such as this one, told by Ken Barham, a young magician of today, about a show he put on for his family when he was just fourteen:

> I was doing the vanishing silk. This uses a thumb tip to do the vanish. Once it is gone, you must "show your hands empty in a natural manner." To me that meant rotating your hands as quickly as possible to show both sides. On the third or fourth gyration, the centrifugal force was enough that the thing flew off my hand and sailed ten feet to drop behind the couch. It then rolled out from under the couch stopping at my feet.
>
> I calmly stooped, picked it up and placed it back on my thumb. I figured that they weren't paying to see me and if they didn't like it they could complain to the management (my parents). My aunt exclaimed, "Did you see that? His thumb came off . . . Oh my God!!!" She completely forgot I had started with the silk . . . to her the trick was my thumb falling off. . . . She is my favorite guinea pig.

The aunt's reaction seems illogical, unreasonable and perhaps stupid—until you realize that it actually is very logical, reasonable and intelligent. She came to the show expecting to see magic. And magic is what she got out of it. Magic is, after all, supposed to defy our expectations.

Sometimes people refuse to catch the magic. They are cynical. They refuse to step into the fantasy world of the magician. By doing so they are refusing to allow themselves to be entertained, and so the magician has a hard time giving them what they want. Because what they want is the complete opposite of what the magician is prepared to give them.

Sometimes magicians have to focus on this aspect of entertainment. It isn't all about "tricking" people and mystifying them. Deep down, the magician is an entertainer, out to make the audience feel good about the show, themselves, and their world. Barham tells a story of the most horrendous working conditions he's ever had to face. He was scheduled to play a variety show in an old age home, but, as it would turn out, his act went on right after a tragic act of God—one of the housemates had died right in his seat in the audience. An old guy in the next chair over kept muttering to himself, "It was that gottdamn corn bread that gottim gottdamn it . . . that's why I won't eat that shit." Barham quickly realized his magic could not lift this saddened audience out of their world of illness and death and into the fantasy of magic. Rather, he concentrated on the humor and laughter that made up their world. He made jokes. He made death jokes. He made bad death jokes. Instead of attempting to pull them from their misery and into his fantasy, he went with the flow—gave them what they wanted and needed—and put humor into their real (not fantasy) world. Whether in magic, sales, negotiating, or life, it's all a matter of Give 'Em What They Want.

May the Force Be with You

Some magicians' techniques may be directly translated to the real world, used in a sales situation for instance, to influence the buying habits of the customer. The card force is one such tactic used by magicians and sales-people alike.

Of course it is up to the customers to make up their own minds about buying products. Like the magician who makes subliminal suggestions to create an illusion, the advertiser can only create a certain image of the product in the consumer's eye. It is up to the consumer to take that image into their mind, mull it over, and whip out their checkbook because of it. As Ogilvy says, "It is no use fatuously remarking that [the product] is 'not really expensive.' You must be specific, definite and factual. The prospect is not interested in your personal opinion."[13] No matter how good it is, a "force" is only as good as the salesman's confidence, verbal dexterity, preparedness, and knowledge of human nature.

When a magician forces a card, he asks a question that appears to introduce randomness into the act, but in reality only obscures the fifty-two possibilities, of which the magician knows the outcome to all of them. Barham quips that magicians "are prepared for all occasions. Of course, fate has a way of knowing which occasions we have neglected." Randomness is a charade. People who design sales scripts follow the same rules as magicians. For instance, Disney phone operators are allowed to suggest only three choices, even when more are available. They also use false names.[14] Barbara Garson's *The Electronic Sweatshop* explains how even the tiniest conversation with an airline reservation agent (as well as other sales clerks you encounter throughout the day) has been thought out, managed, and controlled by overseers. Like the magician who knows beforehand how his act will proceed, conversations with ticket agents are prepared as carefully as a show. The agents are controlled, limited to certain dialogue clues and cues that must trigger in them specific questions, which in turn trigger from you an answer that has been carefully controlled. Kenny, one of these reservation agents, told Garson, "You never ask a yes or no question. . . . Never say, 'Would you like to book?' It's, 'Which would you prefer, the 10 o'clock or the 4 o'clock?' "[15] This is like the magician asking, "Which would you prefer," (holding up two cards), "the ten of clubs or the four of clubs?" This is similar to the childcare books that recommend such tactics as, "When would you rather clean your room, before or after dinner?" rather than simply ordering the child to clean the room. The parent is in control, forcing an answer he or she wants to hear. Even with the force at work, the speaker seems to be especially conscious of the listener's needs, courteous, and respectable—a person whose orders he wouldn't mind following. But he's not giving any orders, only asking the listener to choose for himself what he would like to do: four o'clock or ten o'clock? Before dinner or after? I get to choose—he's not making me! I get to live my life the way I wish! So he believes.

The forced-moved tactic is good to use on stubborn folks, especially those who value their freedom. (Listen up women, this is a way to control the men in your lives!) Men are known by psychologists to be focused on their personal freedom and lack of it. If you need a favor and you think you're unlikely to get one, then you're in a position to force an answer you will like to hear. One petite and sweet young woman got me to help her move furniture around by asking, "Nate, I need your big strong man muscles this afternoon . . . or would tomorrow be better for you?"

Sales Dodge, Magic Dodge

All of these misdirecting tactics are attempts at underselling the idea that you're being deceived. If a magician has something hidden in her hand, she will use the least restrictive method possible to hide the object. A tight fist won't be used if a loose palm will do. Actions must be seen as natural and unpremeditated. The idea is to show, not tell. Show the audience you are being open with them, because if they form that conclusion in their own minds, their conviction you are not tricking them will be thousands of times stronger than if you were to merely tell them. A picture is worth a thousand words—and a picture is something the magician can present to the audience without them being aware she is consciously presenting it to them. If she says, "This is a real, solid bottle of wine," they will have reasons to doubt the authenticity of the bottle:

- Why did she point out the obvious?
- Why did she say it was solid?
- Is it wine, or just colored water?
- Suspicious!

On the other hand, if the magician accidentally knocks it against a microphone stand, she has proved its solidity without raising suspicious hackles—she is underselling the ideas she wants to present.

* * * *

Money makes the world go round, perhaps more than we think about day to day. Advertising is the controlling force behind what we see in magazines, on television, by the roadside, and on our clothing. Since salespeople are the power behind the force of advertising, it would stand to reason that the sales techniques they have developed work well, and perhaps have a bit of magic to them. Indeed they do!

The first rule of selling is to get the customer to like the salesperson. The magician obviously is little different from the salesperson in this regard. The magician is selling you a false mental process, leading you to believe that magic, rather than some natural process, has accounted for the strange effect unfolding before your eyes. Sandorse pointed out the unthought-of mental process that may be at the heart of all magic believability issues—likability. Sandorse, an experienced magician who also rose in his field as a master salesperson, discussed with me his winning selling technique. Mostly he sold by underselling the product and overselling, his personality. Making himself friendly and open, and even throwing in a magic trick to liven things up. "It's an old sales dodge. You have to sell yourself first, then you sell your product. After you sell yourself, you can sell the guy the Brooklyn Bridge."

The way Sandorse talks about selling is similar to the way he talks about performing magic:

> I have to go out there and in the first ten or twenty seconds, I have to sell myself to the audience. I have to sell myself—not my tricks, not my table, not my rabbits, not my birds. I have to sell *me*. I have to get them to like me, and I can't say, "Hey, please like me." So what do you have to do? You have to have some kind of a trick or some kind of a gag or bit of business to get you off the ground. And once you've done that, all of a sudden they, "Hey, he's a regular guy. He's one of us."

This is the issue of magic as performed by the magician, versus magic experienced around the magician. Here Sandorse allows himself to be a regular guy so that magic will happen around him, rather than because of him. Lest you think this is unimportant, the value of friendliness in magic has been touted for a long time. In 1948, magician Al Leech said virtually the same thing: "Making people like YOU is the easiest way to sell your magic, because you sell yourself first." This is on the first page of a manuscript Leech typed on a manual typewriter and stapled together fifty years ago. Back then magicians would put together their thoughts on paper and distribute them (for a small fee) the way rock groupies put out fanzines today. In this one, *Don't Look Now! The Smart Slant on Misdirection*, the author's entire approach to magic is based on this simple but valuable point: The audience should be relaxed and open to suggestion, not critical, and not skeptical. Who are we more critical of—friends or enemies? Of course, we are more easily critical of our enemies. Therefore it is in the magician's best interest to have the audience as his friend. Friends are more willing to follow the procedures and mental processes that magic requires for it to appear magical. And, as Leech points out, "If people like you, they may even overlook or forgive a minor slip."[16] Sociologist and magician Peter Nardi wrote that modern audiences "are more skeptical and adversarial than in past eras. . . . If a positive rapport is established between the performer and audience, this disbelief is often suspended."[17] And don't forget the title of the classic Dale Carnegie book, *How to Win Friends and Influence People*, which boldly points out the close link between being liked and influencing the minds and decisions of others.

Unfortunately, these very facts may mean that influencing minds is more easily accomplished by the "psychic" charlatan, whose motive is often pure greed. As psychologist/magician Richard Weibel pointed out, the classic stage magician has an immediate problem in that the audience may not like him very much. After all, to be fooled by a magician can be frustrating, a blow to one's ego. However, off-stage magicians, psychics, tarot card readers, psychic surgeons, and the like can use the very same tricks as magicians but don't run up against the same wall of skepticism as the stage magician. After all, with a psychic there is the desire to believe that the power is coming from the person, not from a trick.[18]

Robert Cialdini, who wrote the book on influencing people with psychological principles, declared, "Few people would be surprised to learn that, as a rule, we most prefer to say yes to the requests of someone we know and like. What might be startling to note, however, is that this simple rule is used in hundreds of ways by total strangers to get us to comply with *their* requests."[19] So, just as a magician's illusion will be more readily accepted if we like him, the salesperson's pitch will also be more readily eaten up. Awareness of why you believe in something is the first step toward taking back control of your own destiny.

THE LIKABILITY ACCIDENT

Some salespeople have reported they have trouble "making friends" with potential clients, because they happen to be extremely big and tall. Their large size sometimes makes clients uncomfortable, and perhaps even a bit fearful. They may think that because the salesperson is a giant that he'll boss them around, try to hardsell them into buying product. But these huge salespeople have learned a compensating tactic. One ex-football player turned salesman explained the approach he uses: "When I walk into an office and I sense the man on the defensive, I simply drop my papers all over the floor and start groveling for them. Often the man comes around and helps me, and when he does, I usually have a sure sale."[20] Another huge man was confronted by his boss: "If you scare people [by your size], how the hell do you get them to buy so much?" The man demonstrated with a pratfall, then explained, "When I walk into a man's office and I catch that glimmer of fear in his eyes—which I've become very sensitive to lately—I simply fall down. I pretend I've hurt my leg and have him help me. That puts me in the defensive position and enables me to make the sale."[21] In these two anecdotes we see traces of many of the magician's tools:

- *Choreographed moves* that look accidental but are in fact intentional.
- *Restricted choice.* As described earlier, the magician (or in these cases the salesperson) leads the spectator into acting a certain way, when the spectator thinks it is his own doing (in these cases, the salesperson is leading the client into a dominant position over his subservient one).

- *Emotional direction.* The salesperson is sneakily attempting to induce a particular emotion in the client, while reducing fear.
- *Bumbling.* Good old-fashioned bumbling that helps let down the client's guard somewhat.

These anecdotes are from John T. Molloy's *New Dress for Success.* This is the revised edition of a classic book that taught the business community how to dress itself. (People used to not know about "power ties" and stuff like that.) Molloy's focus is on dressing well to influence those around him. For example, Molloy ran experiments to test how secretaries would react if a stranger came in and made some small demands, like asking them for letterhead or a pencil. The variable in these experiments was how the stranger would dress. Molloy found that the better-dressed the man, the more likely the secretary would respond politely to the requests. When the stranger made a more demanding request (asking the secretary to retrieve certain files for him), the clothing affected the secretary's compliance with the request even more readily and with less pejorative comments directed at him. Another study of Molloy was the famous "black verses beige" raincoat experiment in 1971. Molloy entered a number of randomly chosen offices wearing a black raincoat and a *Wall Street Journal* under his arm, and asked permission to deliver the paper personally to the man in charge. He then did the same wearing a beige raincoat. It took him a day and a half to deliver twenty-five papers when wearing the black raincoat. The same task took but a single morning in the beige raincoat. Molloy's conclusion: "You cannot wear a black raincoat, and you must wear a beige raincoat—if you wish to be accepted as a member of the upper middle class and treated accordingly."[22] (Note: Raincoat rules might have changed somewhat since 1971.)

These tactics of influence are worth mentioning because it's certainly true that our clothing affects how we are perceived, and others' clothing affects how we perceive them. It's something to keep in mind, that the way a person dresses may play a role in how we react to their attempts to control us. Molloy mentions other facets of dress-deception and influence, such as that a young businessman might want to look more mature by graying their sideburns.[23] Certain props—yes business people have props just like a magician does—such as certain brands of pens, wallets, umbrellas, and gloves can help project a successful, powerful image. Molloy mentions a black minister who carried an expensive attaché case even though he didn't use it for anything: "Without it I'm just another black; with it, I'm a black gentleman."[24] Molloy also details some interesting cases of how the dress of lawyers and criminal defendants can help or hinder their cases. Example:

> In a case on which I was consulted, involving three men accused of corporate shenanigans, my client took my advice and dressed much differently from the other two. He was found innocent while the others were found

guilty. On the facts presented, one of the other two was clearly innocent, but he looked so much like the third man who was clearly guilty, that the jury lumped them together in their verdict. Any experienced lawyer can cite many cases when clients were found guilty simply because they dressed incorrectly.[25]

This anecdote illustrates the lazy ways that our minds work, and how illusions result from that laziness. It is common to lump "like with like," and if one blue-suited man is clearly guilty, then *naturally* the other blue-suited man is guilty too. We use faulty heuristics like that every day without realizing it! These illusions abound because our minds are imperfect. It's worth noting that Molloy himself is doing a bit of suggestive influence while telling this anecdote. He leads you to believe that his client got off scott free *because* of the way he dressed. Of course we have no way of verifying that. See what I mean about people trying to influence you everywhere you look! This kind of non sequitur is the same tactic the gum company uses to sell its gum ("Three out of four dentists . . ."). It is very hard to be critical of everything you read and look at and experience, especially when you've fallen into the trap of liking someone, for example, an author and the concept the book presents. It's hard to get past one's liking to critically determine whether what you're being handed is truth or garbage. But it must be done. If you don't want to be fooled and influenced by the people in the world who try to fool and influence you, you must consciously seek out explanations for why you feel the way you do. If it turns out your feelings have no logical basis ("I trust him because he looks like he can be trusted, he wears nice clothes") that's a sign that he may be leading you on, whether intentionally or not.

UNDERSELLING

One problem with the hard sell is that people like having a free will, so they rebel against a salesperson trying to pressure them into buying. When you're talking about magic, you're talking about a person who is trying to influence the very mental processes and thoughts that flow through your brain. Certainly no one wants their brains hard sold! And so magicians will resort to soft sell, underselling techniques.

Sucker tricks are like underselling tactics, where a salesman lets you make up your own mind about a product, not trying to influence you, and perhaps in fact even dissuading you from the product. But as you fill in the gaps, you find that his explanations for the product's badness can be reconciled in a good way, in your mind. You convince *yourself* that you want the product, and that is the most convincing convincing in the world! The product does not have to be a material thing. It can be a religious idea the "seller" is trying to convey. It can be sex: "You don't have to do that to show me you love me. I know you love me." *Hmm, he's so sincere, I think I'll show him how generous I am....*

Or it may be a chore. For instance, one time when I was a teenager I didn't want to dry the dishes, for two reasons: (1) It was boring and (2) I didn't want to break them. If I asked my sister to do them, she would say no. So I started using a technique that solved all of these problems—an interesting and safe dish-drying method that would also guarantee my sister taking over the job! I put the towel on a countertop, placed a dish on it, then wrapped the dish in the towel. Then I pressed down to soak up the water. This annoyed my sister so much she smirked, "Don't you know how to dry dishes! Give that to me—I'll do it!" Fine with me! My method for drying was perfectly valid, and in fact safer than the usual technique of holding a dish in your hand to dry it (my dish was sitting on the countertop, so it couldn't drop and break). This action is similar to the magician lifting one end of the die box and allowing the die to slide across to the other side. I purposely present a method of drying dishes that—while getting the job done—makes me seem incompetent. My sister fills in the gaps to conclude that I am a hopeless barbarian. She, like the audience volunteers who jump at the chance to prove the magician wrong, comes to my rescue (ego is involved here too!) and saves the day by performing the trick the way it was meant to be done—her way—the way her brain fills in as the correct way for doing the dishwashing trick. I got out of mowing lawns the same way.

Chapter 4 described "discounting," the psychological component of magic in which a smart audience dismisses solutions to the trick because they seem too obvious, too simple, or too silly. Advertising works the same way, and it may even have an easier time of it than magic. It is well known that most people find most advertising to be silly, outlandish, and using obvious ploys. However, some critics have argued that although we are not convinced by most ads, a "sleeper" effect takes place. "While viewers are not persuaded, they do alter the structure of their perceptions about a product."[26] If television viewers actually believed in the importance and relevance of ads, their minds would swell with "perceptual defenses" and a barrage of logical objections against the advertising message. Instead, as writer and critic "Northrop Frye has argued ... advertisements, like other propaganda, 'stun and demoralize the critical consciousness with statements too absurd or extreme to be dealt with seriously by it.' "[27]

Outs

Magicians use "outs" to help them get out of a bad jam. Let's say Merlin loses track of the selected card. It would look bad if he admitted he flubbed the trick. A better solution is to regain control of the situation by throwing the deck of cards in the air and causing it to vanish! Salespeople are familiar with this concept. They make a sales pitch and then the customer starts in with objections. Ogilvy the ad man advised his salesmen to have replies ready to every possible concern that the customer may have. He recommended patter to follow, alternate strategies for selling the product, depending on the interests of the client. Outs are important enough in selling that numerous books and audio programs have been developed around the concept. There's even a biweekly newsletter called *Objections* that tackles the subject. Make no mistake, the best salespeople are manipulative magicians who attempt to wrangle their control over the situation of selling, while creating an illusion of a product custom-tailored to your needs.

Nonspecific Words

Nonspecific words are a technique used by magicians (especially mentalists) to enhance an illusion, to shift the audience into the magician's mental wavelength, and sometimes to direct the actions of a volunteer. It is also used by advertisers. I'll explain what it is and then you'll be able to detect it in action as you're watching TV. The concept is explored in Kenton Knepper's informative *Wonder Words*, an audio program that explains how magicians can use words to deceive and manipulate spectators.[28]

Suppose a magician said to you, "Everyone believes in psychic powers, and now I'm going to show you why..." How would you react? Most likely you would be skeptical of this claim. "*Everyone* believes in psychic powers? *Really?*" You would start doubting the magician, you might think he's a moron for saying such a thing. Even if you believe in psychic powers, the statement is so egotistical and assumptive as to be off-putting. The audience suddenly gets a lot of frowns on their faces, and their minds are running wild with objections. "I don't believe in psychic powers! And you're sure not gonna fool me with that!" The problem is, the statement is too specific. A better way to phrase it might be: "*Some* people believe the mind has special abilities, if only we practice using them..." Now the statement is unspecific. Instead of the outrageous claim that "everyone" believes, we have "some people." And what is it they believe? They believe "the mind has special abilities." What are those special abilities? We don't know exactly, but we are curious, and drawn into the discussion. As Knepper says, "The key words are all unspecified references. Some noun, some person, place or thing, that is *not* specific enough. If it's not specific, the audience has to find some way to apply it to their own lives. And once they do that, you've got 'em." Instead of the audience raising objections, they are actively contemplating how the sentence applies to their own core beliefs. Instead of objecting "That's not true!" they are in agreement: "Oh yeah, that is true because...." The magician has captured their attention, and captured their thought patterns into his own. They are primed and ready to discover the mysteries the magician will present to them.

Nonspecific words are also used in predictions: "You will overcome adversity . . ." Of course you will! Everyone does! And nonspecific words are used in cold readings. James Randi wrote about one psychic who uses the word "dook" in his mind readings. "I see a dook! What about the dook?" The subject is allowed to interpret this however he or she chooses. Maybe they have a pet dog, or they remember an incident from their youth when they were bitten by a duck. Or for that matter, perhaps they are going to visit the doctor. Dook can mean anything the subject wants it to mean, which allows the psychic to seem brilliantly talented.[29]

Advertisers use this same technique. Look at the catch phrase used by Trojan brand condoms: "Helps Reduce the Risk." Helps reduce the risk of *what?* Of AIDS? VD? Unwanted pregnancy? The risk you won't get laid? The consumer is allowed to make any interpretation he or she wants.

What if the catch phrase was "Helps Reduce Unwanted Pregnancies." That would very narrowly target one segment of the market—people who buy condoms for birth control. Further, it would turn off all the other consumers. "Hmm, maybe it's only for birth control but doesn't stop diseases." And, of course, such a catch phrase would be offensive to those who are against birth control. Instead Trojan uses nonspecific words that consumers can choose to interpret in whatever way they want. It allows each consumer to create the ultimate product illusion in his or her own mind.

Here are some more examples of nonspecific advertisements:

- *Get your burger's worth.* What does this ad for Burger King really *mean?* Whatever the consumer wants it to mean: a cheap burger, or good value, or a big, thick burger with toppings piled high. Instead of forcing a particular marketing slant, it allows consumers to come up with their own.
- *Coke is it!* Coke is *what* exactly?—Whatever you *want* it to be.
- *Say it with flowers.* Flowers are the magic word, but what exactly are you saying with them? Will those flowers help your first date run smoothly? Smooth over an argument you've had with your spouse? Perhaps they're meant as a mother's day gift. Other variations have the consumer saying "it" with chocolate, wine, roses, beer, and you name it. And that's the point: the consumer's the one naming exactly what "it" is.
- *It's Miller time!* A magic spell that transforms "ordinary time" into the special magic of "Miller time."
- *Say Seagram's and be sure.* Be sure of *what?* Another magic word that is so powerful, its incantation will allow you to be sure of whatever you want to be sure of.
- *A different kind of company. A different kind of car.* This motto is from the Saturn car company, and once again it touches the pulse of every and any concern the consumer may have. One consumer is fed up with high prices; another wants safety; yet another wants a snazzy design. Whatever the concern, Saturn proclaims it is different from the others. Different has

to mean better, and specifically it has to mean better in the ways that each individual person wishes.

In all these cases, consumers end up creating an illusional ad campaign in their own minds. It is illusional because it's not particularly what the ad agency had in mind, but rather, whatever the consumer infers it to mean.

Another technique shared by advertisers and magicians is the use of questions. A question is another way of drawing listeners emotionally into what you're saying. Even if a question is asked rhetorically, even if it's a silly question, the listener invariably answers it mentally. Even if the listener doesn't come up with an answer, he or she thinks about it a little, and perhaps they wonder how the speaker is going to answer the question. "In every interpersonal situation," business adviser Brian Tracy propounds, "here is the most important rule you will learn. . . . It is that the person who asks questions, has control. Whenever you ask questions of another person, they will almost invariably answer or feel compelled to answer. We've been taught from childhood to answer when we are spoken to. When you ask a person a question—even if they don't speak aloud, in fact—they will answer the question to themselves."[30] Tracy gives this example: Suppose a salesperson approached you and asked, "If you could go anywhere in the world on vacation all expenses paid, where would it be?" Even if you don't answer the salesperson, very likely you would be thinking "Hawaii!" or "France!" or whatever vacation paradise you dream up in your head. "So when you ask questions you have complete control of the conversation until he or she has answered the question, one way or another. When you ask questions it's the equivalent of grabbing the other person by the lapels of their jacket and jerking them toward you. Questions arrest and hold attention. Questions are the most powerful form of communications technique if you want to strongly influence people."[31] Of course, magicians routinely ask leading questions, in such situations as forces, magician's choice, and sometimes to get a certain idea in the spectator's heads, or to provide a believing frame of mind so the magic will seem more mysterious ("Do you believe some people have extraordinary powers of mind?"). In these ways, questions are used to control your mind.

Advertisers are asking questions left and right. The U.S. Postal Service asks, "What's your priority?" McDonald's wants to know, "Have you had your break today?" What is interesting is that *any* answer is good for McDonald's. "Yes" means you have had your break today—in other words, you bought the product. "No" means you haven't bought the product yet, but come to think of it, yeah it sure would be nice to have a break right now. Even if you don't go out and buy some artery-clogging grease patties right away, you have made a mental connection between "break time" and a certain product line.

Magic in Negotiating

Negotiating a contract, a business deal, or a prenuptial agreement can require nerves of steel and a swiftly working mind. And a competitive edge doesn't hurt either. One negotiator uses the magician's tool of a pocket index to help gain that edge. A pocket index is a utility gimmick normally used in psychic predictions and also in some card tricks. The pocket index is like a small card catalog with divider flaps that is hidden in a jacket pocket. During the show, the magician can reach into the pocket and seem to pull out a random card, when in fact he is "letting his fingers do the walking," counting tabs on the index, and thus positioning his fingers at a particular card in the index, inside his pocket. How did a negotiator use this technique? Well, one of the basic tenets of negotiating is that you don't want to reveal your lowest offer. If I can sell you the house for $200,000, then you're not going to want to pay a penny more for it. This negotiator prepares a few "best offers" on pieces of note paper and arranges them in his jacket pocket. For example, let's say he wants to sell the house for $200,000. He will prepare one paper that says $200,000, another that says $250,000, another that says $275,000, another that says $300,000, and another at $350,000. During the negotiating, he talks with the other party and tries to get them to deal their hand first. Let's say they mention a price that's less than he expected ($150,000). He can say, "Sorry guys, my wife says I can't sell for anything less than . . . Gosh what was that figure again?" He reaches into his pocket and pulls out the $250,000 figure. He knows that if their offer is that low, then they're not going to go for the higher $300,000 figure, but they're likely to buy at $200,000, so he pulls out the "best offer" that matches what he thinks they'll buy at. If they happened to overbid at $250,000, then he's prepared for that instance too, by pulling out a higher "best offer" of $350,000. By having several "best offers" preconfigured in his pocket and arranged so that he can pull one out, it seems that the number on the paper must really be his best offer. The written word is a lot more persuasive than whatever comes out of the negotiator's mouth, especially words that were written before the bargaining began.

The tactic of deferring to his wife is a variation on the "accidental tap." It is a way of making the magician—whoops, negotiator—seem less competent, and thus someone you don't have to watch as carefully. In this way, accidents, stumbling and bumbling, create a seeming incompetence that is actually controlling. Related is the subtle/accidental revelation of information that works in your favor—like the magician's planting seeds of misdirection, it's up to the audience's brains to piece the clues together and form an illusion inside their heads. For example, some negotiators allow the other side to "overhear" a phone conversation in which they check with their supervisor. "Okay, so you're authorizing me to go as low as $250,000?" he says softly into the receiver. Now the other side thinks they know something they can use to their benefit—they don't realize that if they wheedle him down to this "best offer," then he's actually making a $50,000 profit!

A ruse similar to the pocket index was used by Peter Guber while he was vice president of Columbia Pictures, the movie company—or so the rumor goes. In order to bolster his reputation, he allegedly wrote up two memos about each movie Columbia made during his reign there. In one memo he recommended the picture, in the other he advised against it. After the movie came out he would destroy the incorrect prediction.[32] In that way he created an illusion of infallible prediction. The guy could be Kreskin's opening act!

Gimmicks

Advertisers often talk about a sales gimmick. As we know, there are gimmicks in magic too. How is a sales gimmick or advertising gimmick the same as a gimmick in magic? A gimmick is a device, a trick, a means to an end that the consumer or audience doesn't realize is there, or is not supposed to notice, anyway. Or even if they do know it, they are "helpless" against it because of its great persuasiveness. Like my duel with the grease truck woman, even if you recognize it for what it's worth, it is worth something to you either monetarily or emotionally, so you end up going with it.

Fig. 44. An illusion of an overflowing barrel of candy. Actually the candy only fills a shallow pan that rests atop the empty barrel.

There is a classic illusion called Ink to Water in which a glass of black ink is transformed into clear water (often with a goldfish swimming about happily inside). The illusion uses a number of gimmicks to achieve its effect, one of which is a black rubber "shell" that is placed around the inside perimeter of the glass to give the appearance that the glass is full of ink (similar to the confetti shell described earlier). Some candy stores use the oil/confetti shell gimmick to create an illusion that huge transparent containers are filled to the brim with candy and happiness. The containers are not as filled as they appear. The candy is held between thin double walls to give the appearance of a full container. Other stores portray a fantasy land where barrels overflow with sweets (see figure 44).

Ban deodorant uses the technique to give the appearance that there is more deodorant in the container (see figure 45).

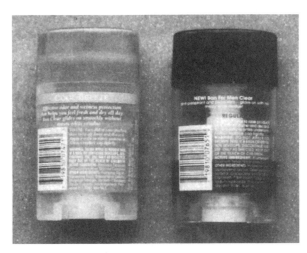

Fig. 45. The product container on the left appears to be transparent, but the bottom is colored to match the deodorant inside. It looks like you are getting more product than you actually are. An empty container at right shows that the seemingly transparent container was really colored. Similar techniques are used by magicians to show a full glass of liquid—when really the liquid is only painted on the sides of the glass.

Note that the deodorant's gimmick will ultimately be discovered when the deodorant runs out, so its creators must cleverly balance trickery with innocence, so consumers don't end up frustrated with the product. Ideally it would be designed so when the illusion is revealed people say, "Oh, cool!" rather than "How disappointing!" This, you'll notice, is the dilemma magicians always face.

I am fascinated by the similarities between the magician's stage and a supermarket. Both have containers and fancy boxes. In a magic show, the magician wants his boxes to look smaller than they are. For example, in some variations on the cut-the-woman-in-half trick, the woman hides inside the table. You don't suspect she's in there because it looks too small and skinny to house a person. In a supermarket, similar physical gimmicks are used to make it look like the boxes are *bigger*, that you're getting more for your money. One common ploy is to put a stripe of bright color at the top of a box ostensibly to show how much more you're getting. Actually the box hasn't changed size at all, but subliminally (or perhaps liminally) we're fooled into thinking that the box used to come up only to the bottom of the stripe. I've seen the stripe ploy used on all sorts of dry goods boxes, as well as toothpaste tubes and candy bars. Notice how similar the stripe trick is to the Zig Zag Woman illusion or other effects where a band of color is used to distort size.

Fig. 46. The stripe technique is used on many products to make it look like you're getting more. The contrasting stripe makes the box look bigger, and it seems to represent an additional layer of food that was not there before.

I've always been suspicious of those potato chip bags that aren't filled up all the way. Someone who doesn't fear the moguls of the potato chip industry could make a case that *air* is being used to create an illusion of larger size! And is it always so necessary to make the indentations at the bottom of wine bottles so large? Hmm, I'm starting to get more suspicious than Miss Marple!

The back page of *Consumer Reports* is always covered with stories of various products whose packaging has been enlarged while their contents remain the same (or even shrink!). The Wendy's hamburger is intentionally square so that the corners stick out of the bun. Grocery stores use mirrors to create an illusion of a multitude of fruit down the produce aisle. It doesn't mean you'll buy more fruit, but certainly the store that has an abundant supply gets a better reputation than one with threadbare shelves. The same trick is used in the amusement park's "claw" games. A glass case houses hundreds of stuffed animals and toys. The player maneuvers a claw into position and tries to grab hold of one of the prizes. In some versions of the game, mirrors adorn one or two walls, to give the impression of prizes galore. All these tricks make consumer goods look bigger and better than they actually are—supermarket illusions!

Salespeople use a verbal analogue of this technique to make prices look smaller than they are. The price is made to seem inconsequential by comparing it to something from everyday life that we buy without thinking: "It costs no more than a container of milk." Another technique is to break up large prices into smaller, digestible portions. A $49.75 CD box set becomes only $9.95 in five monthly installments. Or consider the familiar television commercials where you are asked to sponsor a child "For just 52 cents a day, the price of a cup of coffee." In this case the two techniques are used simultaneously; the price is first broken down into a small unit, and then compared to an everyday cup of coffee. To make a competitor's price look higher a company might quote its cost as a full $100.00, adding the extra cents zeros, while stating their own price as only a tiny $10. Another price ploy is misdirection. A mattress company advertises, "Great service and great value too! A [Brand X] mattress is $400 less at our place than the competitor." The ad directs your attention to that mattress only—who knows what all their other prices are?

When magicians talk about gimmicks they're often referring to a prop or object that looks genuine, but is in fact bogus, or has some trick about it. For instance, a quarter that looks like a real piece of coinage but is gimmicked with two hinges so that it can fold up and fit into the tiny neck of a wine bottle. (This is good for a climactic finish to a vanish-the-coin trick.) Other times a container of some sort is gimmicked to look real when in fact it is fake as an honest politician. For instance, a magician might rig up a false bottom in a box of Corn Flakes to do a color-changing silks effect. Or the magician might have bought a gimmicked Tic Tac box so he can make a disappeared wedding ring magically appear inside the small plastic case. Or maybe he picked up a sealed bottle of aspirin at the magic store (one that's really not sealed; it has a secret method of secreting things inside it). Or he might have gotten himself an invisible thread dispenser that looks like a pager he can wear on his belt. In any case, it is not what the audience believes it to be, even though it looks very genuine. Recently we've seen similar products come on the market for nonmagicians. You can buy cans of household products like shaving cream and bug spray that are hollow inside and have a secret hiding spot to store your valuables. There's even a fake head of lettuce that opens up at the bottom to hide jewelry in.

Siegfried and Roy use similar tactics to disguise their touring trucks. They put the words "flammable liquid" on the trucks so people will be extra cautious when driving the trucks, or driving near the trucks.[33] I imagine they in part decided to use that bit of deceit after the incident of their first visit to New York City, when some low-life stole their truck and made off with some of their tigers. The same sort of deception was used in the ominous movie *Close Encounters of the Third Kind*, where the government used trucks painted to look like they were carrying innocent cargoes like Coca-Cola, Baskin Robbins ice cream, or groceries from the Piggly Wiggly food store, when in fact the trucks were carrying the equipment to build a massive structure to communicate with space aliens.

At least one professional magician has mused, "I have often wondered how many purchases the CIA has made of manuals, books, coins, wallets, and boxes from the major [magic] mail-order suppliers and retailers."[34] By "coins" and "wallets" he's referring to the gimmicked sort of coins and wallets that can be purchased from magic shops and catalogs, and may be useful in spywork. A gimmicked wallet might contain two sets of ID cards so a spy can maintain two different personalities. While showing off one set of ID, the other set remains hidden in the wallet. As another example he points out an episode of "Mission: Impossible" in which a mirror rigged up like an Owens table is used to conceal a person.

Remember the fake beepers mentioned earlier? (Some magicians use a fake beeper to hold invisible thread on their person.) Well, the Miami Field Division of the U.S. Drug Enforcement Agency found drug smugglers using gimmicked beepers in their own nefarious way—the beepers were modified as weapons and concealed ammunition. One of the rigged beepers could fire a small-caliber bullet.[35]

Drug smugglers have certainly put deception to hearty use in the many ingenious ways they've come up with to smuggle drugs into the country. Cocaine has been hidden in such items as a motor home's sewage tank, and inside hollow baby dolls. Heroin has been concealed inside floral-decorated plates, tennis racket handles, suitcases with false sides and bottoms, aerosol cans of deodorant, and even inside a D cell battery being used to power an electric shaver. The battery trick was especially shrewd. The smugglers hollowed out a D cell battery and filled it with 50 grams of heroin. But they also inserted a smaller AA size battery so that the D battery would function properly (albeit at a lesser power). The shaver seemed to function properly, it looked genuine, contained real batteries inside, but it was merely an illusion for passing drugs across the border. Thus a magic trick was created, complete with camouflage, gimmicked props, built-in proofs, and misdirection. Another drug smuggling ring made use of hidden compartments in automobiles; the compartments were electronically remote-controlled, and hidden under false walls and swatches of matching carpet. A hidden trunk compartment was made by welding and bonding into place the trunk floor of a matching car, thus offering few clues to the deception. The compartment made this way was five inches deep, therefore the car trunk was shrunk by five inches.[36] All these devices are reminiscent of similar illusions used by magicians, such as false backs on boxes, or the fishbowl illusion where no one in the audience realizes that the table has shrunk when the fishbowl appears. The fish bowl had been hidden beneath the table cloth.

Magic for the Sake of Magic

Up to now we've been discussing how magic is used in a "sneaky" way, without the audience realizing that they are being affected by the magic, or even that there is magic going on around them, for example, the child who is influenced by advertising, or the adult who visits a psychic. Both of them may be experiencing a magic show and not even realizing it, as the advertisers and psychics work their secret magic upon them, to influence them, to prod beliefs into their minds.

But I would like to conclude this talk of magic off stage and out of the theater with a few words about magic that is done out in the open. Because you see, magic can also be done blatantly in order to influence those who are watching. For instance, my sister related to me how her student body president was elected: all the candidates got up to speak. One guy accompanied his speech with an amazing magic trick (he poured milk into a newspaper cone and it disappeared). They elected him not because they were awed by his politics—they were simply entertained by his magic. Some religious leaders and clergy have taken to using magic in their services. Often called gospel magic, these displays make use of biblical stories and allegories. I suppose the point is to instill a spiritual reverence in the flock. Both Sandorse the Magician and the proprietor of Diamond's Magic, Inc., told me they would open a sales pitch by performing a little magic trick to loosen up a tight situation. Nothing underhanded or secretive about it. Magic is used to break the ice, the way a comedian might use a joke, or a Playmate might show her kinky passport photo. Magicians are now routinely hired to sell products at trade shows and conventions. There is an instructional video on the market that teaches the viewer how to flirt with magic. Not everyone has the gift of gab and a sparkling smile, so perhaps this is the technique needed by some to communicate with others.

Siegfried, of Siegfried and Roy, writes of a time when he was a boy and he wanted to prevent his father from driving home drunk from a bar. Siegfried moseyed into the bar and sat with his dad and his friends until "he was no longer suspicious of my presence" (standard magician's technique: the audience's guard is down and not paying suspicious attention to the magician). Little boy Siegfried gleefully announced he wanted to do a magic trick, and he asked his dad for the car key. He tied the key on a string, placed it under a handkerchief, and made it vanish. The adults were amused and surprised, and Siegfried quickly left the scene of the crime, mission accomplished, the car key in his pocket. Now his daddy couldn't drive home dangerously drunk. Later that night he would get the beating of his life from his father, but for a little while it was a triumph of magic over the evil of drink.[37] Real-world magic, that is, off stage and out of the theater.

How Humans Entertain Themselves

Throughout these pages we have talked about magic and the illusions found in magic. But we have also talked about advertising, politics, ventriloquism, gardening, television, pantomime, acting, reacting, music, art. What is going on here? It is true that magic consists of certain techniques and skills. Some of those skills are borrowed from other artforms, such as mime, music, storytelling and acting. Furthermore, it is true that the other human endeavors, such as advertising and politics, make use of techniques of magic; but they also make use of acting, music, visual illusions, storytelling, and so on. All of these artforms borrow from each other. An actor can put on a good act, but an actor who makes use of voice skills, gesture skills, and all the rest of it, will be a great act. If it is a politician doing the acting, then it is a great act to a dubious end.

We can think of the great collection of human accomplishments as a box filled with techniques and skills. No matter what endeavor the human undertakes to do, he or she reaches into that same box and pulls out one or more of those techniques. The human storyteller will pull out the gift of narrative, plot, climax and character. If an advertiser, narrative and character, colorful images and attractive wording. If a movie director, then perhaps he or she will also pull out narrative, plot, colorful images, and maybe leave out some of the others, skills not yet mastered. A mime will leave behind sounds. A novelist may take the box's full supply of character and narrative, but ignore physical abilities such as double-jointedness. Each human, for each endeavor, takes a little of some, a lot of others. Most take some illusion too.

True, an actor could take only a little piece of "acting ability" and nothing more. But who could bear to watch acting that was devoid of character, conflict, or emotion?

And the magician. The magician takes all of the above. A lot of illusion—the illusion is emphasized. In other endeavors the illusion is there as well, but it is not emphasized by the actor, or the director, or the musician.

These entertainments and endeavors are all based on the need humans have to try and fulfill the desires that we feel in our hearts. We all reach into the same box with the same skills. Some pull out a little of this, others a little of that. And we try to fulfill desires by using different combinations of those same skills.

I believe that's how it all fits together. If you look at it that way, when watching a performance of magic—or the performance given by an advertiser, politician, cult leader, psychic, etc., etc., you can decide which of all the basic human techniques and skills the particular performer has pulled out and what dubious end they are attempting to achieve with it.

17

When the Curtain Closes

There is much more that can be said about magic. Whole books have been written on practically all of the subjects touched on here. There are a few simple—but secret—points that I have attempted to express in this book:

(1) Most magic is based on very simple tricks, but it is not the simple tricks themselves that produce an amazing performance. It is the accumulation of all of these simple tricks, taken with a large dose of showmanship, stage presence, atmosphere, storytelling, and motivations, that produces an effective performance. It is often possible to analyze a trick and figure out partially how it is done, but a *true* understanding can only be gained by looking at this larger picture.

(2) Magic is tricky in ways that most people don't think about. Tricks start before the audience is even aware they are starting. They may start before the show, or during the previous trick. Trusts are broken. The magician lies. These techniques are especially deceptive in off-stage magic because it leads gullible people to incorrect conclusions about what is possible or impossible for magicians to accomplish. If a trick seems impossible through ordinary means, then probably part of the trick was done before you arrived, backstage, or otherwise out of your view.

(3) Magicians are tricky! And they are skilled at what they do. If a psychic or other supernatural charlatan has convinced you that their powers are real—then you have been fooled. Remember *they know more than you do about deception.* Of course you're going to be fooled by it.

Effectiveness of Magic

An amusing anecdote with magical overtones appears in Lynn Snowden's book *Nine Lives*. She tells how in an animated TV commercial for a children's cereal, one of the cartoon creatures lifts up his shirt . . . and a giant erection pops out. "You'd never notice it normally, because it happens so fast and your eye is being diverted by something else."[1] I used to have an acquaintance who worked at an ad agency designing print ads for magazines. One day we got into a discussion of subliminal advertising. Subliminal advertising is the use of subconscious meanings and symbols to induce people to purchase a product. My friend said that people at his agency actually did airbrush in "subliminal" images; a breast in the ice cube, a penis in the shiny chrome of a sports car. "It's definitely out there," he said. "I know because I've done it myself."

Fine. But that doesn't mean it works. Should any of this magic we've been discussing actually work? All of these little things magicians do—the subtle spatial and temporal misdirection, small gestures, flicking some cigarette ash off the table, a glance at a fist, using particular words and giving particular directions—all of this seems so minor, so slight. How could these little things add up to an illusion taking form in one's brain? Indeed, we all remember cramming for exams at school. If it's so hard to intentionally remember specific information, how can we possibly pick up and remember, unintentionally, these little bits of abstract clues and piece together the clues to form the illusion that the magician wants us to create in our minds? The magician is taking a big gamble, isn't he? On television, David Copperfield can select the viewing angles he wants you to see. But when he performs live, he has to trust that his spatial directional clues will cause you to look at the appropriate spots from your vantage point in the theater. The magician who crumpled up the wine bottle and tossed it over his shoulder was taking a gamble that the accidental tap against the microphone stand would be noticed and that the audience would recognize it for what it meant—that the bottle was real and solid. So very often the magician throws out these little clues, and we are expected to subconsciously pick up on them. But to what extent does this apply to real-world magic? To what extent are these subtle indicators effective? Does our brain really have a mind of its own?

I believe that yes, to a large extent, our minds are quite capable of picking up a lot of these clues. We may never know how effective some subliminal clues, like the stripe at the top of the Wheaties box, are unless we talk to the lab manager at General Mills. But I have two stories that illustrate how a mind will unconsciously, without effort, do things you really wish it would not do!

SUBLIMINAL MUSIC

I don't listen to the radio. I want to hear the music that I want to hear. I don't want to search for something good; I don't want to listen to commercials. So I don't listen to the radio. If I want to hear music, I play one of my tapes or CDs. Consequently, I don't hear new songs and new groups. Luckily I have a source of new music to which I turn. This source supplies me with any piece of music I want. And since I am of curious nature, I take advantage of my source, and listen to lots of new tapes and CDs, all different kinds of music, of bands I'm familiar with and bands I am not. The funny thing is, very often I will pop in a new CD by a new group, and one of the songs will be very familiar to me. Certainly I've never heard that song before! I don't listen to the radio; how could I possibly have heard it? And yet this happens time after time.

The answer is simple and scary: Even though I've never heard the song before, I actually have heard it—I just don't remember. If it's a new popular song, I've heard it in the mall, on television, from passing cars on the street. Even though I never really hear the song, I end up learning it and memorizing it and *getting it in my brain.*

How much different is it to get a piece of propaganda in your brain? Not hard at all, I'm sure. Probably you can think of many world views you hold that are quite the same as those your parents held. Ideas wear off on you, even if you don't realize it. Similarly, the little clues that are presented, the sly misdirections, the gestures, the timing, the unusual covers, are picked up by your brain, analyzed, sloshed together, and finally spit out into a neat package called an "illusion." And if your reality is based even partially on some sort of illusion then you have been affected by real world magic.

I can think of several examples off the top of my head how my mind has been captured and bent by magic. For instance, remember the silly notion at the beginning of the last section that perhaps we are being affected by magic and don't even realize it—and perhaps that is part of the magic as well? It seemed silly when I first presented that idea. Now consider the story of my remembering music I've never heard before. Not so silly anymore, huh? I don't think I am affected by advertising and hype, but if I'm restricting myself from listening to music and still find the music affecting me, there is clearly something wrong with the dividing line between reality and my perception of it. This must be true to some extent for all of us.

BEER

I was sitting on a train, on my way into the city for a cocktail party, and I was casually eyeing a poster on the wall. The poster showed a can of Fosters, Australian beer. My mind was wandering. The train rode along. Just then the familiar *ksssxxxx* sound of a beer can being tabbed open filled the train car. I heard the beer bubbling up, and the passenger taking a guzzle of frothy brew. Then I thought, *Waitasecond, that can't be beer, it must be soda.* I turned around to see a man a few seats back chugging down a Pepsi.

He wasn't drinking a beer, and it was illogical to think that he was when a soda fit the context much more appropriately. Furthermore, I personally barely ever drink beer, but I do often drink soda from cans. So it would seem to me that just by hearing the sound of a can opening and some liquid fizzing up, that I *should* have associated those sounds with *soda,* not with beer.

Ah! But it wasn't just the sounds. Coincidentally, I was looking at the can of beer painted on the wall at the exact moment when the passenger opened his Pepsi. My mind fused together the picture and the sounds, and came up with the idea "Passenger opening can of beer." What was previously an illogical thought (that a person would be chug-a-lugging a beer on a train ride), now becomes completely understandable. A visual image of beer, coupled with a sound that can represent beer, equals—what else? Beer!

Again, we see the mind unconsciously putting clues together to build up a very real illusion. I had no real reason to believe the man was drinking beer behind me, and yet, if I hadn't given it any thought, I would still probably, to this day, believe that's what he was drinking.

My advice to you is this. Don't underestimate the power of suggestion. It can be very strong. Keep in mind the sucker effects and the underselling tricks we mentioned earlier, because they can lull you into a complacency that will add more "proof" to the suggestions being offered. And always remember, you are susceptible to these illusions, even if you believe you are not—*especially* if you believe you are not, because when your guard is down, that is when you're not putting up barriers to protect against these mental intrusions. Be prepared for them; be wary of them. Consider the advice of one professor of psychology:

> You don't expect to get persuasive information in the middle of a book. It turns out, though, when you take a step back and think about it a little bit, it turns out it should be the case that you should always be on your guard for persuasive information. Because you would be hard pressed to find a situation in which whatever information is being given to you is not intending to change you in some way.[2]

Normally when we think about information being given to us, we think of someone talking directly to us, or of reading information in a newspaper article or book. But the whole point of magic, and magical techniques of communicating with people, is that not all information is given on the surface. Much of it is given as subtle clues (particular words or gestures), much of which may easily be overlooked by the recipient of that information. Our brains are like adding machines, silently and quietly adding up the data being fed in. My sister told me that she is repulsed by the idea of getting her ears pierced. "Mom brainwashed me!" she said. "For years I wanted to get them pierced, but she told me I was too young, and she badmouthed it. Now I look at people with holes in their ears and think, 'Boy that's disgusting.' " Brainwashing can be explicit, like a parent who by rote force conditions her children to have certain beliefs. Or brainwashing can be implicit, the way a magician feeds beliefs "on the sly." How many times has your mind "gathered evidence" without you realizing it, and come up with an answer when you least expected it? For example, how often have you tried to remember a person's name, but then later on (even though you're not thinking about it anymore) it suddenly pops into the forefront of your mind? The adding machine's at work!

Furthermore, much of our brain works on reflex principles that are very hard, if not impossible, to control. Magic, especially sleight of hand, relies on exploiting our instincts. Sociology professor Peter Nardi explained that when he lectures his students he sometimes throws in some sleight of hand as a way of demonstrating how humans can fall into such traps. Even when he explicitly tells the students how the sleight works, they are still fooled by it, they still look at the wrong hand, and they are still surprised when the sleight works.

Because we have this great brain of ours that can think when we don't think it's thinking, we have to be careful, and cautious, and understanding, of the thoughts and beliefs that we do have. This is especially true in today's society where our popular media and entertainment is more and more intertwined with advertising. We have:

- Infomercials that get higher ratings than the scheduled programming they're up against
- Product placements in movies
- Corporate sponsorships of amusement park rides
- Talk shows where the entertainment is actually advertising for upcoming movies and music
- Advertising inserts in magazines that contain more information than the magazine itself
- Characters from advertisements crossing over into cartoons and video games.

Some of this stuff uses the magic techniques we've been discussing. Other times it's just plain deceptive. All this leads to one important question:

What Are the Effects of Real-World Magic?

The effect of stage magic ranges from the disappointment felt at witnessing an unconvincing performance to a deep reverence of the mystical in the world. Real-world magic may be this and more.

As paranormal investigator and magician James Randi says, the supernatural "are products offered you by charlatans who think you are not the marvelous, capable, independent being you are."[3] In our context we may extend this to all forms of off-stage magic, including misdirecting advertising, product design, sales pitches, public relations, and all the other examples we've discussed herein. The sellers mean to suck up your creativity and your passion for your own abilities. They feed you images of your horribleness, and glorify their own exaggerated goodness. They want you to be passive, except when you are buying their products and services and ideas and thoughts. You are no good unless you buy my product. Why think on your own when I can sell you my ideas, which will give you hope and instill magic within you? But it is a false magic, and false hope. Attributing the pyramids to space aliens, you get the feeling that you are not worthy—that you're not as good as those higher-ups in power, in the media, those who write books. Did we say there was no motive to a hoax? There sure is one: it gives all this power to the one perpetuating the hoax! Remember that actors are the most consummate fans, and similarly magicians are the biggest idolaters of other magicians. The false prophets and psychics and supernatural leaders can only be the most adoring fans of the leaders who came before them. And in being their fans, they feel the weakness and the emptiness within themselves.

But we cannot let this all get to us! We must be aware of it when we encounter it, and realize that the reality we see may be a secretly altered illusion.

How to Deal with Magic

Let's end on a happy note, by starting the conclusion with a joke.

> A magician goes to K-Mart to buy some props for a trick he's working on. He picks out a large and sharpened knife, then goes up to the counter to pay for it. At the counter he realizes he also needs a costume for his assistant. "Do you have women's bathing suits here?" he asks. "One-piece or two-piece suits?" the clerk asks. The magician looks at his knife: "Three."

The humor of jokes is based on surprise, and a joke's power to be funny is based on the amount of surprised contained in the punch line. A joke told twice in a row will not amuse as much (or at all) as the first go around, for the simple reason that the surprise has been lost. No punch in the punch line. Mystery stories are the same way. In a mystery, suspense is vital, and must remain with the reader until that crucial last chapter when the jig is up, the trick is revealed.

Like jokes, like mysteries, in magic the surprise is everything. The suspense is everything. Unlike a mystery story, in a magic trick the suspense should be endless, everlasting. You should never know how it's done, because then the magic is lost. So in certain ways, what this book has done is taken the punch out of magical punch lines. It has revealed who done it, even before the murder is committed. Ah, well, I did warn you in the beginning about that. The jig is up. Not for the magician—he can continue performing shows for those who still hold interest in the art of illusion. No, the jig is up for you. With knowledge comes understanding. With the knowledge in this book, you have the understanding of how it's all done. The mystery is gone. The joke is not funny. The magic and the illusion and the awe and the mystical reverence are gone for good.

The techniques magicians use to deceive an audience are useful to know for real life, but ultimately they detract from a magical performance. Use your knowledge of them wisely, when confronted with a seedy used car salesman, or a door-to-door evangelist. But when going to a magic show, I say enjoy the show! Why destroy your feelings of amusement, of entertainment, of tingly wonder about the world, by analyzing it to death? It may be interesting to know what goes into magic, but when you find the answers it's like discovering what they put into hot dogs: You'll never want to take in another one.

When in life, beware. When in show, sit back and enjoy.

Glossary

Magician Jargon

The nonnormal use of words is another way in which magicians control the audience (see the definition for "illusion," for an example of this). And like any group, magicians have a language they use to describe the objects of their profession. Note that these objects fall into two groups—things we know about (scarves), and things that remain hidden from us (servantes). In that vein, this lexicon of magic will help get the thought of magicians into your own mind, because these words are as impressioned into their skulls as the fancy sleight work is practiced into their fingers. This is by no means a complete list of jargon, but it should be a useful start toward understanding the magical realm.

Abracadabra—A magic word. Magic words are used to focus the audience on a particular place and time, which neatly covers up the fact that the trick actually took place at a different place and a different time.

Angle—As in "watch your angle," "bad angles," and angle-proof trick. This is something magicians must watch out for, that a trick may be given away because a spectator is seated in a location where they see something they should not be seeing.

Apparatus—Any object seen by the audience that has been prepared in some way to achieve an effect. The object may appear perfectly normal to the audience, but it is still apparatus.

Arrangement—The ordering of cards in a stack of cards. Card magicians often pre-arrange a stack of cards before a show.

Assistant—A person on stage who helps the magician perform magic, and whom the audience recognizes as a member of the magician's show. (As opposed to a *volunteer* or *confederate*.)

Back palm—To conceal a card, coin, or other object from the audience by clipping it between the fingers behind the hand, while showing the empty palm to the audience.

Billet—A small piece of paper that contains a message and is folded up so the writing remains hidden. In mentalism acts, the magician attempts to know the contents of a billet using psychic powers.

Bizarre magick—Loosely defined, this is a branch of magic that tries to create a weird atmosphere both ancient and mystical, and perhaps even a bit horrifying, using old relics as props, and with spooky music and lighting setting the stage. Bizarre magick tends to be serious, intense, and intended to invoke an emotional response in the audience. While mostly unknown to the general public, this kind of spooky magic has a loyal and growing following amongst magicians.

Black art—Covering an item in black so that it is hidden from the audience as it is situated in front of a black background, on a dark stage.

Body load—An object or number of objects hidden on the performer's body or in his clothing, in a pocket, clipped under the jacket, etc., to be magically produced later during the show.

Bottom deal—Secretly dealing a card from the bottom of the deck. In card hustling, known as "dealing bottoms."

Bullet—In faith healing, a piece of animal tissue or bloody cotton that is made to appear to have been removed from the patient's body.

Bush—Another name for a *plant*. Get it?

Cardician—A magician skilled in card sleights.

Cave—Tongue-in-cheek term for the area in which black art magic is to be performed, because the area must be darkened and enclosed like a cave.

Chop cup—A gimmicked cup with a magnet inside that draws balls up inside it to give the appearance they have vanished.

Chops—Technical mastery. "He's been practicing that sleight all day. Now he's got the chops!"

Confederate—A person who assists the magician, but who the audience does not realize is part of the act. Confederates are often used in psychic performances, mentalism, and occasionally in conjuring tricks to provide a gimmicked prop.

Coolers—In card hustling, prearranged decks of cards that are switched in for the game deck. Also called "cold decks."

Crimp—To mark a card or deck of cards by slightly bending or folding certain cards.

Daub—Any substance used to *mark* cards, such as a smidgen of lipstick or rouge.

Ditch—To secretly get rid of something. ("They're so amazed by the appearance of the silk, they don't see me ditching the thumb tip.")

Double duke—In card hustling, prearranging a deck so that two people receive good hands as the cards are dealt.

Dropper—A clip or holder worn under the clothing that secretly dispenses items to the magician. There are droppers for coins, billiard balls, cigarettes, and thimbles.

Effect—A magic trick as viewed by the audience. ("Then he did a great lady-to-tiger effect.")

Evanishment—An effect where an object or person is made to disappear.

Fake—The *gimmick*, or *apparatus* that has been secretly altered to create the illusion.

False cut—A simulated cut of a deck of cards, carried out to maintain the current order of the cards.

False finger—A rubber or plastic finger slipped in between the real fingers on a magician's hand and used as a secret storage place for a small silk or other items.

Feke—Variation on the word *fake*.

Fair shuffle—A genuine mixing of the cards.

False shuffle—A simulated shuffle of a deck of cards, carried out to maintain the current order of the cards.

Flash paper—Chemically treated paper that, when lit with a match, explodes into flames for a moment and just as quickly vanishes.

Flashing—To accidentally allow a spectator to see how a trick is done. ("I didn't realize she was sitting at a bad angle! I must've flashed the gaff to her!")

Gaff—A physical alteration to an item. The alteration remains hidden to the audience and is thus used to produce the magic trick, for example, a gaffed playing card that is hinged in the middle so it can fold down and turn into another card.

Gimmick—An item used by the magician, unbeknownst to the spectators, to create an illusion.

Hocus pocus—A magic word. See *Abracadabra*.

Illusion—A deception of the senses.

Impressionment—To draft a *volunteer* into becoming a *confederate*, usually by covert means, during a performance.

Impromptu—An effect performed off the cuff, at the spur of the moment, in some odd setting such as the dinner table, and not as part of a magic show. The word itself is a ploy, for there is no such thing as a truly impromptu trick—they must all be learned, planned out, and rehearsed ahead of time.

Induction—Drawing a general conclusion from a few facts. In magic, the magician offers some facts but neglects to point out one or more critical facts or clues that would help explain the mystery. The lack of those facts causes the viewer to induce that magic has transpired.

Juice—To mark a deck with large dashes and dots across the back, using a liquid that discolors the card.

Key card—A card known by the magician that is used to determine the volunteer's selected card.

Lapping—When the magician uses his lap as an accessory to a trick, either to vanish an object or make it appear. Lapping is often used with Cups and Balls routines.

Levitation—An *effect* in which the magician causes a person or object to rise in the air and float. Levitations are usually done with hidden pipes, tubes, or cables.

Load—An item or collection of items that is stored in a secret place (under the table, in the lap, in a pocket, in a thumb tip), that will later be produced by the magician. ("These rubber hot dogs compress down into a tiny load that fits in the palm of the hand.") To load something means to secrete it into a special compartment or receptacle so it can be produced. ("She loaded the rabbit into the hat.")

Magician—Someone who performs magic tricks or practices deceptions for an audience.

Magician's choice—A supposedly free selection made by a volunteer that is in fact controlled by the magician. Also known as "conjurer's choice."

Magick—In this book, used specifically to refer to the kind of magic practiced by people who really believe in real magic.

Mark—A means of secretly identifying a card, either by smudging something on it, crimping an edge, or making an indentation with a fingernail.

Mentalist—A magician who performs psychic, mind reading, or telekinesis effects.

Metamorphosis—Another name for the *substitution trunk*.

Misdirection—The routing of spectators' attention and perception, usually to hide a crucial move or *sleight*.

Nail writer—A small piece of graphite that clips to the fingernail and used by mentalists to covertly scratch an answer on paper before the eyes of the audience.

Office—In card hustling, a verbal or gestural signal that relays information to one's partners. Also called "officing."

Palming—A sleight of hand in which an object is held in the palm by the fleshy parts of the hand. There are many variations on this including the thumb palm, finger palm, back palm, and more.

Paper—In card hustling, a marked deck of cards.

Peeking—Covertly looking at cards in a deck while dealing.

Penetration—See *Solid penetration*.

Plant—A *stooge*.

Pocket index—Used by some mentalists and some cardicians, and perhaps a good gift for the anal retentive office organizer in your life. These are small card filing systems that fit into one's pocket. The magician can organize playing cards, predictions, or any items in the index. With practice, the magician can place his hand in his pocket, flip through the tabs of the index, and come up with the appropriate item.

Production—An effect where an object or person is made to magically appear where previously there was nothing.

Proofs—Techniques the magician uses to show the audience that no trickery or deception is involved in an illusion, for example, when the magician rolls up his sleeves or passes a hoop around a levitating assistant. Of course, trickery and deception are very much involved in the illusion, so proofs are really shams.

Property change—The alteration of intrinsic traits of an object or person, such as color, size, weight, or speed.

Psychic—A magician who performs psychic, mind reading, or telekinesis effects, but claims not to be a magician.

Pull—A length of elastic attached to the inside back of a jacket. The other end has a clip or cup into which the magician pushes an item that he wants to vanish. The contraption is hidden in the fist, and the magician takes the item and pushes it seemingly into his fist, but really into the pull. When he lets go, the stretched elastic whizzes invisibly up the sleeve or jacket. The hand is opened and shown to be empty.

Read paper—To read the markings of a marked deck of card and to use them to infer the face value of the card.

Reel—A mechanical variation on the *pull*. When a button is pressed, the thread or elastic is reeled in, under the jacket or coattails, similar to a retracting tape measure. Used for many effects, such as the magical untying of a knot in a silk.

Restricted choice—A choice that appears to be unlimited and completely up to the choosing of the audience, but is in fact controlled by the magician.

Roughing fluid—A sort of paste that is painted on cards, causing the surfaces to stick to each other.

Routine—A scripted plan for a trick or series of tricks.

Run-around—When a magician "runs around" the audience, back stage or off stage, and reappears unexpectedly in back of the audience or on the opposite side of the stage. Used after trick escapes or disappearances to garner an extra "oooh!" from the audience.

Run up—Stacking a deck so that when it is dealt a particular player will get a good hand.

Salting—Hiding items around a room in which you will later perform. Often the term is used when the magician will be performing impromptu later. Notice how deceptive this is—the audience thinks the trick is spur of the moment, when really it has been carefully planned!

Seconds—Dealing the second card from the top of the deck.

Servante—A ledge, box, basket, or bag hidden behind a table. Objects are secretly dumped into or scooped out of it.

Shade—A distraction designed to assist a card shark.

Shell—An item that appears to be some genuine, solid thing, but is in fact hollow. There are shell balls, coins, wands, assistants, and many more.

Shill—A con artist's accomplice who aids in the con by pretending to be an innocent bystander. Similar to *stooge*.

Silk—The magician's word for a silk scarf or handkerchief.

Sleight—Any special, learned move that produces an illusion. Typical sleights are those showing the hands as empty when in fact they conceal an object, and seeming to move an item from one hand to another but actually retaining it in the first hand.

Sleight of hand—General term used to describe methods of manipulating items in ways contrary to appearance, to produce an illusion.

Solid penetration—An effect where two solid objects seem to pass through one another. A common example is the Linking Rings.

Steal—To secretly get possession of an item. For instance, the magician shows her hand empty, steals a lollipop from her pocket without the audience noticing, and then reveals the lollipop in her previously empty hand.

Stooge—An accomplice of the magician who pretends to be an ordinary member of the audience. Also called a *plant* or *bush*.

Sub trunk—Short for *substitution trunk*.

Substitution trunk—A stage illusion in which the magician and an assistant change places inside a sealed trunk. Also known as *Metamorphosis*.

Sucker trick—A *routine* in which the audience is led into thinking it knows how the trick is done, but then is proven wrong.

Takeup reel—Another name for a *reel*.

Talking—Accidental sounds that the magician doesn't want you to hear. For instance, if a card scrapes against a tabletop as it is being dealt out, and the spectator hears a metallic sound, the card is "talking" that there's a coin hidden underneath.

Tell—What professional gamblers and magic analyzers look for. The tell is the subtle facial expression that gives away the trick. Does the magician grimace at one point? Does his smile seem a bit more forced? Are the eyes suddenly dilated? His body is unconsciously telling you that something is going on at that moment that he'd rather not let you in on. Be on the lookout! Reference: the movie *House of Cards*, available on video.

Thumb tip—Sometimes metal, sometimes plastic or glass, sometimes called by the code name "witches nose" when speaking of it in public. This is perhaps the most top secret of all top secret implements in the magician's trade, because with it and a degree of skill, dozens of astounding magical effects can be performed.

Transposition—A magical effect in which two objects exchange places.

Trick—A lay term for what magicians do. Magicians are more apt to use the word "illusion," since they feel a trick is something hookers do.

Volunteer—A member of the audience who is invited to take part in an *effect* with the magician.

Bibliography

These are the books, magazines, newspapers, journal articles, and other sources that were used for research in preparing this book. Information was also collected from on-line sources, including some magic-related Worldwide Web pages and various Usenet newsgroups, primarily alt.magic. I have cited these sources whenever possible to give credit to the original poster. However it should be realized that most newsgroups are unarchived, and these postings are thus long gone. Another wonderful source of information was interviews with magicians, psychics, and others, for whose assistance I have the utmost gratitude. The addresses and phone numbers mentioned throughout this book were checked for accuracy at time of publication.

Books

An asterisk indicates a particularly informative, useful, or great book.

Bader, Robert S. *Groucho Marx and Other Short Stories and Tall Tales: Selected Writings of Groucho Marx.* Beverly Hills, California: Dove Audio, 1994. The source for Groucho's story about plants in his audiences was taken from this collection, but originally appeared in the March 1933 issue of *Redbook.*

Bandler, Richard. *Using Your Brain—For a Change.* Moab, Utah: Real People Press, 1985, p. 115. Lectures on using neurolinguistic programming to influence thoughts and behaviors in other people.

*Bannon, John. *Smoke and Mirrors.* Silver Spring, Maryland: Richard Kaufman and Alan Greenberg, 1991. This is a wonderful book of tricks, written for the well-practiced magician who is as good at manipulating cards as buttering bread. Bannon really knows his stuff.

411

Barreca, Regina. *Sweet Revenge: The Wicked Delights of Getting Even.* New York: Harmony Books, 1995.

de Beauvoir, Simone. *The Second Sex.* Trans. H. M. Parshley. New York: Alfred A. Knopf, 1982. The roles women play in this world. Source for some of the information from the section on women in magic.

Bellman, Willard F. *Scene Design, Stage Lighting, Sound, Costume and Makeup: A Scenographic Approach.* New York: Harper & Row, 1983. Comprehensive technical manual on subjects mentioned in the title. Used here for background information on wires and rigging in levitation effects.

Berrett, James, Chief Inspector. *When I Was at Scotland Yard.* London: Sampson Low, Marston, 1932. This is the source of the story of the woman who was convinced by a "psychic" that her husband was having an affair.

Blackstone, Harry. *200 Magic Tricks Anyone Can Do.* Avenel, New Jersey: Wings Books, 1995. Reprint of a text Blackstone wrote back in 1949. The two hundred magic tricks were collected from Blackstone's earlier writings on magic, and they include a variety of standard conjuring effects. Anecdote about Blackstone Jr. learning telepathy code is taken from the preface.

Brenneman, Richard. *Deadly Blessings: Faith Healing on Trial.* Amherst, New York: Prometheus Books, 1990. A reformed believer in the supernatural showing why faith healing is bunk.

Buckley, Arthur. *Principles and Deceptions.* Las Vegas, Nevada: The Gambler's Book Club, 1948. Excellent professional instruction for anyone interested in deceptions with coins, cards, and billiard balls, as well as "head stuff." His principles of magic from pp. 25–27.

*Burger, Eugene. *The Experience of Magic.* Silver Spring, Maryland: Richard Kaufman and Alan Greenberg, 1989. An outstanding treatise on coordinating patter and gestures with one's routine to achieve an experience of magic and mystery.

Burris-Meyer, Harold, and Edward C. Cole. *Scenery for the Theatre: The Organization, Processes, Materials, and Techniques Used to Set the Stage.* Rev. ed. Boston: Little, Brown and Company, 1971. Contains some diagrams of complicated rigging schemes for levitating actors in plays. See pp. 298–99.

Cader, Michael. *Saturday Night Live: The First Twenty Years.* New York: Houghton Mifflin, 1994, p. 178.

Chambers, Karen S. *Trompe l'Oeil at Home: Faux Finishes and Fantasy Settings.* New York: Rizzoli, 1991. A colorful romp through the subject. You'll want to, as I did, keep showing photos in this book to people and saying, "Doesn't it look *real?*" when in fact all you're showing them is a painting of bookshelves on the wall, or a lifesize naked plastic woman.

Charney, David H. *Magic: The Great Illusions Revealed and Explained.* New York: Strawberry Hill Publishing Co., Inc., 1975. A new edition of a tell-all book first published in 1897.

*Christopher, Milbourne. *Fifty Tricks with a Thumb Tip: A Manual of Thumb Tip Magic.* 3d ed. New York: D. Robbins & Company, 1948. Slim primer demonstrating the many uses of this valuable tool of the magician.

———. *Magic: A Picture History.* New York: Dover, 1991. Christopher, a former national president of the Society of American Magicians, is one of magicdom's most prolific authors. This volume was used for the information on "doctors" and "professors" of magic in the eighteenth and nineteenth centuries and other historical data. The David Devant quote in chapter 1 is from pp. 153–54.

*Cialdini, Robert B. *Influence: How and Why People Agree to Things*. New York: William Morrow and Company, Inc., 1984. An easy-reading text detailing the social psychology that permeates our interactions with other people, often causing us to act in ways we don't believe, and to believe in ideas we find inconceivable.

Clute, Cedric E., and Nicholas Lewin. *Sleight of Crime*. Chicago: Regnery, 1977. This mystery anthology contains fifteen stories about magic and magicians and is my source for the Leacock story mentioned in chapter 1. An interesting relation between magician and detective: one obfuscates, the other delineates.

Coleman, Earle Jerome. *Magic: A Reference Guide*. Westport, Connecticut: Greenwood Press, 1987. A comprehensive review of the magic literature up to 1987.

Cruickshank, Charles. *Deception in World War II*. Oxford: Oxford University Press, 1981.

Drabelle, Dennis. *The Art of Landscape Architecture*. Washington, D.C.: Partners for Livable Places, 1990.

Dunninger, as told to Walter Gibson. *Dunninger's Secrets*. Secaucus, New Jersey: Lyle Stuart, Inc., 1974. The mentalist Dunninger talks about psychic shows, reveals methods that have been used, and continuously claims his telepathic ability. Lots of clever secrets revealed about how mentalists read our minds. The quip about the time bomb is from page 10.

Edelstein, Andrew J., and Frank Lovece. *The Brady Bunch Book*. New York: Warner, 1990. The episode mentioned, called "Lights Out," originally aired February 19, 1971. Mike and Carol Brady encouraged Cindy to be Peter's assistant in his magic act to overcome her fear.

Edmonds, I. G. *The Magic Makers*. Nashville: Thomas Nelson Inc., 1976. A fantastic journey through the history of magic, revealing many of its secrets along the way.

*Ekman, Paul. *Telling Lies*. New York: W. W. Norton, 1985. Quintessential survey of psychological research into lying.

Engel, Joel. *Screenwriters on Screenwriting: The Best in the Business Discuss Their Craft*. New York: Hyperion, 1995. The source for the stereotype of character in *Sleeping with the Enemy*.

Engel, Peter. *Scam!: Shams, Stings, and Shady Business Practices, and How You Can Avoid Them*. New York: St. Martin's, 1996. Shows the many methods of fleecing innocent people.

*Feynman, Richard P. *"Surely You're Joking, Mr. Feynman."* New York: W. W. Norton, 1985. An instant classic and wonderful book from an amazing and brilliant character.

*———. *"What Do You Care What Other People Think?"* New York: W. W. Norton, 1988. The extraordinary follow-up to above, and source for the quote on advertising designed to fool the customer.

Fischbacher, Siegfried, and Roy Ludwig Horn, with Annette Tapert. *Mastering the Impossible*. New York: William Morrow, 1992. A colorful biography of the two magic superstars of Las Vegas. No magic secrets are revealed, but we are given many wonderful and mystic stories of Roy communing with the animals. Sample story: One of the leopards is operated on to have tumors removed.

Everything turns out fine, the most difficult part of the surgery being at the end, while sewing the animal up: they had to line up the spots correctly.

Fromm, Erich. *The Art of Loving*. New York: Harper & Row, 1956.

Gardner, Robert. *Magic Through Science*. Garden City, New York: Doubleday, 1978. A good sourcebook for magic of the Property Changes, such as crystals and liquids that change colors, as well as other scientific feats of mysticism.

Garson, Barbara. *The Electronic Sweatshop*. New York: Simon and Schuster, 1988. A different sort of control: managers controlling their employees down to the last finger flick and vocal inflection, in an effort to cut costs and hopefully control consumers as well.

Gibson, Walter B. *Magic with Science*. New York: Grosset & Dunlap, 1968. A book of magic based on scientific principles. The chapters are entitled "Physitrix," "Optrix," "Equilitrix," "Arithmetrix," "Hypnotrix," and the like.

————. *The Original Houdini Scrapbook*. New York: Corwin Sterling, 1976. Ephemera, posters, anecdotes, and photos documenting Houdini's extraordinary life and career.

Goldberg, M. Hirsh. *The Book of Lies*. New York: William Morrow, 1990. Compendium of lies, hoaxes, frauds, tricks, and illusions through history.

Gregory, R. L., and E. H. Gombrich, eds. *Illusion in Nature and Art*. New York: Charles Scribner's Sons, 1973. Fascinating collection of essays on illusion in the world, including how insects and animals use illusion for camouflage to protect themselves against predators. Also includes essays on illusion in art, physiological roots of illusion, and an analysis of illusion across cultures.

Griffin, Nancy, and Kim Masters. *Hit and Run: How Jon Peters and Peter Guber Took Sony for a Ride in Hollywood*. New York: Simon & Schuster, 1996. Jealousy-inducing story about an ex-hairdresser who makes fortunes in the movie business. Contains the anecdote about Sony's trick with the pocket radio, and the story of predicting a movie's success with two memos.

Harris, Geraldine. *Gods & Pharaohs from Egyptian Mythology (World Mythologies)*. Vancouver, British Columbia: Schocken, 1983. Used for further information on the story of King Khufu and the magicians.

*Hay, Henry. *The Amateur Magician's Handbook*. 4th ed. New York: Harper & Row, 1982. A complete and wonderful guide to performing magic.

Hooker, Richard. *M*A*S*H*. New York: William Morrow, 1968.

Hyde, Margaret O. *Brainwashing and Other Forms of Mind Control*. New York: McGraw-Hill, 1977. An introduction to psychological knowledge related to brainwashing.

The Illustrated Art of Lock-Picking: An Educational Trade Manual. Asbury Park, New Jersey: Mentor Publications, 1976. A clear, concise guide to how locks work and how to pick them open.

*Itoh, Teiji. *Space and Illusion in the Japanese Garden*. New York: Weatherhill/Tankosha, 1973. Many fascinating ideas that are ancient and yet oh-so-new to an American mind. The chapter 12 information on capture gardens was borrowed from this absorbing book.

*Jillette, Penn, and Teller. *Penn & Teller's Cruel Tricks for Dear Friends*. New York: Villard Books, 1989. A great collection of all sorts of bizarre stuff, including how the duo cut and restored a snake on "Saturday Night Live."

Jones, Jan, et al. *The Magician's Assistant.* Sierra Madre, California: Magical Publications of California, 1982. Covers all aspects of being a magician's assistant, including makeup, poise, handling props, appearing on television, and a pictorial history with anecdotes of assistants.

Kaye, Marvin. *Catalog of Magic.* Garden City, New York: Doubleday, 1977. Descriptions and ratings of commercially available effects. While the book is now probably somewhat dated, it contains valuable information on the tricks, as well as (sometimes) a brief hint at how the trick is accomplished.

Kelley, Harold H. "Magic Tricks: The Management of Casual Attributions." *Perspectives on Attribution Research and Theory: The Bielefeld Symposium.* Dietmar Görlitz, ed. Cambridge, Massachusetts: Ballinger, 1980. Chapter on how attributional psychology can be used to analyze a magic trick. Especially interesting is Kelly's comparison of how a magic trick is like a scientific experiment.

Knox, Michael, with Mike Walker. *The Private Diary of an O. J. Juror.* Beverly Hills, California: Dove Books, 1995, p. 76. Anecdote about sneaking a pocket knife past the deputies when being detained for the jury.

Kreskin. *The Amazing World of Kreskin.* New York: Random House, 1973. Kreskin talks about his alleged powers of ESP.

Letts, Malcolm. *Mandeville's Travels: Texts and Translations.* Vol. 1. London: The Hakluyt Society, 1953. An old book with ragged pages, in my copy many pages yet uncut. Includes Sir John Mandeville's visit to the Great Kahn, and his witnessing of feats of magic there.

Lifton, Robert Jay. *Thought Reform and the Psychology of Totalism: A Study of "Brainwashing" in China.* New York: W. W. Norton, 1961. The author interviewed victims of Chinese Communist thought reform ("brainwashing") over the course of many months, and proposes his analyses and theories on brainwashing in this highly readable text.

Loeschke, Maravene Sheppard. *All About Mime.* Englewood Cliffs, New Jersey: Prentice-Hall, 1982. Wordier and more academic than the Stolzenberg book.

Majax, Gerard. *Secrets of the Card Sharks.* New York: Sterling, 1977. Reveals all the tricks of card hustlers, including marked decks, misdirections, sleights, gimmicks, and more. Instructive stuff for those interested in this area.

Mastai, M. L. d'Otrange. *Illusion in Art: Trompe l'oeil, a History of Pictorial Illusionism.* New York: Abaris Books, 1975. A beautiful (but mostly black and white) stroll through the subject matter through the ages.

Matalin, Mary, and James Carville, with Peter Knobler. *All's Fair: Love, War, and Running for President.* New York: Random House, 1994. Two lovebirds on opposing sides of the presidential race.

Molloy, John T. *New Dress for Success.* New York: Warner, 1988. I think Molloy goes a bit overboard with his claims about what effect clothes can have on the wearer, but it is thought-provoking for those interested in how clothing may be a factor in off-stage magic and influencing behavior.

Mulholland, John. *Quicker Than the Eye.* Indianapolis, Indiana: Bobbs-Merrill, 1927. An out-of-print tome with thick paper pages. Mulholland gives away the tricks as performed by the Red Man, Hindoos, the Chinaman, and other denizens of the 1927 world. He doesn't, however, give away tricks of the Western world.

Negroponte, Nicholas P. *Being Digital.* New York: Knopf, 1995. Engaging rumina-

tions on modern technology's place in the world. Source for quote about virtual
reality from p. 118; quote on HDTV from pp. 125–26.

*Norman, Donald A. *The Psychology of Everyday Things*. New York: Basic Books,
1988. Lively writing in an interesting examination of how humans interact with
the products around us. You'll never look at a store door the same way again. At
the end (p. 188) Norman offers some guidelines for the design of everyday
things. For our purposes it is intellectually amusing to note that these guidelines are the exact opposite of what a magician attempts to do. This book is
good.

Ogilvy, David. *The Unpublished David Ogilvy*. New York: Crown, 1986. A compendium of previously unpublished writings by this leader in advertising.

Paladin Press. *DEA Classified Intelligence Reports: Inside Secrets of the Smuggling Trade*.
Boulder, Colorado: Paladin Press, 1988. Photocopies of classified documents
from the U.S. Drug Enforcement Administration, obtained "by covert means"
by "an unnamed source" in the DEA. Fascinating deceptions abound!

Peary, Danny. *Cult Movies*. New York: Dell, 1981. The first of an indispensable series about cult movies. Used for information on *Plan Nine from Outer Space*.

Petroff, Tom. *Baseball Signs and Signals*. Dallas, Texas: Taylor, 1986. Fascinating
guide to the secrets and symbols of baseball signalling, including a great
chapter on how to steal signs.

Phillips, Sue. *Creating a Cottage Garden*. London: Weidenfeld and Nicolson, 1990.
Contains some information on illusion of space in a garden.

Pickering, Samuel F., Jr. *Let It Ride*. Columbia: University of Missouri Press, 1991.
Essays by the man who inspired the John Keating character in the insipid *Dead
Poet's Society*.

Playfair, Guy Lyon. *The Geller Effect*. New York: Henry Holt, 1986. Playfair gushes
over Geller's powers.

Plotkin, Mark J. *Tales of a Shaman's Apprentice: An Ethnobotanist Searches for New Medicines in the Amazon Rainforest*. New York: Viking, 1993. Source for the information on Christian missionaries using Western medicine to convert the native
tribes of the rainforest.

Popeil, Ron. *The Salesman of the Century: Inventing, Marketing, and Selling on TV: How I
Did It and How You Can Too!* New York: Delacorte, 1995. Fun and fast read about
the man who brought us many legendary products of the TV age. Popeil mentions
here the industry's use of fakery such as paid audiences and telemarketing scripts.

Poretz, Mel. *What Would You Do?* New York: Fawcett Columbine, 1994. A survey in
book form, best played as a game, to see how "normal" you are compared to the
2,810 subjects who took part. This book was the source for the anecdote about
using physical misdirection to remove a toilet paper tail off a woman in a library.

*Poundstone, William. *Big Secrets*. New York: William Morrow, 1983. The first in a
great series that reveals all on a number of topics, including magic. This volume
contains information on the dancing handkerchief, the floating ball, sawing a
woman in two, blindfold drives, the vanishing horse and rider, and various Kreskin stunts.

*———. *Bigger Secrets*. Boston: Houghton Mifflin, 1986. The Indian Rope Trick,
firewalking, levitating a woman, headline prediction, Zig Zag illusion, and the
Statue of Liberty vanish.

*Poundstone, William. *Biggest Secrets*. New York: William Morrow, 1993. Pulling a rabbit from a hat, various escapes, the catching a bullet trick, Siegfried and Roy's white tigers, and stage hypnosis.

Prus, Robert C., and C. R. D. Sharper. *Road Hustler: The Career Contingencies of Professional Card and Dice Hustlers*. Lexington, Massachusetts: Lexington Books, 1977.

Project on Disney. *Inside the Mouse: Work and Play at Disney World*. Durham, North Carolina: Duke University Press, 1995. Also see interesting description on p. 14 of a thoughtless mixing of symbols.

*Randi, James. *The Faith Healers*. Amherst, New York: Prometheus Books, 1987. Revealing look at the scams and magic tricks used by faith healers to make money for themselves and destroy people's lives.

*———. *Flim-Flam!* New York: Lippincott & Crowell, 1980. A comprehensive bashing of all manner of paranormal gobbledygook. I do believe Randi's $10,000 is quite safe.

———. *The Magic World of the Amazing Randi*. Holbrook, Massachusetts: Bob Adams, Inc., 1989. Randi goes around the world, asking magic friends from different countries to donate an illusion to this museum of magic. A good idea not carried off so well, since most of the tricks are old hat, or have little to do with the magician's country of origin.

Regardie, Israel. *The Golden Dawn*. Llewellyn, 1994. A mish mash of signs and symbols, rituals, and floorplans. A world of law in which to revel for those wanting to escape the real world.

Rodriguez, Robert. *Rebel Without a Crew: How a 23-year-old Filmmaker with $7,000 Became a Hollywood Player*. New York: Dutton, 1995. An exciting and engaging story showing that sometimes schooling does not pay off. Used here for the anecdote about imposing the sound of machine gun fire over single-shooting guns.

Rowell, Lewis. *Thinking About Music*. Amherst: The University of Massachusetts Press, 1983. Information on illusion in music.

Rydell, Wendy, and George Gilbert. *The Great Book of Magic: Including 150 Mystifying Tricks You Can Perform*. New York: Harry N. Abrams, Inc., 1976. This book runs through a short history of magic, then continues by explaining variations on effects originally performed by famous magicians.

Schudson, Michael. *Advertising, the Uneasy Persuasion: Its Dubious Impact on American Society*. New York: Basic, 1984. Explores the role of advertising in "the culture of our consumer society," touching on issues such as the efficacy of advertising, and how it might influence us.

Seger, Linda, and Edward Jay Whetmore. *From Script to Screen*. New York: Henry Holt, 1994. How a movie is made, with a lot on how movies create illusions of reality.

Sisti, Jim. *The Magic Menu: The First Five Years*. Tahoma, California: L & L, 1995. Contains the contents of *The Magic Menu*, "the international journal for restaurant and bar magicians." Reviews, articles, and tips all geared toward magicians who work in this field of magic. The topit-in-tuxedo information was from an article by Stuart Bowie called "Secret Support." The pro-stooge rant was from "The Full Bottle Wipe Out" by Simon Lovell.

Snowden, Lynn. *Nine Lives*. New York: W. W. Norton, 1994. Participatory journalism: The author takes nine jobs in the course of a year. She works for an ad agency, a chocolate company, as a roadie for a heavy metal band, as a stripper, a housewife, and, oh, um, four other things I can't remember.

Stadelman, Paul, and Bruce Fife. *Ventriloquism Made Easy: How to Talk to Your Hand without Looking Stupid!* Colorado Springs, Colorado: Java, 1989. Everything you need to know to engage in the entertainment industry's "nerdiest" profession in a few short chapters.

Stebbins, Robert A. *Career, Culture, and Social Psychology in a Variety Art: The Magician*. Malabar, Florida: Krieger, 1993. Stebbins's interest is less in magic than in the social-psychological makeup of a subculture, professionals, hobbyists, and amateurs.

Sternitzky, Julius L. *Forgery and Fictitious Checks*. Springfield, Illinois: Charles C. Thomas, 1955. A retired inspector of the Oakland, California, police department reveals all he learned in his thirty years investigating crimes of check fraud and forgery.

Stolzenberg, Mark. *Be a Mime!* New York: Sterling, 1991. Everything you need to know to engage in the entertainment industry's second nerdiest profession.

Sutton, Caroline. *How Did They Do That?* New York: William Morrow, 1984. Fascinating inquiries into all sorts of amazing actions throughout history. Description of Houdini's underwater packing case escape detailed on pp. 97–99. Also contains a fascinating account of how Houdini used a double to fool the Liverpool police.

———. *How Do They Do That?* New York: William Morrow, 1981. Sawing women and sword swallowing, pp. 220–21.

———. *More How Do They Do That?* New York: William Morrow, 1993. Pulling a rabbit from a hat, pp. 125–26.

*Tarr, Bill. *Now You See It, Now You Don't! Lessons in Sleight of Hand*. New York: Vintage, 1976. If you wish to learn sleight-of-hand skills, this one is a sure bet. With profuse illustrations and clear descriptions, it covers sleights with cards, coins, thimbles, billiard balls, and cigarettes.

VanFleet, James K. *21 Days to Unlimited Power with People*. Englewood Cliffs, New Jersey: Prentice Hall, 1992, p. 114. Sometimes hokey, sometimes grandfatherly, sometimes needlessly wordy, but often very correct advice.

Warlock, Peter. *The Complete Book of Magic*. London: The Abbey Library. A potpourri of conjuring tricks for beginning warlocks.

Weiner, David L. *Brain Tricks: How to Cope with the Dark Side of Your Brain and Win the Ultimate Mind Game*. Amherst, New York: Prometheus Books, 1993. A long book, but easily managed in forty-five minutes by simply reading the summaries and ignoring the rest of it.

Wheeler, Elmer. *Sizzlemanship: New Tested Selling Sentences*. Englewood Cliffs, New Jersey: Prentice-Hall, 1940.

Williamson, Judith. *Decoding Advertisements*. Great Britain: Marion Boyars, 1978. Williamson deconstructs magazine ads in surprising ways. Sometimes she may go too far in her musings, but she is always insightful and entertaining.

*Yeager, Wayne B. *Techniques of the Professional Pickpocket*. Port Townsend, Washington: Loompanics Unlimited, 1990. Slim enough to fit in your pocket, this is a quick but thorough guide to the methods pickpockets use to ply their craftiness.

Young, Martin, and Robbie Stamp. *Trojan Horses: Deception Operations in the Second World War.* London: The Bodley Head, 1989. Cool photos and stories about fakes, blow-up tanks, and subterfuges during wartime.

Periodicals

Also used as valuable sources of information were magic catalogs. For names and addresses, see chapter 7, "Crashing the Clan."

Applebaum, Michael. "The Usual Suspects." *Spy,* May/June 1995, p. 16. Discusses David Copperfield's use of stooges in the audience.

———. "The Usual Suspects." *Spy,* July/August 1995, pp. 16–17. Discusses Copperfield's use of video and shadow in stage performances.

Cornish, Edward. "Six 'Teleshocks' for Workers." *The Futurist,* March–April 1993, p. 39. Information on beeps from a laser scanner as a way to dumb down employees.

DeCurtis, Anthony. "Woody Allen: The *Rolling Stone* Interview." *Rolling Stone,* September 16, 1993, p. 50. The quotes from Woody Allen and magic used in chapters 3 and 13.

Drosnin, Michael. "Mind Control in Waco?" *Village Voice,* March 2–8, 1994, p. 18. Three cheers for the *Voice,* which, instead of throwing away unsold copies, distributes them on college campuses. That's how I got this issue, and all the issues I've read. After all, if an article is worth reading this week, it will still be worth reading a week from now.

D., J. "Do Trailers Tell Too Much?" *Us,* March 1992, p. 83. This article contains the quote about how movie audiences deduce how the movie will make them feel from the background music.

Frankel, Daniel. *Men's Fitness,* November 1995. Short article in which coach John Robinson offers some football plays to use when the family comes over for Thanksgiving.

Fricke, David. "Smashing Pumpkins." *Rolling Stone,* November 16, 1995, pp. 52–53. Contains the revealing photographs of band members in magic apparatus. In fairness to the photographer, I doubt the casual observer will notice anything amiss with the pix; only us super-analyzers will spot the discrepancies. Furthermore, the photographer pulled off a nice levitation shot on p. 50, with no wires or pipes visible.

Gardner, Martin. "Thomas Edison, Paranormalist." *Skeptical Inquirer,* July/August 1996, pp. 9–12. Contains the information on Bert Reese mentioned in chapter 4, as part of a detailed investigation into Edison's supernatural beliefs.

Hanscome, Barbara. "The Play's the Thing." *Game Developer,* December/January 1995, pp. 50–55. An article that attempts to answer the question "How do you keep a [computer] game interactive and also weave in a good story?" Mentions use of Pavlovian conditioning, sound cues in Asteroids, and stereotyping to quickly impart information to the player.

Jillette, Penn. "You Probably Didn't See This." *Mofo Knows: The Penn and Teller Newsletter*, September/October 1996. Penn tells the tale of a trick gone awry. They recover and no one's the wiser.

Kolbert, Elizabeth. "Hawkeye Turns Mean, Sensitively." *New York Times*, May 18, 1994, p. C1.

Martin, Douglas. "Poof! Quick as Smoke, Questions About Magic Just Seem to Disappear." *New York Times*, December 26, 1996, pp. C11, 22. The trials and tribulations of a *Times* reporter on the trail of David Copperfield's secrets.

Mikla, Pete. "A Magical Marriage." *What's On*, August 29–September 11, 1995, p. 83. A Las Vegas tourist magazine.

Nardi, Peter M. "Toward a Social Psychology of Entertainment Magic (Conjuring)." *Symbolic Interaction*, 7:1 (1984): 25–42. Once you get past the first two pages, this is an easy-reading and idea-rich discussion of many of the topics covered in this book.

———. "The Social World of Magicians: Gender and Conjuring." *Sex Roles*, 19:11/12, 1988, pp. 759–70. An analysis of gender and the magician using historical and sociological perspectives.

Nickell, Joe. "Sleuthing a Psychic Sleuth." *Skeptical Inquirer*, January/February 1997, pp. 18–19. Nickell examines some claims psychic detectives have made and finds them to be lacking.

Robertson, Chuck. "Scanning Televangelists: Listening-in on the Behind-the-Scenes Chatter, Wireless Mikes, Two-Way Transmitters, & More! Here's Your Hidden Frequency Guide to the Electronic Church!" *Popular Communications*, December 1992, pp. 12–15.

Sieks, David. "Void Pirates on Parade." *Game Developer*, October/November, pp. 61–64. Mentions use of darkness to cloak the fact that the game designer couldn't afford to add touches of detail to the game.

Singer, Mark. "Secrets of the Magus." *New Yorker*, April 5, 1993, pp. 54–73. This article, on cardician and magic scholar Ricky Jay, is well worth looking up for such intellectual delicacies as the Sprong Shift, the Master's Advice to His Pupil, the sense of how a mere trick is glorified to become an emotional tale, as well as some cool anecdotes about Jay.

"Skeptics on Oprah." *Skeptic*, 3:4 (1995): 17–18. Oprah Winfrey's skepticism of a psychic, revealing that a debunking of the psychic was edited out of the show.

Smith, Warren Allen. "Debunking the Mystical in India." *Skeptical Inquirer*, May/June 1996, pp. 6–7. Contains anecdote about Indian swami whose magic trick was accidentally recorded on film.

Stashower, Daniel. "The Fun of Magic Is in Figuring How the Tricks Work." *Smithsonian*, June 1991, p 108. Used here for information on the Ohio collector who couldn't find the trick to his trunk.

Teller. "My Search for Donna Delbert." *New York Times Magazine*, April 24, 1994, pp. 44–47. Teller tells about the AWOL, transvestite, "Rosie the Riveter" of magic.

———. "What Teller Blabbed at the Magic Castle." *Mofo Knows: The Penn and Teller Newsletter*, July/August 1996. Teller's acceptance speech as the duo won their Magicians of the Year award from the Academy of Magical Arts. Teller explains how Cups and Balls took them from sidewalk performances into the big time.

Tierney, John. "Fleecing the Flock." *Discover*, November 1987, pp. 50–58. Article on James Randi verses evangelist Peter Popof. Randi uses a shortwave radio receiver to listen in to Popof's backstage assistants.

Trevor, David. "Siegfried and Roy: Mysterious Satan Worshippers or Tiger-loving Men?" *Bikini*, November 1995, p. 24. Information on S & R's tour trucks and the 7-11 woman who believes the duo are possessed by Satan. But truthfully, who in some small way, is not?

Whaley, Barton. "Covert Rearmament in Germany, 1919–1939: Deception and Mismanagement." *Journal of Strategic Studies*, 1982, pp. 26–27. Source of the story on Hitler's general using a magic trick to make an aircraft look more powerful than it really was.

Wiater, Stanley. "Truth's Bodyguard." *Twilight Zone*, June 1988, pp. 32–35, 45. Interview with James Randi on faith healing.

Wiseman, Richard, and Peter Lamont. "Unravelling the Indian Rope-Trick." *Nature*, September 19, 1996, pp. 212–13. Study supports the view that testimony changes over time to become more elaborate and amazing.

Zehme, Bill. "Shazam!: How David Copperfield, a Relatively Average Guy Who Makes about $26 Million a Year and Can Also Fly Whenever He Wants to, Won the $10 Million Heart of Claudia Schiffer, the Most Fabulous Übermodel in the World." *Esquire*, 121:4 (April 1994): 90–95.

———. "Siegfried and Roy." *Us*, March 1993, pp. 41–46, 63. This article contains the information on SARMOTI, as well as this handy tidbit: Siegfried is the blonde; Roy is the brunette. In photographs they stand with Siegfried to the left of Roy so that the photograph can be read like a book. (For Israeli magazines do they pose reversed?)

Manuscripts

Most of these are photocopied, one-page sheets describing how a trick is done. Some are longer, consisting of a few sheets stapled together, forming a small pamphlet. Some are self-published by the magician. Some are out of print, others can be purchased from magic suppliers.

"Egg Bag Plus." Peabody, Massachusetts: Diamond's Magic. A routine for use with an egg bag and egg vase. Used as background for the discussion on the egg bag.

Elmsley, Alex. "The Elmsley Count." Peabody, Massachusetts: Diamond's Magic. Used for the description of the Elmsley Count in chapter 10, this is a photocopied manuscript describing his famous way of counting four cards as four cards without showing one. Although the byline on this paper gives Elmsley's name, it is doubtful that he wrote it, since Elmsley is mentioned in the third person.

Koons, Jon. "Prestidigitation." Indianapolis, Indiana: H-O, 1983. A short booklet for children by the H-O company, maker of oatmeal cereals. The cereal packages explained magic tricks, and this booklet was obtained through a write-in offer. It details some of the important fundamentals of magic, such as patter, misdirection, and categories of tricks.

Leech, Al. "Don't Look Now! The Smart Slant on Misdirection." Chicago, Illinois:

L. L. Ireland, 1948. A manuscript typed up on one side of each page and stapled together. This is the kind of homespun work I wish we could see more of.

"Side Show Tricks Exposed: How They Do It at Those Carnivals." Peabody, Massachusetts: Diamond's Magic. A quick page of tidbits.

Supreme Magic Co. "X. L. Sealed Letter Reading." Bideford, Devon: Supreme Magic Co. Photocopied sheet describing one use of carbon paper to achieve an amazing psychic effect.

"Valuable Tricks Exposed (Things You'd Like to Know)." Peabody, Massachusetts: Diamond's Magic. Another page of quick tidbits.

Online, Audio and Video Sources

The Usenet postings are listed primarily to give credit where credit is due, for the articles themselves are long vanished. Also listed here are videos and audio cassette programs used as sources in this book.

Barnett, Bruce. "Re: Re Re Bruce Barnett," alt.magic, July 14, 1994. Describes how David Copperfield makes notes on his illusions after performing them.

BayPad. "Re: A Question for Coin Workers," alt.magic, June 22, 1994. ProGrip recommended for sweaty palms.

Cohen, Michael. "Look, My Hands Are Empty......," alt.magic, May 14, 1994. A member of the studio audience at the Penn & Teller special, confirming that the entire audience was taught to perform the trick with the thumb tip.

Close Encounters of the Third Kind. 1977. Directed by Steven Spielberg and starring Richard Dreyfuss, Teri Garr, Melinda Dillon, and François Truffaut. Eerie and frightening sci-fi classic, here used for its depiction of military trucks disguised under comforting brand names. Good movie, but try to get the original version without Spielberg's additional footage that merely lengthens the film while lessening its impact.

Colossus: The Forbin Project. 1970. Directed by Joseph Sargent and starring Eric Braedon and Susan Clark. Melodramatic and outdated story of two all-knowing computer rivals striving to take over the human world. Humans use a magic trick to try and deceive the computers.

Frazier, Jeff. "Tricky Plane," alt.magic, circa June 13, 1994. Anecdote about engineer dinner lecture on how the airplane was made to vanish.

Gerrig, Richard. *The Life of the Mind: An Introduction to Psychology.* Dubuque, Iowa: The Teaching Company, 1992. Eight spirited lectures on psychology on audio cassette. Psychology obviously plays a big role in a magician's ability to produce an illusion in your mind. Thus, a good knowledge of psychology, especially social psychology, and the psychology of perception, is helpful to the budding (or experienced) magician.

Harwood, Mark. "DC Flying in Australia," alt.magic, May 8, 1996. Notes about David Copperfield's flying routine and prop man ready in the wings.

Hotz, Leigh. "Tiping [*sic*] Gaff at Magic Shop," alt.magic, May 13, 1994. Discussion of one store owner's occasionally revealing a trick to a potential customer.

Isozanki, Jeff. "Re: Sharing Performance Secrets," alt.magic, April 10, 1994. Mentions the Gary Kurtz lecture notes, as well as a video, *Let's Get Flurious*, by A–1 Multi-media, that discusses the use of shifting weight for misdirective purposes.

Jeannie. Usenet posting on alt.magic, circa 1994. One poster's comments as to why it is wrong for a magician's assistants to meet with audience volunteers before the show.

*Knepper, Kenton. *Wonder Words*. Vol. 1. Phoenix, Arizona: 1996. An excellent audio program that explains Knepper's methods for improving and creating improvements by careful words choices. I highly recommend it for anyone interested in the use of words to manipulate thought. The quote about nominalizations was from tape 4, side A, "Psychic Readings." The quote about unspecified referential words was from tape 1, side A, "Unspecified Words."

Mobbs, Robert. "Furthermore (David Copperfield)," alt.magic, July 1, 1994. Describes Copperfield's stereo blasting "Rock the Cradle of Love" by Billy Idol "loud enough so he wouldn't have to listen to us as we tried to talk to him" while filing out of the theater.

POSNACO. "Re: Swetty [*sic*] Palms," alt.magic. June 23, 1994. Describes how the author uses Arid XX Clear roll-on deodorant on his palms.

Roth, Chris. "The CIA and Magic Secrets," alt.magic, April 16, 1994. Roth's ruminations on the use of magic by spies.

Tracy, Brian, and Colin Rose. *Accelerated Learning Techniques: The Express Track to Super Intelligence*. Miles, Illinois: Nightingale Conant, 1995. Quotes on influence via questions from tape 10, "Power Communicating."

Ward, Paul. "How David Copperfield Vanished the LearJet (?)," alt.magic, May 26, 1994. Speculations on the jet vanish.

Interviews and Assistance

In writing this book, I talked with magicians: experienced magicians, hobbyists, "psychics," magicians who believed their magic was real, those who were out to get the audience, and many who simply wanted to entertain. Much thanks to all who were willing to reveal secrets or just to talk about their art.

Before speaking with a magician, I explained fully the intent of this book. Only one declined to speak. The rest understood that the secret is but one aspect of a skillful performance.

My thanks and gratitude to the people—magicians, laypeople, psychics, wizards, magickians, mediums, and assorted others who helped by giving of their time and of their thoughts on the subject of magic and illusion. Quotes throughout this book that are not footnoted are the result of interviews with these people.

In nonpartisan alphabetical order they are: Robin Allen, the king of crop circles, for his look at magic and board games—Ken E. Barham for his honest tales from the front—Herbert L. Becker for his explanation of the lawsuit—Robert Cialdini for a fine book and for pointing me toward Harold

H. Kelley—Dad, for his help with the photos—Matthew Dwinells for being my very first interview and a fine one at that—Charlie Ellis, for his recommendations—Francine, for her help with photos—Eddie Gardner for his cheerful explanations while I cost him a fortune tying up his 1-800 line—Jessica for her photographic brilliance—John, the computer consultant who believes he has psychic powers, for his comments—Patricia Ju for her help with the music stuff and just for being cute—Harold H. Kelley for his articles and pointing me toward Peter Nardi—Marcus C. Ludl for his thoughts on magic—Max the Mad for his thoughts on magick—Sol Messler for his time and patience—Kalelkar Mohan for his gracious and lucid explanations of physics—Mom for research assistance—Peter Nardi for his enlightening look on the subject—Harley Newman for his view from inside the Saran Wrap—Scott Parker for information on the flying trick—Piyush M. Patel for his perspective—William Poundstone for his help with fact checking—Prometheus Books for having the guts—James Randi for taking the time to share his experiences—Sandorse the Magician for revealing some tricks of the trade—Eric Schulzinger at Lockheed Corporation for procuring the World War II photos in the midst of a move—Suzanne the Magician for her insightful comments—Teller for speaking his mind—Venu for an excellent recognizance mission—and to all those who wished to remain anonymous, as well as anyone else whose name inadvertently has been left off this list but whose gracious advice has contributed to this work—and to you the reader: thank you.

Endnotes

Chapter 1: The Foundations of Deception

1. Christopher, 1991.
2. Randi, 1980.
3. Bannon, 141, italics added.
4. This is not to imply that this entire trick is based on the switching of the duplicate card box. The full illusion, described in John Bannon's *Smoke and Mirrors*, relies on a good deal of sleight-of-hand skill.
5. It can work the other way as well. There is a magic trick done by comedy magicians called Flight of the Paper Balls, in which an audience member is invited on stage while the magician makes tissue balls disappear. Actually the magician throws the wads away without the volunteer seeing. As the volunteer's confusion grows, the audience laughter grows too, because the audience sees the balls being tossed aside. In this case the audience is sacrificed for the good of one person—and for comedic effect.
6. See William Poundstone's *Bigger Secrets* for an explanation of that event.
7. For example, Randi, 1980, 157.
8. This quote is a mixture of ideas expressed publicly on alt.magic, the Internet magic discussion forum, and in personal correspondence with the author.
9. Stashower, 108.

Chapter 2: A Magician's Dozen

1. A popular card trick called Do as I Do relies on imparting this feeling of magic to the volunteer and spectators. The magician hands a deck of cards to an audience volunteer. The volunteer is told to do exactly what the magician does. Step by step, the magician leads the volunteer through a card manipulation. At the

climax of the trick, the magician reveals that some magical thing has happened to his cards, while the spectator (who has been manipulating the cards exactly as the magician) does not have the magic happen. It *looks* like anyone should have been able to create the magic—but they couldn't.

2. A local ski shop plays ads that show home movie footage of a boy shoving his eyeglass earpiece up his nose. It is unrelated to the product they're selling, but very attention-getting.

3. Sutton, 1981.

4. Burns-Meyer, 299.

5. Ibid.

6. Ibid.

7. Edmonds, 39.

8. Ibid., 47.

9. Ibid., 39.

10. Kreskin, 21.

11. Dunninger, 21.

12. Blackstone.

13. Gibson, 1976, 13.

14. Knepper.

Chapter 3: What Is Magic Made Of?

1. VanFleet, 204.

2. Kolbert, C1.

Chapter 4: The Art of Chicanery

1. Gardner, 12.

2. Isozanki.

3. Stolzenberg, 107–108.

4. Loeschke, 94.

5. Ibid., 141.

6. Stolzenberg, 117.

7. Cornish, 39.

8. Norman, 103.

9. Seger, 289.

10. One of the local television news broadcasts has been using the same technique to bolster its ratings. They play booming, exciting background music in order to "pump up" the viewing audience, getting them to feel an intensity about this news show that more sedate news shows don't elicit. Commercials use the technique all the time. Is it really *that great* that you can now mix Original and Extra Crispy chicken in the same bucket? The music makes you think so!

11. Matalin, 330.

12. Stebbins, 51–52.

13. This is true for persuasive essays and speakers, and other arenas in which

words are the foundation for a way of thinking. I could tell you a story about a furry woodland creature who was hungry and yet the other animals would have nothing to do with him. You would feel sorry for this creature. But if I switched the focus, altered the wording, you would see that this creature was really the Big Bad Wolf, and he was hungry for cute little piggies to eat. Your attitude changes due to a word change. This is the basis for much of persuasive arguments, advertisements, and yes, magic. Nardi, 1984.

14. Christopher, 1991, 155.
15. Zehme, 1993, 42.
16. Kelly, 24.
17. Lifton, 82.
18. Ibid.
19. Ibid., 23.
20. Ibid.
21. Ibid., 28.
22. Ibid., 29.
23. Randi, 1989.
24. Cialdini, 121.
25. Sisti, 179.
26. Fischbacher, 289.
27. Bader.
28. Popeil, 211.
29. Sisti, 214.
30. One magician described one of her card tricks like this: "A spectator chooses a card . . . I tell them to sign it. (I usually get 'You mean you want me to write on it?' Well, that was what I said, wasn't it?) . . ." It seems to me if she repeatedly gets this kind of response from her volunteers, she needs to rethink the way she handles her dialog with the volunteer, to avoid a potentially awkward and show-slowing moment. (On the other hand, she could also milk the subject's response for comedic effect.)
31. Coleman, 19.
32. Bannon, 127.
33. Seger, 143.
34. Martin, C22.
35. Harwood.
36. Barnett.
37. Stebbins, 55.

Chapter 5: Analyzing the Action

1. Ekman, 92–93.
2. Ibid., 123.
3. Ibid., 130.
4. Ibid., 126.
5. Ibid., 279.
6. Ibid., 87.

7. Applebaum, *Spy*, May/June 1995, p. 16.
8. Hay, 364.
9. For a look at the photographer see Fischbacher, 260.
10. Smith, 7.
11. Robertson, 12.
12. Applebaum, *Spy*, July/August 1995, 16–17.
13. Feynman, 88–89.
14. Ibid., 90.
15. Ward.
16. Frazier.
17. Mobbs.
18. Seger, 125.
19. Ibid., 275.
20. Peary, 267.

Chapter 6: Things to Look for When Watching a Magic Show

1. Poundstone, 1993, 187.
2. Martin, C22.
3. Cader, 178.
4. Coleman, 19.
5. Poundstone, 1986, 214.
6. Charney, 96–99.
7. Nardi, 1984.
8. It occurs to me that if I were the magician performing this trick, I would make use of an additional principle to further ensure that everyone focuses in on the green band. I would select off-colors for all the strips except for the green. The other colors might be maroon, marigold, navy blue, and burnt umber. But the green would be classic, pure green. People should be more likely to concentrate on the color that they are most familiar with, and less likely to look at the colors that are hard to categorize.
9. Martin, C22.
10. Harwood.
11. Mulholland, 81.

Chapter 7: Crashing the Clan

1. Mulholland, 20.
2. Ibid., 27.
3. Hotz.
4. Fischbacher, 46.
5. Mikla, 83.

Chapter 8: The Audience

1. Kelley, 25.
2. Bannon, 102.
3. Ibid, 12.
4. This reminds me of commercials that admit a flaw in their product or political candidate. They point out that particular flaw because that's the one they have a witty response to. Meanwhile you're not focusing on the flaw for which they have no excuse.
5. Seger, 9.
6. Warlock, 7.
7. Kelley, 26.
8. Harder to guess might be the actual method employed: an assistant backstage would "trigger a flow of hydrogen gas and send an electric current through thin wires spaced just far enough apart for a spark to jump at each turpentine-soaked candlewick, causing it to leap into flame." Rydell, 63. Spooky stuff.
9. Letts, 164.
10. The darkened night was likely due to the fact that the viewer's irises would have contracted while watching the fireworks display. When the fireworks were done it would be difficult to see until their irises adjusted to the light by expanding.
11. Dunninger, 18.
12. Mulholland, 81.
13. Wiseman.
14. Dunninger, 85.
15. Magus, 58.
16. Burger, 101.
17. Randi, 1980, 7.
18. Coleman, 15.

Chapter 9: The Stage and the People on It

1. POSNACO.
2. BayPad.
3. Yeager, 49.
4. Ibid.
5. Pickering, 18.
6. Charney, 183.
7. Sutton, 91.
8. Stadelman, 7.
9. Zehme, 93.
10. Stebbins, 15.
11. De Beauvoir, 164.

Chapter 10: Grrrrrrrowlll!!! The Animals of Magic

    1. Most of this information came from Edmonds, pp. 17–19—the Snapple I made up. A more elaborate, and slightly different, telling of the tale can be found in Harris, pp. 53–59. The ox trick is probably an embellishment added in later retellings, either that, or a different method was used to perform it. Any ideas?

    2. Rydell, 63.

    3. Fischbacher, 161.

Chapter 11: Props and Gimmicks

    1. Randi, 1989, 95.

    2. Buckley, 175.

    3. Hay, 111–12.

    4. Coleman, 66.

    5. Teller, 1996.

    6. Jillette, 130–51.

    7. L&L Publishing magic catalog.

    8. Gardner, 1978, 36–37.

    9. Hank Lee magic catalog, September 1996 supplement, p. 6.

  10. Christopher, 1948, 3.

Chapter 12: Illusion Outside of Magic

    1. Mastai, 11.

    2. Rowell, 144.

    3. Ibid., 170.

    4. Ibid., 144.

    5. Drabelle, 39.

    6. Phillips, 56.

    7. Itoh, 56.

    8. Negroponte, 125–26.

Chapter 13: Translating Magic into Desires

    1. DeCurtis, 50.

    2. Michael Drosnin, *Village Voice*.

    3. Barreca, 253.

Chapter 14: The Use of Fakery and Magicians' Psychology Out of the Theater

1. Kreskin, 16.
2. Ibid., 17.
3. Edmonds, 5.
4. Trevor, 24.
5. Berrett, 107.
6. Ibid., 111.
7. Brenneman, 160.
8. Randi, 1980, 43.
9. Ibid., 159.
10. Nickell, 18–19.
11. Regardie, 130.
12. Ibid., 117.
13. Plotkin, 213.
14. Randi, 1987, 114.
15. Weiner, 28.
16. Playfair, 248.
17. Wiater, 45.
18. Engel, 43.
19. Ibid., 41.
20. Popeil, 207.
21. Ekman, 245–46.
22. Sternitzky, 69–70.
23. Frankel, 94.
24. Hooker, 172.
25. Petroff, 5.
26. Ibid.
27. Ibid., 10.
28. Ibid., 14.
29. Prus, 85–91.

Chapter 15: Misdirection Magic in Everyday Life

1. Fromm, 14.
2. Cialdini.
3. Bandler, 115.
4. Lifton, 420.
5. Ibid., 422.
6. Mulholland, 85.
7. Lifton, 428.
8. Ibid., 429.
9. Ibid., 430.
10. Ibid., 431.
11. Bannon, 142.

12. Edmonds, 27.
13. Goldberg, 52.
14. Edmonds, 100–104.
15. Whaley.
16. Goldberg, 57–58.
17. Feynman, 1985, 143.
18. Knox, 76.
19. Ibid., 76–77.
20. Engel, 4.
21. Hanscome, 55.
22. Ekman, 165–66.
23. Negroponte, 118.
24. Sieks, 64.
25. Hanscome, 52.
26. Poretz, xi–xii.
27. Yeager, 30.

Chapter 16: Magic in Selling and Advertising

1. Feynman, 1988, 218.
2. Williamson, 140.
3. Ibid., 141.
4. Ibid.
5. Wheeler, 216.
6. Ibid., 218.
7. D., 83.
8. Ibid.
9. Ogilvy, 9.
10. Griffin, 193.
11. VanFleet, 84.
12. Dunninger, 15.
13. Ogilvy, 14.
14. Project, 126.
15. Garson, 15.
16. Leech, 1.
17. Nardi, 1984.
18. Coleman, 14.
19. Cialdini, 19.
20. Molloy, 202.
21. Ibid.
22. Ibid., 26–28.
23. Ibid., 198.
24. Ibid., 241.
25. Ibid., 302.
26. Schudson, 227.
27. Ibid., 225.

28. Knepper.
29. Randi, 1980, 271.
30. Tracy.
31. Ibid.
32. Griffin, 80–81.
33. Trevor, 24.
34. Roth.
35. Paladin Press.
36. Ibid.
37. Fischbacher, 10–11.

Chapter 17: When the Curtain Closes

1. Snowden, 76.
2. Gerrig.
3. Randi, 1980, 326.

Index